"I CAN'T IMAGINE"

The Powerful Story of a Micro-Preemie Named Emilia Quinn Sears who was born in a pandemic at 22 weeks old. *I Can't Imagine* is about her life, her fight for a chance in this world, and how her legacy lives on through her father as he tries to live up to his 1 pound, 1 ounce hero through their now shared life mission!

Written by Emilia's father, Chris Sears

For My Daughter Emilia Quinn Sears
"And Though She Be But Little, She is Fierce"

CONTENTS

Part II: Chris' Story

Part III: Rebuilding our New City with Purpose and Together

INTRODUCTION

The What, When, Why, and How of Our Journey

The What

My daughter, Emilia Quinn Sears, is my hero! She is my why! She is my role model! She is the bravest, most courageous person I've ever met in my life!

What is this book about? This book is about the remarkable story of an amazing little micro-preemie named Emilia Quinn Sears, who was born at 22 weeks and 6 days old, weighing in at a whopping 1 pound, 1 ounce. This story chronicles her fight for a chance at life just as a worldwide pandemic was beginning to grip the country in March of 2020. This book is also about her parents' journey of learning how to navigate the crazy world of a micro-preemie and the rollercoaster of daily life in the NICU as we fought to give our daughter a chance for life. Sadly, this story is also about losing a child and all the pain, suffering, questioning, heartache, and devastation that tragedy can unexpectedly bring to a family. Finally, this book is also about the lessons, wisdom, and growth that can sometimes follow the worst events you can ever imagine happening in your life.

I, Emilia's father (Chris Sears), will be your guide on this journey.

In PART I, we will begin our journey with Emilia's story, where I will do my best to be the voice for my child and tell the story of my infant daughter's courageous battle for a chance at life.

In PART II, we will take a look at my personal story, which details my life after losing my daughter, along with my quest to find purpose and meaning in my life after my world was blown to pieces.

In PART III, we will discuss how Emilia and I were able to find each other again. We will take you on a tour of the new world we've created and imagined together through our shared mission and purpose.

Finally, we will conclude our journey together with a whimsical story demonstrating all that is possible in this world if you are lucky enough to understand your mission, your core values, and living your life on purpose while always remaining open to following the omens in life and letting the compound effect of your daily actions work their magic in this world.

The When

The events, stories, and lessons shared in this book all took place beginning two days before Emilia's birth on 3/13/2020 through her first birthday on 3/15/2021.

The Why

Why are we writing this book?

- We are writing this book for Emilia.
- We are writing this book for ourselves and to help in our own healing process.
- We are writing this book to tell Emilia's story to her future siblings.
- We are writing this book to share Emilia's incredible life and story with the world so her name isn't lost to eternity.
- We are writing this book for all the parents out there in this world that didn't have the perfect pregnancy, lost a child, and had to figure out how to re-imagine their worlds after suffering a life-altering tragedy.
- Finally, we are writing this book for everyone else that has the privilege in life to say the words, "I can't imagine," when they hear stories like that of my family. We hope to challenge them to embrace stories on the other side of the human spectrum around pain, suffering, and

tragedy for the beauty, wisdom, and lessons that can sometimes come from the worst things you can imagine in life.

For Emilia

As I mentioned in the beginning, my daughter, Emilia Quinn Sears, is my hero and my why! This whole story was never supposed to be seen by anyone other than Emilia, Felicia, and whoever Emilia chose to share it with in the future when she was older. When we started this unexpected journey together, Felicia and I decided to write every day and keep a journal of our experience until Emilia got home from the NICU. The goal was to leave a documented journal so Emilia could one day read about her incredible journey, understand how much her mom and dad loved her, feel the experiences she once went through on a daily basis, and realize just how strong and brave she truly is. Let me be clear, from day one, I was resolute in my belief that my daughter was going to make it home safe and sound even when all the statistics and odds said otherwise. I never had a single doubt in my mind that she wasn't going to survive this unfortunate situation that had been thrust upon her. I could sense how strong she was from the moment the NICU nurses and doctors told us that they were able to successfully revive her. That little tiny cry that came out of her mouth when she was born said it all. To me, that was a mighty lioness' roar. I still don't know if I remember exactly what it sounded like, but I remember it happening.

I don't know at what age we were planning to share this journal with Emilia. In my mind, I envisioned when she was in her early teens, maybe just about to enter high school, and starting to grow into a young woman who was unsure of herself. I imagined that she would read this and understand just how strong and brave she is and how much she can endure in this world. If she could tackle being born at 22 weeks and 6 days old, survive the NICU, NEC, all the surgeries, and whatever else was to come after we got her home, then high school and the rest of her life would be a breeze. There were a few times during our stay in the NICU where I remember having a vivid conversation in my mind with Emilia as she became a young woman. I remember telling her this very story, handing her this book of journal entries, walking her through her old stomping grounds in the NICU at Riley and IU Methodist, and giving her a tour of the old hospital rooms she spent the first few months of her life in. It allowed us to instill so much more strength in her by telling her own story back to her when she was able to truly understand what all this meant. I swear those moments between Emilia and I felt so real when they played out in my mind. They were so vivid and real that I almost can't imagine that it didn't really happen.

The first of these conversations happened when we were three days into the NICU experience, and her blood sugar levels had spiked to 500+ overnight. The nurses had just told us they needed to move her from IU Methodist to Riley's Hospital for Children to get her to a level 4 NICU (the highest there is) for her continued care as she required more intensive support than they could offer. As I sat there waiting in that tiny little parent's room at that little table Felicia and I had turned into a makeshift workstation, I could see Emilia and me having a future conversation in this very room as she was departing for college. I was telling her about the time when she was in a really bad spot, we were all really scared, and we had to move her to Riley's to get her better access to care. I showed her the videos of her being wheeled out in the mobile NICU lifeline cart, talked about what the doctors told us, and how delicate and urgent her situation was. I remember seeing us both start to cry. It felt so real. Who knows? Maybe in another universe or timeline, it was and still is real. These impromptu "conversations" happened a few other times as well throughout our stay in the NICU. They mainly seemed to spring up when pivotal and really scary moments in her journey occurred. Like when she had her first intestine perforation one week in at 3 a.m., when she had her first ostomy surgery, and a few other times in the final days of her life. Every time it happened, I still felt like it was so real and that these events were truly going to happen in the future. This book has taken on many meanings since those first few days of journaling, but at the end of the day, it was and will always be for Emilia.

For Felicia and I

After we lost Emilia, writing this for her took on a whole new meaning for my wife (Felicia) and me. The story had changed and the purpose had grown. The mission became to keep ourselves moving, to process what the heck just happened, to do our best to make some sense of our family's tragedy, and to do what we could to help anyone else out there unfortunate enough to have to go through the same thing we were going through. I can honestly say that writing this book truly changed my life. This book was my therapist, my comfort zone, my way to slowly process what had happened to us, my way of finding God, my way to stick to a routine, and, ultimately, my way to grow from this traumatic and tragic set of events that were thrust upon us. I can't tell you how many times tears poured out of me as I was typing in the early morning hours at my desk before work, telling my daughter's story over the past year since we began. It helped me stay connected to my daughter and always will.

Learning the new daily habit of writing led me to some crazy, weird-in-a-good-way, and unexpected compounding outcomes that we will talk about throughout the story. If I was going to write every day, I'd need inspiration. So, I read every single day as well. I would read a daily scripture reflection every morning and then write my thoughts. Before I knew it, my relationship with God had blossomed and we were talking every day. While my family is very religious, I've never really been a "religious" person by any means. I did go to Catholic grade school and high school but never really engaged in any of the religious aspects during my schooling. Catholic schooling clearly didn't make a huge impression on me because, at 36 years old, I don't think I've been to church more than five times since high school. So, writing this story made me explore my spirituality again and I'm so glad. Writing this story reignited my curiosity in all kinds of other new topics and dimensions of life as well. I started reading every day about things relating to psychology, happiness, resilience, humanity, tragedy, business, biographies, ancient cultures, science, religion, spirituality, and much more. My mind was opening up to new concepts I had never been exposed to. I was learning so much about a myriad of topics while learning more about myself as well in the process. The discipline of reading and writing every day led me to add in daily exercise. Because why not? I've always considered myself a fit person and exercised fairly regularly, but never on a daily basis. Daily exercise goals led to nightly walks with Felicia, where we would talk about our thoughts and feelings. Exercise also led to me running all the time and embracing nature more. I even ended up running a half marathon the day before Emilia's original due date, which never would have been even a consideration in my prior life. I've always hated running! Never, in a million years, could I have imagined running a half marathon. I've always played sports and loved competition. That is my comfort zone. The concept of running a marathon is something I could never understand. It's such a boring and awful activity with no real objective. It just never made sense to me. I watched Felicia run half marathons many times in the past and I was always so impressed because I knew that I could never do that. I just wasn't made for distance running. Well, I guess I was wrong.

The point being, these activities all started to snowball and compound over time until I was living a whole new life that I had never imagined before and, honestly, didn't even mean to create. I was just trying to figure out how to keep existing every day as I fought through the most traumatic thing I could have ever imagined in losing my first child. So, because of Emilia, we started writing. Because we started writing, we changed our lives. Emilia truly changed our lives now and forever in so many unforeseen ways. These lessons, thoughts, and self-improvements aren't stopping with this book. I'm never going back to my old way of life. I always knew that fatherhood would change me in some profound way. I could never have imagined that this would have been the change. Emilia was so strong and courageous and had such a powerful, lasting impact on my life that I truly feel that we will be together forever in some way. Every time I sit down to write, I think of Emilia. Every time I run, work out, or play tennis, I think of Emilia. Every time I read, I think of Emilia. If she could go through what she went through, I owe it to her to try and push myself to live up to my daughter's example. What kind of father would I be if I never came even remotely close to achieving the example that my 40-day old daughter set for me on how to live a purpose-filled life no matter how long you have on Earth? I like to think I'm "living for two" at this point, a topic we'll dive much deeper into later in this book.

For Emilia's Future Siblings

We are writing this book so Emilia's future siblings can learn of the amazing story and life of their big sister, Emilia Quinn Sears, that their mom and dad never shut up about. These poor kids are going to have so much to live up to that I almost feel sorry for them. Emilia certainly set the bar crazy high for her future siblings to have to try and jump over. That is what big sisters and the firstborn children are supposed to do. They are the leaders and set the tone for their siblings on how we are going to attack this thing called life together. During this past year of reading and learning, I read a book called *Originals* by Adam Grant. It's about unique people (originals) in this world and the societal, organizational, and psychological reasons of how they may have come to be. One of the sections of the book was about the importance of sibling birth order and the impact it can have on one's originality. Firstborn children are often the least likely to have this "original" label because they are raised in an adult world for the most part with only their parents as their examples and role models. Due to firstborns being raised in an adult world, they are typically very responsible, play things by the book, are rule followers, leaders, and follow more traditional life paths toward success. Last born children are raised in a kid world with their older siblings serving as their role models; they have fewer rules thrust on them by their parents, and in turn, often become a little more creative and rebellious, which is why they tend to have greater odds of becoming more "original" per the book's thesis. Emilia had all the makings of an amazing oldest child. She was strong, courageous, responsible, reliable, followed the rules, and did what she needed to do. She would have been the best big sister and role model to her future brothers and sisters. Sadly, she'll never get to be that physical example for them in this world to model their behavior after. I figured that this book could serve as her future siblings' blueprint to learn a little more about how amazing their big sister, Emilia, truly is/was. The hope being that in some small way, with this book, she can still carry out that sacred duty of being the oldest child and take the pressure off her siblings to free them up to be the originals that they will become.

For Posterity

We are writing this book so the name, Emilia Quinn Sears, isn't only remembered by her parents and immediate loved ones in the annals of time. While Emilia's time here on Earth was brief, she had more of an impact on so many people than most of us will ever have in a lifetime. She went through a lifetime of pain and suffering in under 40 days that most of us, God willing, will never have to endure. She showed so many people what life is really about and how to make the most of the time you have here on Earth. One of the things that I think parents that have lost children hate the most is when people stop speaking their name in the world. It hurts just a little more every day when you are around friends and family that know of Emilia and don't talk about her. It's like she never really existed, which couldn't be further from the truth. She not only existed, but she also lived and experienced more than most people will ever get to in any lifetime. I totally understand that people are afraid to say her name in our presence, thinking that it will inflict some unintended pain on us but, sadly, the opposite is true. WE WANT TO TALK ABOUT HER TO ANYONE AND EVERYONE WILLING TO LISTEN! We don't want to keep Emilia to ourselves. We aren't ashamed of our daughter. We are so proud of her! The last time I checked, people love to talk about stuff that they are proud about. People don't like to talk about stuff that they are ashamed about. I think we should all remember that as we approach people in our own lives that have lost loved ones in the future and always remember that they most likely want to share! Writing this book is one way Felicia and I can share Emilia's story with the world and make sure that no one will ever forget our daughter's beautiful name, Emilia Quinn Sears. Her name is so beautiful that it hurts not imagining others seeing it in this world. To that point, one morning in which Emilia and I were together on the treadmill in our basement, I got the brilliant idea as I looked out on the bookshelves staring back at me and viewing all the famous authors and their names down the spine of the books. I started to envision my daughter's name on the spine of one of those books and thought about how amazing that would be to behold someday in someone else's library. I could visualize the name, Emilia Quinn Sears, sitting on a shelf in someone else's basement, staring at a random guy on a treadmill getting in his morning workout. The thought of it made me smile. I couldn't think of a more beautiful way to honor her and ensure that people will know her name and remember her story for as long as books are still in existence in this world. After all, we are all just stories once we are no longer here and Emilia deserves credit for her story even if it was cut way too short. In my mind, she was the true author of this story the whole time anyway (as you will see in later chapters). So, I made the decision, right then and there on my run, that Emilia would be named the author of this story and I'll include my name in the opening section, so people know the role that I played in sharing our story with the world.

For Bereaved Parents

Most importantly, in my mind, we are writing this book for other parents that may be going through their own traumatic experiences surrounding the most basic human function of having children and growing a family. We always see in the movies or on our Instagram feeds, how easy it is to build a beautiful family in this modern world. A man and woman meet, fall in love, get married, buy a house, produce two or three beautiful kids, and then they spend the rest of their lives happily ever after together as they explore the world and watch their children grow, play sports, graduate college, and build their own families filled with grandkids to enjoy. That life certainly does exist out there, and for those lucky enough to have that be their reality, don't take it for granted. That's the Instagram version of having children and parenting. If you follow along with the Kardashians, the Hadid's, and Emily Ratajkowski's of the world, you know exactly what I'm saying. For them, pregnancy is all fun baby bump photoshoots, cool new wardrobes to model, and getting to tell the world "just because I'm pregnant doesn't mean I can't work out and be a business mogul at the same time." The whole thing seems perfectly planned and orchestrated until one day, out pops a beautiful baby, and they get back to living their fabulous lives as we all watch their kids grow from afar in tiny snapshots of their lives. I guess that is the dream or something if you were to believe that narrative.

Felicia and I were certainly on that similar path in our lives until we hit the childbearing portion of our own Hollywood story. I had no idea that just the pregnancy and getting a child to the crib at-home portion of the journey could be so challenging. It is mind-blowing to me how naïve I was as I look back on all of this. For years we had this grand plan on how we were going to start our family. We had it all laid out. We had devised when we would start trying for children based on what milestones we had to check off before we began first (travel, career, age). We were doing what Hollywood tells us to do until, all of a sudden, we weren't. That is when you realize that we aren't in control of this one! While creating human life is our fundamental job function, the end outcome is truly out of our control beyond the initial act of having sex. After that, everyone's story is unique and different. That is the basic lesson I've learned from this whole journey. Let go and just be present. Life is random and the only thing you can control is what you value in life and then trying to do as many actions each day to reflect those values. You never realize how truly helpless you are and what little control you have until your wife goes into labor at 22 weeks and 6 days into your first pregnancy. After our dose of reality in this world, that is when we learned that so many others have stories and experiences just like our own. As our journey progressed, people kept coming out of the woodwork to share stories around their own traumatic pregnancy and parenting experiences. We heard so many stories about children being born premature and thriving, of miscarriages and stillbirths, and so many more tragic and beautiful stories. I started to wonder if it is more common to have a traumatic experience versus the Kardashian/Instagram /Hollywood ideal. Again, never in my life had I heard of anything like these stories that were being shared with us about people's troubles with this basic human function. Before Emilia, I once had a friend who confided in me that he and his wife had a miscarriage. My uncle tragically lost a child at birth as well. Those were both tragedies and something I was aware of but certainly didn't seem to be commonplace. That seemed to change after our own family trauma with pregnancy and childbirth.

The more people told us their stories, the more I realized how very common it is for pregnancies to go imperfectly. I had this picture in my mind that your wife gets pregnant, she complains about her back hurting and how tired she is all the time, the guy jokes around about it and tells his friends how lucky he is to have a designated driver for nine months, you argue about the nursery and getting all the things you need ready, your child gets here at nine months, and that is when the craziness starts. That's what Hollywood tells us! I think that is literally the plot of *9 Months* with Hugh Grant. I couldn't have been more wrong. I couldn't help but feel sad hearing about all these stories after we joined this club, knowing all these people suffered in silence for the most part. It seemed they would only talk about their experiences when someone else tragically joined the club. I wish I would have known their stories for so many reasons before ours began. I wish I would have known to grieve with them and be a better friend. I wish I would have known so they could have the opportunities to talk about their deceased children with us and keep the memory of those children's names in the world. I wish I would have known so I wouldn't have been so naïve to this whole process from the start. I wish I would have known and realized that this is part of the human experience and always has been. It is only recently, in the past 100 years or so, that modern medicine has made that Hollywood experience so commonplace, leading us to believe that is how it has always worked. The privilege of having healthy children has been a battle throughout our existence as a species. While it may be the most basic thing in humanity, it is probably the hardest thing that we can do and, sadly, the thing that we have the least amount of control over. Hell, even Queen Anne of England had 18 pregnancies from which only one child made it to infancy but then still passed away. 18 PREGNANCIES! Think about that for a second. She experienced the loss of 18 children in her lifetime, and she was a Queen with the best care you could buy during that time in our human history. The one loss of Emilia was enough to change my life forever. I CAN'T EVEN IMAGINE (and this is from the co-author of a book named I Can't Imagine), losing that many children in one lifetime. I read once in another Adam Grant book, called *Give and Take*, about a concept he referred to as "uncommon commonalities." As soon as I heard this term, I couldn't help but think about this unfortunate club that we had just gained membership to after we lost Emilia. These uncommon commonalities lead you to immediately form an instant bond with people that have a similar shared experience in which they feel compelled to give and share with even perfect strangers. When something is uncommon, and you share a similar experience with someone else, you feel instantly drawn to them and it creates a meaningful connection. Well, fertility issues, pregnancy loss, miscarriages, and infant deaths are certainly no longer common in our modern society and sadly fit well in the uncommon commonality description. So once you join this tragic club, we now have something deeply personal in common. That connection makes me want to give, just like all those other people that gave to Felicia and me when we experienced our own loss. I have to write this book for anyone else out there that walks into that NICU on day one and has to stare at all of those machines, hear all the noises, see the flurry of activity, and feel that overwhelming fear that permeates your entire being as you watch your child fight for their life. I have to write this story for anyone else out there that has to eulogize their child, to let them know that they aren't alone. I have to write this for anyone that is struggling to figure out what life is all about after they lost everything. It is my duty to try and help them through this in some way, shape, or form. Even if I can't be there with you in person, I hope this story helps you in some way that will give you the courage and strength to keep fighting and trying to be the best person you can be for your children, living and deceased. If I can do that, then maybe my family's crazy journey won't have been for nothing.

For Everyone Else

Last, but not least, we are writing this book for everyone else out there that has the privilege to say the words "I can't imagine" as a response when they hear stories like you are about to hear in the coming chapters of the book. I hope to offer a look into a new paradigm in which they can view life where we don't run from other's life tragedies and pain; but rather embrace them with open arms to understand the whole spectrum of life and benefit from the wisdom, lessons, and growth that can sometimes be gained from the darker side of the human experience.

Let me explain what I mean by that.

When I first started writing this book, I wanted the title to be 22 and 6.

That stands for 22 weeks and 6 days old. That's how old my daughter was the day she unexpectedly made her dramatic entrance into this world. 22 and 6; I had no idea what these words meant before March 15th, 2020, when I heard the emergency room OBGYN say them to a colleague as my wife, Felicia, was being admitted into the hospital as she went into preterm labor. Hell, I didn't even really know a full-term pregnancy was 40 weeks (I thought it was nine months or 36 weeks). I should have read the books Felicia asked me to read. I didn't. I regret that so much now because I was so unprepared for the world I was about to experience and what our life was about to become.

22 and 6 was the title in my mind from the first day I started even thinking about writing this story about my daughter's life as we sat in the NICU after she was unexpectedly born and survived the birth. My mind was dead set on this title as I felt that it truly represented the essence of Emilia's story. I thought the words 22 and 6 said it all. 22 weeks and 6 days! Just think about those words for a second. 22 weeks and 6 days old! I didn't even know a child could be born that early, let alone have an actual chance at survival. About 10% of all children in this world are born "premature," meaning before 37 weeks by definition. That equates to about 15 million kids worldwide. Of

those 15 million kids, only about 6% are born before 28 weeks. Even less still, only around 5,000 children in the US are born at 22 weeks each year and the survival rate is only 10%. Being born at 22 weeks is extremely rare. Surviving birth at 22 weeks is even rarer. Being able to make it through all the trials to come and live a happy and healthy life is unfathomably rare. Of course, we didn't know these numbers when Emilia first arrived on March 15th, 2020. As I said, I didn't even know that full-term meant 40 weeks. Early on, this story was conceived to be a triumphant one about a special little girl born at 22 weeks and 6 days old, weighing in at 1 pound, 1 ounce, and overcoming all the odds to make it home and live a happy and healthy life with her mom and dad. That was my dream from the day this book idea was hatched, on day two of her life, sitting in the NICU as I watched my daughter fight for her shot at life. In my mind, these two numbers personified who Emilia was and the journey that she and our family were embarking on. She was born in a thunderstorm where most babies would have little to no chance of even surviving a few hours. Emilia didn't just survive; she came out ready to fight and was feisty as hell. She was kicking and flailing from the moment she was out of the womb and was ready to give this chance at life everything she had. Emilia didn't ever question her circumstances. She took what was given to her, fought like hell, and NEVER QUIT! These two numbers, 22 and 6, reminded me of the mountain she had to climb for her chance at life. They reminded me of how rare and special Emilia's existence in this world truly is. That was until this story shifted from the triumphant ending of her beating all the odds and making it home safe and sound to the ending we ultimately got, which was Emilia losing her battle unexpectedly just when we thought she was really about to make it.

After we lost Emilia, seeing the words "22 and 6" at the top of this book when I sat down to write every morning no longer felt right. While they once filled me with passion, excitement, courage, and the urge to fight on with everything I had just like I had witnessed from Emilia, this title no longer seemed to fit the story that was developing as we tried to figure out life without our sweet angel. After ten months of writing this book, I decided to make the switch to *I Can't Imagine*. Why? After almost a year of rebuilding my life without my daughter, searching for meaning and purpose again, and doing my best to be the dad that Emilia could be proud to point out to her best friends up in heaven, the words "I can't imagine" wouldn't leave my consciousness. I had been thinking about them since shortly after Emilia passed away. "I can't imagine" are the first words you hear from almost everyone when you tell them that your daughter was born at 22 weeks and 6 days old, at the beginning of a pandemic, fought like crazy in a NICU for

39 days without ever getting to meet anyone besides her mom and dad, and ultimately lost her battle due to complications from emergency surgery after it looked like we may have a chance at a miracle and making it home. I heard this reaction time and time again whenever I would share this 30-second story of Emilia. People's eyes would open wide and then fall to the floor. They would then let out a heavy sigh and say, "I'm so sorry...I can't imagine what you are going through." It happened without fail to every person I would share Emilia's story with as I slowly started to re-enter the world and see people I had known before March 15th, 2020. Every time I heard those words, "I can't imagine," something didn't sit right in my mind. The more and more I heard this phrase from others, the more I started to catch myself saying the same thing whenever I was in a similar situation and it made me start to question why do we do this as humans?

Around seven months or so into this whole journey, I read a book that had a profound effect on me, called Sapiens by Yuval Noah Harari. The book is fantastic and I devoured it as quickly as I could take it in. One of my most important takeaways was listening as Harari explains how almost everything we do in our world is built from pure human imagination. From religion to money, to corporations, to Nation-States, to cultures, etc. These staples of humanity started in someone's imagination as just a tiny idea that would go on to eventually be embraced by humanity in mass. These ideas were then internalized and interpreted by other humans, spread like wildfire, and then formed cultures and societies around them and ultimately were used to allow us all to collectively grow far beyond the limitations of our biological selves to build the world that we know and live in today. This idea, that our unique ability as humans to leverage our imaginations to create whatever world we wanted to create had a profound impact on me as I was in the process of searching for answers to the meaning in my own life after Emilia's passing. I kept thinking, our imaginations are basically our superpowers and the most treasured thing we have in this world as humans. I started to realize how long ago I had stopped using my imagination in my life. This singular idea prompted me to start to question everything around me, its origins, and how and why it came to be. This rabbit hole of internal reflection and searching ultimately kept bringing me back to one question that began to burn in my mind. If our collective imagination as a human race allowed us to build and sculpt the incredible world that we see all around us and people can accept that as a reality without thinking twice, why couldn't people "imagine" what my family was going through whenever I would tell them about Emilia's story? Why is that always our first response when we hear about a tragedy in someone's life? We have no problem happily imagining flying to another planet, scaling the tallest peaks in the world, jumping out of airplanes, winning the lottery, or whatever other "good" and incredible things we could dream up in our minds. Imagining all the fun and exciting things humans can do in this world is as easy as eating ice cream on a hot summer's day. When the first astronauts got back from landing on the moon, I'm 99% sure that the first response they encountered from friends and strangers was, "I can't imagine." I'm sure that people's minds were dreaming about this new world that they saw, asking as many questions as they could think of, and wanting to soak it all in so they could imagine what that experience might have been like. Then they would go home and talk to their families, perhaps even dream about it in their dreams, and envision themselves on that spaceship.

So what was so different about my life and my family's journey? That is all I kept thinking this past year as I read more and more into topics about the human experience and how our brains work. It didn't seem that hard to "imagine" what my family's journey must have been like. Hell, 10% of all babies in this world are born prematurely technically, so it's not even that rare. There are only 48 active astronauts in NASA right now, but that seems easier to imagine to us than a premature birth, apparently. Imagination is our superpower, right? I started to wonder, were people really saying, "I can't imagine?" or was it actually, "I don't want to imagine?" If it was, "I don't want to imagine," then why? We regularly dream of pleasant things that are about as rare as having a baby born at 22 weeks old, like becoming a billionaire, starting a successful business, galavanting around the world to new and exotic places, living in a castle, becoming a prince or princess, etc. Everyone imagines and dreams all the time. We even willingly accept completely crazy ideas like a little piece of green-tinted paper (money) having such immense value that we have our lives run on it without even blinking an eye. However, when we are forced to confront a real, painful, and tragic human experience that can happen to anyone, we just can't muster up the imagination to think what that life might be like for that unfortunate person going through it. We run as far away from pain and tragedy as we can, put it as far out of our minds as possible, and pray that this will never happen in our own lives.

As my thoughts around this question became more refined as I was deep in the middle of my own re-imagining of my life and existence, I concluded one day that this story needed to pull back the curtain on one of life's tragedies so that people could never say "I can't imagine" to me again. Now, when they said this, I had a way to combat and challenge people. I could ask, "Well, do you want to imagine? If so, here is my family's story." For those brave enough to want to take a look into things that we don't like to think about and see some incredibly important life lessons that can be gained from some of our worst human experiences, here is your chance. I promise to hold nothing back as I take you through our journey step by step in hopes that you will walk away from our experience with the ability to imagine what our life was truly like. Hopefully, you'll take away whatever lessons you can apply to your own life going forward.

Unfortunately for me, this whole journey was thrust upon my life. I was never given the option to imagine what it was like to meet the most beautiful person in the world and then have her taken away almost as quickly as we met. As I watched my precious daughter die in my wife's arms and my world collapse around me, I was forced to stop everything, question my life, and re-imagine my world. As I sat in the rubble of my former life, I found myself searching for answers to life's questions. What is this all about? Who am I? Who do I want to be? Is there a God? If so, why would he do this to our family and me? The more I questioned, the more I searched for answers. The more I searched for answers, the more I learned. The more I learned, the more I reflected. The more I reflected, the more I noticed my imagination returning and all the joy and hope that brought back to my life. I also started to wonder why it's so hard for people to imagine? At what point in life do we stop imagining? Are we just afraid to imagine bad things? How can you have any empathy if you are never willing to imagine someone else's reality?

To be fair, "I can't imagine" would have been the first comment out of my mouth as well before this happened in my own life. This experience was a wake-up call to me. I hope that it can also be a bit of a wake-up call to you if you find yourself no longer imagining much in your own life. Kids ask A LOT of questions. Some studies show that four years olds ask as many as 200-300 questions per day. Warren Berger, the author of A More Beautiful Question, says kids ask an average of 40,000 questions between ages two and five. When we are young, our minds are full of imagination, questions, and a never-ending search for new knowledge. Berger also found that over the next couple of years, as kids go to school, the number of questions they ask dramatically declines. The reasons vary. It can range from exhausted parents that can't answer any more questions, teachers being measured on making sure kids know answers versus asking more questions, or kids being afraid of being seen by peers as stupid because asking questions means you don't know anything which can make them appear uncool. Whatever it is that drives the dramatic decline, we all know it happens. As we get older, we slowly start "knowing" a lot more and stop learning and thinking. We stop asking questions and using our imaginations. I don't know about you, but I stopped questioning and using my imagination long ago. I had it all figured out and was on the "right" path to success or whatever that means. I had a happy life, a successful career, happy marriage, etc. My hamster wheel was pretty dang nice, and I had stopped asking any of the big (and little) questions in life long ago. Too often, once we get our hamster wheel of life going in the "right" direction, we hop on for the ride and pray to God that it all doesn't fall apart. Well, unfortunately for me, my family's hamster wheel didn't just break down; an atomic bomb fell on it and left nothing in its wake. I was forced to stop, think, reflect, and start to use my imagination again to do anything to shield myself from the searing pain of my reality.

So, that is why this book is now called I Can't Imagine instead of the original title, *22 and 6*. This story will walk you through my daughter's harrowing battle for a shot at life, look into my search for the answers to life's burning questions that are forced on you after a tragedy, how that search changed my life and got me imagining again, and how this whole journey helped me to find purpose to try and keep "living for two" to carry on the legacy of my hero and daughter, Emilia Quinn Sears.

Which brings everything back full circle on this journey which we are about to embark on together. The goal is to help anyone reading this story that isn't in the uncommon commonality of the bereaved parents club to fully be able to imagine my family's life and all that we went through after hearing our story. I hope that maybe it will open their minds just a little bit more to remind themselves when they find themselves saying, "I can't imagine" in the future to be more open to embracing the human experience for all the good and bad that it has to offer.

THE HOW - Structure of the Book and the Two Selves (Remembering and Experiencing Self)

The day Emilia was born, we had no clue what to do or how to act. Who knows how you are supposed to handle your seemingly healthy wife all of the sudden going into preterm labor and your firstborn child arriving almost four months earlier than expected? From the moment we heard that Emilia survived the birth, we had no idea of what was to come or how we were going to get through this as a family. It truly was the first time in my life where I felt completely helpless toward any future outcome that was to occur. As parents of a child in the NICU, you don't have any real job or responsibilities in the process. The care team provides around-the-clock nurturing, care, cleaning, and medical treatment. We learned quickly that your main job is to do everything you can to keep yourself from mentally falling to pieces. I'm a bit of a control freak overall. I like structure and consistency. It keeps me calm and at peace. Trauma has a way of forcing things on you, whether you like it or not. In this case, trauma made me triple down on my focus around structure and consistency. With that idea in mind, I devised a plan to control whatever I could control within the first few days after Emilia was born. The goal was to try to stay focused, healthy, calm, and present for ourselves and our daughter. We needed to keep our minds sharp, our bodies energetic, and our emotions in check as best as possible to prepare for the long journey ahead. A few of the actions we decided to try were to do our best to journal every day to document what was happening around us, read as much as possible, maintain our energy every day, keep our emotions in check by honing in on our faith, and SUPPORT THE CRAP OUT OF OUR CARE TEAM with anything and everything we could do.

One of those activities, our journaling, eventually evolved into a daily log of what we were observing, how we were feeling, what was medically going on with Emilia, etc. As I mentioned before, the plan quickly became to keep this practice up in the hopes to one day give her our journals, when she was big, strong, and old enough to understand, so that she could relive the amazing journey she endured. Again, in the NICU, you don't have a lot to do, so I took up the practice of reading each day. Daily reading wasn't a normal habit for me, but it quickly took hold as a staple in my life and provided a small source of joy as I sat around a hospital room most of the day. I started reading like it was my job and the pace only accelerated in the months that followed. To date, I've read more in the last year of my life than I have in all of my other years prior, combined.

In my newfound love of reading, I came across an amazing book written by Nobel Prize-winning psychologist Daniel Kahneman called, *Thinking Fast and Slow*. In this book, I discovered, according to Kahneman, that we have what he calls our two selves: the experiencing self and the remembering self. The experiencing self is an example of the fast, intuitive, unconscious mode of thinking that operates in the present moment, focusing on the quality of our experience IN our life – living life rather than thinking about it. The experiencing self knows only the present moment and what is going on right in front of us. We often ignore how the experiencing self perceives things upon reflection, and it doesn't impact our utility of an event very much, if at all. Essentially, what is happening to us at the moment is fairly irrelevant in the long run toward our happiness or memories. The remembering self, on the other hand, is our storyteller. This is where all the memories of our experiences are stored. This is how we think about and perceive a moment in time or an event in our life. We typically only remember the beginnings, the peaks, and the ends of events, and those are what we use to shape an experience upon reflection. After encountering the concept of two selves along the journey, I devised a plan to try and combine the two selves into one work of art that would become this book. By leveraging both our journals to illustrate the experiencing self and my internal narrative for the remembering self, this book is a rare combination of the two selves colliding for a unique look at our family's journey, so any reader can truly fully imagine our experience. Each section of the book is structured with a story of the remembering self-thoughts of our NICU experience, losing our daughter, and our quest to regain purpose in our lives. After each remembering self-story is shared, the journals will be chronologically placed for the reader to consume to see a different perspective from our experiencing self as well to serve as an anchor for life being lived in real-time.

Now, with the what, when, why, and how of this story complete, let's begin our journey together.

PART I

Emilia's Story

CHAPTER 1

The Birth

Our crazy journey began on Friday, March 13th, 2020. One of Felicia's best friends, Brittany, was in town to help her to pick out a venue for Emilia's baby shower which was supposed to happen in just a few short weeks. We all met after work, at a place in Broadripple (a bar and restaurant district in Indianapolis), with some of Felicia's other good friends for some barbeque and a few drinks (not for Felicia, obviously). Everything in our life seemed to be in perfect harmony. We had just had our most recent ultrasound the day before (March 12th) and had not heard a peep from the doctor. Her only advice to us was to have fun on our upcoming trip to Hawaii, don't get coronavirus, and eat as much sushi as Felicia can handle because it is super fresh there, so no need to worry. Felicia had just started to show a little baby bump that everyone could see. She was always so self-conscious about her lack of a baby bump. Side note, it's so funny how different pregnancy can be for everyone. I never in my wildest dreams thought I'd have to calm Felicia down for not looking too big. That Hollywood imagery of a "normal" pregnancy is so strong and powerful.

I was recently looking at a photo Brittany shared with me of that Friday night out at the restaurant called Half Liter. Before I had arrived, someone at the party had gifted Felicia with a tiny pair of cute pink sneakers as a gift for our future daughter. When I got to the restaurant after work, arriving a little later than the rest of Felicia and her friends, someone showed me the cool sneakers that had already been opened. I'm a big sneakerhead and loved them. I pulled them up close to my face, jokingly pretended to flip my hair back, and Brittany snapped a goofy photo of me holding them up while cheesing for the camera. It hurts a lot seeing that photo today and thinking what was to come over the next 48 hours and subsequent months. Everything seemed so normal that Friday night. The pregnancy was coming along nicely, it finally felt like Felicia was starting to feel a little better, and no issues from the doctor at our last ultrasound the day before. It was the typical Hollywood pregnancy at that point in time and we were all feeling great. Little did we know what was just around the corner.

Saturday, March 14th, 2020 – Brittany and Felicia were out all day trying to find the perfect venue for Emilia's upcoming baby shower. They were gone all afternoon and I think I remember being told later that night that they had officially found and booked a venue. I can't say for certain because everything that happened after that was such a blur, and the idea of a baby shower became so irrelevant just 24 hours later. Once they returned from their day of searching, we were supposed to go to dinner again with a few other friends. Around 4:30 p.m., Felicia started to voice that she wasn't feeling too great and didn't know if stressing herself that night would be a good idea. That was pretty un-Felicia-like, so my ears perked up a little bit when she said that. I asked her what was wrong and she said, "Nothing much. Just feeling a little off, but it's not a concern." After 30 minutes or so of debating whether we were going to leave or not, the decision was made to stay in by Felicia, Brittany, and me. We decided to shift to plan B and go down the street to the Whole Foods grocery store, buy a bunch of organic junk food snacks (you know, bad food that is super expensive but still says gluten and dairy-free on it), and rent a few movies to watch at home from the Redbox. As I'm writing this, I'm laughing at how funny my generation has become and how much things change yet stay the same. Somehow places like Whole Foods, which started an organic counterculture movement, are now a shining example of overindulgence, excess consumerism, and selfishness. We spent like $50 for oat milk ice cream, a few gluten-free cupcakes, gluten-free corn puffs (i.e., Cheetos), and a dairy-free frozen pizza. It's packaged as health food, but it's really just $50 worth of junk food. That's not what this book is about, though...that was just a tangent. I swear to you that what I just described isn't anything like our everyday life. We aren't one of those typical millennial couples. We certainly did things like this every once in a while, but it truly was few and far between.

As we're walking around Whole Foods, searching for bougie junk food options, I remember looking over my shoulder and seeing Felicia wince in pain a little as she was walking down one of the aisles. I stopped her and asked, "Are you sure you're okay? Do we need to call a doctor?" She responded that she had a little pain, but it was only once every few hours, and the pain didn't last long, so no need to worry. We kept going through Whole Foods until we had picked up all the goodies and snacks we had wanted for the night.

Something felt off the whole time we were there and we all could feel it. Felicia had already had some issues earlier during the pregnancy that scared us both, but it always seemed like it was okay, and we were just panicking first-time parents afterward. This night felt like something was actually wrong and we were all just afraid to admit it. As we checked out, got in the car, and headed back to the house, it was clear Felicia wasn't feeling great. We got home, watched our movies, and ate our bougie snacks until about midnight, when we all went to bed. A few times throughout that night, she had a few little episodes of pain, but we continued to chalk it up to not being a big deal and went to bed.

Sunday, March 15th, 2020 - This was the best and worst day of my life. I woke up around 7:30 a.m. and looked over at Felicia, who was already awake. I immediately asked how she was feeling. She said, "Much better than last night." She only had to wake up in the middle of the night once with the pain she was experiencing and then it went away after a few minutes and she was able to sleep through the night. I was so relieved. Brittany, who had stayed in our guest room, came into our bedroom to check on Felicia after she woke up. I remember saying something stupid like, "I'm convinced she is just having some stomach issues because of eating too much bad food Friday and Saturday." We usually have pretty strict diets. I'm a Celiac who also chooses to eat dairy-free. Felicia follows these diets as well, partly because she likes it and partly because I'm so picky that it's just easier that way. My go-to response when someone isn't feeling well is to immediately blame what they eat. I did this for everything. I'm like that dad in *My Big Fat Greek Wedding* that carries around a bottle of Windex and sprays it on everything because he thinks it is the cure-all. That is me with food. In my mind, everything can be solved by what you are eating, and I am always quick to say that whenever someone is having unexplained issues with their body. I couldn't have been more stupid and naive! As the morning began to take shape, I got up, and I was replaced by Brittany next to Felicia on my spot in our bed. Brittany and I kept asking Felicia how she felt, keeping a watchful eye on her. It seemed like the little painful episodes were occurring more frequently now after she had awoken, about once an hour.

It was about this time that I snapped a photo on my iPhone of Felicia and our dog, Lea while laying on her pregnancy pillow. This huge pregnancy pillow is a giant U that takes up a large portion of our king-sized bed. Felicia was sitting at the top of the U toward the head of the bed, while Lea was lying at her feet at the opening of the U. It looked like Lea was worried and protecting her. I thought they looked cute together, which is why I took the picture. Lea and Felicia have a special bond. She protects Felicia and is like her bodyguard all day, every day. Normally she gives her a little more space, but this day, she was right on top of her. It turns out she probably knew something we didn't. Dogs are amazing like that; they can really sense things that humans just aren't capable of feeling or seeing. It was about 10 a.m. at this point, and we decided that we needed to call the doctor's office for some advice as we were all officially a little concerned now. Unfortunately, we couldn't get anyone on the phone. We literally tried for an hour to talk to someone, anyone, and couldn't get through. Finally, around 11 a.m. that morning, the OBGYN on call was connected to us. We told her about Felicia's last 24 hours or so and the pain she was experiencing. After five minutes or so, her recommendation was, "everything is most likely fine, but if you feel like you need to come in, do so." I don't know what we were hoping for, really. That was like the 3rd time during the pregnancy that we had made an effort to call someone because Felicia was scared about something and the answer was basically always the same. You should be fine but come in if you feel like you aren't. She was so freaking helpful! I honestly can't even imagine.

Time out (in my best Zach Morris from Saved by The Bell voice)...

I want to take a second to call out the words "I can't imagine" in my own writing throughout this story. As I was proofreading my own words, I started to realize how often I found myself saying these words as well, about a whole lot of different topics. I wanted to let the reader know that they are not alone and show that I'm not perfect either. We are all human and it is hard to try and imagine life from someone else's perspective. The goal isn't to make the reader or myself feel bad; rather, it is to point out the areas where we have the opportunity to grow as we strive to open ourselves up to thinking about as many different types of human experiences as we can. Throughout the story, I plan to call out every time I say, "I can't imagine" myself and will point it out with a parenthetical "there it is again" each time it occurs.

Time in...

I honestly can't even imagine what women must go through during pregnancy. So many new things are happening to their bodies and they probably have no idea what to make of them: so many questions and concerns with no one there to really help. Keep in mind that we were literally at the doctor's office getting a routine ultrasound just 48 hours before this phone call was made. Nothing was off during that visit. How could things have changed so quickly?

We went back to waiting around the bedroom for Felicia to hopefully start feeling a little better and for this dark cloud of worry that was hanging over all of us to lift. As we were waiting, I was getting restless (like I always do). It was a Sunday afternoon and we were wasting the whole day sitting around in the bedroom. I'm a busy body and always need to be doing something. I thought to myself, "Well, the doctor said not to worry. We've done this song and dance before and nothing bad happened. It is probably just gas or an upset tummy from the bad food this weekend." I asked Felicia if it was okay if I went to the gym and got a workout in? What an asshole!!! My thinking was that I knew Brittany was there so Felicia wouldn't be by herself. That was the justification in my mind, along with all the other reasons listed above. The truth is that I was being a selfish jerk and I'll forever regret making this decision. Around 11:30 am, I got changed and headed off to the gym. I arrived around 11:40 am. I went up the stairs to the cardio area, put my stuff in a cubby, put my AirPods in, and went off to start my workout on the treadmill. I was only a little over a minute into the run when my phone rang. It was Brittany. She said, "Felicia just started bleeding and we need to get her to the emergency room ASAP." I said, "Oh my God. I'll be right back in five minutes!" I hit the emergency shut down on the treadmill, ran to get my stuff, and sprinted down the stairs and out of the building. I drove as fast as I could to get back to the house, and when I arrived, Felicia and Brittany were in the driveway.

Brittany looked like she had seen a ghost and had no idea how to process what was happening in front of her eyes. Felicia was keeled over in pain, crying, and visibly terrified. Brittany got Felicia into the front seat and then hopped into the backseat of the car. We took off for the emergency room toward our hospital at IU Methodist in downtown Indianapolis. I still remember pulling up to the driveway so vividly. I was terrified. I thought we had already lost our daughter and was preparing myself for the worst. I was so scared for Felicia, who looked so devastated and in so much pain (physically and mentally). It was all really hard to process and still is even as I type this, trying to find the words to describe the scene.

In the car on the way to the ER, everything was eerily silent except for Felicia's light sobbing and occasional apologetic comments. I kept telling her that this isn't her fault. Then, everyone would stop talking again as we drove silently with our thoughts. I can't imagine (there it is again) what Brittany and Felicia were thinking during those quiet moments. I know that all I was thinking the whole time is, "We lost her! We lost her! We lost her!" I was coming to terms with the fact that Emilia was already gone and how devastating this was going to be after officially receiving the news in hours to come. It was a coldish early spring morning and no one was really out and about on the roads because it was a Sunday. We were able to cruise to the hospital in a relatively quick fashion in about 10-12 minutes. Ironically, this is the first and only time that we ever made that hospital run.

I had always envisioned that, as we got closer to Emilia's due date, we would have done a few trial runs to nail this process. Felicia would say it's time, and we'd grab our go-bags, jump in the car, call our families on the way, take every shortcut, and get her there safe, sound, and excited to meet our new baby girl in a few hours. It definitely didn't go like that. We had never made that run from our house to the IU Methodist emergency room entrance before. I had no idea where I was even going, to be honest. We had the GPS going and Brittany was looking for signs to the ER. We didn't have any clothes packed. We literally just hopped into the car and went. We were all robbed of so many little things during this process, I know this may not seem like much, but it was. Nothing about this experience to come was anything like I could have imagined (there it is again) in my wildest dreams the day that Felicia told me she was pregnant. Literally, I couldn't have dreamed up this story because... who the hell would want to do that?

Those 10-ish minutes in the car felt like an eternity. As I pulled up to the emergency room entrance, Felicia and Brittany got out, and I went off to go park the car. By the time I got back to the ER entrance, Felicia was already in a wheelchair and they were waiting for someone at the desk to come get her. A few minutes later, we were wheeled back to the ER. It was around 12:30 p.m. at this point. We were sitting in the emergency room waiting for the OBGYN on call to come over to evaluate Felicia and tell us what I already knew...that we had lost the pregnancy and our dreams of starting our family were over before they began. I don't think Felicia and I spoke much at all during the time we sat there waiting for the OB on call to come. I remember that it was a tiny little room. Felicia was sitting on the bed and I was sitting in a chair tucked into the corner, kind of behind her where I could only see the side of her face. All we could really do was hold each other's hands and wait. Felicia apologized a few more times and I assured her it wasn't her fault. That is about the only thing that I can remember during this time.

My most vivid memory is just of that damn tiny, little room. It was so small with a lot of things and equipment packed into one little area. I was stuck in the back corner of the room and could barely see my wife's face as she faced forward toward the entrance curtain/door. For the rest of my life, I will be terrified of ER rooms after this experience. You are behind a curtain, in a tiny room, just waiting for someone to come help you during an EMERGENCY! Sitting and waiting for what feels like an eternity while your mind is racing with all the worst thoughts you can imagine. Finally, someone came in and calmly started asking Felicia some questions about what was going on. I don't really remember what they spoke about other than Felicia telling her about the past 24 hours and the bleeding that had just started at home a few hours prior. I wanted to ask if our daughter was still alive, but deep down, I already knew and couldn't bear the thought of saying the words out loud. After a few questions, the doctor said they were going to start with an ultrasound to see if they could still find a heartbeat. She pulled out the ultrasound equipment and began to hover around Felicia's belly, searching for a heartbeat. Circle after circle, we waited and waited for an answer. In my mind, there was about a 1% chance that Emilia was still with us. I had never gone through anything like this before, but hearing Felicia say she was bleeding gave me all kinds of red flags that something had gone horribly wrong with Emilia and that she must have had a miscarriage or something. The doctor finally says, "I think I hear a heartbeat, but I can't tell if it is the mom's or the baby's" HUH??? There is a chance she's still alive? My heart jumped a little, thinking that maybe a miracle was still a possibility. I didn't want to get my hopes up, though. Because ER's aren't set up with the most state-of-the-art equipment, the doctor was having a hard time pinpointing what she was hearing. A few more circles and a few minutes later, she finally said, "Yeah, I think this is the baby and we still have a heartbeat." Holy shit! She was still alive! That was the first illustration of this child's never-quit approach to life. Emilia was not to be denied an opportunity to enter this world and get her chance at life.

The doctor began to examine Felicia and determined that she was already fully dilated and going into active labor. At that point, the whole conversation changed. They discussed with us what was going to happen and that we needed to get Felicia admitted into Labor and Delivery ASAP! Felicia was prepped for delivery and rushed out of the ER and over into the Labor and Delivery section of the hospital. Little did we know that the craziness of the day was just beginning.

LDR 20. I still remember seeing the sign on the door of this room as we were wheeled in around 2:30 p.m. to prepare to bring Emilia into this world. For some reason, I made a mental note of this number and wrote it down in what was to become my daily journal, an app on my phone I used called Evernote. LDR 20 will be forever burned into my brain for the rest of my life. That is the place where our little Emilia was born and given a chance at life. Just a little over three hours since this whole thing started, we were officially sitting in a delivery room preparing to bring Emilia into this world. I don't exactly remember when, but at some point early on, after we made it into LDR 20, I stepped outside to call my parents and family for the first time to let them know what was going on. That was one of the hardest conversations I can remember. I had no idea what to tell them, how to explain what was going on, what was going to happen, etc. I literally just called them and told them to get to the hospital as we have no idea what is to come. I remember walking around the hallway and trying not to cry, but I couldn't stop myself as I was talking to my mom. I was so scared. I was scared for Emilia, for Felicia, and for myself. That was the first time that I really had a moment to step away from all the action and speak to my mom. I tried to keep it together, but I couldn't. My mom told me that they were on their way and that they were praying for a miracle. Felicia's mom lives in Texas and she was on her way to the airport to hop on the first flight. Fun note, this was all happening at the beginning of the COVID-19 pandemic. It wasn't a full-blown panic everywhere just yet, but the concern was certainly known by all the medical community. The US was in a bit of a holding pattern at this time, waiting to see how things would play out, and we were at the tipping point on March 15th, 2020. Business was still normal at hospitals, but they were beginning to tighten up the reins on who would or wouldn't be allowed into the hospital on a situational basis. Because they didn't know how our event would turn out (meaning Emilia could possibly not survive), they told me that they would allow my parents to be in the Labor and Delivery area and wait with us in the unit. THANK GOD! Little did we know at that time, this would be the ONLY time that anyone in either of our families would actually get to meet Emilia in person.

As I went back into the room, I sat down next to Felicia and held her hand as she laid on the delivery bed. We listened to our delivery nurse, Allison, give us instructions and get Felicia all situated in the room. They asked Felicia if she wanted some magnesium to help protect Emilia and warned that it might make her sick. Felicia, of course, said yes. A few minutes later, she was puking in a bucket. The anesthesiologist then came in to talk about an epidural. She told Felicia she was fully dilated and if this pain was tolerable, then really no need. Felicia decided not to get it. Felicia, just like Emilia, is incredibly strong and her pain tolerance is unreal. As this story goes on, you will see where Emilia gets her brute force strength and endurance from, and it certainly isn't me. Emilia gets her optimism from me. Endurance and optimism are pretty powerful things and that is Emilia in a nutshell.

Then, we waited. It was now around 4 p.m. At one point, two NICU doctors came in to sit down and talk with us about what was to come when Emilia arrived. They asked us the weirdest question, I thought. They said, "Once Emilia is born, do you want us to try and revive her?" I don't know why, but that question baffled me. Felicia and I both looked at each other with a bewildered look on our faces and turned back to the doctors and said, "Why would we not?" The thought hadn't even crossed our minds that we wouldn't try to give Emilia a chance at life. Who in the hell would do that? I didn't know that you could even do such a thing? The doctor said, "Oh, we agree. We just have to ask that as some people say no." I couldn't even believe that someone could literally deny a tiny child a chance at life as they entered this world. All I know is that certainly wasn't happening in this situation. I'd give my own life for Emilia to have a chance at life in this world. She was going to get every ounce of support we could get for her.

Over the next hour, we waited around and talked to our nurse to keep ourselves busy and our minds occupied. I paced around the room, met my parents out in the hallway, filled them in on what was going on, and tried to keep busy as best I could. Around 5 p.m., our delivery nurse said she was going to step away for a minute or two, but wanted to show me first what to do if Felicia starts to go into delivery and how to signal the whole team. She showed me this button on the wall and said, "All you have to do is hit this button if I'm not in the room, and the whole team will come running."

What freaking timing! Less than a minute later, as our nurse was preparing to leave the room, Felicia's water breaks and yells, "She's coming!" The nurse ran to Felicia and told me to hit the button. I sprinted across the room and smacked it as hard as I could. A few seconds later, a team of like ten people swarmed into the room. The NICU nurses and doctors were at the ready, so the minute Emilia was out, they could try and revive her. Felicia screamed and pushed. I held her hand as hard as I could. I couldn't bear to watch what was about to happen. I literally had no idea if our daughter was going to survive or not and couldn't muster up the courage to actually watch what was going on. I turned my head to face the back wall and would every once in a while look at Felicia's face as she pushed. I couldn't look at what was going on in the rest of the room. I cried. I RARELY cry, but I just couldn't hold it back at that moment. I was so scared and worried about what was about to happen.

At 5:16 p.m., our beautiful little daughter was born. I heard the tiniest little cry out of her when she was born, and then she was whisked off to the other side of the room for the NICU specialists to get to work on trying to revive her. Felicia and I were scared and crying. The delivery nurse asked us if we had a name for her. We both looked at each other and immediately said in unison, "Emilia." They asked, "Amelia with an A?" We both looked at each other again, and I replied, "With an E," and Felicia smiled because that is how she always wanted it spelled. The previous few weeks, we had been debating back and forth between Emilia and Amelia. I was in the Amelia camp. Felicia was in the Emilia camp. We still hadn't really made the final call until that split-second decision when the nurse asked us for her name. We are both so happy we ultimately went with the E!

We hadn't done much in terms of traditional prep for our daughter's arrival. The nursery wasn't done, the baby shower hadn't happened, hell, we hadn't even announced our pregnancy on Facebook yet. The only thing we had done was pick out her name, Emilia Quinn Sears. What a beautiful name! We waited for what seemed like an eternity to get an update from the other side of the room to learn if Emilia survived. About five minutes later, I looked at the back of the room and could see three of the NICU nurses smiling a little bit as they stood watching what was going on behind the curtain we couldn't see around. They seemed super calm and unworried about what they were watching on the other side of the curtain. That gave me some faith that maybe we would clear this next big hurdle and hear that our daughter had survived. Finally, about 10 minutes later, the doctor wheeled over our little daughter in her isolate for us to meet her. She was alive and had a chance at life. "Incredible!" is all I could think.

My parents came into the room to see their exhausted daughter-in-law and to meet their newest granddaughter. I don't think any of us really knew what to do. I never in my wildest dreams imagined (there it is again) my parents meeting their newest grandchild in this fashion. We all knew how delicate this situation was but didn't want to say it out loud. Felicia was exhausted from just giving birth. I was exhausted from the mental strain of not knowing whether my daughter was dead or alive for the past six hours. I remember someone, maybe my mom, asking to take a picture really quick of Felicia and me with Emilia in her isolate in the background. That was, I think, the only picture we took that whole day of any aspect of the birth. I look at that picture every once in a while and can still remember trying to figure out whether to smile or not before it was snapped. The picture looks exactly like that for both Felicia and me. It was awkward. Were we happy? Of course, we were happy that Emilia was here, but we certainly were probably more exhausted and scared of the unknown to come than anything. I feel like the first moment you get to hold your child is always portrayed as the moment that you will remember for the rest of your life. That's the moment that your first child steals your heart and you realize you will never get it back. That moment is a smiling from ear to ear moment of euphoria. Our first few minutes with our daughter were anything but that mental image. That is probably why I remember feeling so weird about that picture. I almost didn't even want it taken. I'm glad we did because, as it would turn out, we wouldn't get very many moments over the next 40 days together in the same room as a family. It is one of the rare photos that I'll ever have with my beautiful wife and daughter together with me. For that, I'm so grateful that we took it and it exists.

After getting to spend a few minutes with Emilia near us, they had to whisk her off to the NICU to get her all set up for the LONG stay to come. We were told we'd have to wait a few hours before we could come in and see her. As they wheeled her away, I took another picture on my phone. That picture would turn out to be probably the most impactful picture I will have ever taken in my life. When a micro-preemie is born, they don't have much body fat to protect them and keep them warm. They will literally freeze to death if they aren't wrapped up and placed in a heated incubator immediately. Emilia was born at only 1 pound, 1 ounce. She was REALLY tiny and needed all the warmth she could get. The reason I mention this is when we first saw her in the hospital room in the isolate, she was wrapped in this plastic bag with a beanie on her head. You could barely see her as the plastic wrapping was covering her almost entirely. As she was being wheeled away, she pushed her tiny little hand in the air and it barely snuck out from all the plastic around her. It was basically all you could see: all this plastic, a little beanie, and the tiniest little hand sticking out of the top. I was lucky that I snapped a photo at that time. As I looked back at it, it almost looked like she was saying, "It's okay, mom and dad. I got this!" as she was being wheeled away. I have to believe, after getting to know Emilia over the next 39 days, that she was saying exactly that. That photo hangs up on the wall in my office and I look at it almost daily. It gives me the chills sometimes when I see it and think of all the strength, courage, and fight that little baby would show us over the next few weeks as she struggled for her chance at life.

After Emilia left the Labor and Delivery room and was whisked off to the NICU, my parents stayed around for another 30 minutes or so to comfort us and then left to give us some time to rest and recover. Eventually, Felicia and I were moved to the Mother/Baby portion of the maternity ward, where we waited for the call of when we could officially go see Emilia over in the NICU for the first time. I don't really remember much during this time. The only thing I remember is calling Brittany to see if she could gather up some of our stuff back at the house and bring it over to the hospital for us. I walked Brittany through, on the phone, where to find everything that Felicia and

I would want/need for our stay the next three days. Remember, we hadn't made our "go bags" yet because we thought we still had four months left to go before Emilia was supposed to get here. I was planning on waiting until May or June before we did this step. We had absolutely nothing with us. We just ran out of the house and got to the hospital as quickly as we could earlier in the day. Brittany followed my instructions, nicely packed everything up for us, and brought it to the hospital. I went down to the lobby to pick it up from her and the security team wouldn't let her in, not even into the lobby, because of coronavirus concerns. We went outside instead to make the exchange. I hugged her and thanked her for everything she did for us on this day. It was an awkward encounter overall. Neither one of us knew what to say. Everything just felt weird. It felt like we both wanted to say, "What the hell just happened?" Neither of us seemed to know what feelings to express at the moment. I went back into the hospital and waited with Felicia until we were able to go visit Emilia.

CHAPTER 2

She's Here, She's Great, She's Adorable, and She's Loved!

The Journal Begins - Dazed and Confused (Day 1)

Around 9 p.m., on March 15th, 2020, we finally got a chance to go into the NICU to see Emilia for the first time since her birth. We walked up to the NICU door, hit the call button, and someone replied, "What's your code word?" We asked, "What code word? We're here to see Emilia Quinn Sears. We are her parents." They buzzed us into the washing-up space and told us through the door that in the future, we needed to pick a code word that only we would know for us to be able to come and go from the NICU. They asked, "What would you like?" I looked at Felicia as if to say, "Do you have a preference?" She didn't seem to have anything top of mind, so I immediately chose the first word that came to my mind and said, "Lion." The word lion didn't really come out of nowhere; I'm really big on lions. I don't totally know why, but lions are one of my two spirit animals (trash pandas, i.e., raccoons being the other). *The Lion King* was always my favorite Disney movie growing up, my Zodiac sign is Leo, and I've always just loved how regal, strong, and majestic lions are in the wild. Lions are fearless, courageous, strong, playful, they care for their pride, and they are leaders. Even though I had only known Emilia for a few hours, she already seemed like the prototypical lioness to me. I thought that code word personified her and I was happy to donate my spirit animal to my daughter.

We scrubbed in and went through the NICU door for the first time. I didn't really know what to expect. There were doctors and nurses everywhere. We had to walk by all of them sitting at their computers in a tight little corridor before entering the open floor plan NICU. One of the nurses offered to help us find our way and walked us over to Emilia's little section of the shared

NICU space. Anytime you walk into somewhere new, there is always this incredibly awkward feeling. That feeling when you know you just went behind the curtain into the unknown, and you have no idea what's about to happen. The NICU might be the weirdest place to get adjusted to. Nobody actually wants to be in there. The first time you enter the NICU, the sites, noises, and activity are all a bit overwhelming. I personally was expecting to see a bunch of parents and families there and was really surprised to find out that it was just Felicia and me, surrounded by like 30 beds filled with babies and a bunch of nurses and doctors. As we slowly made our way over to Emilia's isolate in the corner of one section of the NICU, we walked up and were introduced to her first nurse. She was so nice and welcoming.

Quick aside, NICU nurses are living SAINTS on this Earth. They truly are the most patient, kind, loving, and caring people you will probably ever encounter in your life. Thank God for them and what they do every day! I still remember telling them multiple times a day how much I was in awe of them and what they do every single day. They deal with some of the most intense and pressure-packed environments most people could ever even imagine, and they do it all with patience, grace, and a smile on their faces. Some of them became what felt like best friends, older sisters, and mentors to us throughout our time with them. Treat them like you would treat your closest family and friends, and you will be rewarded beyond your imagination with over-the-top care for your child and emotional support and coaching for the parents. They deserve to be loved and supported just as much as they are about to love and support your child. There will be a ton more in this book dedicated to Emilia's care team as we go. For now, back to the story.

As we were welcomed by our first nurse to Emilia's new home, we approached Emilia's isolate with an incredibly scared and timid look in our eyes. There are so many buttons, tubes, machines, noises, monitors, etc. It is so overwhelming that you don't even really want to get too close because you feel like you will break something and hurt your child. I remember her asking us if we have any questions. She said, "We love to answer questions, and don't worry if they are stupid." I LOVE asking questions normally; it's basically what I do for a living. I'm perpetually fascinated by pretty much everything in this world. However, on this day, neither Felicia nor I could think of anything to ask. We were speechless and our minds were literally in a fog. I still couldn't quite figure out how we even got to this moment, sitting next to our child when she wasn't due for another four months. By this point in the day, it was somewhere around 9:30 or 10 p.m. We were exhausted, overwhelmed, scared, anxious, confused, terrified, etc. The last thing on my mind was trying to figure out what all these buttons and machines did. Eventually, we were still able to get out a few questions and started to become familiarized with our first NICU jargon and vernacular that would become a second vocabulary over the coming weeks. Words like blood gas, the jet, oxygen settings, sats, RT's, NP's, central lines, TPN, and PICC lines, eventually became the norm. All these words didn't really mean anything to us yet. We asked a few more questions when something would beep and she would take time away from what she was doing and try and explain it to us. Eventually, we sat down in the little chairs near Emilia's isolate, held hands, and watched the nurse do her thing in silence. I feel like we sat there quietly for about an hour or so while just taking it all in and snapping the occasional picture. Finally, we decided it was time for us to go get some sleep and do our best to recharge for the fight to come in the morning. We headed back to the Mother/Baby room that we would be staying in for the next 48 hours, and we crashed. That was officially the longest, happiest, and saddest day of my life, all wrapped up in one.

The next morning, as we woke up, I could hear the babies crying and new parents tending to them in the rooms next to us. I have no idea what that experience is like to have your daughter actually with you in your room in the Mother/Baby section of the hospital. It's little things like this that most people take for granted in life. Those other new parents are probably all just as exhausted and tired as we were. The big difference was that they were exhausted from taking care of a newborn. We were exhausted from worrying about whether our daughter was going to live or not in the room down the hall. We left the room as quickly as we could to get back over to the NICU to spend time with Emilia. We wandered back through the halls and followed the signs to the NICU entrance, said our codename "Lion," scrubbed in, and walked back over to Emilia's isolate in the corner of the unit. This morning felt a little different. We were no longer in shock from what happened the day before. We were no longer physically exhausted. For the first time, we were able to truly just be in the presence of our daughter and try to figure out what this parenting thing was all about. We met our new nurse, asked some questions for a few minutes, and then we just sat down and stared at her in her isolate covered in blankets. After 10 minutes in the NICU, the thing I can tell you I remember the most is all the dinging, bonging, alarms, etc. JUST when you feel like you can relax and let your guard down, some alarm goes off and brings you back to the reality that you will never relax in this environment. That is the NICU in a nutshell. Every time there is an alarm, another question comes up. Is that bad? What does that mean? Should we be freaking out? Is she okay? What do you do to fix this? What is this monitoring? Luckily, these nurses are freaking saints and are always willing to answer your questions. I came to find out that they actually love to answer these questions because, sadly, most parents aren't too nice to them apparently. I can totally understand how the stress and anxiety of the situation can get to people, but there is NEVER a situation where you should take out your anger and concern on others. From what they told us, it happens all the time. That is so sad because they are such amazing people. Over the next 38 days, I think we would ask so many questions that I feel like I could probably be a neonatologist or a NICU nurse by the end of our stay (I'm kidding…sort of). The beeping and alarms seem funny to me now because I miss them so much, and I'd give anything to hear them again because that would mean that our daughter is still with us. I remember I made a joke to Felicia after we had been home from the NICU for a few weeks after we lost Emilia. I said, "You know what the WORST sound in the world is? The alarms in the NICU!" Then I asked, "You know what the BEST sound in the world is? The alarms in the NICU!" She agreed. Those alarms will never leave your memory, and I still miss those alarms to this day.

After about an hour of visiting, Felicia decided to go back to the room as it was so hard to sit in the NICU and be immersed in this environment. It was truly chaotic. Not only was it hard to see our daughter fighting for her life, but you are also hearing all the other babies' alarms going off as well. So even when you don't need to be worried about your own child, you are still constantly on edge. There were nurses and doctors everywhere. It was incredibly overwhelming. I stayed a little longer by myself until I was out of questions to ask and couldn't take my own heightened anxiety levels before heading back to our room to decompress. Back in the Mother/Baby room, Felicia and I were able to talk about a lot of things. We made a promise to keep each other positive if either one of us started to slip. I'm so glad that we got those first few days of time together alone in the Mother /Baby room to connect, gather our thoughts, and support each other. No one could visit because of coronavirus concerns, and we could turn off the whole outside world for a time when we needed it the most. It was just us, and we were able to talk a ton in-between visits back and forth to the NICU. We were in our own little bubble and didn't have to think about anyone else but ourselves and Emilia. We did a few more visits back and forth to the NICU throughout the day whenever we got up the courage to go back into that environment and last as long as we could before needing a break. Each time we went back, the nurses kept telling us how well Emilia was doing, how her oxygen levels were almost normal and close to breathing room air, that she seemed to be eating well, and that she was fussy and feisty, which is a great thing. This little girl kicked and flailed constantly. It was adorable to watch and I was so proud to watch my feisty little fighter.

Around midday is the first time I heard the words "honeymoon phase" come from the lips of one of the nurses. I still get PTSD thinking about those words. We asked, "What is the honeymoon phase?" The first nurse told us that the honeymoon phase refers to the first few days a baby is out of the womb and they appear to be doing really well. At this point, they aren't really resisting any of the equipment or support, and everything to the baby feels like they are still in the womb for the most part. The baby's brains and bodies don't know what is happening yet and the fight that is to come. They are supposed to be still developing and learning all the basic skills, like breathing, digestion, and organ functions, while safe and sound in mommy's womb where they can fail and be protected. They haven't quite figured out yet that they no longer have that safety net. It is just a matter of time before reality kicks in and the real battle starts. Basically, in my mind, this meant that all the good updates we were hearing were just temporary until the honeymoon phase wore off and the real shit started coming. All I could think about was when the honeymoon phase was going to end? It was like telling us that we WILL be getting into a car wreck in the next few days; we just don't know when yet. The funniest thing about that phrase, every nurse we met for the first three weeks kept moving the goalposts on the duration of how long this "honeymoon phase" actually lasts. At first, we were told it was the first 48 hours. Then, after we were moved to Riley's Hospital for Children (I'll touch on this here soon), we were told it was the first week, really. Then the respiratory therapists told us it was actually the first few weeks. After a while, I just think they were all hedging their bets, waiting for the craziness to begin. What they were really trying to say is that shit will get real, so don't relax. As I look back while writing this now, I'm so proud of little Emilia for extending that honeymoon phase longer and longer. She wasn't normal. She was so ready for this challenge that was thrust upon her. She held off the craziness for a lot longer than most of her nurses normally saw from babies born at 22 weeks and 6 days. After knowing her, that all makes so much sense. If there is one thing I would learn about my little lioness through this journey, it's that SHE IS A FIGHTER!

Monday, March 16th, 2020, 5:16 p.m. – Emilia turned one day old. We OFFICIALLY made it through our first full day together. I remember sitting in my little wooden rocking chair and staring into her isolate, just feeling so happy and scared at the same time. So happy that she was here for the first whole day and things seemed to be going somewhat okay, and so scared about what the hell was to come and if she would still be here tomorrow. From going to the hospital the day before and thinking she was already gone to being here the next day celebrating our daughter's first day of life, it was almost too much to comprehend at the time. 5:16 p.m. is a number and a specific time that is burned into my mind at this point in my life. When Felicia first told me about being pregnant with Emilia, I was obviously super excited and couldn't wait to meet my first child in July of 2020. My biggest fear at that time was, "Where am I going to move my office to in the house since that will now have to become the nursery?" Never in my wildest dreams did I think my ACTUAL biggest fear would be if Emilia would make it to her second day of life after being born. That is why this specific time, 5:16 p.m., took on so much importance for us during this journey. This time each day was a reminder to us that we were able to celebrate a new, unexpected day with our little miracle. Think about that for a second; my biggest fear before I met Emilia was moving furniture from one room into another and having to lose a personal space I held dear. It was a genuine fear and stressor in my life. I was pretty angry about it, to be honest. It is embarrassing now to say it, but it was so true at the time. Juxtapose that with our current situation, and it really puts life in perspective. We worry about such stupid things in life and don't take advantage of the truly remarkable moments like spending time with the ones that we care about and celebrating each and every new day together for the blessing that it truly is. 5:16 p.m. was the reminder for our family to cherish each and every day while we were in the NICU, and continues even to this day. I can't remember the exact day when I first did this, but I set the alarm on my phone to go off at 5:16 p.m. every day as a reminder that Emilia is still here with us and to celebrate and cherish it. I also found the perfect song to play as the alarm. The song was "Alive" by Sia. This song personified everything that Emilia was to me. The song starts off with the lyrics, "I was born in a thunderstorm. I grew up overnight." Those lyrics sounded like they were literally written for my daughter. Emilia was born in a thunderstorm, but she survived and wasn't ever going to give up on herself. Every day at 5:16 p.m., when that alarm went off, it almost brought me to tears as I listened to Sia's words while looking at Emilia over in her isolate. I still have that alarm go off every night at 5:16 p.m. to remind me of our sweet little angel. The song isn't "Alive" anymore, though. It's now "Lullaby" by the Dixie Chicks. I couldn't take hearing all that anger and rage in Sia's voice as she sang her heart out, letting the world know that she wasn't going to be dictated to no matter what. I will still always love and cherish that song for the rest of my life because of how many days it added just that little extra boost of energy for me to keep fighting with Emilia. Every time I accidentally hear it, it brings back warm memories of my little fighter. These days, it will pop on while I'm listening to my headphones on a run, and it feels like Emilia is running right there with me. I get this wave of electricity that flows through me, and it almost feels like I'm floating while listening to the words and remembering all the times it came on at 5:16 p.m. in the NICU while I was sitting next to Emilia. I highly encourage you all to do the same thing. Find that perfect song and create some memories. Celebrate each new day with your growing family and cherish those moments because you never know what might happen in the future.

The Journals:

Day 1: 3/15/20

- I love you
- You made me a Dad. That's the best job I could ever ask for.
- That was the scariest thing I've ever been through in my life. Emilia was so strong and so was her mom. I'm overwhelmed with emotion, tired, scared, frustrated, positive, happy, optimistic, pretty much every emotion you can have.
- That was the longest day of my life as well. It started off with Felicia cramping and not concerned. Like an idiot, I told her to call a doctor and went to go on a run...wtf. Thank God Brittany was there when she started to feel bad.
- We got to see her as she was rushed to the NICU
- LDR 20
- 22 and 6...22 weeks and 6 days, I had never heard this term before today.
- Our first visit in the NICU, she waved and we got an awesome photo. It's like Emilia was telling us to chill and she's got this.
- I'm glad my parents were able to be here and sad that Genie couldn't because of all this coronavirus stuff.
- I love you

"The Honeymoon" (Days 2-4)

As we woke on our 2nd day with our beautiful daughter, the haze and fog of the past few days and nights were slowly starting to lift. It is in this honeymoon timeframe, back in our hospital room, that Felicia and I adopted the phrase that would become our mantra the rest of the time in the NICU, "She's here, she's great, she's adorable, and she is loved!" To be clear, this whole NICU life with a 22-week old baby is INCREDIBLY SCARY! Every minute your mind can wander in about a million different directions about all the bad things that can happen. Thoughts can range from her possibly dying any second to her triumphantly coming home. When you have nothing but time on your hands, sitting in your hospital room pondering what's to come can become a pretty dangerous mental situation for yourself. That's where this mantra helped to get us back on track and keep us there. Felicia and I came up with this one day while we were still patients over in the Mother/Baby section of the maternity ward. Felicia was really starting to break down with anxiety, fear, and anger, and who can blame her? I looked at her and said, "She's here, she's great, she's adorable, and she's loved! Let's just focus on that for now and say that to each other whenever our mind starts to wander to a bad place." That is exactly what we did and here is why those words mattered so much.

She's here. You often can forget that your daughter is ACTUALLY in front of you sometimes in this crazy environment. You can get so wrapped up in your thoughts about the future and what can happen that you forget to live in the moment and realize what is actually right in front of you. Every waking moment with her is a blessing and not to be taken for granted. As I write this today, what I wouldn't give to be back in this very moment again because that would mean I get another day with my daughter.

She's great. Let's be honest, the survival rate for a baby born at 22 weeks and 6 days is like 10%. Even with that reality staring us all in the face, Emilia couldn't have been more adorable while flailing and kicking around all day long. The nurses all kept telling us she is "FIESTY" and how great of a sign that is. Emilia was a fighter from the moment she was born. If there was any little baby that could defeat these odds, it would be this little girl.

She's adorable. I'm going to let you in on a little secret. I've secretly always thought babies were ugly. Every time I'd meet my friends or family members' newborns, I just wasn't impressed. I typically only really get googly-eyed when I meet a dog or puppy. I'm a sucker for animals; I can't walk by a single dog without baby-talking to them and trying to pet them. Babies, on the other hand…meh. However, little Emilia was the most adorable thing I had ever laid eyes on. I can't really describe why, but she just was. I think in the back of my mind, I always knew that Felicia and I would make some beautiful little babies someday. It was just really cool to see her in person. I couldn't get enough of looking at her whenever I could. Even with all the tubes and everything, she still stole my heart.

She is loved. By this point in time, without even announcing to the world what had even happened, we could already tell how much love and support this little family had outside of those hospital walls. The love from the outside world for Emilia, Felicia, and I was palpable and energizing. Knowing that we had a little army of supporters out there was all we needed to stay present and in the moment as best we could.

She's here, she's great, she's adorable, and she is loved! Every time one of us would slip up and start to break down, we would repeat our mantra and try to right the ship. Keeping those negative thoughts at bay was incredibly hard in this environment. Sometimes you will be sitting there in the NICU feeling good and relaxed just watching your daughter live, and then, all of a sudden, alarms start going off all around you, your heart starts racing, your mind starts wandering, and your anxiety goes through the roof. You can go negative REALLY fast. That phrase was our way to help each other through those tough moments.

Something to note here, Felicia and I stayed in the Mother / Baby section of the maternity ward for the first two nights and three days of Emilia's life. It was during this time that the coronavirus pandemic was in its very infancy. The US was just starting to see its first few cases and viral spread. No one had acted on anything yet, but we all knew something was coming. We were seeing what was happening in Europe and the havoc it was wreaking over there. However, at this time, the hospitals were still allowing two parents in the maternity wards, and the world had not locked down on us as of yet. We could still freely walk around the hospital, staff grumbled at what was to come, and wearing a mask hadn't been mandated yet. The hospital wasn't allowing visitors, and the NICU, in particular, was only allowing one parent in at a time unless you had just delivered and were still staying in the hospital. Basically, it was during these first three days of Emilia's life that Felicia and I were still, at this time, allowed to see Emilia together in the NICU until Felicia was discharged from the hospital. Little did Felicia and I know, those first few days would be the last time that our entire family would be together in the same room, at the same time, until the last few days of Emilia's life. More on that to come in the future. The reason I bring this up now is because of how important helping each other out through this process truly is. You have to be there for each other and support each other as much as possible. This whole thing is hard and will never get easier. As I reflect back on it, I'm truly grateful that we had those three short isolated days together to get our minds right for the battle that was to come. Without this honeymoon phase and time to reflect on how to best support each other, I can't imagine (there it is again) how differently this journey would have gone.

When Felicia and I awoke on our 3rd day as a new family, we found out that we had a missed call from the NICU in the middle of the night. The thoughts that go racing through your mind are endless at that moment when you realize what could have happened and why they were calling. Is she still alive? What the hell happened? I needed to get dressed and run over there ASAP! Something we learned over time but weren't aware of at this point, The NICU will NEVER call you in the middle of the night unless they absolutely have to. They don't want to terrify parents, and nothing can be more terrifying than going to sleep after a long day of fighting in the NICU and being woken up to hear that something really bad is happening to your child. After the initial panic of the missed call wore off, I started to think, "We are in the hospital. If something truly tragic happened, they would have come into our room and woke us up." That thought ruled out the worst-case scenarios running through my mind. The next thought was, "Well, what the hell did happen last night?" The third thought was, "I WILL NEVER LET THIS HAPPEN AGAIN!" Immediately after we awoke and saw the missed call, Felicia and I saved the NICU number in our phones and set the number to bypass the silent mode so it would always ring through no matter what. We did the same thing for each other's numbers as well. Once we addressed all of this, we were off to the NICU as fast as we could to figure out what had happened to our daughter in the middle of the night.

When we arrived, a nurse calmly told us that Emilia's blood sugar had spiked to something like 500 mg/dl overnight, and that was a huge cause for concern which is why they called us. Keep in mind, a normal blood sugar level is between 70 and 105 mg/dl, and diabetes is diagnosed at 126 mg/dl and above. 500 mg/dl is off the charts high and extremely dangerous. By the way, I obviously didn't know any of this information at the time. We just asked a lot of questions of the care team as warranted to learn as much as we could about what was going on with our daughter. We will touch on this much more in-depth later, but don't be afraid to ask questions and become involved in the care team's plan. As parents, you are part of the care team for your child. It is your responsibility to learn, understand, ask questions, and challenge (politely) when things are being done to your child. Your care team will appreciate it, and it will help you keep sane as well. When you are in the NICU for long enough, you will learn more than you can ever imagine about the human body, the way it functions, the wonders of modern medicine, and what it can do in a traumatic situation. By no means am I a doctor, but after our time in the NICU, I definitely went through what felt like the equivalent of at least the first year of medical school.

And so, with that, the honeymoon phase was officially over. We were really in the thick of it and Emilia's little body was starting to realize she was no longer safe in her mother's womb. The nurse practitioners and doctors told us they were going to try and put in a PICC line to help give some extra protection to Emilia and an additional source for medication should another event happen. A PICC line is a thin, soft, long catheter (tube) that is inserted into a vein in your child's arm, leg, or neck. The tip of the catheter is positioned in a large vein that carries blood into the heart. The PICC line is used for long-term intravenous (IV) antibiotics, nutrition or medications, and blood draws. Inserting a PICC line into a child that small is incredibly challenging. Emilia's little arteries and veins were so insanely tiny. They told us a specialist from Riley's Hospital for Children would be in later that day to try and do the procedure and they would let us know when they arrived if we wanted to observe. To be honest, I still had no idea how serious any of this was at the time. Emilia still looked feisty and was doing her normal kicking and flailing that I had seen the past few days. The rest of her vitals looked okay. No one seemed to be panicking, and a plan was in place. In my mind, the crisis was averted. I went back to sitting in my rocking chair, listening to a book, getting up every so often to watch Emilia kick and flail and take some pictures.

As I was sitting in my little rocker bedside with Emilia, a huge group of nurses and doctors, at least six to eight of them, began to gather around Emilia's isolate. This was my first "rounding" experience. One of the nurses that I hadn't met yet leaned down to talk to me while the rest of the group was going through Emilia's charts. She told me how beautiful Emilia is and talked me through what was happening in front of me. I didn't ask for any of this, but she talked me through it because she could see it was overwhelming to have all these people flood in around your child. These nurses are amazing. They are so patient and kind. I have so much more to write about them later in the story. After she got done volunteering this information, I stayed in my chair, sat back, and took in what I was observing in front of me silently in amazement. ALL OF THESE PEOPLE WERE HERE TO HELP MY DAUGHTER LIVE! That moment was not lost on me at all. I made a note in my journal at the time to always remember to say thank you to these miracle workers every single time I got the chance. In my mind, it became my job to take care of them as much as they were taking care of my daughter.

It was also in this moment of reflection and journaling that I got the inspiration and courage to want to tell the world about our amazing daughter and formally announce her to everyone via social channels and every mountain top I could find. I started to think in my head about all the amazing thoughts and emotions this little girl had unexpectedly brought to us over the past few days. I started to write these thoughts down in my Evernote journal while sitting next to Emilia. Then I began to realize I have to tell the world about my amazing daughter! She deserves it and we owe it to her. I'm not sure if this is just us, but one weird emotion that, I think, Felicia and I both got from the day Emilia was born was almost a feeling of shame. The definition of shame: a painful feeling of humiliation or distress caused by the consciousness of wrong or foolish behavior. It felt shameful and humiliating to tell the world that our experience in childbirth and pregnancy wasn't normal. It was messy, scary, sad, joyful, and uncertain. I felt ashamed that we weren't going to get to announce Emilia to the world the way that all of our friends got to after their beautiful children arrived. I felt ashamed knowing that I may lose my daughter tomorrow and I'm not sure if I should tell anyone about that. I felt ashamed that I was ashamed of our situation. The truth is, all of that thinking was centered around Felicia and me, and life was no longer about just the two of us anymore. Then I looked at that amazing little girl fighting for her life, and at that moment, I knew that I owed it to her to make sure the world knows about her and her story. I jumped out of my rocking chair and walked as fast as I could back to our hospital room, where Felicia was resting. I was full of energy, excitement, and inspiration. I burst into the room, and I worked up the courage to tell Felicia that I wanted to tell the world about Emilia. I read to her what I wrote down while sitting in the NICU to get her thoughts on messaging. Felicia and I agreed it was time to announce our daughter to the world. I felt so good for the first time since the day before March 14th, when everything about this pregnancy experience still felt "normal." I felt like we were taking back control of the situation in our own little way. I felt like we were honoring our daughter the best way we could by sharing her story with the world. After all, the mantra said, "She's here, she's great, she's adorable, and she's loved."

The "She's loved" portion of our mantra needed some more work. We had to tell the world about her so they could send their thoughts and prayers to help her through this fight. After a few more revisions to what we wanted to say, what photos we wanted to share, etc., I finally worked up the courage to hit "post" on Facebook. Immediately, I felt a wave of relief for us all. Prior to this moment, this was all our little secret that we had been hiding from everyone since March 15. It felt incredible to call for some help and resources for our little family to fight this battle. It isn't lost on me the power of a tool like Facebook. I'm not a huge social media user, but I certainly respect the amazing power of spreading a message to your world with the push of a button. This small act, posting a picture and some words on Facebook, was a monumental thing for us to do in my mind. It is a time-honored tradition amongst people in my age group that we get to share our pregnancy journey through a platform like Facebook. My generation is literally the Facebook generation. I'm the same age as Zuckerberg. Facebook was invented and started for college students when Felicia and I were in college. We've literally grown up with this thing and made it what it is today. As we've all gotten older, basically all our friends' posts these days are about their children in some form or another. New pregnancy announcements, gender reveals, baby showers, birth photos, first few month's pictures, and updates, and then every other child milestone that follows. This is the way having a child is supposed to go in our Facebook/Instagram generation. You get pregnant, announce with a cute ultrasound picture with a little funny pun description or something, share your whole pregnancy journey along the way, and then finally get to announce your beautiful child's birth upon arrival and talk about how in love you are and how tired you feel. Emilia, Felicia, and I got none of that. We never even got a chance to announce that Felicia was pregnant. We had been planning to do that later in March. Felicia and Brittany had literally just solidified the baby shower venue and date the day before Emilia was born. Nothing about our journey was going according to plan. That is probably where a lot of that feeling of shame I mentioned really comes into play. We are hammered over the head with how life is supposed to work and what is "normal." These social norms become our expectations and we think that this is how it all works. When that doesn't happen, the shame creeps in and we don't even know why. As dumb as this sounds, announcing Emilia to the world this way was the first normal thing that we were able to do as a family. After looking at that little girl's face and seeing how amazing she is, the last emotion I felt was shame.

I say all of this to make the point that you can't, and shouldn't, make this journey alone. You will need every ounce of strength and endurance to make it through this marathon. That love and support for your child and yourself will help to carry you through the hard times and make you smile and enjoy the good times just a little more. We, humans, are social creatures, and we need each other. You certainly don't want to shut people out when you need them the most.

The rest of that day was pretty uneventful. We spent as much time with Emilia as we could. Then we called in the grandmas with a request for some help to get us a few lion and Sheltie stuffed animals that we could bring tomorrow to make Emilia's little section of the NICU feel a little cozier. And with that, we were discharged from the hospital and sent home. We went home that first night away from Emilia and slept in our own bed, excited and anxious to get back to the hospital first thing in the morning to see our precious little girl.

The next morning, it truly felt like we were going to work and starting a new job in a good way. Felicia and I got up, got changed, packed all the things we would need for the day, and headed off to the NICU. I couldn't help feeling, as we pulled into the garage at IU Methodist, that this moment was truly the first day of a LONG marathon to come. This was the first time we would park at this garage, make this walk, check-in at the front desk, and walk into the NICU to see our daughter. This would be our new normal for the next four months at least. We'd wake up, pack up our stuff, get to the hospital, sit in the waiting area as we each took turns going to visit her throughout the day, repeat. We held hands as we walked through the parking garage. We didn't know where anything was, where to park, how to get into the building, where to go, what to do, etc. We'd been living at the hospital for her first three days, and we only really knew how to get back and forth between the Mother/Baby section and the NICU. This was a whole new feeling.

One important thing to note, IU Methodist is a level 3 NICU and not a very big space. The level 4 NICU, Riley Hospital for Children, is less than a mile away and is usually where the most serious cases are sent, should they be warranted. IU Methodist's NICU was one large shared room overall. There were no private spaces, and it has a very communal feel. The doctors and nurses were all together in the same room, along with the babies and the parents. There is a whole lot of activity that goes on in that space. It can be chaotic at times, but it also feels very family-orientated since nothing is private. Remember, Felicia and I were no longer both allowed to be in the NICU together due to coronavirus restrictions that were put in place a few days prior. We were both allowed to be in the hospital at the same time, but not together with Emilia. One of us would have to spend time outside the NICU, in the family waiting area, while the other was visiting Emilia. The family waiting area was very small, with only one table, a few extra chairs, a mini-fridge, and an old TV. I don't think that space was originally designed for people to be spending all day there. Obviously, if you were visiting your child in the NICU at normal times, you would probably be actually visiting your child. Sadly, this was not allowed now. This tiny little area would be our new home for the next four months while the other parent was over in the NICU.

As our first day on our new job went on, we were told that the nurse practitioner specialist from Riley would be over around 2 p.m. to try and place the PICC line that was needed to help Emilia with her high blood sugar concerns and other needs. This specialist only ever came over once a day, and that is when they would try to get this procedure done. We waited all day for this to happen, and then the time finally came. Placing a PICC line is a "minor" procedure in the grand scheme of things. Doing this for a baby that is 1 pound, 1 ounce, however, is incredibly difficult. Nothing with a baby Emilia's size is minor and routine. Felicia and I were incredibly scared. Felicia didn't feel very comfortable watching this procedure happen. She said she just couldn't stomach the thought of watching someone operate on our daughter. I volunteered to sit with Emilia and watch as the NP did their thing. I sat in the corner of the NICU and observed as he tried to put a tiny line inside the arm of a 1 pound baby. It was no easy task. It was pretty nerve-wracking and fascinating to watch him operate on Emilia. The skill and training it must take to perform this task are inconceivable to me. In true amazing NICU nurse fashion, he was incredibly patient and kind as he talked me through everything he was doing. Part of me honestly felt weird with him talking while operating because I wanted his focus 100% on my daughter. The other part of me was very happy because he was calming me down at the same time. These nurses have probably interacted with 1,000 nervous parents before and instinctively know that it is probably in everyone's best interest to focus almost as much on the parents as their patients. After over an hour of him trying to place the line, he said that he couldn't get it today and wanted to give Emilia a rest. He would come back tomorrow and try again - all that for nothing. I walked back to the waiting room to fill Felicia in on what happened.

A few hours passed until the resident neonatologist came to visit us in our little visitor lounge, where Felicia and I both were sitting at the time. She sat down at our little table and looked very serious. You could tell she had some news to share that we all needed to discuss. She told us that Emilia's blood sugar levels were still pretty high, in the 300's, and that is still a huge risk. They were coming down slowly from the peak they hit a few nights before, but were still at very scary levels. Because the PICC line wasn't successful earlier in the day in helping control this, it was their recommendation that we move Emilia down the street to the level 4 NICU at Riley's Hospital for Children. There, she would have access to much better equipment and personnel where they could intervene faster if something bad happened. After she told us this, I felt compelled to ask for the first time, "What does this mean? How serious of a situation is this?" She explained that this was very serious. If they couldn't get her blood sugar levels to normalize, she could die. For the first time, Felicia and I felt the true gravity of our situation. Just that morning, we strolled into the NICU, ready to take on the marathon of the next four months. By 5 p.m.

that night, we didn't know if Emilia was going to live to see the next day. Such is life in the NICU; every minute, every hour, every day is a battle. You literally never know what you are going to get the moment you clock in for your new job each day.

After the doctor shared her recommendation of moving Emilia and the severity of her current situation, she left Felicia and me to ourselves to make the first major decision of this journey for Emilia. We were told that she would come back in a few minutes to hear what we wanted to do. Moving a child that small and in such a precarious state is no small task. Nothing is riskless. We had a lot to think about. Do we stay at Methodist and risk the possibility of not having the level of care needed should something urgent happen, or do we potentially endanger our daughter by embarking on a risky move to get her to Riley for additional support? Then there was a third thing to consider. While we had only been at Methodist for three and half days, it had already started to feel like a second home. We had gone through so much in this place already. We were getting used to the nurses and doctors. We knew where everything was and how to get around. We were learning people's names and had started to make friends. We had adjusted to our chaotic environment. While three and a half days might not seem like a lot of time, it truly felt like we had already been there for months. Riley was totally unknown from our perspective. What would that place look like? Would Emilia's accommodations be better? Is the staff better? I'm one of those people that, when I get comfortable with something, it is the best thing in the world, and it would take a lot to convince me otherwise.

I like to think of it like this, let's say you drove a basic car like a Honda Accord or something. That Honda Accord, to me, would be the best thing ever. I would sing its praises to the world, and I would find a way to maximize my personal value with that car for as long as possible. Even if you gave me a Ferrari to replace it one day and forced me to drive it, I would find all the reasons why that Ferrari isn't my Honda Accord, and it would take me months to adjust before I felt comfortable again. It is just the way I am. In one way, it is a great thing because I'm extremely happy with what I have and I rarely think about what I'm missing out on. On the other hand, I may miss out on a lot of better things in life due to my resistance to change. In this instance, Riley was unknown to me personally. However, this was the first time in my life that my decision-making process wasn't about me at all. This was about Emilia and what was best for her. I guess that is parenthood in a nutshell. You do what you have to do for your children no matter what it does to you personally.

When the doctor came back to get our decision, we informed her that we were giving the thumbs up for them to move Emilia to Riley based on her recommendation. She said she would call the LifeLine people and we should expect to have Emilia on her way in a few hours. We were terrified and scared beyond belief. There is so much equipment and stuff to transport. All I could think is, "How in the hell do they do all of this?"

We were on the clock. Felicia left to go sit with Emilia before her journey. I was left alone in the visitor room. It was at this time that I had my first conversation with Emilia from the future. I swear to God, I'm not crazy! As I sat there with my thoughts and worried about Emilia's upcoming dangerous journey, I had this flash forward to 20 years from that day where Emilia and I were in this same space, talking about her first car ride and how scared we all were for her. I told her the story of her first few days, showed her the room where her mom and I sat, and took turns going back and forth across the hall to visit her all day. I showed her where she lived. I told her how strong she is and all the strength and courage she showed in her fight to be here. We had a magical conversation and it felt so real. As I sat in that tiny visitors' room and envisioned the conversation in the future with Emilia, a wave of emotion hit me for really the first time since the moment she was born. I think that was the first time I truly let myself believe that it was possible for that moment 20 years later to actually be a reality. I was ready for this next step, this journey, and whatever was going to come next.

Emilia's first car ride

After a few hours of anxiously waiting for the LifeLine team to get her all ready for transport, we were finally ready to embark on the journey to our new home. I remember joking with her care team that I had to get her first car ride on video. I pulled out my phone and recorded everything I could as they wheeled her out of the NICU and down the hall toward the LifeLine vehicle. I think I caught one of the LifeLine ladies off guard as she jumped back and said, "Whoa," as I was right there with the camera on as soon as the door opened. As Emilia went by us, it was pretty clear that she didn't care at all about what was happening and was just doing her normal Emilia thing. That was such a relief. Emilia was always able to roll with just about anything you threw at her. She is truly the strongest and bravest person I've ever met.

Just like that, our family was off to our next stop on this crazy journey at Riley's Hospital for Children about a mile down the street. Felicia and I packed everything up from our little visitor room at IU Methodist and got over to Riley as quickly as we could. We were only at IU Methodist for three and a half days overall, but it felt like a lifetime. This is where our daughter was born, where they saved her life, where she spent her first few days, where Felicia and I had so many long talks about what was to come, where Emilia and I had talked 20 years in the future, and where we had met all of our first care team members that had treated us so well. It honestly wasn't easy at all to leave that space and depart into the unknown that was Riley. As we were walking out, I stopped Felicia and said we need to go back into the NICU one more time and thank everyone that had helped Emilia and us these past few days. We walked in, started choking up, and expressed our gratitude to everyone that was at their stations. You could tell that they really appreciated it. Like I mentioned earlier, you don't have a lot of actual tasks to do as a NICU parent. The one thing I would encourage you to always do is be overly thankful to the care team. They are true heroes and deserve every bit of our gratitude for the sacrifices they make for our children. After we said our goodbyes, we were off to Riley.

Everything was new again. Everything was different. I didn't know where to park, how to get through security, what elevators to take, where to go, or who to talk to. We were exhausted and I just wanted to see my daughter safe and sound again after her first car ride. I was just about at my breaking point for the day.

Do you know that moment when you're the new kid to a class, or walking into the first day of the new job, or meeting your significant other's family for the first time? That moment when you realize you just walked into someone else's world, you're the odd person out, and they aren't going to adapt or go out of their way to change for you? That is exactly how the first few hours at Riley Hospital for Children felt for me. Riley couldn't have been more different than IU Methodist. From the moment you walk in there, you can tell that these are SERIOUS people that care for children's health and ONLY children's health. These are the pros! They are the major leagues of caring for kids. Everything in the place reflects that image and sets that tone. It's so clinical-looking. IU Methodist's NICU felt like a ragtag tight-knit little minor league team...like the Bad News Bears or something. They were a scrappy family that just got the job done. Methodist's NICU was really an afterthought to all the other operations that go on in that hospital. This was like getting called up to the big leagues of children's healthcare. We were now walking into Yankee Stadium and you were going to respect this sacred space.

As we slowly got our bearings and made our way up to our new home on 4 West, we were greeted by the NICU welcome desk staff outside the NICU. This was a first. They had a NICU welcome desk that was manned with staff at all times. They welcomed us to the NICU, gave us our badges, and told us that they would help walk us through all the NICU protocols we'd have to do every time we got here each day. "NICU Protocol? What the hell is that?" At Methodist, we just said our codeword and walked in to see our daughter. They went through all the stickers we needed, where everything was, how to scrub in every time we walked in, what our code pins were to get in and out, etc. This was all too much for my brain to take. I was slowly getting angrier and angrier. I just wanted to see my daughter! I finally hit my breaking point, not out loud but in my head, when this poor lady stood over my shoulder and watched me scrub every portion of my arms from elbow to hand for the minimum three minutes that was required to enter the NICU. She watched me for the entire three minutes. She wouldn't let me miss a spot. FINALLY, a few hours after we left Methodist, we were escorted into our private room, where Emilia was now all set up.

As we walked in, I thought, "Holy shit! We have an entire room all to ourselves?" There was a couch, recliner, refrigerator, places to store our stuff, etc. Emilia's isolate probably only took up about 10% of the space. This was like a palace compared to Methodist. We had a tiny little area of the shared NICU space over there. At Riley, we had two nurses AND two respiratory therapists in the room when we arrived. It looked like they were teaching or something. They were pointing out certain things and talking about how this and that worked. They greeted us and immediately went back to teaching. My brain was about to explode. EVERYTHING WAS SO DIFFERENT AND I WAS SO TIRED! As we were putting away our stuff, I pulled out Emilia's lion and Sheltie stuffed animals that her grandmas had gotten her to keep by her bedside. I started to put them on a shelf in the room until the front desk lady that had watched me scrub every area of my body said, "You can't have stuffed animals in the NICU because they aren't sanitary." That was it! I had had enough for the day! First off, those aren't just stuffed animals to me. The lion is my spirit animal and, in turn, was already proving to be my daughter's spirit animal as well. Having that lion watch over Emilia meant a lot to me! The Sheltie is our family dog that was supposed to be watching over Emilia at our house in a different universe where all this didn't happen. That also meant a lot to Felicia and me.

Lea, our Sheltie, is 13 years old and an incredibly important member of our family. Felicia and I bought her together after only a year of dating. We had always dreamed that one day she would be there to take care of our future children. She might never get a chance to meet Emilia, and now you are telling me I can't even have a freaking stuffed animal in here to represent her love and support? What kind of a place is this? Methodist didn't care! What was so special about this place? I gave up because I didn't want to argue or make a scene. I packed the stuffed animals back up in my bag. The front desk lady finally left the room, and we got all of our stuff put away. As soon as she left, I took out the lion and Sheltie and put them secretly in a little cubby hidden behind the recliner in the room. I wasn't going to let them keep Lea or the lion away from Emilia. I took a picture of it to show Felicia after we left that night; she wasn't surprised and laughed. That was a very typical Chris move in her mind and such a Trash Panda thing to do (my other spirit animal). We finally said goodnight to Emilia and headed home. I remember telling Felicia as we were driving back how much I hated everything about Riley and how much I missed Methodist. Either way, this is where we were.

The Journals: Days 2-4

Day 2: 3/16/20

- I love you
- I can't believe she choose to be born during the coronavirus outbreak... what a total Sears move.
- The bells and alarms in the NICU are overwhelming. Trying to understand everything. Tons of questions.
- Keep hearing "honeymoon phase" and that scares me about what is to come here in the near future.
- The nurses are all so nice and helpful.
- Felicia and I got to talk a lot about everything and help each other through this. We made a vow that we will remain patient and positive and only think happy thoughts. If we go negative...we promised to speak to each other to help.
- We officially made it through her first day. I was there with her and it felt great. All the nurses keep saying that she's doing amazing which is great to hear.
- This is going to be my ultimate marathon (which I've always hated long-distance running). I feel like I've been training for this moment since the day I left Angie's List a few years back. I'm 100% clear and locked in on being the rock of this family for both Felicia and Emilia and everyone else.

- I gave Felicia my health wristband to keep for Emilia. I'm going to only wear my Felicia (happiness) and Success wristbands.
- I love you

Day 3: 3/17/20

- I love you
- I've decided to journal about this whole process and put down my thoughts every night before saying I Love you and goodnight to Emilia.
- We got a call at midnight while we were asleep from the NICU...we missed it...never again.
- Emilia's a fighter. I can't wait to talk to her about all of this when she's older, and we are playing tennis together or dropping her off at college.
- Maybe I'll write her a little book she can read that includes all of our journaling. It would be cool to combine photos and her mom's notes as well. Might make it a book to publish someday and help out other parents as well.
- I'm literally crying as I write this one.
- THE BONGING IN THE NICU IS REALLY HARD TO TAKE!!!!
- There were like 7 women around her when I was sitting here. I think they thought it was overwhelming for me or something to have so many people around. One of them kept asking me if it was okay and explaining what was going on. I thought it was amazing to see how many people love and care for her.
- I NEED TO ALWAYS REMEMBER TO SAY THANK YOU TO THESE LADIES. They are doing such an amazing job.
- I let myself slip for a hot second and go a little negative in my thoughts...that won't happen ever again.
- I'm going to spend so much time here with her...I can't wait to be here with her as much as possible.
- The Motto- SHE'S HERE, SHE'S GREAT, SHE'S ADORABLE, and SHE'S LOVED! That's what I'm saying to myself anytime my mind goes negative.
- We made the decision today to announce to the world the birth of our beautiful little Emilia (which I'm going to always call you Quinn btw...that's a fun story for when you're older). That announcement was not taken lightly given the circumstances, but we wanted to have all the people that love us shower down their thoughts and prayers to you because you deserve them. The more people out there

that love you and are thinking of you...the more support you have to keep fighting. I made this decision while sitting watching you in your NICU crib and thought...you're too beautiful and I need to tell everyone about you. You probably won't understand this by the time you are old enough, but there is this thing called Facebook and Social Media in our day. They are ways to connect to the world of people we love through technology. We didn't just announce you to your aunt, grandparents, great grandparents...we told the world and they have all showered down their prayers on you through us. I hope you feel it. For our generation, it's become a rite of passage for us to be able to announce these milestones on these channels. However, you being miss unique, refused to let your mom and I have a "normal" time with your pregnancy from day 1. Someday I'm going to love that unique story because you aren't like everyone else. You're our little baby and we know how unique you are and will become. However, this was our 1 moment to be a little normal and I'm glad we did it. We have to share your story and journey with the world because you deserve it.

- That was a long thought.
- Your mom and I got to go home yesterday for the first time. It was great to finally be able to have your mom see your grandma and help each other.
- This won't make any sense to you, but nobody can visit you other than myself and your mom right now because of this weird coronavirus thing. That really sucks. I wish your grandparents, aunt, cousins, great aunts and uncles, etc. could come in to see you. I'll explain later how you were born in one of the weirdest times our world has ever seen. Google it someday (if that is still a thing).
- Quick note - You'll learn this over time but your dad is weird and superstitious as hell. I gave your mom my health wristband that I always wear so she can watch over your health. I'm going to wear my Felicia wristband and Success wristband to watch over your mom and all of this so we know this whole thing will be a success and we can get you home.
- We Are calling in the grandmas to bring you a bunch of stuffed animal lions and Shelties to watch over you near your bed. Btw... your code word is LION to get in because you're so strong and the queen of the pride lands. Again...your dad is weird and superstitious.
- I feel like God has been training my whole life for this moment to use my superpowers of optimism and positivity to shelter over you and your mom and everyone else as we go through this. I swear to God,

I won't let him or you down. That's why I'm journaling all of this to make sure we watch how far we've come and never forgot.

- I love you.

Day 4: 3/18/2020

- I love you
- We brought your lion and Sheltie stuffed animals to watch over you. They will help you through today.
- You have a BIG day ahead of you. You're experiencing a little bit of concern around blood sugars overnight and early today. The docs adjusted to everything and each passing few hours it slowly went down.
- We had a doctor come in and tell us all about what you are experiencing. YOU ARE SO STRONG!!!!! I can't believe how strong you are. I've never seen anyone stronger in my life.
- They told us 20-30% good outcomes for baby's your age...screw that...they don't know Emilia Quinn Sears yet. God gave you 100% chances of survival.
- Your mom made breast milk today to give you...I was so proud of her. I could tell that made her feel a lot better.
- I had a talk with your older self while you were home from a break in college. I brought you too this room in the IU Methodist NICU where we waited and I told you how amazing you are and what you went through. I'll always say you're amazing and a miracle every day going forward...because you are. That was a fun talk, and I can't wait to have it for real someday in the future. Trust me...this is happening like it or not.
- We are keeping a really close eye on your blood sugars, but they are coming down. Keep it up...you're doing so great. You're doing so well right with everything else. No infections, gut issues, head bleeding, or major respiratory issues. The doctors have said those are all looking amazing for what is to be expected. You're so impressive.
- You crushed it all day with bringing back down your blood sugar levels. You are so strong.
- The doctors made the call to move you from the chaos of IU Methodist NICU to the quiet and serene pros over at Riley Hospital for Children.
- YOU GOT TO TAKE YOUR FIRST CAR RIDE!!! The nurses said you did so well and really enjoyed it. I have a feeling that is where I'll get to you to relax at in the future.

- Selfish Dad moment. After the move to Riley, it took me a while to get adjusted to our new settings at Riley and I was pretty frustrated and a little grouchy with everyone. It felt like we were in a war zone before at IU Methodist, but we had gotten used to it and you were doing well. You'll learn this about your dad in the future, but don't do well with change and new things at the beginning. I come around quick, but I don't love disruption into my daily life unless absolutely necessary. You'll have to work with me on that one in the future. Methodist felt more like much more of an intimate environment. That is where you were born and they had saved you. The nurses were all so nice and did such a great job. I just felt bad leaving. Riley on the other hand is so professional and clinical. You can tell that they are pros. We have more space and you have better care which is all that really matters. For some reason though, it just felt weird to start so I got a little grumpy and tired (which I also do). Either way, Riley feels like a much better place for everyone to run this marathon in the long run.
- I slipped a little yesterday in my optimism. I let the emotions get the best of me and started to complain about your mom's family living in our house and moving all of our stuff around when we aren't there. I need to remind myself that everything is happening for a reason and that everyone cares and just wants to help. That isn't a bad thing at all.
- We found out we get a camera for you at all times in your NICU room...what a relief.
- Your mother had a moment last night where she let herself slip as well and broke down. I was able to help her...which selfishly was nice to know that I could do something for her. I've told her that I have her and the overall success of getting you home...she just needs to worry about you. We're working through all of this and getting better day by day.
- Finally got some potato chips...I was in withdrawal (lol).
- Going to bed. I love you

CHAPTER 3

The NICU Marathon

The Rules of the NICU

Now that we've settled into our new home at Riley Hospital for Children, we have officially made it to day 5 of this wild ride. This makes us no longer newbies at this whole NICU life. Time moves so slowly in the NICU that it is best to think of each day in the NICU as like dog years where one day actually equals seven. At this point, we are practically seasoned veterans. With that said, it is a great time to pause the story and take a minute to illuminate the path forward on some general rules of the NICU that I feel are important for every parent or reader to understand before we rejoin our journey.

Rule 1 – It's a Marathon

If you remember nothing else from this book about life as a NICU parent, always remember that it is like running a Marathon. It is tiring, overwhelming, challenging, and sometimes feels like it will never end. However, just like in a marathon, this journey will come to an end at some point for every parent and family. There is a finish line. Unfortunately, that finish line for each family is unique. You don't know what, where, or how your race will end. Rest assured though, it will end at some point. I can't tell you how many times we heard our nurses say, "Don't forget that this is a marathon" from our first moment entering the NICU, and they were right. These Nurses have seen it all. They've seen pain and heartache, and they've seen miracles. They've seen babies look healthy and happy at the beginning of their shift, only to have them pass away unexpectedly by the end of it. The point is, you never know what you are going to get on any given day, hour, or minute in the NICU, so you have to be prepared for it all. If you are a runner, you'll totally get this analogy. Distance running is miserable. There is no way around that in my mind. Nobody wants to put their bodies through that pain and suffering if they have the choice. So why do people choose to run long distances and put themselves through that? I think they do it because it is a test of the human will, it is a test of your mind and body, and it is a challenge to see how far you can willingly push yourself and suffer along the way without giving up. While the NICU is a little different in that nobody actively would choose this type of test, running a marathon is still a great analogy to what you are about to experience. You will be tested mentally, physically, and emotionally. You will have amazing highs and incredible lows. You will want to quit and give up. You will be exhausted. You will be triggered by a million different environmental factors that are out of your control. There really is no way to sugarcoat any of this. However, there are ways that you can overcome and push through, just like a marathon runner.

A few months removed from our NICU experience, one of the key lessons I unearthed from my newfound love of reading was a concept I came across in a book called *Good to Great*. The author, Jim Collins, in one of his chapters, explained something he called the "Stockdale Paradox," which was named after James Stockdale, a United States Navy Vice Admiral and aviator awarded the Medal of Honor in the Vietnam War, during which he was a prisoner of war for over seven years. During his time as a prisoner of war, the Vice Admiral's theory of the Stockdale Paradox was formulated, which he explained was crucial to his survival in such a traumatic experience for seven years. The Stockdale Paradox states that you must retain faith that you will prevail in the end regardless of the difficulties, while at the same time, you must confront the brutal facts of your current reality, whatever they might be.

In essence, the Stockdale Paradox is somehow learning to live simultaneously as an extreme optimist and an extreme realist, which is incredibly challenging and rare to find in most humans.

How do you do this? Well, it is hard, but here is my best take on living the Stockdale Paradox. Just like any person in any test of endurance, such as a marathon runner, prisoner of war, or NICU parent, you need to have 100% unshakable confidence and optimism that you will make it home safe and sound. You have to BELIEVE that you WILL make it through NO MATTER WHAT! That thought needs to be written in stone in your mind. Once you've convinced yourself that you will get through this test of wills, then you need to put that in the back of your mind and hold it there for the rest of the journey. Don't fixate on it, and don't revisit it. Just leave that there buried deep down in your subconscious. In the meantime and back in the present, your objective is to not set any goals or to think about the past or future. Your only goal is to live in the present and focus on confronting the brutal realities of what is in front of you each and every minute, hour, and day. The key is to always try to stay in the present and not let your mind wander to the future and getting out of the POW camp, finishing the marathon, or leaving the NICU.

This is really hard to do, and you truly need both extreme optimism and realism to survive and thrive in these environments. Why is that? As Stockdale would say, the pure optimists are the ones that died first in the POW camp.

I'm an extreme optimist, so I have some pretty good insight as to why this occurs that I will try to walk you through. We optimists love to always think about the future and dream big. We are propelled forward by dreaming that impossible dream of what life will look like when it all comes together in perfect harmony. In this POW scenario, these optimists would set that impossible dream that they were going to make it home by some arbitrary date, say Christmas or something. I'm sure that date was maybe half grounded in reality and most likely a best-case scenario, to say the least. That random date and vision of release is what kept them pushing to get up and fight each and every day. As soon as that arbitrary target date comes and goes without the outcome they dreamed about for so long occurring, an optimist would be crushed. They built up their mind and used all of their strength to get to a certain date, goal, and outcome. When that didn't happen, they would lose it mentally and then it was all downhill from there.

As an optimist myself, I know this trap all too well. We love to set our dreams and goals for a specific and often completely arbitrary end date on the horizon to keep our spirits high and focused on the prize. That build-up in an optimist's mind, if it doesn't happen, can be soul-crushing for a brief moment in time. Normally, it is no big deal with most of life's scenarios that end this way for an optimist. So what if that deal didn't close for as much money as you had expected, you don't get that promotion, you get 2cd in the tennis tournament, your new business idea fails, etc. Sure, it is a letdown, but it's not like it is life or death. We optimists feel all the pain deeply and then get over it quickly. That is our secret weapon. In most life scenarios, being an optimist is advantageous. After we fail, we pick ourselves right up again, start a new dream, our energy comes back, and all is well. Well, unfortunately for optimists, POW camps and NICU battles are never-ending. You can't get out of it. When you are in it, you are stuck until this thing ends one way or another. Missing that date you set in your dreams is no longer something you can pick yourself up from and go begin another dream. When that dream doesn't happen, you are stuck right back in the same nightmare with no chance of escape. That is why optimists die first. You have no idea when the end will come, what that end will be, etc. You are at the mercy of the gods on this one and stuck in this never-ending saga until it either breaks you, or you can muster the strength to make it through.

That is the most important lesson I can give to anyone unfortunate enough to be in this situation and reading this book. Just like every nurse told us from day one, always remember that this is a marathon!!! Have faith that you will get your child home. Just don't ever think about that again until you are actually home. I personally had to learn the lessons of not properly applying the Stockdale Paradox the hard way on my own journey. Throughout the rest of the story, I will come back to the concept a few times to show how critical it truly is to making it through tests of human endurance and traumatic events such as my family's story.

Rule 2 – You Have One Job

Life as a parent in the NICU is weird. You technically don't have any actual responsibilities surrounding the care of your child. The amazing care teams of doctors, nurses, nurse practitioners, X-Ray techs, and social workers will do everything for your child 24/7. That is their job and they are amazing at it. Most parents of a newborn are probably pretty overwhelmed with all the life-changing responsibilities they have to take on, from what I've been told. Since Emilia is our first-born child, Felicia and I have never really had a chance to understand that feeling of 3 a.m. feedings, round-the-clock care, and all the other things that go into caring for a newborn ourselves. Just like our friends can't imagine our life and experiences with Emilia, we truly can't imagine (there it is again) what their life is like caring for a full-term baby, either. Our only parenting experience includes having two dedicated nurses watching over our child's every movement, alarm, and lab results. The care team is with your child 24/7, so none of the actual care for your child is your responsibility. Even with all of this support, you still have one incredibly important job as a parent of a child in the NICU, in my opinion. That job is to be the #1 supporter of the team of people caring for your child. Keep them entertained, ask about their life, ask about their job, ask questions about the care of your child, and always show gratitude all day, every day, to everyone. If you make this your priority, I promise your child will have a better experience, you will have a better experience, and your care team will have a better experience. I'm not 100% sure, and there is really no way to ever truly know, but I could argue that your child will have BETTER care if you do this than if you didn't. After all, getting your child home safe and sound is the goal of this whole experience. If you could do anything to improve those odds, I'm sure you would.

I was told by several nurses that, shockingly, most parents don't really treat them very well and often aren't very involved in the process. That blew my mind. Emilia was the most precious gift I've ever been given in my life. For me to not care about what is going on with her is the weirdest concept I could ever imagine (there it is again). So while you don't technically have a job to do, I would encourage you to pour all of your efforts into your appreciation and support of your care team. You will make some lifelong friends, you will learn more than you can ever imagine about neonatology, you will be able to add input and contribute, and you will give your child the best chances of making it home safe and sound.

Rule 3 – Don't Be Scared Unless Your Nurses Are Scared

The NICU can be a terrifying place. There are monitors everywhere, constant beeps and alarms, lines running medicine all over the place, sensitive equipment, people constantly coming in and out of your room, and more titles and acronyms than you can ever imagine. It's hard to understand what is going on and which things are the most important for you to be monitoring yourself. I can tell you with certainty that you will never truly understand what is going on. However, that doesn't mean you shouldn't ask or be open to learning. When you don't know what to panic about, you panic about everything. Remember, this is a marathon. You need to conserve your energy and focus on the next step. This whole experience will be miserable if you allow your mind to run wild and be triggered by everything around you unnecessarily. That is why this rule is so important.

Thank God for one of our earliest nurses, Lori, who let me in on this little secret at the beginning of our journey. She was one of the NICU OG's on the 4 West floor. She had been doing this job for 20+ years and had literally seen it all. One of our first nights at Riley, she let me in on this super important unwritten rule when she told me, "Unless you see me scared, you have nothing to worry about!" That simple phrase was probably the single most impactful tip I ever received. Lori was the absolute best! She was like having another big sister with me there to protect and guide us. She always did such an amazing job of helping us to relax and stay loose when she was around. We went through some of the scariest nights that I've ever had in my life with her at my side. Even at the worst of times, when she was working her butt off, she would somehow magically answer all of my questions while keeping things fun and relaxed. It was truly remarkable. I remembered this advice she gave to me throughout our time in the NICU. Every time something new happened, I would always wait first to see how our nurses and doctors were reacting before I made my decision on how to react. It was incredibly helpful. I got so good at it that I started to ask, "Scale of one to ten, how should I be feeling?" They would always answer honestly. Anything over a six is when my ears would perk up, and my heart would start to pump a little harder. Sadly, we did get to see both sides of this rule. 95% of our time in the NICU, using this rule, kept things relaxed and my blood pressure under control. The other 5% of the time, when we saw the nurses and doctors get scared, it was truly terrifying for everyone. I feel like this rule is a great way to look at life in general. Save all of your fears, anxieties, and heartache for that precious 5% when you will actually need it; otherwise, you'll drive yourself insane.

Rule 4 – Control What You Can Control

This isn't just a rule of the NICU; this is also a rule of life. However, in the NICU, the spotlight shines just a little brighter on this rule, and I feel like it needs to be noted and discussed in our conversation. Controlling what you can control is pretty self-explanatory, and at the same time, incredibly complicated. As I mentioned before, as a parent in the NICU, you don't have many responsibilities, and therefore you have very little perceived control. I would actually argue that this is not true. To me, control what you can control means looking outside of what is directly in your face and finding ways to add value to the process overall that may not seem obvious at first. Here are some examples of areas that you have 100% control over every day that can help your child thrive:

- Take care of yourself. You can't keep the mental and physical strength necessary for this marathon unless you focus on keeping yourself happy and healthy every single day. You will need every ounce of energy to deal with what is to come. That means that you need to get plenty of sleep, find time every day for exercise, eat balanced meals, read some inspirational books, keep yourself occupied with productive activities, etc.

- Encourage and thank your care team. See Rule #2. This is an incredibly simple thing to do every day. It will build alliances and make you feel like you are a part of the care team as well. Think of yourself as the cheerleader or a fan on the sidelines rooting on the players in the game. Encouragement helps. Ever wonder why the home team always has an advantage in the eyes of Vegas bettors? It's the fans cheering them on that give them the extra boost to perform.

- Update your friends and family – With everything going on in your life right now, thinking and worrying about keeping other people informed can seem like a ridiculous exercise. All the messages, phone calls, cards, emails, and texts will start to pile up quickly. The last thing you want to worry about is keeping up with this stuff. However, the truth is, you can't do this alone. This isn't about you. This is about your child. It is selfish of you to turn away support from others for your child when they need it the most. You and your family are going to need every ounce of support to get through this. So, suck it up and find a way to get the message out around updates in a clear and direct manner to keep everyone informed. There are a million ways to do this. We happen to prefer Facebook and GrandmaBook (i.e., our moms).

- Ask a lot of questions. Get involved in your child's care! If you have to be stuck in a room with people saying words and doing things to your child that you don't understand, at least take the time to ask and learn. The funny thing is, these nurses and doctors want to explain these things to you. It is enjoyable for them. This is their passion and life's work. Let's think of it this way: If you were suddenly forced to move to a foreign country for four months where you didn't speak their language, are you really never going to try and learn what they are saying? I suppose that is an option, but that sounds downright miserable to me. I can't imagine (there it is again) how boring and isolating that would be for you. This situation is no different, and you have a ton of willing natives that are eager to help you learn their world. Also, as you learn more, you may even discover some insights and surface some ideas that the care team wasn't even thinking about. That certainly happened a few times in our journey. We ended up learning so much and asking so many questions that the doctors started to invite us to the rounds each morning to listen in (because they knew we'd have 500 questions afterward anyway). Doctor Osa, our favorite doctor ever, at one point in time even joked that he'd make a neonatologist out of me yet! Much more on our favorite doctor ever later in the story.

- Take care of your partner. If you are lucky enough to have a partner in this battle, helping to support each other is a MUST! This process is equally brutal on both of you. Think of it as the two of you running your own separate marathons, so to speak. While you may be running an individual marathon, you aren't "racing." This isn't about winning and who finishes first. This marathon is about surviving and crossing that finish line together. You both have to run at the same pace. If one of you is falling behind, slow down and let them catch up. You can't get out of alignment. This entire process will be one of the most trying tests that you will ever experience together. You can easily get off track with each other and let the little things build up, ultimately leading to an explosion. Don't let it happen. Listen to your partner. Understand where they are at in their marathon and slow down or speed up accordingly. Support the crap out of each other.

Note - These are just a few examples of how you can "control what you can control" while on your marathon. There are 100's of other ways as well. Use your imagination and time while you are sitting in that room to figure it out.

The NICU Marathon: Officially One Week Old (Day 5-8)

With the rules of the NICU established, let's resume our story.

As we settled into our life at Riley, one of the first game changers that we were introduced to was this magical thing called the NicView camera. The NicView camera was a Godsend for Felicia and me, our extended friends and family, and anyone else looking to follow along with Emilia's journey. Back in our IU Methodist days (days 1-4), Felicia and I were the only visitors allowed to see Emilia. That isn't how a normal NICU works, but our precious little angel had to decide to be born at the start of the biggest pandemic to hit the world in over 100 years. Coronavirus had essentially locked out anyone that wasn't a parent from seeing a child at the NICU. To this day, we still truly have no idea what "normal" NICU life is like. We'd heard stories from nurses about how hectic it could be in the NICU with a ton of family and friends around and people constantly coming and going. That certainly wasn't our NICU experience or any atmosphere that we ever witnessed. Our NICU atmosphere was simply one of us (Felicia or I) with Emilia and our nurses all day, every day. Felicia and I would change out every few hours during a "shift change," as we called it. One of us would wait in the family area outside the NICU while the other spent time with Emilia. After a few hours, we would do our shift change, tag the other partner in, and repeat all day long. This went on for the first few weeks. Eventually, as the pandemic raged even worse, restrictions got even tighter to where only one parent at a time was even allowed in the building. That meant that our new shift change meant coordinating one person coming from home and seeing each other in the hospital lobby as the other one left the hospital. I say all of this to share how hard it was to manage all of this. Not only was our daughter battling for her life every day, but Felicia and I could also only ever see each other in passing during a shift change, and no friends or family could physically be there to help us during our entire process. That was until we learned about the NicView.

NicView is a camera system that is placed above the isolate so that you can tune in from anywhere via a website to view a patient. It is like one of those camera systems that people use to live-stream the births of baby giraffes at zoos, but for NICU babies. As soon as we found out about this, we immediately shared the link and password with the world so everyone could tune in and follow along. For the first time ever, friends and family could be there with Emilia and us in the room whenever and wherever they were. It was magical! It was also magical for Felicia and me. I didn't have to wait until my shift change to see my little angel. If I got nervous and wanted to peek in on how she was doing, I could look whenever I damn well wanted to. I could go home and eat real food while staring at my phone and not feel that dreaded despair of having no idea of what was going on back in her room. It was the best thing that could have ever happened to us. This wasn't available at IU Methodist; this was just a Riley thing. I came to find out that the whole NicView system was donated by a wealthy family that had a long stay themselves in the NICU with their child in the past. After their time there, they created a grant for Riley to use on this system. I wish I could remember the family and baby's name for this story, but unfortunately, I can't. Either way, their contribution changed our lives in so many ways. It allowed us to sleep at night while in our own bed at home. I can't remember how many times I woke up in the middle of the night and checked the NicView camera to see what was going on in Emilia's room. After five to ten minutes of watching her flail and kick away, I would go back to sleep so I could be fresh to see Emilia in the morning. Most importantly, the NicView gave Emilia's family and our friends the ability to watch her grow. We would get texts and screenshots sent to us all day of people tuning in to watch Emilia and see her kick and flail around in her isolate. It was adorable. I'll forever be grateful for that NicView camera.

On top of the NicView being a game-changer for our family, I discovered a hidden omen in our room that couldn't just have been a coincidence. I don't know about you, but I truly believe in omens, fate, serendipity, the supernatural, or whatever you want to call it. I believe that everything happens for a reason, and we simply have to be open to see it and receive it. You can't walk through life with blinders on. You have to keep your eyes open! There is a fun story I read along this journey called *The Alchemist*. It is a short story from the author Paulo Coelho that tells the magical story of Santiago, an Andalusian shepherd boy who yearns to travel in search of a worldly treasure as extravagant as any ever found. The story of the treasures Santiago finds along the way teaches us, as only a few stories can, about the essential wisdom of listening to our hearts, learning to read the omens strewn along life's path, and, above all, following our dreams.

In one section of the book, Santiago learns of a story about a shopkeeper that sent his son on a mission to learn the secret of happiness from the wisest man in the world. To paraphrase the story, the boy went on a long journey and finally arrived at the castle of the wise man. Upon arrival, the boy found a ton of people at the castle, all vying for the wise man's attention. After waiting hours to see the wise man, the boy finally had his chance. The wise man tells him that he doesn't have much time to talk. He recommends the boy take a stroll around the castle for a few hours and come back, and he should be ready to divulge all the answers he is hoping to learn. As the boy sets off, the wise man stops him and asks a favor. He hands him a spoon and puts two drops of oil in it. He asks the boy to return the spoon with all the oil when he gets back from his walk in a few hours. The boy walks around the castle for two hours and focuses on the oil the whole time to make sure that he doesn't lose a drop as requested. He comes back and shows the wise man that he completed the task and still had all the oil left. The wise man replies, "Great, did you also get a chance to see the amazing castle as well?" The boy says, "No, I was too busy trying not to drop any oil." The wise man tells him to go do it again and, this time, take the time to enjoy the castle and all its marvel. The boy sets off with his oil and walks around the castle again. This time he really takes it all in and marvels, architecture, sculptures, paintings, etc., that the castle has to offer. The boy comes back to the wise man. Upon his return, he is saddened to show the wise man that this time only has half the oil left on the spoon. The wise man asks the boy, "Why?" The boy said he was too busy looking at the beauty of the castle. The wise man then tells him the secret of happiness is "to see all the marvels of the world and never forget the drops of oil on the spoon."

I share this whole story to say that life is such a delicate balancing act between love and work. You have to do both well in order to truly take it all in. In the NICU, you can be inundated by the work. No one wants to drop the oil, so to speak, and have a tragedy on their hands. You also can't forget to look around and marvel at what you are seeing, look for the omens and signs, and enjoy every minute you have with your child and care team.

All of this has been a huge build-up to the amazing omen I saw that first day in our new room at Riley. There was this large photo of a mighty lion just laying around in the grasses of the savannah smack in the middle of Emilia's new room. It sat directly across from Emilia's isolate, almost as if it was staring at her. I can't believe I didn't see this the previous night when we had first moved in. The room was actually pretty big, and the couch area didn't provide a direct view of the picture as a cabinet jutting out from the back wall blocked it from view. I must have flat out missed it somehow. I was too busy trying not to drop the oil on my own spoon, if you will, when we were meeting all the new nurses, learning the new protocols, putting stuff away, etc. When I first saw it, I couldn't believe it! Of all the photos and all the rooms to be in, we got the room with this beautiful lion staring at my daughter and seemingly watching over her. "That couldn't be a coincidence," I thought. I asked our nurse where the photo came from and why it was in the room? She told me that the head of neonatology at Riley loved to go on safaris, apparently. That photo was one that he had personally taken on one of his trips. He had taken pictures of all kinds of other animals, and they were all in other rooms around the NICU. Somehow, we got the lion room for Emilia. I jokingly told her that I'm going to buy that photo for Emilia's nursery when we get out of here. I actually asked her if we could do that and she laughed, not knowing if I was serious. I told her I was dead serious. She said, "You know what? I'll see what I can do. Worst case scenario, just take it and I won't tell anyone!" I couldn't believe she said that, but I definitely knew what I was doing the day we left that place.

We officially hit the end of our first week together. I remember sitting in her room and waiting for my alarm to go off at 5:16 p.m. to hear Sia's "Alive" blasting from my iPhone signifying an end to our first week of life together as a family. What a crazy ride this has been so far. That first week truly felt like a year had passed since Emilia was born. So many things had happened, so many emotions had come and gone, and we experienced so many highs and lows along the way. I actually remember getting a text from a friend asking how things were going around this time and responding with, "Dare I say good???" Emilia was doing so well. She was taking the introduction to milk feedings well, she was growing, her lungs were improving, she was still feisty, and most of all, she was freaking adorable. Just like running any marathon, though, you can never relax or feel too comfortable. I actually look back on this reply I sent my friend and think, "What an idiot! What was I thinking?" This was me letting the optimist inside take over. The realist should have stepped in and said, "My daughter was 23 weeks and 6 days old, on a ventilator, and fighting for her every breath. You need to keep your head down, stay focused, and in the present moment." If I was being a realist and leveraging the Stockdale Paradox rules, my reply would have been, "It's going. Today is okay."

My mental lapse reminded me of something I wrote during this time in my journal. Earlier that week, I had been out on a run around the neighborhood. I was moving well and had reached an extended downhill portion of my running session. I was a few miles into the run and running at a decent pace for myself. I was feeling good and was thinking, "Man, I could run like this for another 10 miles." All of a sudden, I turned the corner to the next street and was starting up at this big hill, and it felt so soul-crushing. I immediately thought, "Well shit...this is going to suck"! I began the climb. I started slowing down, my quads started to burn, my breathing got heavy, and I felt deflated mentally and just wanted to get the rest of this run over with as quickly as possible. How quickly it can all change just by turning a corner. Minutes before this turn, I thought I could run another 10 miles easily. Now I'm thinking, "I can't run ten more miles; I don't even know if I can run another half mile." Your mind goes into a tailspin and the proverbial wheels start to come off. One minute you are cruising along, and then the next, you are ready to quit and your will is broken. To have your mind wander and dream about the past or future is the most natural thing a human can do. Imagining the rewards at the finish line happens to everyone at some point. However, the moment you break that concentration on the task at hand and feel your mind slip into thinking about anything but the present is when you know you are in serious trouble. That's when it all falls to pieces. This letdown is exactly what I was unknowingly setting myself up for with my text back to my friend that read, "Dare I say Good???" I had let my mind wander to the finish line of this race, thinking this was going to be easy. The reality was we were just in an early downhill portion of our NICU marathon.

So what's the trick to overcoming this? This is the Stockdale paradox again of staying in the moment and only working on the brutal facts in front of your face. IT IS REALLY HARD, but the trick is to focus on one thing and one thing only. On a run, it is things like your form, your breathing, the pavement a few feet in front of you, the rhythm of your stride, etc. While playing tennis, it is focusing on the seams of the ball, the rhythm of bounce/hit in your mind, etc. In the NICU...I was still figuring that one out.

It was only a day after this stupid optimistic, "Dare I say good???" comment that I was introduced to one of our favorite nurses, Lori. Little did I know at the time that Lori was introduced to me just as we were all getting ready to turn the corner for our next metaphorical "hill" on our marathon with Emilia. I'm not sure that any of us would have ever made it over that hill had Lori not been there to guide us through it. Lori might be the nicest, sweetest, and most patient person I've ever encountered. She has so much energy at all times. Whenever I asked her a question, it was almost like she dropped everything she was doing to explain the answer, all the context behind it, and answer any follow-up questions. My real big sister, Kristin, couldn't be there because of coronavirus, of course, but I'm sure she would have approved of Lori as a more than adequate replacement should they ever have a chance to meet. Lori was my teacher and guide. She looked out for me. I had only known her for a day, but it felt like I had known her my whole life. I think anyone would feel the same way after spending 5 minutes with Lori.

These nurses have a HARD job. They are on their feet for 12 hours straight, dealing with some of these most challenging patients and circumstances that you could imagine, operating complex medical equipment and instrumentation, around parents and family all day who are watching them perform their job. I humbly say that there is no way I could ever do their jobs. That is REALLY hard for me, of all people, to say because I typically think I can do everything well, and I'm always up for a challenge. I'm sure if you were to ask Felicia (or anyone that has known me for more than an hour), they will annoyingly nod in approval of my last comment and follow that up with, "It's the most annoying thing ever!" I can safely say that being a NICU nurse is not one of those things that I would ever claim to be better at than the pros I watched care for Emilia every day. It takes a very specific person to be great at this job, and Lori has all the skills you need and more. Emilia was always one of the sickest children on the NICU floor, and therefore, she always got the most seasoned and veteran nurses due to the complexity of her care. Lori was about as veteran as anyone could be.

Lori had seen it all and she coached me through so many things. She gave all the tips and tricks of how to survive the NICU. She told me that all parents eventually find their role and where to add value to the care team. She told me the trick of not being scared unless you saw that she was scared. She taught me that we could still have fun in the NICU, and it didn't have to be so serious all the time. She taught me a ton about the care Emilia was receiving and why they did what they did. She truly is an angel, and I'm so thankful she was there during this time in Emilia's care because, little did we know, our first HUGE test was just around the corner that we would face head-on together.

The Journals (Days 5-8)

Day 5: 3/19/20

- I love you
- YOU DID SO GREAT LAST NIGHT. You are so strong and incredible. Glucose is down and everything is in range. Keep getting stronger
- Riley is amazing...your nurses are so nice. I've turned a corner with everyone here and I'm back to not being a grumpy jerk.
- I posted your camera feed so everyone could see you. They are loving you from a distance.
- Your grandma is stressed...I need to help her by helping myself. She's loving so many people right now and overwhelmed herself. Your Aunt and cousins are in town from Germany as they fled back to the US because of coronavirus. They are all living at Grandma and Grandpa's. Your Grandma also works in a hospital that is getting overwhelmed with new cases of coronavirus and that is stressing her as well.
- I called Brittany (your mom's best friend) today to thank her for everything the day you were born. She made a huge impact with everything and I'm sure you'll meet her soon.
- Relax was the scripture message of the day...we are all in God's hands. Great message, but I can't let my mind "relax" while thinking about the future like it suggested. I can relax about the present and that is it for now.
- I found a way to actually get a run in today and find a few minutes for myself. That meant a lot. I'm starting to trust your caregivers more and more. They are so nice.
- Your mom got to spend a lot of time with you today and relax a little with her mom. She's also making more milk for you which is making her feel a lot better. She's here to help you. She started buying you clothes already...it's starting. It's great to see her coming around and

getting back to her normal self. You are going to love her as your mom. I will try to not let her helicopter you too much...I swear.

- Your Riley doctors and nurses are amazing. I can't wait for you to meet them someday. They told me that your graduation day and following your progress are their favorite parts of their jobs. I can't wait to have them see the amazing woman you become. They are saints for all they do.
- You're a little all over the place today, but nothing too bad. It's a constant struggle to keep you in perfect vitals. That is the big challenge we keep hearing overall and we need to expect that more and more over the next few months.
- During my run today, I started to think about all the parallels to a marathon and your journey. Sometimes a run feels easy and you're cruising along and then you turn a corner to a new street and you are staring at this hill to climb and can appear overwhelming. Just like with you; I have to keep telling myself just take the next step (never get too high or low), stay present, and just take the next step. You're doing an amazing job at staying focused on your next steps right now. Just stay focused and we will as well. We're Sears' and we can do anything we set our mind too. Nobody is ever going to tell us what we can and can't achieve.
- I'm not as annoyed at your grandma living in our house. I've actually come to love that they are here for your mom. I need to keep reminding myself of that.
- These bible scriptures have been super helpful. Who would've ever thought...me reading the Bible??? I've always believed in God, but never found a lot of help in formal religion. For the first time in my adult life, faith and religion is actually helping me. I promise to make this a part of your life (along with teaching you other methods I use as well). Personal growth and self-awareness are also critical along with religion. I can't wait to watch you discover your own path and help guide that way.
- I love you.

DAY 6: 3/20/20

- I love you
- Daily Scripture Message - don't go to a dark place.
- I officially (successfully so far) smuggled your sheltie AND a Lion into your room to help watch over you and protect you. You have

your protector in the sheltie, and your strength / courage from the lion.

- The nurses said you had a great night last night. When I got here your little tongue was out and so cute.
- YOU'RE A SPRING BABY....it is actually 67 degrees outside today and humid. Perfect Indiana spring day. Spring brings sunshine and new life…that's you. We're going to have to watch out for you during spring break week when you are older because you'll be celebrating a birthday and vacation at the same time. Your mom and I got married in the spring as well. SPRING APPARENTLY MEANS A LOT TO ME EACH YEAR!!!! It's my favorite season. I used to think it was fall, but you officially tipped the scales toward spring.
- SOOO...I talked to my psychic today and she told me the real reason you came to us early is because you have such a STRONG SPIRIT. Apparently, you knew you could handle what was to come, but you were worried that your mom couldn't because your pregnancy had been so challenging. That makes so much sense to me now. You truly are the strongest little thing I've ever seen. It's really incredible. You're also so selfless to do that for your mom. You took on all the struggles of this first pregnancy and said ENOUGH… I got this from here. It makes sense why you are always kicking and flailing so much. You probably just want out and to go run a marathon or something. You'll get there, but you have to get strong and big first. I'm so scared at what this future is going to look like with you being such a strong spirit. I sense a lot of battles coming and I CAN'T WAIT. Luckily...you're just like your dad. We'll see what happens when 2 lions collide. :). Just remember, I'm always still the big LION and you're my little baby forever. I'll let you roam the pride on your own in time. I promise.
- Btw...yes, I have a psychic and no it's not weird. We all need help and guidance sometimes. Good news is that she helped me to see what this was all about, and I'm officially RESOLUTE that you're coming home happy and healthy. It's no longer just a thought in my mind to stay positive and optimistic...I know. Just like I knew we would get pregnant when we did, that you were a girl, and that your name would be Quinn. I know you're coming home with us from this place happy and healthy. Now for me, this is all about patience and letting this incredible team do their jobs. They are so good at it.
- You're so adorable on your little NICVIEW monitor.
- I tried to read to you earlier and apparently you thought I was too loud. Again, get used to it little lioness. Your dad is super loud, fun,

and a little crazy. I don't blame you though. I'll leave the reading and relaxation to your mom. We'll just play like crazy.

- Man...shit got a little crazy for a minute yesterday. This must be the roller coaster we've been told we'd be on by all of your Doctors and Nurses. I guess you can't run a marathon and always be running downhill.
- Your mom freaked out a little bit. I tried to help calm her, but she is struggling. It was pretty scary in all fairness. The worst part is that I wasn't THERE next to you. I felt so guilty you both had to go through that while I was at home eating chips and queso. These stupid virus rules keep us a part from each other so we all can't be together. When my "shift" ended you were doing great. I went home to relax while your mom had you, and then you immediately got all crazy for some reason. They had to turn your oxygen up to 100 for the first time while one of your tiny lungs had partially collapsed. That won't happen again...I promise that I'll be here if something like that happens again.
- Speaking of your mom, can we give her a break for a day or 2 please. Poor lady has been through so much already. Every day is more and more trauma that she is not processing well. It's not bad...but not great either. Sadly, I don't know that I can really do anything to help her. She needs to fight through this on her own. I can't have her stuck-on March 15th every day of her life. I need her to be present in the moment with you and I and what we are going through.
- I'm sleeping at the hospital for the first time tonight. I never could have imagined being here a week ago.
- You're such a miracle and a fighter...it's unreal.
- I set a daily alarm to go off at 5:16 p.m. to remind me of your birthday time and each new day with you. I'm playing the song "Alive" by Sia on the alarm. It's such a perfect song for you. Strong and emotional. Check it out someday if you want to cry. I'm sure I'll have played it for you a million times by then anyway though.
- I love you

Day 7: 3/21/20

- I love you
- Daily Scripture Message - giving, not getting is the way. War on selfishness. My Thoughts - So true. This is a family of givers. We owe it to the world to leverage our gifts and abilities to the fullest

to make the world a better place. You're going to be the rock star of this family someday.

- Quick Note, these daily scriptures have been really helpful to read. I think we need to go back to church more regularly when we bust you out of here. I mean...You are a little miracle baby and we owe a lot to God for you. No more doubt in my head, not that there really was, that God exists after I've met you and seen what you're going through these past few days and how you're overcoming all the odds.
- Wow...this is hard and exhausting. I've never worked this hard doing nothing in my life. It is a brutal, but I'm happy and honored to do it. Your mom and I need to find a balance for ourselves while we are here for you. We can't be here for you if we aren't taking care of ourselves as well.
- Quiet day so far, but we all know that can change in an instant with you being Miss feisty. It's ironic that the same thing that brings us all joy of watching you flail around all the time is the thing you really need to stop to get better. Just sleep and heal please.
- I can't wait for you to open your eyes. Your little face is adorable. You clearly have your mother's nose.
- I'm listening to a book in your room. It's so weird because it is quiet and we're alone. It's such a serene environment sometimes and bizarre that we're all here. Kind of relaxing, but at the same time I know that I can't relax at all with you because I've learned that lesson already.
- Your alarm went off at 5:16...made me smile. Another day of Quinny Bear.
- I'm learning so much about your care and it is kind of fascinating. You definitely don't want to get into this because I'm going to think I'm a doctor by the end of this. I can't help myself though...it's pretty fascinating stuff.
- They took your little beanie off to weigh you tonight and you had so much hair!!!! I couldn't believe it. Freaking adorable. That made the whole day worth it.
- I'm so afraid that tonight will be another crazy night. Please keep it chill. You're doing so well again. Give your mamma a break please :) when she gets here for her time with you.
- Monday is the big Ultrasound day. I'm feeling great about it, but I can't get ahead of myself.
- You're going to love meeting your nurses someday. I can't wait to introduce you when you are older. Marissa and Lori have been the best so far. Everyone is awesome, but those 2 have really taken a lot of time to help us all.

- Dr. Patel and Dr. Osa have been super knowledgeable and helpful as well. They are all like a dream team. We need to find the Doctors and Nurses that delivered you to thank them. Allie was who was with us in the LDR 20.
- Your mom and I had this overwhelming connection to each other last night. I've never felt that close to her before ever and it is really all because of you. We've always been an amazing team but you've really kicked us into overdrive. I know more and more every day that she and you are meant to be in my life forever and God has put you here for a reason. You 2 are both amazing.
- I love you

Day 8: 3/22/20

- I love you
- Daily Scripture Message - Love is the answer. My thoughts: So true. Love unconditionally, give unconditionally, and you'll eventually get it back 20-fold. You've already given me so much love and joy back that you'll never know. I've never been this unconditionally happy in my life. I'm usually always really happy, but it is tasks and activities that keep me moving and motivated. Sitting in this NICU and doing nothing with you all day and staying patient would normally be torture to me. Oddly enough, I'm the exact opposite right now. I look forward to doing nothing and just sitting around and loving you every day. Seeing you every day, and checking in on the monitors when I'm not there just literally makes everything else go away. You truly make me want to be a better person and share this love and feeling with everyone else.
- You've had about 24 hours of no events and have been pretty stable. You're snug as a bug in your swaddle. It seems like wrapping you up and strapping your flailing arms and legs down lets you relax and has been really helpful. It was entertaining to watch you kick and flail but that wasn't helping you.
- They are all making fun of you during rounds because you are so "wiggly." I'm secretly listening in to them. I feel like I'm about a day or 2 away from just asking to join the team overall and be a part of your daily rounds. We'll see. Your care is fascinating. The technology and team are unreal.
- Can you poop already!!! I'll probably regret saying this in the future, but for right now just LET IT GO!!! :)

- Holy Shit, you're going to be a WEEK OLD in a few hours. What a miracle. It's unreal. This week feels simultaneously like a it's been a whole year and only a few hours at the same time.
- 24 Weeks!!!
- Tomorrow morning is the big day for the ultrasound scan for any potential brain bleeds. Let's be on your best behavior young lady. Go crush your first test. I'll know your mother will love to know that we have another little straight A student in the family (that is definitely from your mother).
- I just remembered, your mom went to the hospital in a Harvard hoodie. I'm sitting here in Harvard shorts. You're crushing your exams every day effortlessly. I think you may be destined for Harvard Medical or Business School someday :). I'd be devastated if you weren't a Boilermaker like your Mom and Dad. However, given the signs and how special you are...Harvard may be the place for you.
- They called you a little flirt because you kept having to get Devin, the respirator therapist, to come over all day today. Lol
- YOU'RE A WEEK OLD! My Sia alarm went off on my way back to the hospital. I listened to it all. I'M STILL BREATHING...I'm ALIVE!!! Way to go baby girl. It feels like the past week went by in like 4 hours. Nurse Lori told me that in 4 months when you're out of here I'm going to look back and feel like it was 2 weeks. It is going to go by so fast. She's been such a great help for me in giving me guidance and advice on what is about what is to come for all of us. I've really enjoyed our conversations. Someday you need to meet her.
- All the nurses are obsessing over how cute you are. They are literally fighting over who gets to take care of you!!!
- You continue to be up and down all day. For 4 hours you're great. 2 hours you're not. The Doctors are worried about x, we did y, which caused z, etc. It's like a never-ending game of a dog chasing its tail. Only difference is they will catch up to you and you will all figure it out. That's the beauty of the human body I guess.
- I'm so excited for your tests tomorrow. You have a big day with the ultrasound and they are deciding on your pic line. It feels like a cliff hanger of a TV show where I can't wait to get back in there to figure out what they decided to do. You're must see TV for me.
- They took the beanie off again to do your care. You're so freaking cute. I usually think babies aren't very cute at all. I've always felt weird about that because I thought I was being a jerk. Everyone always fawns all over babies and I would almost run away. You are legit cute as hell. It's hard to not fall in love. I'm pretty sure I'd say the same

thing even if I wasn't your dad...who knows though. I'll let your Dads' friends give him a reality check when they get to see you. :)

- I actually got to do a real workout today...yeah me. Felt great to finally sweat a lot and get some stress out.
- PS - the world around you is falling apart. It's insanity. The economy is collapsing, people are losing their jobs, most people are quarantined at home, etc. It's a nut house around the world due to this Coronavirus pandemic. I can't wait for that crap to be over so we can all get back to focusing on just you.
- I'm exhausted and going to bed.
- Love you

The NICU Marathon: The First Big Hill, The Honeymoon Ends (Day 9-14)

The moment that would come to define our entire stay together as a family in the NICU was about to occur on this 9th night. I heard a nurse tell me something once that truly defines how hard their job is and how crazy the NICU can be all in one sentence. They said, "You can clock in for your shift and everything is fine; then, by the end of your shift, you have a new angel." Those words are so true, humbling, and always need to be remembered at all times in the NICU. As much as we want to be, we aren't in control of this process. Babies aren't meant to be here at 22 weeks old. Their bodies and brains just don't know how to handle that sometimes. I would come to find how true that statement was on days nine and ten of our own journey.

Felicia and I had done our own shift change for the night around 7 p.m. That just so happened to be the same time as the nurse's shift change as well. Their shifts were 12 hours from 7 a.m. to 7 p.m. Lori was back as our nurse for the night shift. Lori and I had gotten to know each other so well the night before that I was so excited to see she was back with us on this night. As her shift started, everything was going great. Of course, there were always a few alarms that went off every now and then, but nothing out of the ordinary or to be alarmed about. At this point, Felicia and I had become pretty used to most of the alarms and knew when it was a big deal vs. just something routine. Emilia was doing great, and we were all having a fun time together in the NICU as the night began. Around 10 p.m. that night, after Lori performed Emilia's care time and assessment, she noticed her belly was getting a little bit bigger, so she made a note of it while charting. She let the NP and doctor know, and they said that they'd keep a close eye on it. Lori told me that she thinks this was just Emilia not having pooped yet that was causing this as her initial guess. I hadn't even realized it until she said that, but Emilia had never pooped yet. We were nine days into her life outside the womb, and she hadn't pooped. Of course, I asked Lori about this and she gave me all the explanations I could ever want to learn about poop in babies this young. She said that this is pretty typical and that they don't expect preemies to have their first bowel movements for at least the first week. It is different for every baby, but she thought Emilia was getting pretty close to pooping.

I learned that the first poop is actually something called Meconium. Meconium is this black goop that comes out of babies during their first poop. I remember Felicia showing me a NICU baby onesie from a website a few days later that said, "Meconium Happens!" NICU humor is the worst. Lori told me she was concerned with her assessment but not too concerned at this point. She said she'd monitor it closely and keep me posted. Again, remember rule number three and don't get anxious unless your nurses are anxious. Lori had seen everything in her career and I knew Emilia was in good hands. A few hours passed and it was now getting close to midnight. Emilia still hadn't pooped and her belly was beginning to look a little more swollen and distended. They ordered an X-ray to check it out. The X-rays showed that her intestines had a lot of gas in them and that is what was causing her belly to swell. Lori still wasn't nervous, so I wasn't nervous. It was about this time that I asked Lori if I should stay the night? She said, "You may want to stick around as we aren't out of the woods yet with this situation." "POOP!!!!" That's all I could think about. I remember writing in my journal, "Would you freaking poop already?" I called Felicia and let her know the situation. I knew that Felicia didn't handle stuff like this well, so I told her I would handle it and would let her know if anything changes. I told her to go to sleep. It was Dad time! I had to be the one to be here for this situation. I had to be the one to be calm and strong for Emilia. I had to do this for Felicia. I vowed not to call her unless I absolutely had to.

I decided to stay in the room that night. This was a big deal. This was the first time since we left Methodist that I would have stayed the night with Emilia in her room. Even though it had been nine days, we hadn't had a need to stay overnight up until that point. Emilia had been doing so well and we felt it was better to get some sleep in our own beds, check the NicView constantly, and be refreshed for the morning shift. Tonight, I was staying. Lori told me to stay, so I'm staying! I sat on the edge of my chair for the next 2-3 hours as we all kept a close eye on what was happening with Emilia's belly. It was only getting worse. Still no poop, belly getting bigger. The situation had progressed to the point in time where it was really dangerous. Lori was officially concerned. That meant that I was now officially concerned. Lori kept me calm and talked me through all the scenarios that could happen. If they didn't get the gas out, the worst-case scenario is that one of Emilia's intestines could perforate, causing all her feces to escape into her abdomen. This would put her at an extremely high risk of a bacterial infection that could lead to sepsis and potentially death. The best-case scenario is that Emilia poops, the gas releases, the belly goes down, and all is good to go. I was officially in panic mode. I had never been more terrified in my life. Was I about to watch my daughter die? How could this be happening? She was doing fine at 7 p.m. that night, and by 3 a.m., we are talking about death? That is how fast things can change in the NICU.

Around 3 a.m., Lori called up the surgeons, and they came in to evaluate Emilia to see if an emergency surgery would be necessary. The surgeons looked her over, huddled, told Lori something, and then left the room. Lori said that surgery might be necessary and they would be back at 4 a.m. to talk options with me if nothing has changed. I still hadn't called Felicia. I was not going to wake her up and terrify her until I knew what was going on! I was going to see this through by myself and be strong for my ladies. Lori was there for me. She helped comfort me, talked me through everything, kept her energy high, and kept things lighthearted as best as she could. I'll never stop saying this, "THANK GOD for Lori!" I'm so blessed that she was there that night. Besides Staci and Raina, two nurses that we'll meet later, I couldn't imagine (there it is again) going through any of this with anyone other than Lori. These three were all handpicked by God to help us through some of the most trying events in our lives.

Back to the story, it is 3:30 a.m. and I'm officially freaking out. We are all on poop watch and literally praying for shit. The surgeons are only a few minutes away from coming back into the room to "discuss options." I'm literally sitting next to Emilia, just waiting for something terrible or something great to happen. And then it happened...She freaking pooped! Meconium Happens! She had a HUGE blowout! Lori looked at her diaper, looked up at me, and said, "SHE POOPED!" She told me to come over and look. I jumped up out of my chair and ran over to the side of the isolate. I had my camera ready. I took a ton of pictures. I guess this is dad life! I was so happy to see all the poop. I never thought in my wildest dreams that I would be so over the moon happy that Emilia just had a blowout. That was the best poop in the world. I was so relieved. Lori was relieved. They called off the surgeons. We were back on the right track, but we weren't officially out of the woods yet.

Lori told me that they needed to get the X-ray person back to take a look at Emilia's intestines again to make sure there wasn't any damage. They were going to start Emilia immediately on another course of full-spectrum antibiotics preventively and send off a blood culture to the lab to make sure she didn't have a bacterial infection. We wouldn't get those results for another few days. We all just needed to cross our fingers that nothing bad had happened inside her belly and intestines from this incident. I was told the best-case scenario is that everything is fine, we take a break from milk feedings for a few days until the antibiotics course is done, and the X-rays don't show any damage. Worse case, she may have had an intestinal perforation, and Dr. Osa would talk us through what to do if that was the case.

As the morning came, Dr. Osa came by the room to talk about what may be going on with Emilia and how we planned to treat the situation. As he was recapping what we were clinically seeing, he mentioned "NEC" as a potential cause for the scare last night. This was the first time I heard of NEC. I hate those three little letters. I will always hate those three little letters. Those three little letters bring up memories of so much pain and suffering inflicted upon my family. NEC stands for necrotizing enterocolitis. Necrotizing enterocolitis (NEC) is a devastating disease that affects mostly the intestines of premature infants. The wall of the intestine is invaded by bacteria, which cause local infection and inflammation that can ultimately destroy the wall of the bowel (intestine). Basically, the intestines perforate and all the fecal matter in the intestines is released into the abdomen. The doctors don't know why it occurs, and they don't know how to stop it. It is one of the mystery diseases of the neonatal world that they are still learning about. We would come to learn so much more about NEC during our stay. I can't remember how many conversations we had with Dr. Osa or Emily, one of the NP's, about Emilia's belly, NEC, and course of treatment. For now, the acute emergency had been avoided, but the extent of the damage still remained to be understood.

Time Out (In my best Zach Morris impersonation again)...

This is a great time in the story to introduce one of the other main characters that played a huge role for the duration of Emilia's care while at Riley's. His name is Dr. Osa. He is one of the most brilliant, dedicated, patient, and empathetic doctors you will ever meet. This guy really cares!!! You could tell how much he LOVED his job with how he carried himself in every single interaction and task he performed. He was all business and brilliant but had a special flair about him that made him relatable and human as well. The best way I can describe him is the perfect balance of medicinal knowledge with love and compassion at the same time. He was the kind of guy that would spend 20 minutes walking you through, with incredible detail, what Emilia was experiencing and all the options that we have in our toolbox. He'd let you ask as many questions as you wanted and never seemed to grow impatient or dismiss anything you had to say. He then would get up and walk away in his untied Chuck Taylor's while letting you know that he would go research the questions we had asked and would swing back later to let us know what he found. He was just a cool dude. He didn't just know his stuff; he went out of his way to seemingly put himself in the parents' and patients' shoes in the way he administered his treatments and care plans. He was a genius medical practitioner who you could tell really knew everything possible about neonatology but never made you feel like an idiot. He listened, he taught, he provided extra attention to both Emilia and us, and he just made you feel like you knew your child was truly in the best hands imaginable.

One of the first times I met Dr. Osa, he sat down next to me and drew me a diagram of a baby, said, "Here are the four things that we need to watch closely," and then proceeded to walk me through them all.

1. The Brain. Brain bleeds apparently happen pretty frequently in micro-preemies like Emilia. It is something that they can't really monitor or detect early on; however, it can have devastating effects if present and based on the grade of the bleed. Dr. Osa said that after the first week, they can do an ultrasound of the brain and will be able to tell if anything serious has occurred. My fingers were crossed that this wouldn't be an issue and I mentally noted this as our first big milestone to jump over.

2. The Belly. NEC is the primary concern with the belly. Dr. Osa said the digestive system is a complicated mystery in babies this young. You never know how they are going to take to breast milk feedings. You never know if something like NEC will happen. All they know is that NEC can be devastating, and we have to always watch closely for this. The belly turned out to be Emilia's never-ending battle.

3. The Heart. Obviously, the heart is critical to all operations for obvious reasons. Emilia had a perfect little heart. (Of course she did.)

4. The Lungs. The lungs are a perpetual game of whack-a-mole in babies this young. In my non-expert view, it seems like everything else impacts the lungs and their performance. The lungs are a reflection of how the rest of the body is functioning. They can be great one minute, and then things can change

rapidly. Respiratory therapists are constantly in and out of the room and the stupid alarm for her oxygen levels is basically the only thing that ever goes off. Emilia's lungs were strong and she would have been great in this area if her little belly could ever get things on track. It seemed like whenever her belly was good, her lungs were good. When anything changed, her lungs would become a secondary fire to put out throughout her entire time in the NICU.

Dr. Osa and I spent the majority of our time together discussing Emilia's belly primarily and her lungs secondarily. I learned so much from him about what was going on with Emilia. I love to learn and he never turned me down from any theory or question I threw at him. Eventually, he started to just invite me to rounds because he knew I'd have 100 questions for him afterward anyway. I still remember one of my proudest moments during our time in the NICU was when he said to me one day, "I'll make a neonatologist out of you yet," as he walked out of the room smiling. I couldn't have been proud to hear those words from him. This was one of the most brilliant men I'd ever been around in my life, and he thought enough of me to say that. It really made me feel like I was actually adding value to Emilia's care and that I was the best dad I could possibly be, given the circumstances we were thrown into.

Time In...

As I was getting ready to finally leave the NICU in the early morning hours to sleep after one of the most nerve-racking nights of my life, Dr. Osa came by with the X-ray results of Emilia's latest belly scan and wanted to walk me through them. He showed me this little section of Emilia's intestines that might look like it had perforated. He stressed that he wasn't totally sure yet, but the little air bubbles he could see in that section worried him a little. He said, "Air bubbles are a sign that a perforation may have occurred, but we just don't know for sure yet." He said, "We'll monitor this closely, but it looks like we may have dodged a bullet." I walked away, praying that this was truly the case, and went home for some much-needed rest. Much more to come in the future on Emilia's fight with NEC.

The Journals: Days 9-14

Day 9: 3/23/20

- I love you
- Daily Scripture Theme- Show God's love to people. My Thoughts - Don't just talk about it...be about it. The way I'm being about it is to support your care team, your mom, grandparents, family and our friends. Trying to keep everyone calm and informed. Saying thank you to all that help you. Not getting too high or too low for you. That is how I'm showing God's love. Once we are all through this, I plan to show that a little more demonstratively and pay it forward. I'd love to share your story with the world and other preemie parents. This stuff is stressful, and I'd love to be there as a support in some way for anyone else that may be experiencing what we are going through. I also want to be more involved in church for what it is worth.
- ONE WEEK OLD!!! You're already close to the old age of 8 days. Unreal and amazing.
- I think you hate your crying neighbor in the next room. Every time they start screaming it looks like it stresses you out as your heart rate goes up a little it seems. Maybe it is just me...lol.
- You officially have graduated to only one nurse for 2 babies... congratulations. They only give one dedicated nurse to the most special babies like yourself when you were first born. It's a big deal that they feel like you can be one of the normal babies in here that needs less support. That means that you are getting stronger and stronger.
- Funny thing about our nurse having 2 babies is we have your friend's stats now on your monitors. I feel like I have watch over you both now.
- You just got another new neighbor across the hall today as well. It sounds like a complicated case. They closed our door (which they never do) because of privacy concerns as they read out the info on the baby. I'm so praying for that new little baby right now. I know everything your mom and I went through just a few days ago and all of this is incredibly intense. You 2 are both going to graduate out of here together soon and we'll make sure you stay connected and get to meet someday.
- Watching them orchestrate this new move into the next room is unreal. It's a delicate and complicated dance. This must have been what you experienced as well. I can't imagine all you've gone through.

Again, this team of medical professionals are unreal in how talented they all are.

- You got your first tummy time. You were NOT HAPPY when they flipped you, but it seemed to help you breathe easier.
- Whenever it is quiet and calm in the room and I get a chance to look into your little incubator, I can't help but feel so proud that you're here and we created you. I guess this is the Dad life. It feels pretty good.
- Probably the only time I'll ever say this…TAKE A SHIT PLEASE!!!! You're making things hard on yourself. Let it go. It's really important. I'm really praying for this one right now. Keep fighting.
- I'm so glad I set this alarm at your birth time. It's amazing to hear that song every day as it reminds me you're here, you're amazing, a FIGHTER, and I'm your dad.
- Break time is over, it's time for this fight to pick up now. We're going to kick some ass the next few days. Fight my little girl. You need to get past this next tummy/gut hurdle.
- I'm sleeping right next to you and not leaving you.
- Crush this next X-Ray tonight and get this poop out of you.
- Praying for no infections either or if you do that it the antibiotics kick it really fast and nothing serious comes from this.
- I love you and I'll see you in the morning.

Day 10: 3/24/20

- I love you
- Daily Scripture Theme - whatever you can do is worth doing.
- YOU FREAKING POOPED!!!! Like…literally it was at the last minute at 3 a.m. of nurses talking about possible surgery and then you just shit all over them. You're so strong and apparently a jokester as well.
- It's your parents wedding anniversary day! We'll have a lot to celebrate each spring (your birthday, anniversary, spring break, etc.).
- Well Quinny Bear, you've passed your first REALLY BIG HURDLE. I need you to stay strong all day today. It's so important.
- I'm glad I was here last night and not your mom. That one was a pretty scary one. Literally, as the nurse practitioner and surgeons were coming up to discuss options to deal with your tummy…you went ahead and just pooped. It was amazing, and almost a slap in the face to us all letting us know you got this.

- Every nurse that comes in that room always talks about how feisty you are. I love it and wouldn't have you any other way. You have to be a fighter to overcome this challenge and you are.
- I'm having all the feels today. Last night was REALLY INTENSE. This morning / afternoon I was doing that bad thing again where you look to the future and start thinking I have no idea how I'm going to endure this for 4 months. Then I get kicked out of the waiting room because of coronavirus and we are officially only allowed to have 1 visitor now (in the hospital) as that gets worse. Now I'm at home and trying to sleep a little to get back to the hospital and the dog is barking and your grandma decided to stink up our entire house by clean the oven randomly. Then I get stuck at a train crossing on the way back to the hospital. It just all got to me. When you're negative, negative stuff happens to you. It's all about how you respond to the stimuli and your environment. In truth, I'm mad about people protecting and caring for you (getting kicked out of the waiting room for coronavirus), your grandma cleaning our house, and a loving dog barking. That's stupid. All those are great things. I started to tell this to your mom and she talked me out of the negative mindset. For some reason I still couldn't shake it. And then out of nowhere, I got 4 random acts of love from people telling me how they watch you every night and pray for us all. Then your mom gave me a beautiful card she wrote about how great I am as a Dad for our anniversary. I just had to look up to and realize that God is trying to help me right now and accept it. I HAVE TO STAY STRONG, positive, and optimistic for you. THAT'S MY JOB!!!! Thank you to everyone and God for reminding me today as I was starting to get a little frustrated.
- I really think I want to write your story someday and publish it for NICU parents to have at hospitals. There just isn't much to do in here and I know it would help me to be reading another parent's real time thoughts as they were going through one of the most challenging things a parent can go through. I'm going to do this someday once your story is complete and we are out of here.
- YOU CALM ME DOWN SO MUCH!!!! As soon as I walk into this room it seems like I find my peaceful happy place. I honestly don't ever want to leave, but I have to because of the stupid virus rules and I can't be selfish to your mom and take up all of your time with just me.
- You continue to amaze me every day with your strength and resilience.
- Every damn day this song at 5:16 p.m. just makes me so happy. I'm going to do that forever. You'll be so embarrassed eventually, but I'm

not going to stop. That song reminds me of this journey, you and how strong you are, how much I love you, and your mom.

- I love you

Day 11: 3/25/20

- I love you
- Daily Scripture Theme - add flavor everywhere you go. My Thoughts: You certainly do that...so expressive and feisty. Everyone loves watching you, and the nurses all think you're adorable. I added a little flavor today with my attitude and shoes (choose a fun and colorful pair to show off to you :). You'll love to see my "flare shoes," as your mom calls them, when you get older. I like to Peacock a little bit everyone once in a while. I have a lot of them, but it's rare I bust them out because I don't want to get them dirty...I will do it for you though. I'm sure you will be super embarrassed to be seen with me around your friends in the future.
- You're healing nicely from your belly scare a few nights ago. They are checking to see the damage right now and I'm praying it didn't tear anything in your intestines...as that would require surgery (which we don't want).
- Okay baby girl...intestinal wall tear it is but they caught it early. You got to fight hard the next few days and don't let this thing spread. We love you. YOU ARE SO STRONG. NEC ain't got nothing on you girl.
- Every day that birthtime reminder alarm goes off it makes me so happy. Best thing I've ever thought of in my life.
- No matter how much you go through...I just KNOW you're coming home and going to overcome this. You are literally your mother's daughter. I know you'll never quit. I don't know what it is, but I just know. I may just be the HYPE MAN of this family, but I'm watching 2 incredibly strong women do their things and I couldn't be happier.
- I love you

Day 12: 3/26/20

- I love you
- Daily Scripture theme - I was always on my mind. My Thoughts - Switching from being a Taker to Giver. I've probably been pretty

selfish most of my life. Not that I didn't ever care or give to someone else. I just always came first and was the priority. The moment you were born that 1000% changed and I'll never look back. You will always be my priority going forward. I still need to take care of myself, but only so I can provide and care for you. We have to trust in God that you'll be okay...AND I DO.

- The doctors literally let me be part of your rounds today. I think they are seeing how smart your mom and I are and figured it best just to include us as we'd pepper them with questions anyway afterward... just our nature. I'm sure you'll have some of those traits as well.
- The doctor said he'll make a neonatologist out of me by the end of this...lol. I think he can tell that I show my care for you and your care team by being so involved, asking a lot of questions, and learning. Truthfully, I do this so I can calm myself and focus on something so I can help keep your mom calm. If your Mom and I are calm, we can all keep you calm.
- Milk is your best friend and worst enemy right now.
- You started to try and open your eyes today. I got it all on video... how amazing to watch my daughter get to see the world for the first time. I wonder what you were thinking and seeing. I'm glad I was one of your first sites. I think you are starting to recognize my voice. You seem to want to look at me whenever I'm talking near you...show off. Such a little daddy's girl.
- Your Mommy is struggling right now. She can't seem to break free from March 15th and enjoy each moment with you right now. I need us to be a team to combine our super powers for you. While I'm pretty cool...she's the real brains of this operation. Trust me, we both need her a lot. I'm going to get to work on solving this one. That's my priority for sure.
- I love you

Day 13: 3/27/20

- I love you
- Daily scripture theme - the journey toward unselfishness.
- You and your Mommy got kangaroo time today. It was adorable. I can't wait to do that with you as well. Truthfully...I'm terrified.
- The nurses are all in love with you and literally fight over who gets to take care of you.

- Your mommy is struggling and I don't know how to help her. She's scared for you and rightfully so, but that is taking her down a negative road. Anytime I try to help it makes matters worse.
- Not a ton of notes today because I feel like we've finally hit a stable patch in your care and it was kind of "normal" ish today.
- You're going to be 2 weeks old in a few days.
- I love you

Day 14: 3/28/20

- I love you
- Daily Scripture Theme - God is love. My Thoughts – "no privilege without responsibility. We must be patient. The things we are most grateful for are the things we've waited the longest for." This is going to be my ultimate test in patience. Not just the NICU, but the rest of your life. You are the thing I'm most grateful for every day.
- There is a baby in the room next to you that squeals like a little piggy when it cries. It makes me wonder what your little cries are going to sound like. I'm praying it isn't going to be like that young man btw :). I imagine yours will be like little rainbow sighs. You certainly will be trained well to deal with crazy stimulation and stay calm with all that you've already endured in the NICU and will endure in the future.
- Random thought - I wonder how doctors think about your outlook? Is it all statistics and treatment or is it hope, love, prayer, and optimism combined with Science and Stats. Do they BELIEVE in you like we do and with their other patients? I know your mom and I do, but I wonder how Doctors and Nurses process all this as well. It's not easy for your mom and I, but at least we can channel all of our love and optimism into you and ONLY you. That is exhausting already. To do that for all of their patients must be overwhelming. I wonder how they cope overall? How they process their thoughts? I may try to dive into that one with a few of them in the future.
- I'm going to read you the daily scripture and share with you my thoughts. Don't freak out on me please. It seems like my voice excites you...or scares you???
- You and your mom live streamed your kangaroo time tonight. I could see how happy you made her...and nervous. It was pretty amazing to watch.
- I'm getting concerned things are going too well the past few days. We've been told to expect roller coaster after roller coaster on this

marathon. I don't want to relax, but I don't know what to do either. Pretty confusing. Only thing I KNOW is that you're coming home safe and sound no matter what.

- I love you

The NICU Marathon: Hitting Our Stride + a Roo for the Ages (Day 15-22)

After the big belly scare back at the end of Emilia's first week here with us, we had picked up the pieces, assessed the damage, and had charted a course with the care team on how we would combat this NEC thing going forward.

Before we get back to that, a couple of days after the belly scare, the brain ultrasound finally happened to assess if Emilia had any dangerous brain bleeds present that are common amongst micro-preemies. Everything else seemed to be going about as well as we could have expected, and that seemed like the next big hurdle to get through. I had been mentally preparing for this moment for the past week since Dr. Osa first walked me through the four key areas to monitor with micro-preemies early on after our arrival at Riley's. I had been so anxious about her brain bleed test. I had jokingly called that Emilia's first big test in life, treating it like it was a school exam or something. I was already thinking about how I was going to be such a proud dad and tell everyone when she crushed her first exam. Her mom is the academic of the family (she has two master's degrees, after all). I'm pretty sure that Emilia was going to be just as brilliant as Felicia, and then some. It was such an unknown at that point what would happen on the day of her big test. Dr. Osa had said that he doesn't see any visible signs or ways that Emilia is behaving in any manner that would suggest brain damage. Then, the belly issue happened and it put everything back into perspective.

The belly scare was a huge wake-up call and reminder for me that there are no milestones in the NICU. EVERY DAY IS A MIRACLE with your child! Nothing is promised for tomorrow. There are no scheduled tests and checkpoints. The NICU does a remarkable job at humbling you and bringing you back down to Earth any time it senses you allow your mind to think about the future. Just when you think you might see a little bit of hope, you get thrown back into the reality that none of us are in control of this ride. You hear your whole life, "Live every day as if it is your last." Everyone conceptually understands this way of thinking, and I don't think anyone would dispute that sentiment. The sad thing is that 99.9% of us don't actually treat life this way.

We constantly set our goals and sights for the next big milestone so we can check the box and let everyone know about the progress that we are making. We are always evaluating and analyzing the past and making plans for the future. We rarely ever truly live in the here and now. If I asked any parent, I knew what the most important thing in their life is, they would all say their children. That is what they say; however, that probably isn't how they live, though, if I had to guess! In the NICU, every minute with your child truly is a miracle. The situation forces you to live your life in the here and now. You really don't have the option to do anything other than that, to be fair. The moment you start thinking about the next big test and planning for the future is the moment when you will get thrown from this horse and won't even know what hit you. So, if any other parents besides a NICU parent are reading this book, please use this as a reminder to not forget that every day with your child is a miracle as well! For "normal" parents, remembering your child is a miracle has to be intentional and by design, which is even harder and one of the most challenging things any of us can do.

One of my favorite books, *The 7 Habits of Highly Effective People*, talks about the concept of always striving to "put first things first." Putting first things first means organizing and executing your life around what truly matters most in this world. It is living and being driven by the principles you value most, not by the agendas and forces surrounding you. The book breaks down time management into activities that are based on urgency and importance to help you to understand and more easily live the principle of putting first things first. There are four quadrants of urgency and importance.

- Quad 1 – Urgent and Important
- Quad 2 – Not Urgent but Important - (FIRST THINGS FIRST)
- Quad 3 – Urgent and Not Important
- Quad 4 – Not Urgent and Not Important

Quad 2 is the "putting first things first" quadrant. It is made up of those incredibly important activities that reflect what you value most in life yet have no built-in sense of urgency to force action to complete. It is in these Quad 2 activities that we make our lives special by living the lives on how we say we truly want. Treating every day as a miracle with Emilia for me was a Quad 1 activity in our unfortunate situation. It was urgent AND important. I had no choice but to remember to cherish our time together because I truly didn't know if I would have another day with her. For regular parents and regular children that are blessed to not be facing literal life and death each day, treating every day with your child as a miracle is a Quad 2 activity (putting first things first) which is why it is so difficult. You have to intentionally think and find ways to live this way every day. There is no urgency, but you have to find ways to build this in your life if this is truly the way you say you want to live your life. I urge you parents out there to remember this principle and figure out how to make every day with your child a miracle. PS – Emilia did crush her brain ultrasound, in case anyone was wondering.

Talk about treating every day with your child as a miracle. It was around this time that Emilia opened her eyes for the first time. It is hard to put into words how special of a moment this was for Felicia and me. How many people literally get to watch their child try to figure out how to open their eyes for the first time? How Many people get to be the first thing their child sees upon gazing at this new world? It all began one morning when I was standing over Emilia's isolate and being captivated by all her little feisty kicks and flails as usual. I caught a glimpse of her face and started to notice this tiny little slit opening in her left eye. I asked the nurse if her eye was trying to open, and she walked over to take a peek and said it seemed to be. If you don't know, preemie babies born this young still have their eyes fused shut. It isn't until around 25 weeks or so that the baby's eyes start to open, or so I learned. Every baby is different in how long it takes, of course. Emilia was a little ahead of the curve. No way in hell this child was going to be last in the class. It was time for Emilia's eyes to open and she was all in.

From that moment on, we were on eye-opening-watch at all times. That little tiny slit in her left eye slowly got a little wider as each hour passed. You could start to see the color of her little pupils barely showing through. Emilia's little eyeballs underneath her eyelids were moving all around. You could tell she was trying so hard to get those eyes open to see the world. After a few hours of this process, a larger gap between her left eyelids started to open up where you could start to see her eye even more. Her right eye was still fused shut, but her left eye was almost fully opened at this point. By the time Felicia and I's shift change happened that day, Emilia had her entire left eye open, and the right eye was slowly starting to come along as well. I got everything on video and couldn't believe the miracle of life I was observing. I felt so blessed to be there to watch this process. It was even cooler to know that I was the first person my daughter saw when her eyes first opened. I'll never forget that moment. I recorded everything as she slowly spent the whole day trying to get each eye open all the way. I wonder what she must have thought seeing the world officially for the first time. Her eyes were so expressive and mesmerizing. I have some photos of her on my office wall, looking right at the camera with those beautiful eyes. That will forever be one of the coolest things that I will experience in my life and something I will never forget.

As Dr. Osa and his team had finally put together the pieces of what had happened to Emilia a few nights prior, he filled us in on our plan of attack moving forward. He was pretty convinced at this point that we were officially dealing with a case of NEC and that it had caused a perforation in Emilia's intestines. We didn't know the extent of the damage or if it was in multiple spots or just one isolated spot. Dr. Osa explained what the ramifications are if NEC occurs and the treatment recommendation course of action.

The proposed treatment plan was as follows:

Step 1 - Immediately stop all breast milk feedings until we know the extent of the damage and keep her on TPN (total parenteral nutrition). This was a big deal. We had to stop the milk feedings to give her belly a rest so it wouldn't produce more waste that leaks into her abdomen. TPN was given intravenously, so Emilia could still get the nutrition she needed in the interim. While little is known about NEC, the one thing that is known is that breast milk is critical to help build up good gut health in babies this young. TPN is a great substitute, but ideally should never be used long term as it just isn't a replacement for a mother's milk. We can design a lot of things in this world, but some things nature got right, and breast milk is one of them. We are still a LONG way from understanding the magic of breast milk and its importance to the baby.

Step 2 - Keep Emilia on a full spectrum antibiotic to protect her from sepsis and other bacterial infections for the next ten days.

Step 3 – Have the surgical team perform a minor operation called a Penrose, which would place two holes and a little drain on each side of Emilia's abdomen to help all the stuff that had leaked out of her bowels drain out of her body.

Step 4 - Wait, pray, and hope her intestines heal themselves over the next ten days.

Once we were done with the antibiotics course, they would put some liquids in Emilia and watch how it passed through the bowels to see if she had healed herself or not. We wouldn't really know until then what was officially going on inside her belly. We were praying that her intestines would repair their own damage, and then we could all move past this scary event. That was the best-case scenario. The worst-case scenario was that the damage to her bowels was more extensive than originally thought, she hadn't healed herself, and that a more intrusive procedure of an ostomy would need to be performed just above where the perforation happened so Emilia could have a permanent solution in place to prevent the leakage and be able to resume milk feedings through her healthy bowel sections. For those of you that don't know, an ostomy is a surgery to create an opening (stoma) from an area inside the body to the outside. It treats certain diseases of the digestive or urinary systems. Basically, they were going to pull her healthy bowel to the surface, and all of her waste would exit out into a bag. She would have that in place until she was really big and strong, and then they would do another surgery to repair the bowels and reunite them together so she could continue to live a normal life. This was obviously the worst-case scenario that none of us were hoping for.

Important note about NICU surgeons and surgeries performed on preemie's in general – NO ONE wants to operate on a baby that small. Their bodies are just so incredibly delicate, and any additional trauma can be catastrophic. Emilia was born at 1 pound, 1 ounce. Operating on a baby that small is not easy, nor is the decision taken lightly. Surgery, we were told, is the absolute last resource that is available should it have to be deployed.

Time Out (Zach Morris interlude here again)...

Speaking of NICU Surgeons, this is a great time to introduce another pivotal character on our care team that would play a huge role in our time at the NICU. His name is Dr. Rescorla, a world-renowned NICU surgeon at Riley Hospital for Children. I say this in the nicest way possible; we never wanted to meet Dr. Rescorla, but I'm glad we did. The handful of interactions that we had with him were at some of the most critical junctures of care during Emilia's time in the NICU. If surgery had to be done, I don't think I could have trusted anyone more than Dr. Rescorla. Just like so many other saints that work in this NICU world, he is incredibly patient and kind and always took the time to walk us through everything and answer all the questions we had before and after any procedure.

The benefits of rule number two of the NICU (support, encourage, and always say thank you to the care team) truly showed the most during our interactions with Dr. Rescorla. His job is so hard. I can't even imagine (there it is again) what he must go through before performing any operation on a baby the size of Emilia. No one wants to do this, and he is the guy that has to do it. He is dealing with the most innocent form of human life, a brand-new person, and one of the most complex patients you could ever encounter. I can't even imagine (there it is again) how much that must weigh on his conscience before and after every procedure he performs. Felicia and I made it a point not to make his job more complicated by staying patient and thanking him as many times as we could. IT WORKED! I remember him telling us multiple times how refreshing it was to interact with us. I don't know what he normally experiences, but I have to imagine that it wasn't that, or he wouldn't have made a point of saying this to us. I have no idea if that ultimately made an impact on the care Emilia received, but I have to feel like it made a difference when the time came for these crucial surgeries to be performed.

Time In...

With the treatment plan in place and agreed to by all, we began the long waiting game over the next ten days to figure out what the remedy would be (self-healing or surgery). Ten days seemed like it was going to be forever. Emilia was only just a little over a week old when the first big belly scare happened. We were now being asked to wait in limbo for ten more days until we would know whether or not a traumatic surgery was going to be deemed necessary or not for Emilia.

In the meantime, life went on. Emilia was actually doing much better. It seemed as though the belly issue had been causing a lot of complications in other areas that were now starting to go away. The Penrose drain (the little holes in her abdomen) was working well and keeping her abdomen clean to avoid any potential bacterial infections. Her lungs were getting stronger, her feistiness had returned, and she had resumed gaining weight. Things were looking up. We were back on the level pavement and staring at a long stretch of flat road for a foreseeable portion of our run. Not effortlessly running downhill faster and faster; rather, gliding along at a consistent maintainable pace. We were just waiting for the road to turn in ten days and find out if there was another big hill to climb (surgery) or if maybe there was a downhill section (self-healing).

Ironically, it was around this time of the long, extended break from everyday crises that my mental toughness and physical wellness started to break down. We had been basically in crisis mode for the past 15 days. Every damn day felt like life and death. I'm great in a crisis. I'm a sprinter. I love challenges, going really hard at problems, having to make quick decisions, and then do it over and over again until I find the best path forward. During the first ten to 15 days of Emilia's life, I had no choice but to have that mentality. I had to stay locked in, focused on what is important, and be there for my daughter and wife. I was able to tune out all the distractions and just focus on Felicia, Emilia, and what we needed to do that day and the next. That just so happens to be my sweet spot, so it wasn't too far out of my comfort zone. Patience and boredom are where my mind starts to break down and wander. Once we finally hit this patch where things felt a little less crazy, that is when I started to let a lot of the outside influences come back into my mind that caused distress. Watching things like the news and all the doom and gloom around what was going on with coronavirus lockdowns, getting more and more frustrated at how the people at Riley were treating us with new virus related restrictions being imposed every day, and starting to allow myself to begin to think about work again, all contributed to me literally getting physically sick. I wind myself up so much to be able to seem in control and put together during the hard times that I think my body comes to claim its debts for all the damage incurred in the calmer times, I guess. This is why I hate and suck at running and other endurance activities. I can never pace myself, and it always catches up to me in the end.

The long stretches of time where nothing happens are when I mentally fall apart. Thank God for Felicia, the real marathon runner of the family. This is where her talents shine brightest. Felicia actually runs marathons. I do not. She thrives on consistency and staying locked in for long stretches of time of intense concentration. This was her time to take over at the helm for our family, and I was happy to take a back seat and watch the master at work. In a weird way, we complement each other so well. I'm able to be quick, fast, decisive, and thrive in stressful environments that she hates. Felicia is able to be patient, steady, focused, and show incredible endurance, which I hate. It's almost as if the tortoise and the hare got married and were named Chris and Felicia. That should have been our cake topper on our wedding cake. When Felicia first signed up for Teach for America as a brand new teacher with no formal training, I remember watching Felicia come home every night after a long day of teaching in the classroom, work on her master's program homework, and then create new lesson plans on her laptop until 11 p.m. EVERY SINGLE DAY for three years straight! It was truly awe-inspiring as she seemed to never tire or lose steam. I had no idea how she did it. She never stops when she wants something and is able to stay locked in better than anyone I've ever seen as long as she is in her comfort zone.

There is no better illustration of our differences as humans than watching us do something as simple as deciding on what to eat and ordering take-out.

Felicia can never make a decision on anything quickly! Let's just assume, for example, that we've already selected the actual restaurant to order from (I'm sure that was a 30-minute ordeal on its own). Felicia evaluating a menu is like watching water carve the Grand Canyon (it takes forever). She has to look at all the options, goes back and forth debating between which thing she wants, does more research, asks for advice, and FINALLY, she might pick something 5-10 minutes later that ends in an "I can't decide. I guess I'll just go with X." I, on the other hand, will scan a menu in 20 seconds, pick the first thing that looks familiar to me, order that and be 100% content with my decision. I've often wondered what Emilia's personality would have been like. Ideally, she would have become the best mix of the two of us. I can envision her having the endurance and consistency of her mother and the competitive, decisive nature of her father. She would have been a world champion marathoner. She would have been so locked in on the goal and ready to kick everyone's ass in the process. I truly wish I would have been able to witness that, as it would have been something special to behold.

As Felicia took over the reins of Team Sears, I first started to see the signs of the amazing mother that I always knew she would be to our children someday. She was helping to take care of Emilia, pumping a ton of breast milk all day on tap and at the ready for Emilia when she was able to resume milk feedings, reading to her all the time, etc. The best part was watching the magical marathon kangaroo sessions that those two would conduct each day. For those that don't know, kangaroo care is a method of holding a baby that involves skin-to-skin contact. The baby, who is typically naked except for a diaper, is placed in an upright position against a parent's bare chest. Both mothers and fathers can do kangaroo care. It's often used with premature infants while they are still in the hospital. Kangaroo care was developed in Bogota, Colombia in the late 1970s. This type of care was a response to a high death rate in preterm babies, approximately 70% at that time. The babies were dying of infections, respiratory problems, and simply due to a lack of attention. Researchers found that babies who were held close to their mothers' bodies for large portions of the day not only survived but thrived. In the United States, hospitals that encourage kangaroo care typically have mothers or fathers provide skin-to-skin contact with their preterm babies for several hours each day.

That is exactly what Felicia and Emilia did; marathon kangaroo sessions every day became the norm. I can't exactly remember when they started this (a week or so into our stay at the NICU), however, they were so amazing to watch together. Remember, I couldn't actually be in the room with Emilia and

Felicia at the same time, so the nurses would either live stream it via FaceTime or turn the NicView camera toward the two of them so we all could watch. Kangarooing a micro-preemie is no easy task. It takes two to three nurses and respiratory therapists to set up a new space with all of Emilia's equipment, then slowly and carefully get Emilia out of her isolate, and creep over to Felicia, who's waiting in the recliner to receive Emilia and begin the kangaroo time. It is a process. For me, watching was always so stressful. Emilia was so delicate. She was only 1 pound, 1 ounce when she was born. She had so much life-giving medical equipment support covering her body at all times that I was terrified to touch her. I was terrified that I would somehow give her a virus as she was out of her little isolated warm cocoon. I was so afraid of all these things that I don't think I ever even really touched her until well after she had been with us for a few weeks. Felicia, on the other hand, was a fearless mother. She dove headfirst into these kangaroo sessions with Emilia. I don't know if she was afraid, but she certainly didn't act like it. Seeing those two together was the most beautiful, natural thing I could ever imagine. Felicia truly embraced the "control what we can control" mantra in this arena. She and Emilia kangarooed every day for the next few weeks and every chance they could. The sessions kept getting longer and longer as they lounged in that recliner chair in our room. Quick and important note about Felicia – she has one of the most epically annoying bladders of anyone you will ever meet. I can't even barely drive on a road trip for more than an hour, most times, before we have to hit our first gas station for a pee break. It is almost comical. Her entire family makes fun of her for this. Oddly, with Emilia, she was able to sit in that recliner for hours and hours without moving a muscle and never once complained or left to get up and use the restroom. It is truly remarkable the power and strength that a mother and baby's relationship can generate. We'll touch more on this later in the story, as this will become even more clear later.

As Felicia and Emilia continued to master the art of the kangaroo, I sat on the sidelines and watched in amazement. This is similar to how I feel watching Felicia run all the half marathons she has run. She makes hard things look so easy, effortless, and I can't get enough of watching her in action. Being proud watching her run a marathon is one thing. Watching her and my daughter together is a whole other level of wonder and amazement. I love cheering her on from the sidelines and watching her work. She doesn't know this, but it truly is one of the joys of my life watching her operate as I know that I can't do what she does. I'm so secretly envious of how effortless she makes endurance activities look.

I was pretty content with thinking that I was never going to kangaroo with Emilia. I made every excuse imaginable to avoid it. I told myself all the bad things that could happen if I did it. Felicia was so good at it, so why risk it? Over time, the nurses started to nudge me and ask me daily the same question, "Are you ready to kangaroo today?" Felicia would also randomly ask me when I was going to try all the time? Every time, the answer was the same from me, an emphatic "NO WAY!" It was like Felicia and the nurses had organized a coordinated attack on me to get me in the chair and kangaroo Emilia. The pressure and anxiety built. Eventually, I started to want to try this whole kangaroo thing and almost worked up the nerve to pull the trigger. On a few different days, I went into the NICU and was finally ready to give this a try and then chickened out each time.

Finally, on day 21, I decided that this was the day! I don't know why exactly. Maybe it was because all the nurses were politely badgering me over the previous few days, maybe I wanted to show Felicia I could do it, maybe it was because Emilia was just so dang cute. Who knows? Either way, today was the day that I was going to make this kangaroo thing happen. I was so nervous. As I entered her NICU room, I sat down on the couch to write my journal entry and read my daily scripture reflection to write my thoughts. As I opened up the *Trusting God Day by Day* book of reflections, I turned to the day's date and, as fate would have it, the theme was "Fear isn't going away, so do it afraid." God works in mysterious ways. Just like they say in, The Alchemist, when you truly want something, the whole universe conspires to make it happen. I guess I truly wanted this kangaroo session to happen at this moment, on this day.

After I finished reading my daily scripture reflection and starting my journal entry for the day, I told the nurse, "I'm ready to try the kangaroo thing. Can we set that up?" I sadly can't remember this particular nurse's name, but I do remember that she looked at me and her face lit up like a Christmas Tree with excitement. She emphatically stated, "Of course, let me go grab another nurse and a respiratory therapist and I'll be right back." I could tell that I just made her day. Again, these nurses are saints. They work so hard to help protect our most vulnerable children. It is the moments where they get to set up a first-time kangaroo session with a dad and a baby born at 22 and 6 that probably make it all worthwhile and keeps them going.

The nurse came back a few minutes later with Raina, another NICU nurse who we'll meet in more detail later, and Devin, our favorite respiratory therapist. They told me to go hang out and wait on the couch while they got it all set up. I was in it now and not turning back. I anxiously sat down and watched them get the room rearranged to move and reposition Emilia. They pulled the recliner over, right next to the isolate, moved all of Emilia's ventilator equipment, taped down a bunch of stuff to the chair to make sure it didn't fall off, and many other preparatory things. The whole process seemed like it took forever as I impatiently paced back and forth on the other side of the room, preparing for one of the most unique experiences I will probably ever have in my life. This was to be the first time that I held my own child.

Let's stop and think about that for a second. This event was a LONG time in the making. Felicia and I met during my last semester of college, when I was 22, and started dating shortly afterward. I was now 35. For 13 years, Felicia and I have been in an amazing relationship and journey together. I wouldn't change any of it. We've been married for seven years at this point (during which we were asked five million times when we were going to have kids)? We've officially been "trying" to have our own child and grow our family for the past three years. For the past three years, I've been patiently awaiting the moment when I would get to hold my own child for the first time. That time was finally here and now. 13 long years and here we are.

As the setup process continued, Raina told me that I should close the parents' privacy curtain (the area around the couch) and get ready. Getting ready means take your shirt off, get a mask on, put gloves on, wipe down with hand sanitizer, etc. Little known fact, the gloves aren't required, but I made myself do it to be extra cautious. Why? A - I was still terrified that I would give Emilia some random virus, so I wanted to avoid touching her as much as possible. B – My hands sweat prodigiously when I'm nervous. Like, A LOT! They can get so bad that the sweat will literally drip from my hand like a leaky faucet. It has been a life-long source of anxiety for me. I get nervous having to shake anyone's hands for the first time because of it. My best friends from grade school still make fun of me because they all hated having to stand next to me at church, where they would be forced to hold my hand during the Our Father prayer.

With that in mind, this was going to be one of the most nerve-wracking things I've ever taken on in my life. I knew my hands would sweat and I didn't want Emilia to have that be her first experience with me. So, I wore the gloves. I got changed and sat there shirtless, on the stool, and behind a curtain, just waiting to finally get the call from the nurses that we were ready to go. It felt like I was a prizefighter stuck in the locker room waiting for the opening bell to sound and come charging out to the ring. After about five more minutes, they finally told me they were ready for me. I opened the curtain and walked across the room. I was scared out of my mind but managed to find my way over to the recliner that was all set up by the nurses. Before I sat down, they asked, "Would you like to grab Emilia yourself, or would you prefer that we hand her to you once you're seated?" I figured the more that the nurses could do, the better. They have done these five million times, and I've not even done this once. I asked them to bring her to me. I sat down in the recliner and got situated. They reached in the isolate, carefully bringing Emilia out, got all of her tubes readjusted, and then handed her over to me. I reached out to receive her, held her in my arms, and quickly brought her to my chest and put a blanket over her to keep her warm. For the very first time since she was born, we really held each other. I honestly don't remember if I had seriously even touched her at any point in her life up until this moment. I had always been so terrified to even try. She was so fragile and I didn't want to do anything that could possibly reduce the odds of her making it out of this NICU and back to the nursery in our house. I was terrified that I'd get her sick. If I had touched her before, I certainly don't remember now, and I feel like that is a moment that I would remember. It was a pretty magical and terrifying moment for me. The nurses coached me to support her head and don't let it tilt. They said just make sure she has her head turned to the side, so we don't affect her breathing tubes. My arms were LOCKED in place, one behind her head and one underneath her to keep her from sliding down. That is one of the things that I remember most. I don't think I've ever been tenser in my life. Once they placed her on me and in position, I don't know if my left arm or fingers that were holding her from sliding down ever moved an inch the entire time. I asked the nurses to do me a favor and to turn the NicView camera on Emilia and me so we could cast out this moment for Felicia and my family to see. I still remember seeing Felicia later that day after our session and her telling me, "I've never been more in love with you than I was watching that!" Felicia does NOT give me compliments! I mean, EVER! She thinks I'm already arrogant enough or something and refuses to add to my ego. On this day, though, she said those words to me, and it meant a lot. For the first time in my life, I was a Dad holding his child. I'm sure for most new Dads, this moment probably happens within a few minutes or hours after their child is born (assuming they are at the hospital). In my world, this took 21 days for Emilia and me to finally have our moment together. With my free hand, I tried to snap a few selfies of us to capture the moment. One of those is hanging on the wall in my office and I'm staring at it right now as I type. I'm looking down on this precious little being laying against my chest with her face resting on her arm. She is so beautiful. I'm so glad we got this moment together. It was terrifying (for probably both of us), but I don't know how I would have ever gone on to live my life without having this memory.

After two hours (nowhere near a normal Felicia and Emilia 'roo session length), I waved the white flag. Emilia seemed to be having some struggles breathing, her breathing tube tape was starting to loosen, and my arms were about to fall off as they had been locked in the same place for the past two hours straight. I called the nurses and respiratory therapists back over to help us out and they put Emilia back, safe and sound, into her isolate. And with that, Emilia and I had successfully had our first kangaroo session. I was so proud of myself. That was one of the scariest things I had ever proactively volunteered to do in my life. I had originally only set out with the goal of one hour in mind. We had made it two. For our first roo session, I considered that a huge success. I was so happy that I followed that scripture advice that I had read and wrote about that morning and "did it afraid." I still remember that phrase often. It is a great reminder about the amazing moments that you can miss out on in life if you always just sit on the sidelines and watch others. If I hadn't "done it afraid" at that exact moment, I might never have had a chance to do it ever again. With Emilia's big surgery just around the corner, I truly had no idea at that point if I would ever get the opportunity again to hold my daughter while she was relatively happy, healthy, and able to do so. This would turn out to be our one and only kangaroo session in the end, which really hurts just to type those words. To think of how many times I chickened out really sucks. Thank God he was able to give me the strength to do it at least once as I can't imagine (there it is again) never having this memory today.

The Journals: Day 15-22

Day 15: 3/29/20

- I love you
- Daily Scripture Theme: Be a blessing everywhere you go. My Thoughts - this is such an important concept and important change for me personally right now. In keeping with the 7 habits book I recently read, I've gotten really good at the personal habits of 1-3, and 7 over the years which is why I've always had decent success in life so far. The INTERPERSONAL habits, 4-6, are still a huge struggle for me. A key theme to getting better at these is to remember to be a blessing everywhere I go. Through my next 5 years of my 30's, I

want to make this a priority as a Father, a Leader of my own business, and a Husband to excel in these areas. It's not just MY agenda... but ALL of our agendas. I've struggled with this fact for a LONG time and probably distanced myself from a lot of amazing potential relationships because of it through the years. I've made a point to say thank you and MEAN it for all your care team every day since we've been here. I've always been polite my whole life, but even I knew it was often disingenuous and just checking a box of a societal norm. I'm making a point to actually have that gratitude mean something and not just be a polite gesture anymore. Your mom and I will work on some gifts for everyone before we leave here.

- HOLY SHIT...it's day 15 and you are about to hit 25 weeks old. It feels like we've been in here only 1 day and 2 years at the same time. I'm so proud of you. Every day you're a miracle.
- No offense, but I really don't want to come to the hospital today. I've never spent more time in one place other than work or my home in my life. I could use a day off, but I'd hate not seeing you. So I'll go, like every day to come, because I love you and seeing you makes it all worthwhile.
- And I'm here and it's totally worth it. You're so adorable. I just want to fast forward and get you home. I know I have to stay patient, but I can't help imagining the future.
- I've started the process to build your nursery. I'm having fun planning this one out with your mom. We will definitely will have a Lion theme of some kind. I'm going to try and ask your Nurses if I can somehow steal that Lioness photo from your NICU room...we'll see. I'll just have to take it if they don't let me buy it...lol.
- Hahaha - I asked the nurse tonight if we can take the Lion Photo and she said she wouldn't say anything, but will ask to make sure. She said it is a real photo from the head of Neonatology here at Riley. He apparently travels a lot and took a bunch of photos on Safari's. She will see if at worst case we can get the print.
- Dr. Osa said that you are doing well. The biggest areas we need to overcome the next few weeks is getting you off the ventilator and resuming milk feedings. He's checking in on all the antibiotics you are on and see if he can help ween you off to focus on your gut. He's a good dude and I'm glad he's overseeing you.
- I love you

Day 16: 3/30/20

- I love you
- Daily Scripture Theme - Seek to do good. My Thoughts - the key that they mentioned was SEEK!!! Go figure it out. Don't sit around waiting for life to happen. It's in front of us every day. You can find ways to make an impact.
- EVERY DAY WITH YOU IS A MIRACLE...it's so true. I can't believe it's been 15 days and you are officially 25 WEEKS!!! I don't know why, but I feel like 25 weeks is a huge deal overall in my head. I can't really figure it out. Maybe because all the extreme preemie success stories I've heard from friends and family at this point was around 25 -26 weeks when they were born. Either way...I know you're coming home. For some reason, 25 just feels really good.
- For how strong I can be sometimes mentally, this coronavirus thing is really starting to get to me. The news coverage when I go home at night from the hospital is overwhelming with death and dark stories. Only 2,500 people have died, but it feels like a million the way it is being portrayed and discussed. I went to bed last night with the news on the TV, and I think by osmosis I kept hearing all the dark and negative stories and it freaked me out and I woke up in a panic at 3 am and couldn't go back to sleep. It's ironic, the most stressful thing I've ever been through in my life has been your NICU situation and I've only really been scared twice since you got here for about a total of 8 hours. One was when you were born and those tense minutes afterward between when we got to see you again and didn't know if you were able to be revived. The second was your belly issues the other night that led to your surgery. Even those 2 overwhelming events I was able to process well and keep the family positive and optimistic. For some reason, this whole coronavirus thing feels even worse with all the coverage and world shutting down around us. I have to get my mind out the gutter. Death and Destruction are not the state of mind I need to be in right now. I think I'm going to ban myself from the news going forward for the next month.
- One more coronavirus note, the only REAL concern I have is Riley shutting down access to the NICU. It's really not too far-fetched to believe at this point. I don't know what we'd do if we couldn't at least see you. Let's cross that bridge when /if we get there...control what we can control.
- On a weird note, the past few 4 days have been in cruise control with you. You're doing so good. Oddly enough, this has been some of the

hardest few days for me because I don't know what to do. I'm good with crisis, tasks, and constant action to process. What I'm not good at is patience and relaxing. This is why I've mentioned so many times before that I'm awful at marathons and distant running. Sprinting is fun for me. Just go really hard and fast and do it over and over again until you can't anymore. You don't really think…you just do. Then do it over and over again until you achieve your goals. Running the same pace forever is so challenging for me for some reason. I always want to push too hard. My mind races and I get frustrated going the same speed. This is my lifelong struggle. This is why your mom is amazing. She's the marathon runner in the family. I'm the supporter on the sidelines drinking an Aperol Spritz and watching / cheering in awe. This is also why we make an amazing pair. I cover the fast-paced crisis, and she covers the patience and steady pace. I can tell she's so much better the last few days and is coming around. However, she's one new crazy event from a full-blown panic. I'm one more day of nothing to do and mind racing. Kind of funny if you think about it. I wonder how you'll be when you are older. My dream would be that you get the best of both of us, and then you'll be able to RULE THE WORLD!!! A sprinting marathon runner (is that even possible?)

- Gosh - you're been really touchy the past few days. Every time your nurses touch you, all of your sats go nuts. I hope this isn't a sign of the times to come when you're older …lol
- I actually played the Sia song for you at 5:16 for the first time tonight. I've been a little embarrassed to share that with the nurses around up until now. It felt good. We need to play you more music anyway. I'll see how I can incorporate that in going forward.
- Love you

Day 17: 3/31/20

- I love you
- Daily Scripture Theme: Remember the Source of all Truth. My Thoughts: God is the source of truth. We need to believe in him and trust in him. We can only control what we can control in our sphere of influence.
- Every day with you is a miracle. It's something that your social worker, Rachel, reminded your mom and I of yesterday during a conversation. She's been through all of this with her own daughter, and it is really nice and reassuring to hear her story as it gives us

some nuggets to help our journey. That's why I'm writing this story... for you, for us, and others to come. If there is anything I can do to help another family going through this situation in the future I will. That is the point of seeking to do good and doing god's will. We owe it to the world to share our story with others. You're too special to not share with any and every one who wants to listen. That was a decision I made the second day we were here, and I'm so glad we started writing and documenting this journey in retrospect. Sharing your story and our story helps EVERYONE!!!

- Your dad needs to make sure he's taking care of himself physically. I think I've let myself get a little run down, tired, and sick. This is a marathon and we have to stay healthy for you. It's okay for us to sleep in a little, take an extended break at home, focus on exercise or work. We can't be here for you if we aren't there for ourselves.
- Because your mom and I can't be in the room with you at the same time, I keep missing your marathon kangaroo sessions. I REALLY want to be there for them, and it is so sad to miss out. I know it is helping you a ton and I'm so glad you both are enjoying it. I'm terrified to try it myself for about 1000 reasons. I don't want to get you sick and my hands sweat all the time. I'll work up the nerve here soon...I swear
- I love you

Day 18: 4/1/20

- I love you...you're a miracle every day.
- Daily Scripture Theme: worry or trust? It's your choice. My thoughts - I love their quote that "worrying is a waste of time and energy as it will never change your circumstances." Yes - you're in the NICU and a million things can happen to you daily. I could sit around and let every alarm, ding and dong, blood gas result, glucose readings, etc. get to me. I could worry about the next day, week, month, year, 10 years and let my mind go crazy. Or...I can just enjoy that You're Here, You're Great, You're Adorable, and You're Loved. That was the motto I told your mom 15 days ago and it has helped us both through a lot of dark anxiety driven thoughts. I choose to focus my energy on controlling what I can control. That is sharing info with family, thanking your care team, being by your side every day, talking to and helping your mom, thinking about the progress you've made, staying positive and optimistic overall, etc. I think this message is

important not just for today, but for the rest of your and my life. We can't control circumstances and outcomes, those are in God's hands. What I can control all the time is my response to them, and that gives me more freedom and peace of mind than you can ever imagine. I could talk about this topic for days as it fascinates me as to why people always tend to focus on the negative aspects of what COULD go wrong instead living in the present. Ironically, last night your mom and I discussed this very topic for hours after we got home from visiting you. It's amazing how her and I can be given the same set of facts and completely interpret them differently. Everything we've learned and seen with you as positives to me are growth toward daily progress. Your mom sees ALL the other negative stuff. It's not that I don't see them, I just CHOOSE to focus on the positives, read the people around me, and control what I can control. This is one of the reasons your Mom and I have always been an incredible pairing. We balance each other out in all the good ways. My blinding optimism makes me look past key details sometimes that I shouldn't. Your mother always balances me out there. Vice Versa - when she goes too negative and focusing on the minutia, I'm always there to bring her a dose of the bigger picture and optimism.

- 510 grams.... you're gaining weight and officially almost 20% heavier than you were when you were born. You're doing so well. The nurses were excited to report that to me this morning when I got here. You had a great night as well!!! I'm so proud of you every day. You really do have this and I can't wait to get you home.
- You have the tiniest little Mohawk. It's adorable.
- This belly issue is so frustrating...this appears to be developing into the real marathon for all of us. The gut is so temperamental and hard to understand. I'm terrified you'll have to have surgery, but I know you'll be fine. It's just so hard to watch you go through all of this.
- We had a nice heart to heart tonight during our staring contest. Felt nice to talk to you without 20 people around and it seems like you recognize me. Starting to feel more and more connected
- I love you.

Day 19: 4/2/20

- I love you
- Daily Scripture Theme: confidence, no more pretending. My Thoughts: duh...I love this. You be you and we'll get you the hell home. You're so strong.
- Oh, the belly...just the source of all of our problems. I just don't understand it at all. No imminent danger, but it doesn't seem like you're out of the woods just yet. Just a never-ending problem it appears. I can't wait until we are past this issues and get you off the ventilator.
- Your mom and I had a rough night last night. I still can't figure out how to soothe her when she is upset. Her stress is starting to stress me out. I just want to help her and she doesn't seem to want help. She's stuck in a bad place where any little set back feels like Armageddon. Last night, your nurse Reyna let us know that your belly might have a tiny amount of inflammation again. I talked to doctor Osa for 30 minutes about it to try and understand. Bottom Line, it is concerning but no imminent danger (unlike the first time). I debated whether or not to tell your mom who was at home. You 2 had had a lovely day of kangarooing, and you'd been so good for 5 days. I decided I should share the conversation and news with her and did. I immediately regretted it as it sent your mom into a tailspin. I learned my lesson...I can process this stuff and she can't sometimes. Sometimes it isn't the worst thing to keep something from her that I know will put her in a bad place. I need to focus on keeping her spirits up and if that means leaving out some deets that aren't mission critical...then so be it.
- I'm really starting to want to try this kangaroo thing with you. Still working up the nerve, but I'll get there soon. Holding babies has always freaked me out. I don't want to hurt you at all. After seeing all the poking and prodding you take every day, I'm pretty sure I can't hurt you at all because you're so strong.
- New room who dis? We moved to a room with a window...holy shit...I'll be able to see sunlight again.
- Side note on the new move, we went from the lion room to the monkey room. Working on a plan to switch these pictures around because you're a lion after all :).
- I swear I'm starting to feel your pains at night. Let me take that on so you can stay safe. I GOT YOU.
- It was a beautiful spring day today, and I got a bit of a sunburn doing yard work. I can't wait for you to see playing in our yard someday...

it's really an amazing place for that. I'm so looking forward to that. As I was doing yard work all day; it just felt different. I've always liked it, but it always felt like a chore in the past. Today felt like I had a reason to do it now for you. It was interesting processing my thoughts about yard work after I was done. How I feel about yard work is how everything in life feels right now; I just effortlessly get stuff done because I have to so I can spend time with you.

- Since it was so nice out, all the neighborhood kids and parents were out going to the park, riding bikes, jogging with strollers, etc. I saw them all and felt happy, jealous, and scared all at the same time. I can't wait to do that with you, but for a moment I got scared that I might not be able to do that with you. Then I remembered you're so strong and that went away. I can't wait to go take you to the park and play tennis. That will be the day I break down in tears probably as it will mean so much to me.
- I love you

Day 20: 4/3/20

- I love you
- Daily Scripture Theme - be deliberate. My Thoughts – "be deliberate about being a blessing to everyone." I think we can have the most impact with our current situation by sharing updates with everyone that cares about you and treating your care team with the love and gratitude that they treat you. Your mom and I want to try and do something special for all of them at the end of this and probably once a month as well while you are in the NICU. These people LITERALLY are keeping you alive every day, and we should do our part to make them feel special and deliberately be a blessing while working with them to make their lives easier. That could even be as little as a conversation and entertaining them.
- Looking good today...keep it up. I love slow days. A week ago, I hated slow days...now I'm starting to get more used to it. Slow day every day would be a great motto going forward.
- I REALLY wanted to hold you today and chickened out again because I was afraid to get you sick. I hate these allergies and honestly can never tell if it is a cold or just allergies. I would be devastated if I did something to harm you at this point and unintentionally get you sick. I'll get there soon. For now, your mom is better at the touchy / feely stuff anyway.

- Still more wait and see on the belly front. Hopefully we have some answers mid next week. Praying that the best case happened where you healed yourself and no additional surgery is required.
- I love you

Day 21: 4/4/20

- I love you
- Daily Scripture Theme: fear isn't going away, so do it afraid. My Thoughts- SO MUCH to say on this one. It is odd that today, of all days, I'm kangarooing with you. I'm freaking terrified...but DO IT AFRAID. Much more to come on this after we're done as I'm writing this right before we Roo. So nervous, I feel like my hands won't stop sweating and I have to use the bathroom at the same time. Lol
- So, the Roo session, it went great. Not gonna lie...that was SUPER scary. It takes an army of people to move you out of your isolate and reset up your respirator on our Roo chair. The RT's and Nurses were super nice and supportive getting us set up. We had only planned to do an hour and we ended up doing 2. I touched your little hands for the first time, at one point you gripped my fingertip and I could feel your little strength. It was pretty impressive. Your mom was able to watch us on the NicView, which was pretty cool. She said she's never loved me more than watching me do this. That was pretty nice to hear. You'll learn this later on, but I'm not the most touchy-feely kind of person. I'm usually very protective of my space. This was a pretty big step for me to do this and I'm really glad I did it. For some irrational reason, I'm so afraid that I got you sick. I'm sure I didn't, but it is really scary to think about that as a possibility.
- Roo-ing is hard btw. My arms and wrists were locked up in that chair for 2 straight hours. It was certainly worth the pain, but no where near as easy as I saw your mom make it look. I think I'll let your mom do the majority of the Roo-ing going forward for many reasons. I'll try once or twice a week going forward.
- Your mom and I actually watched a movie last night together. We both passed out early, but at least that was progress.
- I love you

Day 22: 4/5/20

- I love you
- Daily Scripture Theme - know you are loved. My Thoughts - this is really comforting to me at this point because I'm constantly struggling with thinking if I'm not there to love and care for you... who will? God will! Your mom will! Your family will! All of our friends and co-workers will! Etc. This is really helpful for me to hear right now as I've been struggling with this one for a while. It isn't all on me and your mom. I need to remember that.
- Your Mom and I are getting really tired from this daily NICU grind. It is emotionally and physically draining. I feel like we are both on the verge of a cold or getting sick at any moment. Constantly getting updates from doctors. Feel tired when we are here and feeling bad when we're not. We're all alone in this because no one else can visit due to this stupid pandemic. It is pretty hard. I don't want to miss anytime with you, but I'm not sure being here all the time is helpful either. It is just a super tough situation. I'm not complaining at all as every day with you is a miracle and I have to remind myself of that. Remember, we control our responses to stimulus. That's my job. I think this is where the marathon really starts to kick in. We are at a point where things are RELATIVELY stable, and we don't have to live in crisis mode all the time. I find that almost harder because I have to try to still love my life and deal with our circumstances as well. It's like we're frozen in time for 3-4 months and each day is Groundhog Day. That is the definition of a marathon. Eventually this will pass, but it is not easy to do.
- Speaking of resuming normalish life...I'm going to try and go back to work tomorrow. I'm really curious how this is going to work. Can I really stay away from you all day and be productive? How am I going to find my groove and how long will that take? I really don't care about work at all. I'm just going back so I don't waste time with you when we finally get you home. I'm so torn. Nothing else really matters at this point, but I have to have balance.
- The more balance I seek, going back to work, working out, sleeping at home, not going back for the late shift bedside, doing yard work, etc... the ickier I feel. It's really a bizarre feeling. I know I have to be selfish for you so I can be present when I'm with you. However, it's really hard to tell my mind that as I'm getting done with a workout, eating food, and watching Tiger King (I'll explain this one in the future as well...don't google it). I feel like a bad Dad at that point.

When I'm in the room with you, I'm always in the know. If I'm not in the know and thinking about something else or myself...I feel really gross. Everyone has told me to stay balanced and I agree. It's just really hard to think that way when you still literally could get worse at any minute. It's a little paradoxical to think that way as on one hand, I know you are coming home and I should just live my life thinking that. On the other hand, I can't stay away because I need to know what is happening at every moment. Every stat, weigh in, blood test result, etc. I really need to find balance. Knowing helps... but I can't know it all.

• I love you

The NICU Marathon: Heartbreak Hill, Or So We Thought (Day 23-27)

Heartbreak Hill is one of the most famous and difficult features of the Boston Marathon route. But at only a 3.3% elevation grade at its steepest point and just 600 meters in length, it's a misnomer in some ways. In itself, the incline is merely challenging, but after 20.5 miles, the effort it takes to overcome becomes the toughest stretch on the course. Once at the summit, however, the Prudential Tower comes into view, the BC band may be playing, and a half-mile of downhill lies ahead to ease your breathing and punishment on your legs.

We were now coming up on our own Heartbreak Hill of sorts in our journey. After Emilia's big scare a few weeks back with her belly, a course had been set to let her body rest, heal, grow, and get stronger before we re-evaluated the total extent of the damage that had been done. We all were praying for the best possible outcome, which was that her intestines had healed themselves and that we could resume breast-milk feedings and proceed as planned with her normal treatment plan. The worst-case scenario was that her intestines had not fixed themselves and we would have to have a pretty invasive surgery (for a child this size) to surgically intervene and create an ostomy to allow her to resume normal feedings. We had waited patiently for ten days. Emilia was doing relatively well. She had done her job of staying strong, growing, and being adorable. It was time to find out what the path would be from her care team. The surgeons had scheduled a check to place some fluids in Emilia's system and let them run through her body. The goal was to see if, on an X-ray, that fluid showed up outside of her bowels or not. That is what will determine if she still has perforations and if she would need surgical intervention.

The surgeons and Dr. Osa pulled us together to let us know the results after the liquid test. Unfortunately, it was determined that the perforations in her bowels were still present and surgical intervention was the recommended treatment. Dr. Rescorla, the chief surgeon whom we met earlier, would be performing the ostomy in a few days' time. We now had a date set for our very own Heartbreak Hill. There are so many things that can go wrong during any surgery. Multiply that by 1,000 for a 1.5 pound 26-week-old baby. We all knew it was coming and had been training, gathering our strength, and mentally preparing for this moment for the past ten days. In our view, the doctor's view, and the surgeon's view, once we got over and through Heartbreak Hill, we could at least start to envision finishing this race together and getting Emilia home as a real possibility.

While we prepared for the surgery to occur in a few day's time, I decided for some reason that now would be a great time for me to head back to work. I didn't have to, but my thought process was knowing how far we'd run in this race already; I felt like this family was pretty well equipped to make it to the finish line. With that as my mindset, I thought that resuming my "normal" life would be important, and I also wanted to preserve my paternity leave for when Emilia was actually back at home with us, safe and sound in her nursery, and we could have somewhat of a normal parental leave experience. I also just so happened to work for the most amazing company in the world, Salesforce, which truly does everything they can to help their employees be seen as human beings and help to overcome complicated situations in life as best as they can. Being a Salesforce employee allowed me to work remotely (from Emilia's NICU room), and they provide up to six months of paid paternity leave that I can take at any point over the 12 months after Emilia's birthday! You read that correctly. Salesforce offers six months of paid leave for FATHERS to spend time with their children after they are born to bond and connect. That is unheard of at any company to my knowledge (at least in the USA). What an amazing perk! I had been looking forward to that time at home with Emilia so much and thought it would be great to save every second I could to spend with her once we got out of this NICU. That was my plan and the logic behind it. So, back to work I went! I thought, "I can do this! I can work from the NICU every day, be here with Emilia, save my PAT leave time for home like it was intended, and do it all like every other Super Dad out there!"

A book I referenced earlier, *The Alchemist*, talks a lot about listening and hearing the omens that pop up in life. These days I'm much more in tune with listening to omens in my life. The fact that I worked at Salesforce at this exact time in my life was not lost on me and was no doubt one of those omens. For ten years prior to joining the Salesforce team, the idea of working at a company that size (50,000+ employees) and just being another number and cog in the wheel would have made me want to vomit. At one point in my career, I had said to anyone and everyone that I will NEVER work for a company like Salesforce (I even used Salesforce literally as my example when I said that). I valued my creativity, individuality, and the ability to make a true impact on the design of systems and processes. In my mind, working at Salesforce would never be able to allow me to do the things I loved, so it was never an option for me. It's a give and take, though. The startups that are so near and dear to me would never have given me the freedom and flexibility to manage this situation with Emilia, even at 10% of the support Salesforce could offer. God always has us in the right place, at the right time, for the right reasons. I truly believe that, and the fact that I was in this NICU with my beautiful daughter and had the opportunity and flexibility to still do my job and save all the time for us to spend together when she got home was not going to escape my grasp. So, if someone from Salesforce ever reads this book someday, THANK YOU FOR EVERYTHING YOU DID FOR MY FAMILY DURING THE MOST TRYING TIME OF MY LIFE (at least so far)! That humanity and support you showed to us meant the world to me. To be able to just simply focus on my family and never have to worry about money or where to spend my time is something that impacts my life in a way I can never truly quantify. I can tell you that, without a doubt, this support from my employer is partly responsible for why I was even able to have the time to write this story and pay it forward to anyone else that might read this someday. None of that is lost on me and will forever be forgotten for the rest of my life.

And with that, I went back to work. Actually, both Felicia and I decided to go back the same day. We had a few days before the big surgery to get readjusted and I would need all of them. I honestly thought that this would all be pretty easy to pull off. I knew how to do my job well, I could work remotely from the hospital, and I had adjusted to our routines in the NICU enough these days that I knew I had the time to do it all. Boy, was I wrong. The chaos of getting caught up from 3 weeks off work, nurses and doctors coming in and out of the NICU, taking care of Emilia, coronavirus shutting down quieter areas of the hospital where previously I could go to take calls, Emilia's equipment spontaneously bonging and beeping in in the background on video chats, etc. was a dose of overwhelming that I wasn't close to ready to take on.

For the previous three weeks, I had gotten into the routine of spending as much time with my daughter as I could, forcing myself to read, exercise, and write every day to stay sharp, keeping our household in order, and dealing with the doctors and nurses. I really enjoyed all of that. It was as if life and my priorities were in balance and harmony for once. Even though we were in the most stressful situation I could have ever imagined, I had been able to find peace and joy with almost all of it. Who wouldn't want to spend all day long with their beautiful child while taking care of your family and yourself at the same time? It's strange how you can find purpose in the weirdest places. I had found my purpose and my WHY in Emilia. And then, like an idiot, I decided to add the chaos of work into that equation that I didn't have to do at all. I found myself distracted (in a bad way) all day long by work. I was physically present in my daughter's hospital room, but my mind was somewhere else. I was letting my new daily reading, writing, and exercise habits slip. I was missing rounds and updates from the doctors and nurses, and worst of all, I was neglecting to spend time with my daughter. It is amazing how much we can let "work" dictate our priorities. In the worst moments of my life, I was able to find peace and comfort because I was able to dictate my priorities. I was able to say what mattered most, what I valued most, and where I wanted to spend my time. As soon as I stepped back into the rat race, I did what so many of us do and let someone else's agenda dominate and dictate my world. I take full blame for this and I'm not putting that on anyone else. My head was spinning, trying to do it all. I was so exhausted at the end of every day, and all joy (what little there was) in this situation had been sucked out of me. This was an incredibly important lesson for me at this time, one which I didn't really even realize until FAR later down the road and long after we lost Emilia. My big takeaway was to truly ALWAYS work on putting first things first in your life and NEVER let someone's agenda or environment dictate to you how you are going to live your life and determine your priorities.

The mentality of putting first things first, the concept we discussed earlier from the *7 Habits of Highly Effective People*, is the habit of focusing on those non-urgent yet vital priorities in life BEFORE you do anything else. Some examples of the activities are things like family, spirituality, learning, exercise, reflection, etc.; things that we all know are the real priorities in life but require you to go above and beyond to be proactive to achieve as there is no urgency forcing the action. Most of us are not proactive. Most of us do what we think we have to do, and then if you have any energy left, you will try to do some of those non-urgent yet vital priorities. Putting first things first sounds really easy in theory until those urgent and vital priorities (like work) take over the wheel and start driving the bus again. That is exactly what I was experiencing and didn't realize. For three weeks, my world had been abruptly halted to a stop with those urgent and vital priorities (like work, errands, maintaining a household). I was unknowingly FORCED to truly live an existence of putting those non-urgent and vital priorities (like family, Emilia, my health, learning, reflection, spirituality) first for the first time in my life.

As crazy as this sounds, I had felt more at peace in the most stressful situation in my life than I had ever had before at any point in my adulthood. Sure, I frequently had moments of panic and worry, but I was doing what I wanted, which was to spend time with my beautiful daughter and take care of my family and myself. I still get a sense of calm thinking about sitting in her hospital room, listening to the sounds of the respirator, and just feeling at ease in her presence. In just a few short days of returning to work, 90% of that had been stripped away from me, and those urgent and vital priorities were back in control at the wheel. I desperately tried to fight it off and keep my priorities right and just couldn't for some reason. Work has an incredible way of doing that to almost all of us. It isn't the work's fault; it's ours. I'm sure most of us blame the work, but we all know that isn't true. Thinking back on it now, I wish I would never have gone back to work during this time period. That was probably my only regret throughout this entire journey. I allowed someone else to rob the precious little time that I had with Emilia, and for what? Either way, the decision had been made, and here we were. I was back at work and running around like a madman trying to fight for precious time and energy to "do it all." Each day got harder and harder to keep it all together, but I managed to do it. We were barreling toward the big tummy surgery full steam ahead, and we all couldn't wait to get past this day and start thinking about healing and growth in the future.

When the big day of the surgery finally arrived, Felicia and I were actually able to be together in the NICU waiting room for the first time in weeks because Emilia's surgery allowed the hospital to bend the strict Covid rules. Dr. Rescorla came by the consultation room to do a final run-through of the agenda and answer any last-minute questions Felicia or I might have. I still remember walking into the NICU that day and making my way down the hall toward our room. It felt like every nurse on the floor knew what was about to happen. They all made sure to tell me as I walked by that, "Emilia's got this" and, "We can't wait to see her after the surgery." My actual family wasn't able to be there, but those ladies are a damn good replacement. It made me feel so good knowing how loved and cared for Emilia was at this moment. It felt like a true team, all focused on winning the game for each other and Emilia.

We had officially reached the base of Heartbreak Hill. After ten days, we've had plenty of time to prepare mentally and physically for the hill we were about to climb. We knew that once we got past this big moment that we all had a great chance of finishing this marathon. "First things first...don't forget to not think about the finish line," I told myself. "Getting up that hill today was the mission. One step at a time. Don't think about anything other than the next step." Felicia and I joined each other in the consultation/waiting room while Emilia's surgery began. I can honestly say that I don't remember a single thing about that entire time period during which her surgery was being performed. I'm racking my brain as to what Felicia and I actually did during this time, and I can't think of anything memorable. All I remember is that I was always adamant that she was coming home, and this was just another hill to climb because I knew deep down we were finishing this race. I was just waiting for that knock on the door and word from Dr. Rescorla that the surgery was a success.

Finally, after a few hours of anxiously waiting, we heard the knock on the door, and Dr. Rescorla appeared in his surgical gown and sat down next to us to walk us through what had occurred. He let us know that the surgery had been a success and that Emilia did great (of course she did). It would take some time, but all signs pointed toward a full recovery. He told us that he was happy to find that the intestinal perforation happened pretty far down in her intestines, so there was plenty of healthy bowels still in place for her to resume milk feedings and that she won't have an issue getting the nutrients she needs to be absorbed in her healthy bowel. He said he also feels really good about no long-term damage being caused by this episode. He said that when she is big, strong, and ready to leave the NICU, the next procedure to repair her intestines should be relatively simple.

Finally, he mentioned something to us that made me feel really proud and grin ear to ear under my face mask. He said something along the lines of, "I would also like to add what a pleasure it has been to work with you two through this difficult situation. I rarely get to work with parents that ask such thoughtful questions and give me the trust and support to do my job well. You two really make it a lot easier for us to do our work!" That one really hit home for me and I'll never forget it. Our strategy of always thanking our care team and treating them like the saints that they are was paying off. We have so little control in this environment over the success of anything going on with Emilia. The only thing we have control over is our emotions and how we treat people. I have no idea whether or not that really helped Dr. Rescorla to perform a better surgery that day, but at least I know that it didn't do anything to hurt her chances, and that's just as important. I know that he went into that surgery not wanting to let us down in any way because of how we treated him. For that reason alone, it was for sure worth it.

So, we made it up Heartbreak Hill! We were so relieved!

Now that the surgery was over and Emilia was in post-op recovery, Felicia and I were no longer allowed to be in the hospital together because of the continued coronavirus restrictions, so I left the two of them to be together for the post-surgery recovery. I would come back in a few hours for the "shift change" later that night. I went home feeling great. When I got back to the hospital, Felicia caught me up on the past few hours of Emilia's recovery post-surgery. She said, "Emilia was a little "puffy" from all the post-surgery fluids. Other than that, things seemed to be doing pretty good." That was such a relief to hear.

Felicia left and I took my spot back bedside in Emilia's NICU room. Jessica, one of our favorite nurses, had been watching over Emilia since her mid-day surgery and everything seemed to be going well per her report when I came into the room around 5 p.m. that night. I chatted with Jessica, checked in on Emilia, and sat on the couch to turn on my audiobook, thinking that we were past the worst of this and could relax a little. At 7 p.m. that night, the nightly nurse shift change happened. Jessica left and said goodbye and passed all of her notes over to Spencer, who was taking over for the next 12-hour shift until 7 a.m. the next morning. Spencer was new to me. We hadn't met her before. Spencer and I chatted for a few minutes, and she got to work on getting everything she needed in order for her shift.

I'm not sure the exact series of events that happened next, so I'll do my best to describe the scene.

About 30 minutes after Jessica left and Spencer's shift had begun, all kinds of things started happening to Emilia. It started with her oxygen sats jumping all over the place and dipping down really low into the 60's and 70's. Then, all of a sudden, Emilia's heart rate started spiking to 200 BPM. Next, her blood pressure started to drop to dangerously low levels. The charge nurse, nurse practitioner, and a doctor came in to help, see what was going on, and set a course of action for treatment. They huddled outside the room and talked for ten minutes. I sat there from the couch watching, trying to figure out what the hell was going on. Why was this happening? Should I be scared? It looked like the nurses were a little scared right now, and I remembered Lori's comments from that first big hill we climbed the night that Emilia NEC first appeared, "Don't worry about anything unless you see me worried!" I could see the worry on everyone's face. Something wasn't right. Looking back on this event, I wish Lori or Staci had been the nurse there with me that night. They always knew how to keep me informed and calm. Spencer was really young; she seemed like she was 24 or 25 and fresh out of school. We weren't really used to having a lot of younger nurses supporting Emilia as she usually needed somebody with a ton of experience, especially when we first arrived. When we first got to Riley, she had two nurses to support her at all times. One was usually extremely veteran, and the other was training with the vet to "level up," as they called it, to a higher acuity level patient care like Emilia. In a way, it was good that we now had nurses like Spencer assigned to Emilia. It meant that Emilia was getting better and didn't need the most senior, tenured nursing vets all the time anymore. At this moment, however, I wanted the department vets, my big sisters, back by my side as things were getting ugly, and I was getting scared.

After the care team huddle broke, Spencer came back into the room and didn't say much. I asked a few questions about what was happening, and she said that Emilia's blood pressure is dropping and we need to fix that ASAP. I asked, "What's the plan?" She said something about giving her Dopa, short for Dopamine I found out later, and that she needs to go work with the pharmacy to get that up here ASAP while she is getting all of Emilia's lines restrung in preparation. Spencer didn't go into much detail beyond that and just got to work. She left me in that room all by myself for what seemed like an eternity after that short interaction and explanation. I had no idea when someone would be back. I think it was honestly about 30 minutes before I saw another person enter or even pass by our room.

I sat there panicked, alone, and not having any idea what was happening. I still remember sitting in that room, on the corner of the couch, and staring up at Emilia's vitals monitor while slowly watching them get worse and worse with each passing minute. NO ONE WAS AROUND! It was just my daughter and I waiting for someone to come back in the room and fix whatever the hell was happening. That was one of the most helpless moments I can remember, thinking back on it. My heart was racing, my head was spinning, I had no way to help, and no one to talk to. For the first time during this whole experience, the pandemic and the isolation rules really got to me. I just wanted my wife with me at this moment so badly. It felt so unfair to make a Dad sit in a room with his infant daughter by himself, not knowing what was going on and if she was going to be okay. I felt so alone. It seemed like each minute that ticked by took an hour. I got up so many times to walk to the door and look down the hall, hoping to see Spencer, or anyone really, to ask, "What the hell is happening?" I decided that I wasn't going to call Felicia until I knew what was happening. Just like I had done when the NEC first appeared a few weeks back, I didn't want to put this stress on her. She was already so fragile that I didn't want to set her over the edge. If I felt this helpless and scared in the room, how bad would it be for her sitting at home? I was going to be the man of this family and hold it together for my wife and daughter.

After about 30 excruciatingly long minutes, Spencer finally came back into the room and started to work on restringing all of Emilia's tubes and IVs to make room for the new medicine that was coming. Spencer worked and worked and worked! These nurses work their butts off, but I had never seen someone work as fast and as hard as Spencer did over the next hour or so. She was a blur of activity, and I didn't want to do anything to get in her way. I sat back on the couch, stared at the monitors, and waited. Finally, the Dopa arrived from the pharmacy, and Spencer got it strung up and started the drip. Once strung up, Spencer finally walked me through why they were doing this. For anyone that doesn't know, as I didn't at the time, Dopamine is a catecholamine drug that acts by an inotropic effect on the heart muscle (causes more intense contractions) that, in turn, can raise blood pressure. At high doses, Dopamine may help correct low blood pressure due to low systemic vascular resistance. Dopamine is used to treat hypotension (low blood pressure), low cardiac output, and reduced perfusion of body organs due to shock, trauma, and sepsis. Emilia's body was in shock due to the surgery, and she was at war with herself. When your blood pressure drops, really bad stuff can happen.

The defense against low blood pressure is FLUIDS, FLUIDS, and MORE FLUIDS! They pumped Emilia full of so many fluids that she was starting to look incredibly swollen everywhere. That was pretty scary to watch the visible transformation occur outwardly so quickly. Within a few hours, Emilia had almost doubled in weight. That would have been reason to celebrate if it was real weight gain, but this certainly was not. After Spencer got all the fluids flowing and the Dopamine drip going, we both just sat back, stared at the monitors, and prayed for the blood pressure reading to stabilize over the next few hours. Spencer assured me that this would work and that the Dopa and fluids would get Emilia stabilized. By 10:30 p.m. that night, Emilia's blood pressure was stabilized, and the crisis had been averted. Spencer had saved the day! I was relieved and scared out of my mind at the same time. What the hell had just happened? Emilia was fine when I walked in, and yet a few hours later, we were here.

After it seemed like the coast was clear, I called Felicia to fill her in on what was going on now that everything had settled down. Once again, I'm glad that it was me there that night. I'm glad I was able to shield Felicia from this stuff. This shit was intense. As I let my own heart rate and blood pressure come down, I reflected on how amazing modern medicine can be. In a crisis scenario, the quick action and team coordination to diagnose what was happening, what drugs can counteract the situation, and get them administered at the right time was incredible to behold. Spencer was incredible. The rest of that team was incredible. That whole event was, in some ways, incredible. Heartbreak Hill truly had lived up to its billing. It was no joke. That was a serious hill and almost broke us, but we got through it. Emilia got through it with the help of her amazing care team. Together, we all got over that hill and this was finally behind us, or so we thought.

Over the next few days, after the chaos and anxiety of that night slowly wore off, I watched Emilia slowly improve and couldn't help but be inspired by her journey more and more each day. Felicia was feeling the same thing as well. At one point, she sent me a text saying, "Our daughter is such a fighter. Sometimes I just stop and think about how much she has already been through in her first 27 days of life. It's certainly more than I have been through in 33 years." I couldn't agree more. Emilia is remarkable! She is a fighter through and through. Watching her battle each and every day showed me a real-world example of what it means to be a true hero and role model. Never in a million years would I think that my four-week-old baby would be giving me lessons on how to live a truly virtuous life, but here we were. As my nightly alarm goes off at Emilia's birth time (5:16 p.m.) and the song that accompanies it so eloquently says, "She was born in a thunderstorm, she grew up overnight, she played on her own...but she survived." Those words couldn't be truer about our precious Emilia. As Felicia had said, she had endured more than most people will ever experience in a lifetime, and we all knew she wasn't even close to done yet. It was incredibly inspiring and probably the only reason I have the ability to even write this story today.

As everything calmed down and we got back to more or a normal routine again, I once again resumed my daily reading goals. One of the books I was reading at that time was called the *Compound Effect* by the author, Darren Hardy. *The Compound Effect* is a short book about the compound effect that can result from making seemingly small changes in your daily habits and the amazing outcomes that come out of nowhere over time if you stick with it. It's a great book! I really enjoyed the message and have applied it to my life in many ways over this past year. I can, without a doubt, tell you first hand that the compound effect is very real and powerful!

As I was reading it and sitting on the couch next to Emilia the following day after the surgery, I came across a section of the book in which the author talks about the importance of having a personal brand and identity. Something that leaves a lasting impression on everyone that you meet and that can serve as your compass in life to help guide your choice in actions and how you live your life. As I sat there on my couch in Emilia's room, feeling inspired by watching her battle, I asked myself the question, "What is my personal brand?" I wrote the question in my journal, and then I sat back and thought. I searched for all the words I could think of that I thought described the essence of me. I thought of what my friends, family, and those closest to me would say about me. I thought about my core values and what was truly important to me. Finally, as I was staring at Emilia, it came to me. NEVER QUIT...THAT IS MY PERSONAL BRAND! Never giving up has been a hallmark of my life. I never quit on anything or anyone I encounter. I endure. If I'm good or bad at something, if I hate it or love it, I always see it through and give it all I have. Most importantly, I thought about what I would want Emilia to know about me and how I would want her to think about me as her father. I would never quit on her, no matter what life brought us. A part of me started to wonder if Emilia's fighting spirit might be coming from me at this point already. I have no idea how genetics or nature versus nurture works when it comes to personality. What I could see, though, is my daughter modeling the living embodiment of the "never quit" brand. That couldn't just be a coincidence. Like father, like daughter. For the rest of my life, if you ever meet Chris Sears, I want you to know that I will never quit on you or anything else we commit to together. Just like Emilia, we will endure and keep fighting!

The Journals (Day 23-27)

Day 23: 4/6/20

- I love you
- Daily Scripture Theme: A Great big happy life. My Thoughts - this is all about giving more than you take. I'm writing this stuff every day with that in mind. This is going to be my gift to you and other NICU

parents when this is all said and done. I hope all of our experiences can help make an impact for someone else in the future.

- Big day for all of us. It's the first day back at work for your Mom and I. AND...you are getting off antibiotics and having a tummy X-Ray to determine the extent of the damage (if any) from NEC infection from a few weeks ago. Praying that you've already healed yourself and we can resume milk feedings. Margo (the psychic), told me that you would overcome the belly issues, but it may be a little longer than we thought. That kind of leans heavily over my thoughts right now; however, I also know you're coming home so no worries in my mind.

- Busy day in the NICU already...surgeries, rounds, X-Rays...I'm not sure how I'm going to be able to work in this environment. We'll figure it out, but this is going to take some time to process.

- I can't tell you how weird it is to be typing a work email while doctors are rounding around your room and discussing care. It's like an alternative universe. Throw in coronavirus and this world is so weird.

- Your mom and I can't seem to get on the same page right now, and have been arguing the past few days about how much physical time we are spending individually at the NICU. We're both here for hours every day. In my view, we can only spend so much time in a day physically being by your bedside. We both want someone here for you ideally at all times, but we have to take care of ourselves and our household as well. Bottom line, we are wasting energy arguing when we have no more to spare. I want to create a positive and optimistic environment around you. To do that, takes a lot of prayer, strength, patience, positive thoughts, etc. All of that is a lot of energy to maintain. Being negative and blaming others is so much easier. Sadly, we've fallen into that trap. I have to get us out of this and I will. Your mother is scared, as am I, but she is letting her fear turn into anger and then directing it at me. She wants to be here as much as she can but she also can't take being in this place for very long stretches of time. She's anxious at the bedside and guilty when she's at home. We need to turn negativity and fear for you into love for each other and everyone around us.

- Tonight, we were speaking pretty angrily toward each other during our "shift change" in the lobby. As soon as I walked into the room, you were in your isolate asleep with this adorable little hand on your head exhausted from a Penrose surgery they just did again. I almost started crying and thought...what are we doing? You're so adorable and strong, and we are wasting time being selfish. You're fighting every day and we need to fight just as hard...in our own ways. Fighting each other is literally the worst thing we could ever do.

- Speaking of surgery, the time has come for the scary "real" surgery where they are going to cut out the bad section of your bowels. It's super scary, and we are in for a long few days of hurry up and wait to see how you recover. I know you're a champ and will be okay, but I thought it was a good time to have another "chat" with your 20-year-old self again just like we did back when you were still at Methodist and having your Glucose issues. This time it was me taking you back to your room at Riley to talk about all that has been going on and reminding you how strong and amazing you are. Ironically, I know you aren't worried or scared. You're just tired of this hanging over you and can't wait to show what you can really do once you have a healthy gut. For me though, I'm not so much scared as sad. I want to take away this upcoming pain from you so bad, but I know I can't do anything other than pray and trust your care team. I look at your adorable little face and that hand resting on your head as you sleep. I see a little fighter that has just had enough for the day and wants to rest and recover. I want to give that to you so badly. We both know though you have a lot more fighting to come and I would do anything to step in there for you. This is your fight and God's plan. I trust you both that you've got this. I need to let my selfish needs go and focus on just being present, encouraging your care team, keeping your mom positive, and updating all the people that love you and are praying for you. I'm really looking forward to that day I can read you this in this room, 4106, and you can see and feel how strong you are inside. I'm sure that day will be here before I can even blink.
- I love you

Day 24: 4/7/20

- I love you
- Daily Scripture Theme - imperfect but perfectly loved. My Thoughts – "God loves me unconditionally and I receive his love." That is the quote she asked us to repeat. It's a gift...acknowledge it and receive it. Everyone needs a foundation and support. God will always be there for us all.
- You'll be proud of your dad today. I not only worked, I did my daily reading, my scripture thoughts, journaled, was there for you, got a great workout, and took the dog on a walk. It's nice to be able to

make this as "normal" as possible. I can't wait to share all of these fun activities with you soon.

- BIG DAY TOMORROW...it's surgery time to heal your belly and get you back to the all-important milk feeding.
- I love you

Day 25: 4/8/20

- I love you
- Daily Scripture Theme - Faith beats fear. My Thoughts - Do it afraid. We can't control our circumstances, but we can control how we respond to them. I choose to acknowledge what is happening and walk fearlessly toward it. Just like you will be today, I have to have no fear and trust in God's plan. That's my conscious decision to control what we can control. Keep giving praise and love to your care team, support your mom, and make sure we are there for you every step of the way.
- TODAY IS THE DAY...let's kick this NEC and move on. Surgery is in an hour. I know you're coming home...so I know you got this. You're so incredibly strong and we love you so much. More to come on my thoughts.
- Speaking of big...you look like you grew a TON the past few days. You look more adorable every day. You were so peaceful when I got here this morning. The calm before the storm. Rest up because you'll need it.
- Man...what a day of highs, stress, fear, etc. You just have to run right at it and be fearless like you are. It's unreal what you've been dealing with and just keep bouncing back. It's so hard to watch you go through this and not be able to do anything other than support and pray. It's honestly one of the HARDEST things I've ever done. Just being patient, waiting, and watching...I've never been more exhausted from doing nothing.
- Our focus on appreciating and giving love to your care team strategy is paying off. All of your previous nurses, (and your guardian nurse, Great Aunt Kristie), are behind you today. They were telling me that as soon as I walked into the NICU...you are so loved.
- You had your surgery on your tummy today. The waiting game was intense. At least your mom and I could wait together this time in the hospital. Dr. Rescorla did an incredible job. He stopped in after the surgery to let us know it was a success, that your healthy bowels

were plentiful, and he doesn't see any reasons for concerns to resume feedings and make for an easy fix when you are bigger and stronger to undo the ostomy. Stupid me...I was ecstatic and thought we were through the worst and wanted to run out and celebrate. I left your mom to stay and watch over you for a few hours post-surgery and you were doing well. We switched out later I think the night and all the sudden...you weren't doing so hot. Your blood pressure was dropping, you were so bloated and retaining fluids, your oxygen was maxed out and we were at a threshold of oh shit. For about an hour, I sat in your room by myself as I watched as your little oxygen stats slowly creep down while your care team put a plan in place to get you back to normal. That was probably the scariest thing I've been through to date. I was all alone in your room, no family, no staff, no Felicia...and just watching what felt like an hourglass get to the point of almost running out. Like I was walking on a mountain edge and could slip and fall at any time. It was terrifying and there was absolutely nothing I could do at all. Then all the sudden, your doctors and nurses put your plan into place, I buried my head into some work, and 2 hours later everything was trending well again. You're my freaking hero. I think this may be harder for me sometimes than you. This must be like what it is like for a parent of a pro athlete to watch their kids play. I bet they are more terrified in the stands than their kids are on the field. I can't believe everything you've gone through. If you aren't the president someday, that has to be my fault for not telling you what you've already done and capable of doing. By the time you're 4 months old, you'll have shown more strength and courage than I'll have done in my entire life up to this point. I'll never let you forget this as you get older.

- I love you

Day 26: 4/9/20

- I love you
- Daily Scripture Theme - stop waiting and start trying. My Thoughts - I'm getting so close to figuring out my path in life. It's been a work in progress for about the past 6+ years. Trying new things, incorporating new strategies, starting new challenges, etc. Spirituality has eluded me up to this point, or better said, I've actively chosen to not focus on it for whatever reason my whole life. I feel like since your birth everything has started to change in me. It feels like I'm discovering

my WHY in life, and it is pushing me to be above and beyond what I've always done. I'm getting closer to figuring out my spiritual calling day by day. Writing this journal to you is my first step.

- What a night! You did great and have rebounded so well. I'm so proud of you. You scared the shit out of me for a while and took your recovery to its limits. Then, you did what you always do, and bounced back great and made everything seem so easy. I don't know why I even remotely doubt you at this point. We love you so much.
- I really love it when we have lazy days with you and can just sit around and joke with the nurses and hang in your room. I'll probably look back on those times pretty fondly once we come out of this.
- At this point in time, I think your stay can safely be summed up in this fashion, first 3 days (chaos and confusion), week 1 NEC scare, week 2 surgery, week 4 major surgery, and everything else is just you being cute and hanging with your nurses with a few de-sats in between. It's amazing how really only 3 bad days out of 4 weeks can require so much energy. You just never really know when those bad days are coming. When they're here, they're terrifying and awful. When you get past them, the next few days kind of feel relaxing. I'm learning how to pace myself. I still can't believe everything you've already been through at only just less than a month old.
- I love you

Day 27: 4/10/20

- I love you
- Daily Scripture Theme: Avoid Comparisons. My Thoughts - I typically don't compare myself to others. I love my unique self and my own unique journey...probably a little too much sometimes (I can be selfish). I will try my hardest to make sure you always remember how special you are and that this is your journey and yours alone. The more you blaze your own path, the more others will follow you. On a different note, I'm actively trying to not "compare" our NICU journey with anyone else's either. I want this to be our unique journey. I'll write it all out and process this our own way.
- Daddy had a bad selfish day today. I'm a little ashamed to admit it given what you're going through. I still did everything I had been doing the past few weeks, but for some reason I was just ANGRY. I was tired, had a ton of work to do, on a call all day basically, worked out in the cold weather, feeling sick, tired of the back and forth with

your mom about how many hours we log at the hospital, etc. I'm just ashamed that I let myself behave that way. I only let this happen because I knew you were okay, but that doesn't excuse it at all. This fight is draining of all energy...this is exactly why people said this is a marathon. I really need to speak with your mom and set some ground rules around keeping ourselves healthy and sane during this process. The last thing I want to do is to be in the room with you and literally not even thinking once about you.

- Going back to work has been A LOT harder than I thought. I've been so busy at work (it's good in some ways), but it has distracted me from EVERYTHING around the routine we had built the past few weeks. I was doing really good being present for you, discussing your care, helping the care team, working out, reading, learning new things, journaling, etc. All the sudden...work blew everything up. I've been able to still do it all, but it's making everything miserable. I've got to get organized and into a routine. Coming to see you should be the highlight of my day. I'm sad to say that today it wasn't and that makes me want to puke.

- Writing all this down has been therapeutic. Dad's are allowed bad days as well. Sorry little girl...I'll get better tomorrow.

- No one is still allowed to see you other than your Mom and I. The world is still on lockdown. What a crazy time to be alive.

- I got chased off a tennis court on Wed by a cop for playing tennis... TENNIS!!! Like I'm a felon or something for hitting a tennis ball, on a tennis court, at a public park. It's like we were punk skateboarders or something. This world is bananas.

- You're so puffed up still from your surgery...it's like a whole new baby with how much bigger you look. Your little face and ears are like 4x what they were before your surgery. You weighed in at 660 grams last night which was like 25% growth day over day. I wanted to celebrate the weight gain but just couldn't because it isn't real.

- Your mom texted me this today "Our daughter is such a fighter. Sometimes I just stop and think about how much she has already been through in her first 27 days of life. It's certainly more than I have been through in 33 years." I think I said those same words in my journal a few nights ago. It really is insane how much you've gone through. It really puts life in perspective sometimes. No matter how bad things get...we know how to struggle, fight, and keep marching along. We're Sears!!!

- I snuck wine in the NICU tonight in a little Yeti mug. Sorry...not sorry. It's a Friday night tradition after a hard week's work. If we have to be in this room all day, at least we can relax and have some fun.
- I love you

The NICU Marathon: The Art of Downhill Running and Signs of Hope (Day 28-33)

With Heartbreak Hill and the big surgery in the rear-view mirror, my family walked into week five of our journey filled with hope and excitement for the future. If you've ever been on a run before, you know how awful it feels to look up at that hill and start the climb. Your legs start burning, your breathing gets heavier, it feels like you are stuck in quicksand and mentally willing yourself to take each next step. Every once in a while, you look up and then think, "Shit, I still have a long way to go. Why did I just look up?" You put your eyes back down on the pavement and try to focus on each next step. Eventually, you realize you officially made it to the top of the hill, and you can relax a little as relief of a downhill portion is on the immediate horizon. That is basically what we had just gone through with Emilia's surgery. For ten days, we had been slowly working up that surgery hill and hit our big final push to make it to the top. We had arrived and could feel the relief coming. The BEST part about making it up to the top of a hill is knowing you get to come back down the other side. Running downhill is my favorite part of any run and the best feeling ever. Your hope is renewed, your legs get a break, your momentum catapults you forward effortlessly, and you can feel the wind in your face as you pick up speed.

Running downhill brings so much hope. You start to think to yourself, "I'm flying here. This is so easy. I can run another ten miles, no problem!" It is a feeling that is hard to describe. Your stride slowly starts to lengthen longer and longer. Your speed gets faster and faster. Everything that you had just experienced running up the hill is now the exact opposite. On the run down, you never want the hill to stop. If I had my dream course, I'd be running slightly downhill the whole time. Unfortunately, it doesn't work that way. The only way to experience the joy of running down a hill is to make it up to the top of the hill and all the struggles that go into overcoming that in the first place. The truth is that in running a marathon, you still always have to just think about the next step, whether it is uphill, downhill, or in a flat section. The key is never to get too high or too low. It is so easy to get emotionally beaten down running uphill just as it is to think this whole thing is too easy running down. Neither is true. Your mindset on any run, just like in life, should be to focus on the next step right in front of you, and that is it.

We were back to running downhill and picking up steam fast. I found myself easily falling into this downhill trap of too much hope and optimism after making it through Emilia's big surgery. Emilia still had another handful of days before she would be fully recovered from her surgery, but each passing day showed progress and improvement. Dr. Osa came by to talk about the future and said the most exciting thing. "It's time to focus on getting her off the vent this week. My hope is that, at the end of the next week, she is breathing on her own. We are ready to try the dexamethasone and see if that will be the thing that puts her over the top." I couldn't believe that we were talking about this already. For some reason, I had envisioned Emilia on the ventilator for many more months to come.

A new hope was in the air. I remember confidently telling Dr. Osa, "By the end of this new week, Emilia will be 2,000 grams in weight, off the vents, and back on milk feedings!" He knew that those were incredibly ambitious goals but smiled and humored me by saying, "Let's do it!" I remember telling Felicia the same thing when I saw her later during our shift change. I said, "This was the big week, and to put all your focus toward setting our sights high." I was ready to kick this marathon up a notch and start running at a faster pace. I had all kinds of hope and energy following her successful surgery and couldn't wait to watch Emilia crush all of her next big hurdles like she had done time and time before.

Spring was officially in the air as well. In Indiana, there is nothing better than those first few 60- and 70-degree sunshine-filled days after a long winter. Everyone and everything starts to come alive again. People start to leave their hibernation and head back outside again. It's hard to put that feeling into words that we all experience when we realize we can finally go outside again. It feels like liberation. Spring means all of our landscaping comes alive, the grass greens up, Easter is near, the Indy 500 and our beloved month of May is just around the corner, and I can finally stop paying for indoor tennis. The dark, short, cold, isolating days of the winter months are behind us, and we have the next six to seven months to look forward to progressively warmer weather, longer days, and fun outside. I've lived in Indiana my whole life, and every winter, I always end up asking myself why I stay here instead of leaving for Hawaii, San Diego, Florida, or somewhere else warm. Eventually, spring hits, and I remember why I love Indiana and the Midwest, and I get hooked all over again. It was around these first few beautiful spring days that it first dawned on me that Emilia was officially a spring baby! I realize how dumb that sounds saying that out loud, but it was true. So much had been going on since her birth that I hadn't really even thought about it until those first few days of glorious sunshine and warmth. I had been gearing up for a summer baby since Felicia told me we were expecting, as her due date was technically July 13th. However, Emilia surprised us all as an early spring baby, apparently, and I was just now realizing it. This was just another reason why spring in Indiana is even all that much better. I was filled with hope that this was going to be the biggest and best week yet.

The doctors gave Emilia the Dexamethasone. Dexamethasone is a corticosteroid that prevents the release of substances in the body that cause inflammation. Basically, it is a super booster steroid that can be the secret weapon in helping patients on a ventilator with additional strength needed to start the process of getting off the ventilator. We were told "the Dex" could be tried only a select few times, so it was imperative that they use it only when they thought the time was right. Dex had a short window of time to show whether it worked well enough to get Emilia off the vents. Again, I was not expecting this conversation to be even a remote possibility at this time, so I was so excited that the doctors were willing to use one of their precious chances with the Dex right here and now. They clearly saw signs that Emilia was making progress as well and wanted to give it everything they had to accelerate her growth and development. So they gave her the steroid, and we waited. They told me we should start to see signs if this was working or not within the next 12 hours. By the next day, we were starting to see signs of hope that the Dex was working. I was looking for any and every sign of success that I could point to. I wanted to believe so badly that this was going to work, and my dream at the beginning of the week of getting Emilia off her vent and to 2,000 grams weight was going to come true.

I was really riding this wave of optimism as we were running back down this hill. As the hours ticked by and 24 hours turned to 48 hours since the Dex had been administered, we weren't seeing the progress that we were hoping for. It was clear that the first attempt of "the Dex" push off the ventilator had failed. Emily, our favorite NP, assured us that this wasn't the only time they would try and that it would work next time. For now, we were going to let Emilia keep healing and wait a few days before coming back to this conversation. This one hurt. We had all the momentum, and we were all ready to take that next big step, but we just couldn't put it all together at that time. Even worse yet, Emilia was actually starting to regress with her oxygenation sats somehow. I remember writing in my journal that this experience feels like we always take 1 step forward and two steps back. Read that again, not two steps forward and 1 step back. Two steps forward and 1 step back implies that you are still making progress. I would take that slow progress all day because it is progress. However, In the NICU, at times it feels like you are somehow perpetually losing ground and going slowly backward. It can be the most frustrating thing imaginable. This is where the disciplined mind is the most critical. Control what you can control. These crushing blows can break your spirit if you let them.

As General Stockdale said, the optimists were always the first ones to die in prisoner of war camps. I'm an optimist, so I know the feeling all too well. I perpetually set these unrealistic goals and pretend to ignore the reality in front of my face as I trudge on like a happy soldier. When the outcomes I had built up in my mind don't occur, it feels so crushing. When you let your mind build up hope for the future, and then it all comes crashing down, it can crush your spirits. When you lose your belief in hope, nothing good happens next. That is where I felt at this moment. I had set this arbitrary date and goal in my mind for this week, and we had failed miserably. I was crushed, and when you are crushed, more bad news is always just lurking around the corner to finish you off.

Sure enough, that was the case for us as well, as we soon found out that a new Mount Everest of a hill was coming right around the corner that would make us pray for the tiny heartbreak hill experience again in comparison.

Day 28: 4/11/20

- I love you
- Daily Scripture Theme: Take Action. My Thoughts - so important, you can't wait around for things to happen. You have to be proactive (the first is the seven habits of highly effective people). You control your mindset and God is always there with you as a foundation. We all could look at what has happened to our family as a tragedy with a mindset of why us? I tend to look at this all as a blessing. I get to spend so much time with you every day. I know more about how your body works than I can ever imagine. Your nurses are training me to be a better caretaker. I'm journaling and writing a book for you, etc. All of that wouldn't be possible without our situation. So, we can sit in here and say "woe is me," or we can be proactive and take action. I'm writing a book, learning about you, and keeping your care team

encouraged and entertained. I could be sad, angry, and anxious. We get to choose and that is the beauty.

- Beautiful spring day today! I was able to not work, relax a little, cut the grass, eat breakfast at home, get a bunch of chores done, work out, etc. I love these lazy days with you. It's so nice when we have these lulls in the chaos. I'm not taking my eye off the prize...I just know I need to save my energy for the inevitable next big fight that comes our way. I'm thinking the next big battle will be the will or won't you take to milk feedings again well. I know you got this so I'm not worried. I'll just take it easy until then.

- I don't want to jinx anything...but it's REALLY NICE to think in terms of days and weeks vs. hours and minutes in the future. I'm 100% not getting ahead of myself, but I'm more looking forward to milestones now vs just being happy your still here every day. That is progress I love.

- Trying to think of what to get your care team as your first month thank you...any ideas?

- Oh...talk about weird things in the world today. Your cousin, Katie (my niece), had a drive by social distancing birthday today. We can't "gather" due to rules from the governor so we all drove by to say hi and honk our horns for some birthday wishes. THAT WAS THE FIRST TIME I'VE SEEN ANYONE OTHER THAN YOUR CARE TEAM IN A MONTH!!! The whole family wanted to know all about you and they said they watch you flail around all the time on the NicView. You really have a fan club. I'm so happy for that stupid thing. At least they all can get to know you a little bit even if they can't see you in person.

- Going home early tonight and I'm eating TACOS from La Parada!!! They're my absolute favorite thing. I can't wait to introduce you when you're older. Plus, you and your Mom are Hispanic so we need to start you early on that good Mexican food. Your Grandma Genie will be really happy about that.

- I love you

Day 29: 4/12/20

- I love you
- Daily Scripture Theme: Choose Carefully. My Thoughts - All day I've been trying to think of my "personal brand." What people think of me, the way I present myself, and in how I live my life. I think I'm

settling on "Never Quit" as my personal brand. I'm not the nicest, funniest, caring, smart, determined, consistent, lovable, passionate, positive, prepared, analytical, etc... but I never quit. Lol. You have to forcibly take something away from me for me to stop. Only things I've ever quit in life were gambling, cigarettes, and 1 job (which was way off brand). Ironically, I've become "never quit" now on never restarting gambling or smoking. With this in mind, I need to be super choosy about what I bring into my life. Only things that match my goals can come into my world. For that...I must choose carefully.

- On the never quit brand thing...that's a great thing for you!!! You know I'm not going ANYWHERE!!! You're stuck with me...and all of my weirdness.
- 4 weeks old!!! Holy shit! I can't believe it's been 4 weeks with you. What a blessing and I'm a forever changed person. I already want more kiddos (I'm sure your mom is excited to hear that one).
- Happy Easter as well. Usually we host Easter for the family every year. We have a huge yard you'll love to play in, hunt eggs in, etc. We can't wait for you to be able to enjoy it and play there. We literally bought our house for you about 6 years ago with this dream in mind. Unfortunately, due to coronavirus, Easter as we normally know it was cancelled. I never thought 2 months ago that we'd be sitting in a hospital during Easter with our beautiful baby girl, not seeing my family, and not hosting Easter like normal because of a pandemic. What a strange few months.
- Speaking of strange, you had another REALLY bad morning again today and we all had no idea why it was happening. Pretty scary stuff really. It just makes me wonder, WHEN IS ALL OF THIS GOING TO STOP!!! It is so hard to develop any kind of a routine. I go to sleep and you're great. I get back to the hospital in the morning and no one has any idea why you are spiraling. I'm making breakfast and get a call from your Mom that basically everything goes to hell in a hand basket. It's a crazy alternate universe. It's so hard to figure all this out.
- I was talking to your Mom today and wondering out loud, knowing that I KNOW you're coming home, would it be better if we just didn't know what was happening sometimes back at the NICU. Obviously the answer is no; however, it's an interesting thought. Probably something we should check with other NICU parents on their thoughts around knowing everything or not. I'm pretty sure they'd say be there...just thinking out loud.

- Is there any better noise than when you are sat-ing high on your oxygen? Just makes me so happy.
- Inversely, is there any worse noise than when you are sat -ing low????
- Lol...it's the same noise btw. One creates a smile, the other makes you poo your pants.
- I love you

Day 30: 4/13/20

- I love you
- Daily Scripture Theme - treat yourself. My Thoughts - Balance. Life is all about balance. Your mom and I have to keep ourselves sane every day by staying physically, mentally, emotionally, and spiritually centered. To do that, we have to be strategically selfish. While you are the most important thing in the world to us, we can't be the role models and care givers you need unless we take care of ourselves first. I often feel selfish when I'm not at the hospital and instead I'm mowing the grass, reading, working out, etc. That's not God's intention for us, we all need balance.
- 27 weeks old...you're like a Grandma! Hahahaha
- We are marching into week 5 like a boss! New week...who dis? You're going to crush it this week. I expect you back to milk feedings by Sunday, post op recovery complete, and MAYBE getting closer to coming off the vent. You got this girlie!
- You did GREAT all day today. I'm so proud of you. We're going to have a great week. I'm back on the positive train with you. Not trying to push you too hard, but I'm going to need you to get off this ventilator by mid next week and start drinking milk again.
- You're getting back to your funny, adorable little self again. All the nurses just love working with you. Your nurse the past few days, Sarah, has been incredible. She talks to you all a day and can't stop saying how cute you are...plus she got you through some really tough days as well. We all owe her big time.
- Finally going home feeling good for the first time in a few days. We've OFFICIALLY turned the corner in my mind and we are getting ready for some fun times the rest of the way out. Keep fighting and getting stronger.
- I love you

Day 31: 4/14/20

- I love you
- Daily Scripture Theme: don't shrink. My Thoughts - when you have a challenge...don't back down. That is when people are made and you see the real person. Are you going to cower in fear, let anxiety take over you and cripple you, etc; or, are you going to face it head on, try harder, be better, learn, grow, etc.? We have this choice every day and even more so right now given our situation. I'm disappointed to say that at one point in my mid-20's, I let fear work the opposite effects on me. It made panic and anxiety a part of my daily life. I fought back though, learned the why, learned how to correct, and ultimately choose to take control of my own actions and thoughts to overcome and be a better person. That training has prepared me for this ultimate battle that our family is facing today. I thank God he put me through that earlier in my life so I could get my selfish reactions out of the way and be there to support you and your Mom today. Remember, your Dad's brand is never quit. I try to live up to that every day.
- Well EQ... today is a great day. You're crushing it with the new steroids and Emily, your NP, is talking about extubating you in a few days as a "remote possibility." What an amazing surprise. You're looking so much better.
- Pretty lazy day overall. Your Momma spends most of the time at the hospital. You 2 got back to Kangarooing and improving.
- Whenever I'm away from your room and the hospital, it is a struggle to keep consistent and focused for some reason. All I can seem to think about it getting back to the hospital all the time. It is really distracting to everything else in my life.
- I love you

Day 32: 4/15/20

- I love you
- Daily Scripture Theme - your change begins with you. My Thoughts - I loved this line "your circumstances aren't your problem. Until you change your thinking, no matter what's going on in your life you'll stay stuck." It's ironic if you read the bullets below that I started writing before reading this today. Those notes sound like someone who feels a little stuck and letting circumstances dictate their mood

doesn't it? Great message to remember. I came into this week knowing it was going to be a great week. Let's keep up the momentum. I'm closing deals at work, voluntarily reading and writing daily for the first time in my life, staying healthy and active, and my little baby is still here and I'm blessed to get to see her.

- I couldn't sleep at all last night. I woke up at 2 a.m. and tried to check your NicView camera, but it was down for like 2 hours. Finally I gave in and called the hospital. I knew something wasn't going the way I was hoping it was when I left. I knew you were fine, but I also knew you were having a setback of some sort. It's so frustrating to watch you yo-yo back and forth. When you are doing good, I get excited and want to watch closely. When I know you're taking a step back...I get so confused and can't seem to figure out why.
- The first few weeks we had big themes and goals to observe and work toward. Now, it feels like every day is Groundhog Day. 1 step forward and 2 steps back. Eventually that has to change right? You can't always go backward??? It will flip to 2 steps Forward and 1 step back. It has to...right? In the meantime, it's just so hard to watch and live.
- We live in such a now society, this is the ultimate test in patience.
- I walked back in this morning and you were doing better, but I knew that was coming off a bad night. I could already tell on the nurses faces. I feel so bad for them that they have to deliver this news to parents all the time. They're saints. The worst part is I definitely can't tell your Mom this...she'll freak out and think the sky is falling. I can't do that to her again. I won't "lie" to her, but I also won't go into details.
- I had a deep thought and then I forgot it...damnit. Lol. The charge nurse happens to be the wife of a childhood friend and stopped by right as I had my epiphany. Oh well, I'm sure it will come back.
- I love you

Day 33: 4/16/20

- I love you
- Daily Scripture Theme: know your strengths. My Thoughts - a book I recently read, 7 habits of highly effective people, talks about the how habits 1 through 3 are all personal habits to master of knowing yourself, your core values, and to be proactive and intentional with how you move about your life. You can't master these principles, or how to interact with others (habits 4-6), unless you know yourself

first. I can't wait to be a role model for you to teach these skills and watch you grow and develop as you get older. This is an area of life I'm very passionate about and can't wait to share with you. Also, knowing my strengths (specifically optimism, competitiveness, and never giving up) have really helped me to be positioned to manage this current situation we find ourselves and stay focused on the prize of getting you home safe and sound. I feel like God really has indirectly been training me for years and honing my strengths to prepare me literally for this exact moment. I won't let you down.

- Still up and down this week on the ventilator. I'm choosing to be optimistic. I KNOW you're going to make your big breakthrough still this week. You've got this...you're the strongest person I've ever met and that is not hyperbole. I can't imagine anyone being able to endure what you've gone through. You just keep fighting and never give up. I often wonder what's in your mind that keeps you going and where it comes from? I'd love to know how babies handle all of this, and why some fight and survive, like you, while others don't. You truly will have endured more than any single person I know by the time you're 4 months old. It's remarkable. I wish you could walk me through your mindset.

- I was looking through my video and photos yesterday from the last week. It's amazing seeing your progression, coloring, physical growth, mannerisms, etc. It may only be 5 weeks, but it feels like 2 years in those photos.

- BTW - we know you can tan...whew! When they had that light on you for a week...you got super dark. It really showed in the pictures. I was worried you'd get your Mom's inability. Lol

- Speaking of your Mom, your Grandma sent a photo of your Mom as a baby to us yesterday. You 2 looked identical. I guess that debate is settled. I'm just glad you got my tanning genes at least.

- I love you

The NICU Marathon: The Real Heartbreak Hill (Days 34-36)

Like I said before, the ease, speed, and thrill of running downhill always comes to an end eventually. For my family, after our week of downhill running, we turned the corner onto the next street and found ourselves unknowingly staring up at a mountain to climb this time that we didn't even know was a part of the course. I still don't know exactly why this day was different, but it was. Since only one of us could be at the hospital at a time,

Felicia and I had gotten into the routine of me taking the "morning shift" with Emilia. I would work from Emilia's room, stay until around 1 p.m., and then Felicia would come in to finish the afternoon. Around early evening, we would decide who was going to stay late that night, and then that person would finish up the day until around 10 p.m. and head home.

For the previous week, the morning and late shifts had fallen on me. I didn't mind at all; my happy place was always right next to Emilia for as much time as I could possibly get. I specifically loved ending my days in the NICU because now that I was back at work, my mornings were usually total chaos. I was overwhelmed trying to hop from virtual meeting to meeting as nurses and doctors came in out of the room asking questions and caring for Emilia. I didn't really even get to spend much quality time with just Emilia and me in the mornings after I went back to work. I really missed that quality time we had together with just us before the work interfered. Nonetheless, it had become my new role to take the late shift, and being that I had been doing double shifts for a while now, I think I had it in my head that I deserved a break or something. I asked Felicia the night before if it would be cool if she took that morning shift and let me work from home, and then I would come in for the afternoon change. She, of course, said that was fine, and we went to bed. At this point, we had been running downhill for the past week following the big surgery, and things were looking up. Were we successful with the dex and getting Emilia off of the ventilator? No. Did that mean that she wasn't recovering well? Not at all! She was getting bigger, her swelling had gone down, and we were slowly starting to reintroduce milk back into her system. Things were progressing well in the grand scheme of things. Felicia and I had no reason to believe that today would be anything other than that similar trajectory.

So, on day 32 of our journey, Felicia headed to the hospital for the early shift, and I stayed home that morning. Around 10 a.m., Felicia calls me and lets me know that Dr. Rescorla and the surgery team had come by to check on Emilia and didn't like something they saw in their clinical assessment. They decided to do an X-ray of her belly and saw an air bubble forming again in her small intestines in the healthy bowel section that was above the ostomy. Dr. Rescorla told Felicia that he thought it might just be a kinked bowel and likely not a big deal, but he wanted to correct it, so it didn't cause any more damage. He said it shouldn't take him more than 20 minutes to do this, and he'll be in and out. He asked Felicia for permission to open up some of Emilia's stitches from her previous surgery to go back in and unkink her bowels for the quick fix. Felicia said yes and signed the paperwork for Dr. Rescorla to perform the minor operation. She called me to let me know that because this is technically another surgical procedure, the hospital will allow us both to be there together in the consultation room and forgo the Covid regulations. I had some meetings and customer calls that morning, but I told her I would just take them from the hospital. I got in the car and headed over to Riley to wait with Felicia in the consulting room outside the NICU.

I have to stress that at this point, neither Felicia nor I thought this would be anything other than a minor thing that would take 30 minutes max. By the time that I arrived at the hospital, Dr. Rescorla had already begun setting up for the procedure, and I immediately went to sit with Felicia in the consultation room. I pulled out my laptop and got back to work. It was probably around 10:30 or 11 a.m. at this point. I nonchalantly hopped on a few routine team meetings, took a customer call that had already been scheduled, and joked around with Felicia. I was just waiting for Dr. Rescorla to knock on the door again to let us know that everything was all good and he'd fixed the kinked bowel so I could head back home to get back to work in my home office. After about an hour passed, I started to wonder what the hell was taking so long. After an hour and a half, I remember walking out of the room, into the NICU, and looking down the hall at Emilia's room to see if the surgery stuff was still up. It was. I didn't understand why this was taking so long. I walked back to the room and officially started to get a little concerned. I thought this was just supposed to be a quick procedure.

Finally, around 1 p.m., Dr. Rescorla knocked on the door to the consultation room. He said, "We had initially gone in to unkink the bowels, but when we got in there, we discovered that it wasn't a kinked bowel at all." Emilia had apparently developed a bunch of scar tissue in her intestines that was blocking her healthy bowel above the previous ostomy. Dr. Rescorla continued, "At that point, we felt our only option was to perform a second new ostomy above the area of concern to correct the problem we were seeing." After the first surgery, Dr. Rescorla had told us Emilia had a lot of healthy bowels remaining, and that was a really important thing as it would allow her to continue to milk feed, have normal nutrient absorption, and it less cause for future long term effects, etc. Now, with the second ostomy, he was concerned about how much healthy bowel was left to work with. "It could go either way," he said. However, that was the least of our worries at this point. Dr. Rescorla had just informed us that Emilia just had another major intestinal surgery without being fully recovered from the first one.

Emilia had been so strong during her first ostomy and recovery. While we had a few hours of low blood pressure followed by a few days of extreme water retention and bloating due to the treatments, she was mostly recovered but nowhere near fully recovered at this point. I would put her at like 60% recovered. I was extremely worried about what this new trauma could do to her body. Dr. Rescorla was extremely apologetic, and though he didn't say it, I could tell that he was worried about what had just happened as well. When a surgeon with the experience and knowledge of Dr. Rescorla has some concerns, that is a bad sign. After our first surgery, he was pretty upbeat and optimistic. This consultation felt way different. I'm still haunted by this conversation and the whole entire experience as I replay it over and over in my mind. How in the hell did this happen? Why did this escalate so quickly? Why wasn't I there to ask more questions of Dr. Rescorla before he operated on Emilia that morning? Why did no one come and tell us that the original procedure we agreed to was turning into this whole huge other major surgery? Emilia was fine that morning, relatively speaking, and yet here we were again with another huge post-surgery experience to overcome.

I don't have a lot of regrets or anger from our experiences with our daughter in the NICU, but this one is my #1. It took me a while to process and get through this one over the coming few months. I'm not an angry person at all, and I typically NEVER dwell in the past or hold grudges against others. I have a million examples of this in my life I could share to back this statement up. However, I won't bore you with that stuff here. If you know me, you know that I would NEVER want to hurt anyone or anything, and I'm always quick to forgive and move forward. Here's a quick example of how much I hate wishing ill will on anything. I recently caught a mouse in our kitchen, and it took me about a week to get over the fact that I killed a mouse in our kitchen. He had been leaving little turds all over our counter for weeks, and I had been letting it slide. One day, I found a little turd in my eggs that had come from a pan that I re-used on our stove. That was the final straw! I went to the hardware store and got one of those little old-school wooden mouse traps, went home and set it, and then went to bed that night. Almost five minutes after I turned all the lights out, I heard a loud snap sound and thought, "Holy shit! Did that really work so quickly?" Sure enough, there was a little dead mouse flipped upside down on my countertop. I was devastated seeing his little body stuck in the trap that I had set. Thinking about his little mouse family that would never get to see their dad come home ever again really messed with my head. All he was trying to do was get a little food for himself and his family on our kitchen counters, and I killed him. That seems like an unfair price to pay. How could I honestly do that? This is the kind of crap that goes on in my mind. However, this whole situation still angers me when I reflect back on it. It just never sits well with me when I think about why Dr. Rescorla did what he did that day. I know it isn't his fault, and I know he did his best to do everything he could to save our daughter, not once but twice. He's a great man, and I don't hold anything against him. I can't imagine (there it is again) what his life must be like doing what he does every single day.

Living Dr. Rescorla's life must be incredibly difficult. If I have this many tormented thoughts from dealing with a little mouse, I literally can't imagine (there it is again) what he must think about when reflecting on the stuff he does every day. Most of my anger that came from this event in the weeks to follow probably stems from the fact that I had no control over anything that ultimately occurred. I WASN'T THERE! That's really the problem that I had to face. I feel like I let Emilia down. I was supposed to be her protector. I was the one that was supposed to ask every possible question of her care team before they laid a finger on her. It was my job, and I wasn't there. Why? The real why is because I let those quad one priorities, the urgent and vital priorities like work and meaningless life-stress, win. I was tired that morning, and I asked Felicia to fill in for me because I needed a break. Emilia is and will always be my quad two, first things first, priority, or at least she should have been. That is why quad two activities are the hardest to maintain. It is so easy to let those urgent things consume all of our energy. At this moment, I let life beat me down and dictate my priorities to me, and I paid the price. Look, I get that this "wasn't my fault" or whatever other things that someone wants to tell me to try and make me feel better, but it was my fault. I was supposed to be there that morning, and I wasn't. I'm not sitting here and writing all of this, letting this impact every moment of my life or something, so don't feel sorry for me. If anything, I learned from this moment and made the changes in my life to make sure this never happens again. I will NEVER let anyone else's priorities trump what is truly important in my life ever again. I can say without hesitation that I've lived this principle in my life from this exact day forward with every ounce of my being, and it won't stop until I'm gone.

Regardless, here we were again, back to where we were ten days before today and starting the road to recovery from another major surgery. After Dr. Rescorla reported back that the second surgery was completed and spent a few minutes talking through Emilia's outlook going forward, coronavirus restrictions dictated that one of us had to leave the hospital now that the surgery was completed. Since Felicia had been there all morning, I volunteered to take the first shift after Emilia's surgery to watch over her in recovery.

By this point in time, it was around 1:30 p.m. Felicia left, and I started to walk down the hall and enter back into the NICU to go see Emilia. As I re-entered the NICU and got closer to our room, the curtain was still up over the doorway, signaling that the operation was still ongoing and it was a sterile environment that no one could enter. The nurses told me that they were going to try to put a new PICC line in while Emilia was still all set up for surgery and under anesthesia. I didn't really like this but didn't have a choice. I just wanted them to leave her alone at this point. They had been asking us for the past few days to preventably try for a new PICC line as the old one showed signs of needing to be replaced. They had held off as they didn't want to take any unnecessary risks with Emilia still recovering from her last surgery. I guess with this situation, they took the opportunity to try and do it at this time, so I was told to continue waiting outside the room. I went down the hall and into the shared kitchenette and just sat there staring out the window. I remember feeling helpless, scared, and frustrated. I'm not sure if I can put my emotions into words, but I just felt defeated. I was stuck in this stupid little kitchen by myself, with my mind racing and praying that I could see my daughter. I sat there for 30 minutes, which felt like three hours. I got up every five minutes to look down the hall to see if they had removed the curtain. It was still there every time I peeked out of the kitchen. Another 30 minutes went by, and still, no one left the room. At this time, I called my mom to give her an update and to just talk to someone. I was tired of sitting there alone, scared, and isolated in this stupid hospital kitchenette. I didn't want to call Felicia and worry her any further. I remember talking to my mom and crying. I rarely cry, but this situation really hurt, and something felt different and bad. I was scared as hell for little Emilia and thought there was a real chance that we were going to lose her. My mom tried to ease my concerns, but there were no words that anyone could give me at this time to make this feeling go away. I was terrified. I still vividly remember that traumatizing experience from the first surgery's postoperative recovery. That was scary as hell, and Emilia went into that one about as healthy as she had ever been. This time, she was still weakened from the last surgery, and I was thinking, "How is she going to fight through this one?"

Finally, after about an hour and a half of additional waiting, they let me back into the room. The new PICC line still wasn't in. They had tried their best, but the procedure had failed. I took my place in the room, and I honestly don't remember much at all after this point. By this time, it was around 3 p.m. in the afternoon. This had all begun around 11 a.m. that morning. This had become an unexpected day from hell. I remember it was a Friday, and at least the work week was done so I could focus all of my time and attention on Emilia. I thought to myself, "We did this once and we can do it again!" Remember, I was the one there after the first surgery and had watched Spencer work her magic on Emilia when we saw the post-op recovery taking a nosedive. I had seen and felt what it was like to walk on that edge of the mountain top where we could either fall off or make it back down safely. I was at least prepared for what was to come. Our favorite NP, Emily, was there that day (Thank God). She was always such an awesome source of knowledge and guidance. She told it like it was but in an incredibly kind and caring fashion. She would give us the real talk in all directions. What is the best case, worst case, and everything in between? She was incredibly calming for both Felicia and me anytime she was around. Luckily for me, Emily was overseeing all the medical interventions and directing traffic this time for Emilia's second big surgery recovery. It was nothing against Spencer, but she didn't have the bedside manner that some of the more veteran nurses and NP's had acquired from their years of experience. It is clear that nurses like Emily, Staci, Lori, Joni, Allison, Jessica, Raina, etc., all know that managing the parent might be just as important as managing the patient. This time it wasn't me, left in a room by myself, slowly watching Emilia's oxygen sats dipping and wondering when the hell someone would be back to help like last time. Emily was with me every step of the way this time, always providing counsel and talking me through what was going on, and didn't leave that room unless someone else was there with me. I would need all of that and then some to get through this second post-surgery recovery.

Remember, rule number three of the NICU. "No need to be scared unless your nurses are scared." Well, the nurses were scared! Emilia's blood pressure was really, really, low. The Dopamine wasn't working its magic this time as it had before, and we weren't seeing the bounceback that we all were hoping to see from Emilia. They were pumping her full of more and more fluids to try and keep her blood pressure up. Emilia's body was becoming incredibly swollen again from all the fluids, even more so than before. She was almost unrecognizable from that sweet, little, beautiful face that I had left the night before. Her ears were like four times the size, and her whole head was like twice as big. I remember talking to Emily at this time and asking her, "On a scale of one to ten, how worried should I be right now?" This time, when I asked, Emily's response was, "This is really serious, Chris!" That sent shivers through me, and I was officially terrified. Emily would NEVER say something like that if it wasn't the absolute truth. I had no idea how critical blood pressures were to the body. I would come to learn so much more about all the bad things low blood could do to a body in the next few days. Up until this point in my life, the only thing I had ever heard of concerning blood pressure was when it was too high and its correlation to a heart attack. In this situation, we were dealing with extremely low blood pressure. I came to learn that when blood pressure drops, it causes an inadequate flow of blood to the body's organs which can lead to things like heart attack, stroke, kidney failure, etc. The longer the blood pressure remains low, the more damage to organs is caused. The first line of defense is fluids. When blood pressure is low, the body pulls all the fluids it can find into the veins to help increase pressure and flow. So, the idea is to give the body more fluids, and the blood pressure hopefully stabilizes. If that fails, the next line of defense is medicine. The first medicine intervention is the Dopamine that we heard about before after her first surgery. Luckily for us, the Dopamine worked like a charm the first time, and nothing more was needed. The next line of defense was the drug name I was about to hear for the first time from Emily called "Epi." Epi, I learned, is the "last resort drug," per Emily. She said, "Epi is the last tool in our toolbox. If the Epi doesn't work…"

In case you were wondering, "Epi" is short for epinephrine which is also known by the more familiar name, Adrenaline. They only pull out Epi in the most severe situations in a hospital setting. They needed to give Emilia an Epi drip to help her heart beat harder and harder in hopes that it would get her blood pressure up to stabilize her body. There are different levels of Epi that can be given to a patient. If the first level fails, they bump it up a little, and then they do it again. At a certain point, it is maxed out, and there is nothing more that they can do to stabilize blood pressure. Emily informed me that they had to put Emilia on Epi as the Dopamine was no longer strong enough to turn this around. She sent the order to the pharmacy. Emily told me that they would start Emilia out on the lowest levels of Epi and see if it worked. I was terrified. I was slowly watching my daughter slip away before my eyes. Modern medicine in an acute situation is incredible, but it has its limits eventually. There are only so many interventions that can be done before there is nothing else left to do. Luckily, Emilia is the strongest person I've ever met, and she had the support of the best in the business with her care team at Riley. I was left on the sidelines praying that the Epi would do its job (just like the Dopa had worked after the first surgery). If the first surgery had felt like walking along the side of a mountain ledge where you could fall off at any moment, this one felt like we were walking a tightrope crossing over the grand canyon. This could literally go either way at this point.

They strung up the Epi drip and let it start to do its thing. Then we all waited and watched her monitors for the blood pressure update that popped up in 30-minute intervals. Her monitors would display the last four readings on the monitor for you to view. I honestly hadn't ever even noticed that the monitors tracked blood pressure until this point, as it had never been a concern. We had been in the NICU for 30 days staring at those monitors all day long, but it had never occurred to me to even ask what those tiny little numbers in the bottom left corner were. The only numbers I cared about usually were her oxygen and heart rate sats. That's all the whole care team ever talked to us about. Now those little hidden numbers in the bottom left of the monitor were the star of the show. Every 30 minutes, I prayed and prayed, wanting to see some progress and hoping that we were heading in the right direction. 30 minutes would come and go with no progress. More fluid was ordered and administered. The cycle continued for the next hour or two. Finally, around 8 p.m. that night, we started to see her blood pressures tick up just a little. Eventually, the next few readings were all slowly and steadily increasing. After another hour, we were finally back in a normal range for her blood pressure. We were stable, but the question that was on everyone's mind was what damage had been done to our little angel, and would this progress hold?

It was around this time that future Emilia and I had our next father/daughter chat. As I was sitting in her room and praying for a miracle to keep my daughter safe and alive, future Emilia and I started to talk about this exact moment in her journey. If you remember earlier in the story, this had happened once before in the parent waiting room at IU Methodist when they were readying Emilia for her trip across downtown Indianapolis to Riley Hospital for Children. In my previous vision, Emilia would be heading off to college shortly, and I brought her to visit the waiting room so I could talk her through her own amazing journey and remind her how strong she was. Here we were again, at another crossroads, and I was in a trance again talking to future Emilia. I was always resolute that she was coming home, so this didn't feel weird to me at all. This time, my little college-aged Emilia was back visiting her room at Riley with me 18 years later, and I was telling her all the crazy things that were happening to her and starting to cry. "I can't believe how strong you were to go through all of this," I told her. "You are seriously the most courageous person I've ever met." It's truly unreal to think about what this little girl was going through from the moment she was born. If she can survive this and thrive, she is going to change the world in my mind. Slowly our conversation ended, and I felt more at ease knowing that the future Emilia was still out there to give me hope that those weren't just hallucinations. I have no idea why, but I still felt like we were all going to pull through this one again and be back to normal in a few days to resume our pursuit of the finish line of this marathon and get her home.

Back to reality. For the moment, the crisis had been averted. The epinephrine had done its job, and Emilia's life-and-death crisis was in the rear-view mirror. The toll all this had taken on my poor Emilia was incredibly visible for all to see. You could see it on her face. Even though she couldn't cry because of the breathing tubes, I could tell she wasn't happy. I can't even imagine (there are those words again) the pain she must have been experiencing at this point. It is easy to take for granted that since she is a baby and doesn't have any words that her pain is somehow less than an adult who could describe it. I didn't take it for granted for one second; she looked like she was in incredible pain. Our feisty little girl, who was always kicking and flailing around all the time, was basically motionless. She was left incredibly bloated and retaining so much water and fluids that she could barely move at all. She would need to pass all this extra fluid quickly if her recovery was to continue on a good path like last time. The only problem was, this wasn't just like before. This was ten times worse than before.

The hopes of just a few days prior of getting her off the ventilator, growing to 2,000 grams, and resuming milk feedings that I had envisioned at the start of the week were almost a sick joke at this point. We had a battle for her life on our hands. Her blood pressure may be stable now, but that could change at any point. It was still TBD on what damage this whole episode had done to her lungs and other organs. The only positive was that her blood pressure was stable again, for now. They took her off the Epi and left the Dopamine strung up to keep her stable. It was around 10 p.m., and I was exhausted. Felicia and I made the switch, and she would watch Emilia through the night. I finally headed home to lay down and rest. What began as just another day had turned into our worst nightmare. Even with all of that, I drove home that night thinking that we were through the worst of this and ready to march back up that hill together just like we did before. We've seen this hill already. We know what it takes to make it back up to the top, and we will live the Sears brand, never quit, with each and every day. My mindset was still the same; she was coming home! After all, this is the strongest little person I've ever seen in my life. No way was she about to give up her fight, and neither was I.

The next morning, Saturday (day 33), I arrived back at the hospital to relieve Felicia of her night shift duties. She looked exhausted and tired. If we were both this tired, I can't even imagine (there it is again) how exhausted our little Emilia must have felt. As I walked in, I was greeted for the first time by a nurse that we had never met up to this point, named Jodi. Jodi was another seasoned vet that was apparently really good friends with Staci (so that meant she was already good in my book). Jodi had a fight on her hands the moment she stepped foot into the arena and reported for work that morning. While Emilia's blood pressure had been stable for the past 12 hours, it was beginning to drop again steadily. The constant Dopamine drip wasn't working anymore to maintain her levels, so the doctors and NP's made the call to try a new drug called Dobutamine in conjunction with the Dopa. Dobutamine is another drug that helps the heart beat harder to hopefully increase blood pressure. Think of it as a step down from the Epi that we had to use the day before. If the Dobutamine didn't work, we all knew what was next. We'd go back to the Epi drip. Jodi was ready for the challenge and got straight to work on Emilia.

The next few hours were a blur of watching Emilia's monitors for signs of hope that her blood pressures would begin to increase again, nurses scrambling around the room stringing and restringing new drugs up to administer to Emilia, etc. Emilia's oxygen sats would fluctuate all over the place, and the RT's would have to be called in constantly to evaluate and counteract. Basically, it was a never-ending string of problems. We would fix one problem, and four more would pop up ten minutes later. Emilia was all over the place. Nothing seemed to be working at all to get this blood pressure stabilized once and for all. By midday, the Epi was ordered once again to see if that could get Emilia back into balance. It was at this point that Felicia and I were told by the medical staff that, "As long as Emilia is on epi, which the hospital considered as severe as you can get in an acute situation, Covid restrictions would be waived, and both parents were allowed to be bedside." "Oh my God! We all get to be together again! Holy shit!" That is all I could think about. This was the absolute worst nightmare that either Felicia or I could imagine going through, but at least we'd finally be able to be together again as a family to support each other in person. We hadn't really spent more than five minutes with all three of us in the same room since Emilia's second day of life when we were all together in the mother/baby section while still over at IU Methodist. It had been 31 days since my family, going through the most traumatic experience of our lives, had been able to be together in the same room: no support, no family, no nothing. Felicia and I had been fighting this battle with one arm tied behind our backs since the jump and didn't even realize it. Most parents probably never have their child away from them for more than five minutes in their first 33 days of life. Felicia and I have never been together with our child in 31 days. I can't tell you how much being together would mean to us over the next coming days, which would come to be the hardest of our lives.

Emilia was put back on epi, and Felicia came to join us. It was a truly magical feeling to have my partner in life next to me and our daughter, right where she belonged. We felt like a family for the first time, and it was a shot of energy to keep us fighting for our daughter. The last time we were all together, we were both still in shock from the unexpected birth, and Felicia was recovering from pregnancy. This time together felt different. We had all already been through so much, but we'd been running our own individual marathons. We were all finally in the same race and running this thing together.

One of the oddest things that I noticed when Felicia and I were able to be together bedside was discovering how weird it felt to have the nurses we've all come to know and love see us together as a couple for the first time. We had been carrying on relationships with these nurses individually, and we all had become friends, separately. As a couple, most of the friends you meet post-marriage get to know you as a pair. These nurses had gotten to know us each individually, and now we were getting to meet them again as a couple. It is subtle but different. We all knew each other so well, just not in this way. It had to be just as new and different for the nurses as well seeing us together for the first time, really. They only ever got to really see half of Felicia and I's lives as the other was never there. It was great to finally have the dream team together, as we would need all of our powers combined to get through these next few trying days.

Now that we were together again doing the stupidest little things like reading a book to Emilia together was a blast. Sitting around and talking about how adorable our little daughter is was so much fun. Holding little Emilia's hands together as a family meant so much more. Everything in life is better when you have others to share it with. I realized at this moment that I don't need much in life as long as my family is together.

For the first time in our lives, we were all together in the same room, operating as a family. It was cool and weird at the same time. It was ironic that the first time Felicia and I could be together in the NICU over at Riley, our collective favorite nurse, Staci, was with us for that Saturday night. As I talked about before, Staci was like our surrogate big sister and helped to comfort us individually the most anytime she was around. She was fun, energetic, compassionate, empathetic, patient, included us, treated Emilia like a queen... just the whole package. Thank God she was there! Not only was she the Emilia whisperer, but she was also the Felicia whisperer. She helped to calm Felicia down so much, and I'll forever be grateful that she was with us during this section of our marathon. Joni had fought amazingly hard all morning, and now Staci was being called in to keep the momentum on the recovery going. We were still playing whack-a-mole at this stage, and they were throwing everything they could at Emilia to try and get this blood pressure stabilized once and for all. We would take one step forward and two steps back this whole entire night.

Felicia and I both stayed at the hospital together overnight on that Saturday. That was the first time that we had both slept in the same room as Emilia together in our entire lives. What new parents never get to actually sleep in the same room as their child until 34 days into their life? Felicia took the pull-out bed, and I slept in the recliner. Staci and the team kept fighting the never-ending fires that were popping up all over the place surrounding Emilia's post-op complications as Felicia, and I slowly drifted in and out of sleep.

It's always impossible to get a good night's sleep at the hospital, but it's especially hard when you are scared out of your mind, and there is a barrage of people coming in and out of the room all night. I remember that night, in particular, felt extra strange. It felt as if my dreams and reality were blurring together. I kept randomly waking up in the darkness of the hospital room to people wearing masks and gowns, standing over my daughter, with a red-glowing light coming from behind them. I had accidentally fallen asleep with my contacts still in. As anyone that wears contacts knows, they get super dry if you sleep in them, and whenever you wake up, it takes a few minutes for your eyes to come back into focus. You have to blink a lot in an effort to get back the moisture needed for your normal eyesight to resume. In my half-asleep, slightly delirious state, with eyes that I couldn't fully open, everything looked like we were in a sci-fi movie. I learned in the morning that they were trying once again to put another PICC line in from like 3 a.m. until 5 a.m. When I close my eyes, trying to piece together what I was seeing, it is like one of those foggy flashback scenes you see in a movie when a person can't really remember what happened but knew something weird was going on. It was pretty bizarre, to say the least, and an image that still haunts me.

We all made it through the night and into the next morning. Staci had fought the good fight, left it all on the field for our daughter and our family, and it was time to call in the next reliever during the 7 a.m. shift change. It was Joni again. At least she knew what she was up against this time and was ready to get to work. After that morning shift change and until around 2 p.m., things slowly started to improve for Emilia. Things were finally starting to look up, and there was some hope again in the air. Emilia's blood pressure had officially stabilized back to normal levels. We were no longer fighting new fires that were springing up all over the place. Emilia was still in awful shape, tons of pain, poked and prodded all over the place, but was no longer at critical levels.

The relief in the room was palpable. It felt nice to finally take a breather and relax a little after being on edge for two days.

We actually had some time to really get to know Joni a little more with this newfound positive energy in the room. Yesterday was the first time we had met and spent the day with Joni. Under normal circumstances, we always had a chance to spend some time getting to know our new nurses and developing a bit of a rapport. Unfortunately for Joni, she was immediately thrust into maximum effort and laser focus which was required to tackle the care Emilia needed from the moment she clocked in the previous shift. There was absolutely no time for chit-chat at all, so we had hardly even really spoken. Today, with things thankfully calming down a bit, we had a chance to talk a little more. Turns out, like all of our nurses, Joni was cool as hell, and I could see why she and Staci were such good friends. We learned that outside of the hospital that she was a powerlifter, had all these cool tattoos, and had a teenage daughter that lifted with her. She and I connected in particular on our love of the stupid new game sweeping the nation called pickleball. Joni and her daughter had recently taken up playing this new sport and were loving it. I, as a life-long tennis player, had recently been introduced to the sport in the past few years and played regularly myself. I was becoming a big fan of pickleball, and we had some fun conversations around the shared love of this new sport.

It felt nice to get back to our "normal" feelings in the NICU. This was indicative of 97% of our time at Riley than anything else I've written detailing our past few days. Those lulls in the action where we got to talk with our nurses, get to know them personally, spend time with our daughter, and just hang out are really what I will always remember most about our time in the NICU. There was a lot of fun that was had there, and I will forever cherish those memories.

By the time that Staci came back for the night shift, Emilia was back in relative cruise control mode (so to speak). It was back to care as normal at this point. I remember the weekend surgery team coming by to do a check-up on Emilia right after the shift change occurred. The surgery resident said to us all in the room, "Emilia is looking much better. Rarely do we ever lose patients that are this far removed from surgery. We should be in good shape, medically speaking." That was such a relief to hear in my mind. We had all fought the hard fight over the past few days, and it felt like we were maybe going to pull out of this after all. Emilia, her nurses and doctors, Felicia, and I had all battled and marched back up that hill, and we could at least start to see the ridge where it might end, and the downhill portion can start again. Felicia and I were back to having fun with Emilia and Staci in the room together.

It was around 10 p.m. and WE WERE EXHAUSTED! The past few days of stress, panic, and anxiety were hitting Felicia and me hard. We looked at Staci and said, "Should we stay here tonight or try to go home and sleep"? I will never forget the words that came next from Staci when she said, "Trust me, I've been doing this a long time, and I can tell you without a doubt that Emilia is in good shape right now, and you two should go home and get some rest." This was Staci saying this!!! She's our favorite nurse, a trusted friend at this point, and surrogate big sister. That was music to our ears to hear. She felt like we were in a good place as she would NEVER tell us something like that unless she truly believed it. If she wasn't concerned at all, neither was I. Felicia and I went home and got to sleep.

Day 34: 4/17/20

- I love you
- Daily Scripture Theme: Is your GPS on? My Thoughts – "Prayer is your GPS (guidance, protection, strength)." It IS true...if you don't use it you lose it! I need to start praying at the end of my readings every day. I don't have to do this alone. I can ask for guidance, protection, and strength and turn God "on" each day. You'll never get what you don't ask. One of my life problems has always been to not ask for help and always trying to solve my own problems. You miss out on guidance and mentorship a lot by doing this. That guidance could help prevent you from driving yourself off a cliff. Use it.
- Oh man...belly day drama part 2. So, the surgery team came to check on you routinely this morning and had some concerns. That led to a "minor" procedure we were told. That "minor" procedure turned into a full new ostomy procedure AND a new PICC line for some extra fun. I'm so overwhelmed with emotions and thoughts that I won't do it justice in this writing. Partly because I'm just too damn exhausted to think. This stuff just saps the life out of you.
- It feels like Groundhog Day every day in here. We come in expecting a different outcome, we talk about it with doctors and nurses, we game plan, and then it all goes to shit. Rinse and repeat and do it all again the next day.

- Selfishly speaking...I'm overwhelmed. I can't focus on anything... work, you, errands, etc. It all just blurs together in an endless sea of the same day over and over again.
- I feel so bad for you. I want nothing more than to give you a week... ONE FREAKING WEEK...of no bullshit and see what you can do. It's like we've been stuck in this belly rut for 4 weeks and we all can't move on until this is in the rear-view mirror.
- I need to go back to focusing on day by day and hour by hour. I let my mind get ahead of me again. I started thinking about weeks and months in the future a few days ago. Thank you for the reminder that this isn't possible in this situation. FOCUS and I guess fall in love with the process????? That's a saying I've used to remind myself in the past that NO ONE likes hard work, but if you focus on the process, lock in, and execute on what you can control; then at least it can be somewhat more enjoyable.
- You know what...that's a load of crap. There is NO PROCESS in this environment and that's why it is such a struggle. I think Patience and Faith is the process. I need to fall in love with that.
- I BLASTED your Sia song "Alive" today...I got chills. You're so strong. It just reminds me to imagine you yelling at the top of your lungs so everyone can hear you that you're going to be okay. You're a fighter. You're alive.
- I love you

Day 35: 4/18/20

- I LOVE YOU!!!! I've been writing these 3 words every day at the beginning and end of my writing since this all began; however, the past few weeks I've been forgetting to remember the why behind the words I love you when I type it out. This morning I took some time to think a little deeper about those words so they aren't just words. You're truly the strongest person I've ever met in my life. You're a role model for me to live up to as I try and live the "never quit" motto each and every day. As you know, that's my personal brand I've recently settled on...never quit. You're truly are your father's daughter, and already in one month you have shown more "never quit" than I've ever in my entire life. I'm so proud of you...truly. Watching you has reminded me while I'm running, working, hanging with you, etc. what those words really mean. You are already making me a better person. Hell...I'm WRITING every day. I HATE WRITING!!! I probably haven't ever once in my life written for any other purpose than being forced at school. It's like I'm living in an alternate universe.

- Dad joke of the day - why did the shopping cart quit its job? It was tired of being pushed around. I'm going to start a new trend in my writing, a dad jokes of the day. Hope you enjoy!

· Daily Scripture Theme - break free from other people's expectations. My Thoughts – "Jesus walked his own walk and we should do the same." Don't let anyone make you feel like you need to change who you are. You're super special and God has a plan...let him guide you and be true to yourself.

- I'm also going to actually READ out loud to you the jokes and scripture reading each day. It seems to be working to calm you down today so I'll keep that up going in the future.
- Man... what a day yesterday. You're still recovering from your last surgery and we are back to you being SUPER swollen, low blood pressures, pumped full of fluid to counteract, etc. Rough days are ahead for all of us, but I know you'll get through it because you're the strongest little thing ever. PLUS, in a weird twist of fate, we just did this last week so we all know the drill this time :). Listen to the scripture theme today jn your recovery. Don't let me, your mom, or your doctors and nurses' pressure you to be something you're not. Your recovery is your recovery. You do you. We're here to support you.
- Okay...you're officially scaring the shit out of us. YOU GOT THIS!!!!! I've never wanted something more in my life than to see you pull through this. Please God, get this baby home to us happy and healthy.
- I love you

Day 36: 4/19/20

- I love you
- Dad Joke of the day - did you about the 2 thieves that stole a calendar? They each got 6 months.
- Daily Scripture Theme - Listen to love. My Thoughts - this is very timely for us. The message is all about listen to people around you and give them something special based on this. Your mom and I are still trying to figure out what to get your nurses as gifts to thank them for all of their incredibly hard work. We were just speaking about this yesterday. I think it may be something called Dansko Clogs. They all seem to love their shoes. We'll keep listening though and that will guide us on what to do,.

- What a freaking day and night yesterday. We really almost lost you again. It was a crazy whirlwind of a day where everyone was chasing you around based on your symptoms and throwing everything they had at the problem. You just didn't seem to want to respond and make that breakthrough.
- Ironically, due to all this latest trauma, your Mom and I ACTUALLY GOT TO SPEND TIME WITH YOU AS A FAMILY FOR THE FIRST TIME IN OVER A MONTH!!! How crazy does that sound. We haven't all been together in the same room since basically when you were born. The nursing staff was so nice to let us break the stringent coronavirus rules, yep...that's still a thing, and we were able to be bedside together. Sadly, that was because how bad the situation had gotten, but we were able to have some fun. That was the first time we've truly felt like a Family together since you were born. It felt really good. We read you jokes, stories, held your hand, etc. I forgot what it almost felt like to have a teammate in all of this process because we've been so isolated from each other due to the pandemic. We're way better together than apart. I got to see how amazing of a Mom she is going to be first hand. That is just so amazing to have that opportunity even if it is in this crazy of an environment. I can't wait to get you home safe and sound so we can continue with these amazing little moments.
- You have a huge day ahead of you today. Keep turning that corner and being the strongest person I've ever seen. Your resilience is remarkable. Someday I'm going to tell you this story, and you will be crying your eyes out as you learn what you are truly capable of overcoming.
- You have the best nurses with you today. Stacy is going to be so happy to learn where you are now when she gets back for her shift tonight.
- I love you

The NICU Marathon: The 4 a.m. phone call... (Day 37)

Let's flash back to day two of this whole entire journey when we were all back at IU Methodist and Emilia was on her second day of life in this world. That night, Felicia and I missed a 3 a.m. phone call from the NICU alerting us to the alarmingly high glucose levels that Emilia was experiencing. Felicia and I decided right then and there that we would NEVER miss a phone call from the NICU ever again. We figured out a way on our cell phones to set a bypass of the silent mode for a particular saved number so they would always ring and made sure to mark the NICU as one of them. We then prayed that we would never receive a phone call in the middle of the night again from the NICU number.

Nurses are people too. They don't ever want to call a parent in the middle of the night and tell them that something is wrong with their child. As a matter of fact, I would venture to say that the nurses would probably go to great lengths to avoid that call at all costs until it is absolutely necessary. Well, at 4 a.m. Monday morning, Emilia's 37th day of life, we got our second middle-of-the-night call from the NICU over at Riley. My cell phone rang, and I jumped up out of a deep sleep. I looked over at my nightstand, where I saw the dreaded "Riley NICU" on the caller idea of my cell phone. I quickly answered it and put it on speakerphone for Felicia to hear as well. It was Staci on the other end. Her voice sounded way different. Normally Staci's voice is full of energy, enthusiasm, and excitement. This time she was speaking a little more quietly, reserved, and in almost an apologetic tone. She said, "You know I would never call you guys if I absolutely didn't have to? Emilia's heart rates are jumping all over the place, and you two need to get in here right now!" We were terrified. How could this possibly be happening? We just freaking left there less than five hours before this, and Staci had told us that everything was absolutely fine. We sprang out of bed faster than I've ever done anything in my life. We both threw on the first clothes we could find, brushed our teeth, and ran to the car to make the 12-minute drive back from our house to Riley's Hospital for Children. The silence in the car all the way to the hospital felt eerily similar to the drive we made back on March 15th, the day that Emilia was born. It is that feeling that you know you are in for something awful, and you are bracing your mind to prepare for what you are about to walk into. We got to the hospital, parked in the garage, got through security, and made our way up to the NICU as fast as we could.

We walked into the hospital room to find a lot of doctors and nurses talking and discussing things. A general rule of thumb, you never want to enter into a hospital room with a bunch of doctors and nurses in there discussing things around a patient. If that happens to you someday for any reason, I feel deep empathy for what you are going through. Doctors and nurses are some of the greatest people we have in this world, but I'd happily never speak with them again if I had the choice.

The care team immediately briefed us on what was going on and why everything had escalated so quickly. Emilia's traumatic post-op recovery and blood pressure battle the past few days had done far more damage than we could have imagined. The constant flooding of fluids into her body had left her badly bloated and swollen everywhere. An insane amount of fluid had been pumped into her since midday Friday, which was critical to stabilizing her blood pressure over the past few days. Now that her blood pressure had corrected, her next big battle was to get all this fluid back out of her body as it can cause its own set of catastrophic problems. The doctors explained to us that as fluid builds up in the body, excess electrolytes become a big concern. Electrolytes? How in the hell can electrolytes be bad for you? I thought. All I know of electrolytes are Gatorade and all of those new-age waters that have added electrolytes in them to keep us hydrated. Well, it turns out that electrolytes can be extremely harmful to you if you don't expel them from your body! Potassium specifically was our main concern at the moment. Potassium affects the way your heart muscle works. Too much potassium in your system is called hyperkalemia. Hyperkalemia can cause your heart to beat irregularly and, in the worst cases, cause a heart attack. That's what was happening with our sweet Emilia. Her heart rate was going berserk. Unfortunately, there really aren't a lot of treatments to reduce potassium levels in a human body other than our natural form of peeing it out. There was a drug, we were told, that could possibly help a little, but it interacted poorly with some of the extra blood pressure stabilizer drugs Emilia was on. The plan was to take her off of those other drugs (Dobutamine and epi) and put her on this new drug. In the meantime, the only other thing we could do was wait and pray Emilia pees A LOT AND FAST!

The heart was one of the four areas Dr. Osa told me that he monitors closely in preemie babies along with the head, lungs, and belly. Emilia had never had even the tiniest concern with her heart up to this point in her life. We have had a lot of problems with her belly and a few with her lungs, but her heart was always perfect. She had always maintained consistent heart rates between 130-150 BPM for the most part, which was very typical for a baby this size. Over her entire life, she's only had a handful of bradycardia episodes, a slowing of the heart rate, usually to less than 80 BPM for a premature baby. Watching a "Brady" happen and seeing Emilia's monitors pacing along at 135 BPM and then plummeting down to 50 BPM in an instant was terrifying. All the alarms and flashing lights go off, the nurses come running, the parents are sitting there in shock, wondering what the hell just happened. They can happen for a million reasons, Emilia's breathing tube touched something wrong, the baby is trying to poop, etc.

What was going on right now, in this room today, made a Brady episode look like Yao Ming trying to dunk a basketball on an eight-foot rim. Yao is seven feet, four inches tall if you didn't get the reference. Emilia's heart rate was now averaging between 200-220 BPM. That was dramatically higher than her normal rate. There was a new monitor set up in her room called a telemetry machine. Cardiac telemetry is a way to monitor a person's vital signs remotely. A cardiac telemetry unit usually involves overseeing several patient rooms with vital sign monitors that continuously transmit data, such as your heart rate, breathing, and blood pressure, to a nearby location. Basically, Emilia had a new nursing station remotely monitoring her heart rate at all times because of the situation she was in. Not only was her heart beating faster and faster, but it was also skipping beats every once in a while, throwing off the monitoring machines. The potassium was doing some awful things to our baby girl.

Felicia and I were terrified. Worst of all, I could tell Staci was also terrified. The care team decided to put Emilia on the drug that helps with potassium issues and pulled her off some of the extra blood pressure medication. Then it was just a matter of waiting it out and hoping she would pee this all off and quick.

We waited, talked, prayed, waited, talked, and prayed some more. Emilia was peeing, just not fast enough to make an impact yet. Her blood work was sent off and came back with potassium still reading at max levels (literally off the charts). The labs had no idea exactly how much potassium as their tests only go up to a certain level which Emilia was well past.

As Dr. Rescorla was making his morning rounds, he and his team came in to do their normal post-op surgical check on Emilia. I'll never forget what happened next. He looked me dead in the eyes and said in his normal soft and patient tone, "I'm so sorry. It looks like she won't be able to make it through this." "What? What did he just say? Did I just hear him right?" My mind was blown. He just matter of factly said that my daughter was dying, finished his check-up, and then he and his team left the room. I thought, "Did that just happen? Was Emilia actually dying right now?" I was under the impression that we were just in the middle of another challenge, pulling intervention after intervention to keep this marathon going. We had seen 5-10 nurses and doctors in the room up to that point in the morning, and no one had said anything close to what Dr. Rescorla had just said to me.

Looking back and far removed from this moment, I can oddly appreciate the matter of fact-ness in which he shared his assessment as the next hours and days would become a constant tug of war between us and the care team regarding whether we should keep running this marathon or call the race.

Sometimes we just need to be told the truth and not dance around it. It's our old friend, the Stockdale Paradox, again. Deal with the BRUTAL FACTS right in front of you, and don't run away from them. We were facing some brutal facts at this point, and no one else had addressed just how truly brutal they were until Dr. Rescorla walked in and shared his view with Felicia and me. While the brutal facts are crucial to hear and understand, they are called brutal for a reason. I refused to believe what he just said. I put my optimist hat right back on, pretended that was just one person's opinion, and looked over at my daughter and saw that she was still up for the fight and never thought another second about it. We were marching up this hill, and we were going to give it everything we had. That was the one thing I could always count on was Emilia. This was the toughest little girl the world had ever met. Every single thing that was thrown at her, she took, fought, and found a way through. She lived the never-quit brand better than anyone else that has come or is to come in the future. I knew, just by looking at her, that she would never give up this fight on her own. We soldier on!

The doctor that was with us that early morning, I can't remember her name, was completing her weekend shift and talking us through the treatment options before she departed for the day. This doctor obviously knew how bad the situation was and said to Felicia and me, "Is there anything else I can do for you?" I looked back at her and said, "Is it possible for my parents to be here, please?" I was hoping that if this is the end, I would love for my Mom and Dad to be here to actually spend some time with their granddaughter. The doctor looked at me and said, "Let me go check." She came back a few minutes later, before she departed from her shift, and said with a smile, "I talked to the administrators, and they will allow your mom and dad to be bedside with you, Felicia, and Emilia." I was so happy to hear this and thanked her profusely. I couldn't believe that they were going to waive the Covid restrictions and finally let my family in to see my daughter. I immediately picked up my phone, called my mom, and said, "They are going to allow you guys to be with Emilia and us. Wake Dad up and get down here fast." I couldn't wait to have my mom there with me. My mom is my rock. She is always there for my sister and me and selflessly gives to everyone, especially her kids. Besides Emilia, she is the second-best person I know, and I had been really missing having her with me through this crazy journey that my family had been on the past few months. I wanted my parents to be able to freaking hang out with their granddaughter at least once. I couldn't wait for them to get there.

Staci had left and Jessica had replaced her for the day shift. Staci, who was supposed to be off the next five days, told us that she would pick up an extra shift and be back here tonight to watch over Emilia. She truly is amazing. Luckily, we had one of our favorites in Jessica back with us for the day shift. We haven't talked much about Jessica yet in our story, but she is also one of Felicia, Emilia, and my favorite nurses throughout our time in the NICU. Jessica is so patient, kind, and a great listener. She's a Southsider, like myself, and a little closer to Felicia and I's age than Staci, Lori, or any of the other more veteran nurses we've talked about. Jessica felt more like a close friend instead of feeling like a protective big sister. We were so glad she was here with us those last few days with Emilia and will forever be grateful for everything she did for our family.

By this point, Emilia was being put on every kind of pain drug you can imagine. She had a constant morphine drip, AND they were giving her an extra dose of fentanyl every hour or so on top of that to make her more comfortable. She was in some serious pain and it was obvious. Our feisty and flailing little girl from just a few days ago was now having trouble just laying in her isolate.

Mid-morning, Dr. Matori came in to talk about the plan going forward. Dr. Matori is an amazing doctor with a long and accomplished career in neonatology. Unfortunately for her, we were just now really meeting her for the first time in her care of Emilia. Dr. Osa had spoiled us with his amazing care for Emilia and patience with us. He had been our main doctor for the majority of Emilia's stay at Riley up to this point. Unfortunately, his rotation had ended mid-week the previous week, and Dr. Matori was now the main doctor for the next few weeks. The doctors would regularly rotate so they could spend the rest of their time doing research. Dr. Matori and I had maybe one or two brief chats late in the previous week, and then she was off on the weekend when most of the craziness was going on with Emilia. Now she was back on Monday morning and walking into this mess. She approached Felicia as we were standing together, looking over Emilia's isolate while holding her hand. Dr. Matori asked us, "What would you like to do?" It was asked in this weird tone that made it seem like she was hiding the real question she wanted to ask of should we end this battle now or not. "What the hell did she just ask me? Did she just walk in here and subtly ask if I wanted to end my daughter's life?" is all I could think. I looked at Felicia, and she looked back at me with the same bewildered look on her face. I snapped back immediately, "What are you asking? Are you asking us to make a decision right here and now if we are going to take our daughter's life?" She paused, sensing that I was pretty pissed at how she just approached us, and then said, "There comes a time when we are doing things to Emilia and not for Emilia. I wanted to see how long you wanted to keep this fight going and make sure we are on the same page." I was livid by these comments. We had just arrived at the hospital a few hours before after getting woken up in the middle of the night to come quickly because my daughter's life was in imminent danger. We were still in the middle of fighting the fire and trying to save her life in my mind. Some lady that I barely knew walks up to my wife and me and puts us on the spot about taking my daughter's life while subtly implying that we may be inflicting more damage and unnecessary pain on her by wanting to fight for my daughter's life. Let me be clear; no one had told us that Emilia was a lost cause at this point. Everyone I saw had talked to up to this point was still fighting for her, and that conversation had never been brought up. Before those shocking comments from Dr. Rescorla just a few hours prior, the thought of this battle being over for Emilia hadn't even come into my mind.

For the first time since we had arrived at Riley, I had lost my ability to be empathetic and encouraging toward our care team. I started to get really angry and argumentative with Dr. Matori. I was reverting back to the old Chris (impatient, selfish, and aggressive) that I had been trying so hard to break free from these past few weeks. I had been trying so hard to never get angry, to listen, to be encouraging, to ask questions, and to be empathetic toward them. I couldn't do it anymore with Dr. Matori. She caught me with the wrong approach on the wrong day, and I couldn't stop myself. The room got a little awkward and uncomfortable as I barked back at her and raised my voice. Felicia was looking at me with those, "Just stop!" eyes. I'd seen those eyes many times before from Felicia when I had accidentally embarrassed her by taking things too far in a confrontation. I could see Jessica in the background trying to look anywhere else but at me as if to say, "I don't want to be a part of this." It was uncomfortable for all of us in the room. After the tension died down a little, we decided to talk things over as a family, and Dr. Matori left the room to give us space. If Dr. Matori is reading this someday, I apologize for my behavior that morning. That was one of the worst days of my life, and I can and SHOULD do better. No one deserves to be treated that way. I know you were only trying to do what was best for my daughter based on your countless years of experience as a neonatologist. Thank you for all you did for us.

Time Out (Zach Morris interrupting here again)...

Reminder to always be open to receiving omens in life - this very morning, I received an omen (this morning being in the present as I sat down to write this section of the book before work). Remember the omens that we talked about a while back from the book *The Alchemist*? The ones that show that the universe works in mysterious ways if we are open to receiving the signs when they come. With that in mind, the daily scripture reflection I just read this morning (as of me writing in the present) from a devotional that I read every day called *Trusting God Day by Day* was titled "Love Keeps No Records of Wrongs." These things don't just happen for no reason. I read this reflection immediately after completing this section on Dr. Matori, and it hit me hard. The passage talks about not holding grudges, truly forgiving and forgetting, and wiping the slate clean. I think most of us can forgive, but we often find it hard to forget. I'm trying really hard in my life these days to start each morning off as if it were a fresh start as best as I can. Wiping the slate clean and doing everything I can to live for today and be the best person I can be at this moment. I owe it to Emilia to approach my life in this way each and every day. I owe it to her to try to be the dad that she deserves and will be proud of to look down upon from heaven. I want her to tell all of her friends up there, because I know she has a million, "That's my dad and I'm so proud of him!" as she is smiling and watching me live my life in her honor. Reading the omens, God and Emilia really want me to forgive and forget what happened between Dr. Matori and me. That is what I'm doing by finishing this paragraph. I will never think of how she made me feel or how I behaved at that moment again. I will learn from it and try to be better today. Clean slate every day!

Time In...

After our fiery exchange with Dr. Matori was over and she had left the room, my parents called me from the lobby security saying, "They won't let us up to see you all." I went and found the nurses and doctors to see if they could help and get them past security so they could get up to the 4th floor and the NICU. They made a bunch of calls and came back a few minutes later with a really sad look on their faces and said, "We are so sorry. Apparently, there was a mix-up, and the hospital has reversed what that doctor told you previously. Your parents will not be allowed up here due to the ongoing Covid restrictions. We are so sorry this happened." I could tell how disappointed, embarrassed, and frustrated they were, having to deliver this message at this fragile time in our life. It wasn't worth getting pissed off about as I had a lot more things on my mind to worry about. All I could think was, "Are you freaking kidding me?" I went downstairs to the lobby to tell my Mom and Dad in person that they can't come up after all. My parents had just woken up and scrambled down to the hospital in the early morning because their granddaughter was about to potentially pass away, and they were stopped at the door. I felt so bad for them. My mom, not wanting to worry me or show her frustration, patiently hugged me, cried with me for a minute, and told me it was okay for me to get back up there and that they would just wait down in the common area for as long as they could. I went back up to the NICU.

Once I got back into the room, it was just Emilia, Felicia, and I alone in our room for the first time in a long time. The nurses and doctors were giving us space to talk amongst ourselves and figure out a plan of attack going forward. Felicia and I read stories and dad jokes to Emilia, cried a lot, held her hand, anxiously waited for a really full and wet diaper, and prayed for a miracle. Even with the conversation with Dr. Rescorla and Dr. Matori earlier in the day, my mind was still focused on finishing this race and getting our daughter over this heartbreak hill and back to running downhill with the wind at our backs again. However, I needed to figure out how Felicia was feeling as well so we could make this decision on what to do next together.

One of the things I've always been so excited about regarding fatherhood was becoming a sports dad. Sports mean a lot to me and have, in a lot of ways, helped to shape and mold me into the person I am today. Learning how to challenge yourself, problem solve, lead, endure, socialize, win, lose, prevail, fail, compete, and so many other incredible life lessons and skills are learned while out on the playing field. Practice, training, competing, and hanging out afterward are some of my happiest memories as a kid and still as an adult (I still play competitive sports all the time). Because sports have always meant so much to me, it was only natural to one day hope to share my passions with my children. We live a five-minute walk away from an amazing city park called Ellenberger Park here in Indianapolis. I've dreamt so many times about what it would be like to walk down the street with my son or daughter over to the tennis courts at Ellenberger and just have a blast watching them play and learn the game. Ellenberger Park has everything a sports dad could dream about in terms of infrastructure to help their kids figure out what speaks to them in terms of sports. The park has tennis courts, pickleball courts, a baseball diamond, open fields, a football field, a swimming pool, volleyball courts, swing sets, and playgrounds. I'm constantly over at Ellenberger myself playing tennis and pickleball. Every time I see a father and child playing tennis together out there, it just makes me so eager to be able to do that with my own child someday. When I found out we were having a girl, I was so excited. I would get to watch, coach, and encourage the next Serena Williams, I thought. Just kidding, sort of. My first and forever passion will always be tennis. Luckily, tennis is one of those sports where both men and women can thrive. I couldn't wait to get started with Emilia from the moment Felicia told me we were expecting.

On the idea of being a sports dad someday, I have to imagine that one of the hardest things in the world to do is watching your child fail while out on the playing field. I honestly can't imagine (there it is again) what it must be like to watch your child totally fall apart in a game and not be able to step in and stop it. I don't know this feeling yet, but I'd imagine that it would take an act of God the first few times to keep me from running out onto the court to protect and shield little Emilia from the pain and suffering that can come with loss and failure. Kudos to all of you sports parents out there that have to endure watching from the sidelines while your child fails over and over and not falling into a puddle of anxiety and tears.

Well, in this exact moment, watching Emilia struggle mightily and having all of her doctors and nurses tell me to throw in the towel is the closest thing that Emilia and I will ever have to our very own dad/daughter sports moment. After Dr. Matori's blunt comments earlier in the morning, Felicia and I needed to have some serious discussions on the sidelines about how to handle Emilia's care going forward. After we talked for an hour or so about all that was going on, shared our thoughts and feelings, and cried a lot, I told Felicia about the whole sports dad thoughts going in my mind. I told her, "I will never pull my daughter from the game. I won't do that. I can't do that." The consensus that Felicia and I came to after this discussion was that Emilia needs to be the one that tells us with her actions what we do and when. We agreed that we were not going to pull Emilia from the game of life until she made it absolutely clear that we had no other choice. I may have only known Emilia for a few weeks, but I knew our daughter already. She was the product of two of the most stubborn people you will ever meet in this world. We had already watched her overcome and endure so much to this point. She was a remarkable little being that would have made me so proud on any playing field that she chose. I know for a fact that my daughter was never going to be the kid to quit or give up on anything that she did in life, and neither were we.

We made the decision to soldier on and fight right alongside Emilia. A funny thing happens when you decide to fight. You get this overwhelming sense of strength, power, a surge of energy, and renewed optimism. Your mindset might be the single most important ingredient in determining the decisions you make when it comes to enduring traumatic events and hardships in life. Once you commit to endure and see it through, your mind starts to look at all the little things and signs of hope. Alternatively, once you commit to quitting, you look for any excuse to throw in the towel. When you make up your mind, one way or another, you often set the wheels in motion toward that outcome, and the whole universe conspires to help make that come true. That is what

Felicia, Emilia, and I decided in that room on that Monday afternoon. We were going to fight on and give it everything we had!

A few hours later, a mysterious lady in a suit appeared at our room door and slowly opened our door, gently walked into the room, and sheepishly said her name as she introduced herself. She looked like a business lady or something. In the four weeks we had been in the hospital, I don't think I had seen a single person in a suit anywhere or at any time. We certainly had never seen this lady before, so it was pretty confusing what she wanted and why she was walking in on our private moments with our daughter. Hands folded on top of each other and holding them near her belly as if to show us she didn't mean any harm, she said, "I just wanted to stop by and talk with you all a little and see if I can be of any help and get to know you all a little better?" I'm paraphrasing here as I really can't remember her exact words. Felicia and I said something to the effect of, "Nice to meet you," and went back to looking over Emilia and holding her hand. This lady continues to slowly walk toward the isolate and continues to try and make small talk with us for the next minute. At this point, I'm super confused about what is going on. Is she with the medical staff, administration, social work, etc.? We continued to play along and answer her small talk pleasantry questions for the next minute or so until I finally think I figured out who this lady might be. I thought, "Is she a hospice/palliative care person?" I've never been in a situation before where I ever had to interact with a hospice/palliative care worker, so I had no idea what to expect or what they actually do. I did have some experience dealing with the hospice industry a little through my work history. I had at one point worked at a Healthcare Software company that sold technology services into the hospice space occasionally. From this, I knew the lingo, what they did, but I'd never been around an actual hospice person before in action. This was my best guess at this point as to who this lady was. "Holy shit…this is the palliative care person!" I thought. I finally just skipped all the small talk crap with this lady and said, "What is it that you really want to talk to us about?" She saw that I wasn't in the mood and said, "I'm so and so with the palliative care team here at Riley and my job is to help talk you through how you would like to handle Emilia's potential end-of-life situation that we are currently facing. I'm here to help you talk through any questions, guide decisions, understand your options, and make sure that Emilia is as comfortable as possible." Finally, we got to the point! I looked over at Felicia. We both were still dumbfounded at this line of questioning and struggling to understand where all this was coming from. Dr. Matori had just come in a few hours before and basically said that Emilia was going to die (in a roundabout way). This lady is coming to help us talk through the process of how Emilia passes away or something.

We were still ready to fight! Remember, we had decided not to pull Emilia out of the game until Emilia said it was time. Felicia and I had just talked about this and had come to the decision that we were comfortable with on how we'd like to proceed for our daughter. We were going to fight! As hard as it was to watch all this from the sidelines, we were going to fight on!

We informed the lady that we weren't talking about this stuff right now. She said she understood and said she would be here if we needed her or had any questions. She slowly backed out of the room as gently as she had slid in the door in the first place, and we never saw her again. Side note, talk about a tough job. I can't imagine (there it is again) what that lady must go through every day. She has to talk to parents about helping their children die. She has to interject herself into the most difficult moment of these people's lives and talk logistics about death and suffering. It is an important conversation but messed up all the same. I feel for her.

With the decision clearly communicated to Emilia's care team that we fight on, we all got back to work on keeping Emilia comfortable, focusing on getting these potassium levels back down, and praying that she pees a lot. My parents ended up staying down in the lobby for most of the rest of the day, and a few of my other family members snuck in there as well to keep them company. There may have been restrictions on who could pass by the front desk to go into the hospital, but no one had told us that they couldn't hang out in the lobby. My parents had found a loophole to at least stay in the building and had invited a few other close family members to join them as they waited. My family is amazing, and I appreciate their willingness to "break the rules" and put themselves at risk in the middle of a pandemic to just be in the same building as us. I would pop down from time to time with some updates or thank them for being there and then head back up to the NICU to be with Emilia and Felicia.

Back in Emilia's room, her diapers were starting to get more and more soiled throughout the day, which was a great sign. Dr. Matori informed us that we were going to try to help Emilia pee even more by giving her some drug called albumin, and then follow that up with what they called a "Lasix Chaser" to try to induce more urination and get the potassium and salt out of her body quicker. Albumin is added to improve intravascular volume, diuresis and natriuresis. Basically, it sucks a lot of liquid volume into the veins. Then the "Lasix Chaser" is applied to make you pee a lot. Lasix is a diuretic that prevents your body from absorbing too much salt. This helps to get more of the salt out of the body as quickly as possible. To sum it up, the albumin would suck all the excess electrolytes (salt and potassium) out of Emilia's body and into her veins, then the Lasix would make her pee it all out, hopefully. This made sense to me and I was down to try anything at this point to help Emilia. The care team got to work and we stood by, waiting for each new lab result indicating if there was a reduction in the potassium and salt levels in her body.

It was hard to find any joy and happiness during this time in our lives, but being together as a family and spending time with each other was pretty amazing. Felicia and I had basically been living separate lives the past 30 days. We really hadn't spent much more than five to ten minutes a day talking in passing at the hospital or right before we went to sleep at night. We had been missing each other a lot. Most importantly, we had been missing being together with our daughter as a family. It was amazing to see firsthand how awesome of a mother Felicia was to Emilia. It reminded me how lucky I was to have each of them in my life. It felt so good to just be able to hold our daughter's hand at the same time, talk about how beautiful she was, read stories, and talk about life as a family together. It felt great to be a family, even if it took the worst scenario imaginable to make that a possibility.

As that long Monday continued to drag on, Emilia seemed like she was on every drug imaginable. There were a thousand lines strung up all around the room. They had to bring in an additional mobile medicine holder to add more space to string up all the new medicine she was on. Jessica's shift ended, and she left after battling the good fight all morning. Our surrogate big sister, Staci, was back for the night shift. Eventually, my parents and family went home and awaited phone calls and texts about what was going on with Emilia whenever we had time to update them. Before my family departed, my grandmother, who is one of the most amazing people in this world, strongly encouraged Felicia and me to get Emilia baptized ASAP. I call my grandmother Big Mama. However, she is actually the farthest thing from big that you could imagine. She really is only maybe 5 foot tall and weighs about 100 pounds (if I had to guess). However, the name Big Mama still fits because she has the strangest ability to intimidate anyone when she speaks because you know she means business. She doesn't mess around. When she strongly recommends something, you do it. My grandmother is one of the most fiercely religious and giving people you will ever meet. She's gone through some incredibly traumatic events in her life and used her strength, trust, values, and faith guided by God and the Catholic Church, to overcome and thrive. She's a role model and an example for the whole family. She knew how important it was for Emilia to be able to receive this holy sacrament, no matter what the outcome, and encouraged us to do so immediately. The thought of baptism honestly hadn't even crossed my mind at that point. In my mind, we were still in the middle of the fight, and I had no intention of leaving this hospital without Emilia. Baptism was always going to happen for Emilia, once she was out of the NICU and back safe and at home. However, back to the Stockdale Paradox, my Grandma was dealing with the brutal facts in front of us, and she could tell that they certainly didn't look overwhelmingly promising. If anyone knows how to see the brutal facts in times of extreme trauma, it is her. She's lived through death, trauma, and pain up close and personal in her life more than anyone probably should in a lifetime (more on that to come later in the story). I appreciated her guidance like I always do and forever will, and I'm really glad she brought this to our attention at this moment. Felicia and I took it under consideration and started discussing it when I returned to the room.

My journey with spirituality, God, and faith up to this point in my life has been casual at best. Yes, I went to a Catholic grade school and high school. Yes, I went to church every weekend as a kid with my mom. Yes, the majority of my family is very religious, and I've been around great role models my whole life that lives their life guided by the teachings of the Catholic Church. However, for whatever reason, it never really guided my everyday life in my own journey. If anything, I had somewhat rebelled against the idea of faith and had sworn off formal religion for most of my adult life. The reasons are many and complicated, so I won't bother getting into that at this point in the story. Don't get me wrong, I've always believed in God, or a higher being, that has helped shape and mold this miraculous world. It is all just too amazing and complex for there not to be some higher power that designed all of this. Most importantly, on religion, Felicia and I have always been on the same page in this area of our marriage, and that is all that really matters to me. Our relationship was in no way shaped by the foundation of organized religion. Felicia grew up Lutheran, and to my knowledge, was never really that into it either. Religion was just not something that was important to either of us.

The only thing Felicia or I have ever had even a remote conflict about regarding religion was whether or not to send our children to a Catholic school or a public school. I was pretty dead set on sending our kids to a Catholic School someday, mainly for the strong community of value-driven people and structure. Felicia was pretty adamant, in her own right, that was NOT going to happen. Felicia is an educator in the Indianapolis Public School system. She was educated in the public school system in San Antonio, where she grew up. She is a steadfast believer in the value of the public education system. She is truly passionate about this topic, and passion usually wins. I always, deep down, knew that I was never going to win this battle with our children someday. To be fair, I really didn't care that much. I just remembered my own education and thought it was pretty good. I figured, if it worked for me, why not our kids? As Daniel Kahneman says in *Thinking Fast and Slow*, "What you see is all there is." This sentiment is how most people live their lives, however, I'm always open to trying anything if someone else is more passionate about it than I am. With that said, education is definitely Felicia's jam, so I'll probably defer to her expertise here. Besides this dispute, which is really more about education than religion, Felicia and I are and have always been on the same page around organized religion. I know someday we certainly had planned to have gotten Emilia baptized, and maybe we would slowly make our way back to a religious community. We both felt it is important for our children to grow up around other families that are good influences and core value-driven people. Religious communities certainly offer that and then some. I'm sure we will make our way back someday.

So, back to the question that Big Mama had posed as she left the hospital around baptism and whether we would get Emilia baptized or not in the coming hours or days? After a little discussion, Felica and I came to the dramatic conclusion of, "Sure...What harm can it do?" I think that statement damn near sums up all religion in a nutshell. If God does truly exist, I certainly wouldn't want my baby to not have a chance to enter the kingdom of heaven because her Mom and Dad were "meh" about formal religion for whatever reason. I mean, what are we really talking about here? It is five minutes with a priest pouring water over Emilia's head and blessing her. On the one hand, we do this small act, and our daughter has the opportunity to live peacefully in whatever heaven is, and we get to be reunited someday. On the other hand, I roll the dice, say this is all bullshit, and have to wait until I die to find out if I was right or not. If I was right, what prize would I get? The answer is literally nothing. I don't even get a chance to be reunited with Emilia. If I was wrong, I get to be without my daughter for eternity, and I get to live with the guilt of knowing that I screwed over the most precious and innocent thing in this world because her daddy is an egomaniac and always has to be right. Well, that wasn't happening. We were getting Emilia baptized! We asked Staci to see if she could coordinate with the social worker to get whatever priest we could ASAP. A few hours later, we heard that the priest was on his way and would be there with us later that night to perform the sacrament of Baptism for Emilia. Thank you, Big Mama, for the gentle nudge and reminder to do this for our child.

As the day went on, Emilia was starting to pee a little more and more. I was praying that the albumin and Lasix chaser were starting to work. Her lab results came back with the potassium actually showing a number and not just "max" anymore. That was a huge improvement and a definite sign of progress. We could see the things that needed to happen were kind of happening, but we still had a long way to go. At this point, we were desperate for any positive news to hold on to, and this provided that. The brutal facts were still that Emilia was incredibly bloated and full of fluid that needed to leave her system ASAP. Her urine was starting to show a little bit of blood in it, which meant that her kidneys were potentially starting to fail. Her heart rate was beating 200+ BPM on a constant, which wasn't good at all. Also, her lungs were starting to slowly denigrate, and the respiratory therapists were in and out all day making tweaks to the vents to keep her oxygenation sats in a somewhat stable fashion.

The normal range you want oxygenation to be at is between 92 - 96% with a patient on a ventilator. When her sats would dip for an extended period of time, the RT's would come in, suction out the vent, adjust Emilia's body positioning, and then maybe turn up the dial on the oxygen machine until she re-stabilized. Once she stabilized, they would slowly dial back the oxygen as much as they could and let Emilia do more and more of the breathing until things acted up again and the whole thing started over. That was the normal process we had witnessed over the past month in this journey. However, that was not the process that was going on at this point. Things were starting to get so bad that Emilia was on 100% oxygen at all times. There weren't a lot of magic tricks the RT's could deploy anymore. At this point, this was all on Emilia to get this under control.

The priest finally arrived and we had Emilia baptized. The rest of that night was spent keeping Emilia comfortable, spending time as a family, praying, crying, and closely monitoring her labs and vitals, looking for any sign of hope to hold onto and propel us forward. Remember, we weren't pulling Emilia from this game. She was going to finish her race on her terms. Felicia and I slept in Emilia's room again at the hospital that night.

The Journals: Day 37

Day 37: 4/20/20

- I love you
- Dad Joke of the Day - what do lawyers wear to courts? Lawsuits. Fun story - your Grandma and Grandpa got to read you a few more Dad Jokes today via FaceTime. That was a cool experience. You loved it.
- Daily Scripture Theme - you can cope with criticism. My Thoughts -
- The 4:45 a.m. phone call. Stacy promised us we were okay to go home and finally get some sleep last night. The past few days had exhausted us and we were back in a good place it seemed. Stacy, whom we trusted like a sister, promised you were good and she had this. We went home to sleep. 4:45 a.m., the phone rings, and it was a doctor saying that your potassium had spiked and your heart was all over the place. They said to get in here as quickly as we can.
- Your Mom and I jumped into action and sped off to the hospital. When we got there...it was chaos. Your heartbeat was everywhere and they were scrambling to correct it. The decision was made to try a few more drugs to counteract and wait and see. They worked, but the damage was done and noticeably visible. Your little body's blood pressure had been so off on Fri and Sat and your kidneys were shutting down and not peeing any of the fluids off. They were failing. Your electrolytes were way off as well. We were all sitting around waiting and praying for you to pee. That was the only way out of this mess. It was all on you, but you were still fighting.
- Dr. Rescorla, the surgeon, came by to check on you and said he unfortunately doesn't think you'll make it and there is nothing they can do. That was the first time I'd heard that from anyone. Dr. Matori agreed. I was terrified.
- The rest of the day we waited and prayed for you to pee. We tried everything we could and you started to pee a little...and then a little more...and then a little more. We had hope.
- By the night, your pee was blood red and slowly declining...but still there. We just wanted to make sure you were comfortable.
- Your Mom and I cried and cried. Your grandma, Grandpa, and family came to wait in the lobby (because they couldn't get it because of coronavirus). Everyone else who had been watching your journey prayed for a miracle to happen.

- Your Mom and I got to spend some reflective time talking about how incredible, strong, and how much you exemplified the "Never Quit" Sears brand. You fought and fought and fought!!! I was so amazed and proud.
- The palliative care lady came by to talk about end of life options...our minds were blown. We couldn't process it. Your vitals had stabilized and we weren't ready to wave the white flag...but deep down we knew.
- This day took everything out of us and it started to become real that we might be losing you.
- We threw a Hail Mary of a blood drug to pull fluid into your veins then immediately followed by lasik to help you pee it out...it failed.
- We had you baptized to help you be closer to God if something were to happen.
- We finally went to sleep at the hospital (barely...it was another long night)
- I love you

The NICU Marathon: Making The Call (Day 38)

As we awoke on Tuesday morning at the hospital, things were still bad and only getting worse. Emilia was peeing less and less frequently, while at the same time, what was coming out was getting more and more bloody. Her oxygenation sats were slowly dipping lower and lower, this time down into the low to mid 80's on average. Her heart rate was slowly increasing higher and higher. We were now averaging 210-220 BPM. Worst of all, you could tell she was in so much pain. It hurt so much to look at our beautiful little girl, fighting for every breath. That was probably one of the hardest things I've ever had to do is sit back and let Emilia fight this fight by herself. Everything in me wanted to step in and save her somehow. I wanted to take all this pain and suffering away from her. We had committed to letting Emilia finish her own race, and we weren't about to back out now no matter how much we selfishly wanted to step in. This wasn't our race; this was Emilia's and hers alone. I knew my daughter at this point. Even though I never got to hear her express her thoughts with words, I knew that she would have told me, "Let me fight! I'm never going to give up!" She is the strongest and most courageous little baby in the world, and I had to let her keep trying.

Jessica was our day nurse again on this Tuesday morning. She was doing everything she could to keep Emilia as comfortable as possible. Jessica could give her an extra bit of fentanyl every hour or so and that would always help

Emilia relax just a little bit. You could tell she would start to get restless toward the end of each hour and the pain would become more unbearable until she got her next little boost from the fentanyl. It was so hard to watch.

Around noon, Felicia and I called our parents and told them that this wasn't looking great for our sweet little Emilia. Since they couldn't be in the room, we thought it would be a good opportunity to let them Facetime with Emilia to say their goodbyes should something happen to her. We called them up, turned the camera onto Emilia, and stepped back to let them have their moments with her. What an unimaginable, awful thing to have to do. I can't imagine (there it is again) how that must have felt for my parents to have to Facetime your grandchild, that you've never really met in person, to say goodbye. This world can be so cruel sometimes.

My mom asked me if we would turn the NicView Camera back on so that family and friends could have their own chance to spend some time with Emilia to say their own goodbyes. We had made the decision a few days ago to keep the NicView camera off as there was a lot of constant activity going on in the room that wouldn't be allowed to be shown. There were needles being poked, surgeons, doctors, nurses, RT's, X-ray techs, etc. We didn't want people to have to see all of that, and we also didn't want the camera in the care team's way. With nothing really going on at this point other than pain management and an occasional blood draw, we thought this would be a great time to turn it back on and let everyone tune back in one last time to watch Emilia's final few moments here on Earth and say their goodbyes. We let our parents know that we were turning it back on and to spread the word to anyone that wanted to watch Emilia. I don't know how many people were able to see Emilia that day to say their goodbyes, but THANK YOU if you did! Emilia felt everyone's immense love and support throughout her short life. I know that you all would've wished to be there in person, but at least we had this moment virtually.

The doctors and nurses mostly left us to ourselves the rest of this Tuesday morning and afternoon. As a matter of fact, they actually shut the door to our room to give us some more privacy as a family. In the NICU, no door is ever allowed to be shut unless situations like this were occurring. You never really have any true privacy at all. However, with the door shut, Felicia and I spent the whole afternoon reading to Emilia, telling her stories and dad jokes, crying with each other, and holding her hand. It almost felt like we were in our own home with privacy and space for once. Around 3 p.m., Dr. Matori came into the room and asked us again, "How would you like to proceed? Remember, there comes a time when we are no longer doing things for Emilia, and we start to do things to Emilia. We'll do whatever you advise us you would like to do, but we do need to know if we are continuing on fighting and doing medical interventions or just pain management." Felicia and I huddled and came back with the same message, "We are going to let Emilia keep fighting and pray for a miracle." We told Dr. Matori that we wanted to wait until the blood work came back during the 7 a.m. blood draw the next morning to see what was going on with all the things we were closely monitoring. Based on how those results came back and whether they were trending up or down, we would reevaluate at that time. Dr. Matori replied, "That's fine. However, if that is the case and you are asking us to resume medical interventions, one of you two has to leave the hospital. Resuming "normal" medical interventions would fall under our Covid policies of only one parent allowed in the building at a time. Is this what you are asking us to do?" I couldn't believe she was saying this to us at this moment. I thought, "Are you kidding me? Our daughter is slowly dying in front of us, and they are trying to say that Felicia and I have to choose who stays here by themselves to be with her?" That almost made me want to puke when I finally processed what she was saying at that moment in my mind. "Fine," I thought. We'll play by the rules if this is how they want to treat us at this moment. We all knew what was going on with Emilia and how dire of a situation we were all watching, but if they wanted to play this power move at this moment, so be it. We were exhausted, and I didn't have any more fight in me to give to Dr. Matori. Felicia and I agreed that she would go home, take a shower, get cleaned up, eat a little food, and come back to the hospital in a few hours and relieve me so I could go home and do the same. We would figure out the next steps after that. So Felicia went home, and I took the first shift alone with Emilia.

There I was, back all alone in the room again with just Emilia and me. This time, unlike the past few weeks, it was different. There was silence. No nurses or doctors were coming in and out. The door was closed. The monitor alarms had been permanently silenced by Jessica because they would have been going off constantly if not. The only sound in the room was the noise coming from Emilia's ventilator helping her to breathe and stay alive. It was so calming to hear. It reminded me that my daughter was still alive and next to me. It was just her and I, the dream team, back together again one more time. We had spent so many days and nights in a similar situation. This was my happy place. It was pretty clear to me that I was at the happiest that I've ever been in my life when I was by my daughter's side and just listening to her breath. She brought me peace, calm, strength, patience, and love. All the things I've struggled with in my life, Emilia unconditionally provided to me in droves.

As I sat there next to her, holding her hand, Jessica and Allison walked in and asked me if I'd like them to do a recording of her heartbeat. I said, "Absolutely!" For the next 20 minutes or so, they turned on the sound to Emilia's heartbeat, so it was playing out loud in the room. They then brought this little heart-shaped recording device out to record and capture the sound of the heartbeat playing in the room. They tried the first recording. We all got silent, turned up the volume in the room, and started the recording. That was the most beautiful noise I've ever heard. It was almost meditative as we listened to the rhythmic heartbeat fill the room with sound. It was just Emilia's heartbeat for like three minutes in the quiet of her hospital room. I don't think I've ever listened to a human heartbeat for more than a few seconds at any point in my life. It was an incredible sound to hear and made all the better, knowing it was coming from my daughter's body. It gave me chills. The girls finished the recording and tried to play it back on the little heart-shaped device to check the sound quality. It didn't work great that first time. We tried it again. Same result. They weren't pleased yet and wanted one more try. We tried it again. I was totally happy to have this go on all night because it was such a beautiful noise. The third one worked great. They wrapped the little heart-shaped device up in a box and handed it to me to take home. I'm so grateful to have this memory and memento for the rest of my life. I haven't had the courage to listen to it again yet, as I write this nine months later. I know I will someday, but I have no idea when. However, it is reassuring just knowing that it is there at all when I'm ready.

Felicia returned to the hospital around 6 p.m. that Tuesday night after a few hours back at the house. She was terrified to come back into that room by herself, and rightfully so. Emilia was in a somewhat stable but extremely critical state. Her condition was really bad, but it hadn't worsened all day and was holding steady up to this point. I left the hospital feeling terrible, knowing that I was leaving Felicia with Emilia in this condition. I honestly didn't know when I was going to come back later that night, but I wanted to be back in that room as quickly as I could to relieve Felicia from her stress and anxiety. The plan was for me to go home, eat some food, take a shower, change and pack some clothes for the night. I was planning on being back around 9 p.m. that night. As I got back to our house, turned on the shower, and was about to get in, my phone rang, and it was Felicia. She was in a bit of a panic and said that Emilia's oxygenation levels had suddenly dropped, and her condition was worsening again. She didn't know what to do, was scared, and just wanted me there with them. We talked for a minute about what was going on and what to do going forward. That was the moment that we agreed to officially stop trying for a medical miracle and to just try and keep her pain-free and loved until whatever happened next. Don't get me wrong, I was still hoping for a miracle and that Emilia would somehow turn this all around. I wasn't ready to pull her out of the game, but we also didn't want her to be poked and prodded anymore. Most importantly, we wanted to be back together as a family again. We made the quick decision to tell Dr. Matori and the nurses that we were back on the palliative care plan so I could officially be back in the hospital with Felicia and Emilia. I took a quick shower, changed, and rushed back to the hospital to be with Emilia and Felicia.

I got back around 7 p.m. Her new nurse was Raina. Raina was also one of our favorite nurses that we had grown to love over our time at Riley. I was glad to see a familiar face there with Felicia when I got back. There we sat, just waiting for the sign to call the game for Emilia. It was a crazy change of mindset from when I left the hospital just a few hours earlier. Remember, up until that phone call from Felicia after I got home, we were still mentally in this fight until the end. That meant seeking and clinging to any sign of hope we could hold onto that would give us a chance for the miracle we were praying for. Just an hour later, with our mindset now in pain management mode, the exact opposite was now occurring. We had given up and were now looking for any sign that there was no miracle to be had and a signal to end our daughter's pain once and for all. It's amazing how much mindset plays a part in how we approach life. When we look for signs of hope and progress, we find them. When we look for signs of pain and negativity, we find those as well. That tiny little change in mindset and outlook on life means so much.

This reminded me of a book I read months after this moment on my healing journey called A Man's Search for Meaning by Viktor Frankel. This book is a personal story of Dr. Frankel's time in a Nazi concentration camp and his survival through that incredibly traumatic event and test of human endurance. One of the things I remember most from that book is Viktor discussing when everyone knew that a fellow camp prisoner wouldn't last another day. Frankl stated (paraphrasing), "Whenever they saw a prisoner refusing to leave the barracks in the morning, pull out their cherished cigarettes that they had been holding on to for months, light up and actually smoke it...they knew that guy wouldn't make it through the day. That person had resigned to knowing their fate and had made the decision to throw in the towel on this life. Once their mind was made up, the fight was over, and they were a goner." This is the other side of the equation of the Stockdale Paradox. You can't lose hope. You always have to believe that you will make it out of there. Once you stop believing, it is over before you know it. Felicia and I knew it was over at this very moment in our own journey. This race was not going to have a happy ending. When our mindset flipped and looking for an out, it was just a matter of time before we would find the signs we were looking for to make the call to end this battle.

Things had gone from bad to worse; Emilia was no longer peeing at all. It had been hours since we had even a drip of new urine output out of the catheter. Her oxygenation levels were now in the high 70's to low 80's at all times. Her heart was beating faster and faster; it was now hovering around 220 BPM at most times. Worst of all, the pain meds were wearing off faster and faster, and she would only get a few minutes of relief, and then we'd have to wait until the next hour before she could get any more. Emilia still wasn't ready to give up her fight; she hadn't lit that proverbial last cigarette, if you will, and thrown in the towel. My baby girl would never do that, no matter how much damage she was inflicting on herself. If there was one thing that I knew about her, she was never going to quit! This is why she is my hero. She fought to the bitter end and never gave up.

It is hard to describe waiting for the "right" moment to end your own child's life. I don't really even know if there are words that can truly even describe it, to be honest. This is a situation that I would never wish upon my worst enemy. Trying to balance our own selfish needs to want to end our child's pain and suffering and respecting Emilia's right to fight is a no-win situation. No matter when or how we made this decision, I was acutely aware that this is something that would haunt me until the day I die. If we do this too early, what if we were missing out on a miracle and a shot at a lifetime together? If we wait too long, what if she suffered needlessly? There were only two things for sure in my mind at this point.

1. This decision has to fall on me.
2. There could be no second-guessing once the decision was made.

The first point was a necessity to protect Felicia. Felicia is notoriously bad at making on-the-spot decisions in a no-stress situation, let alone this. We discussed this earlier in the book, so no need to reinforce it with more examples here. Just know that there was no way I was going to put her in this situation that would torment her for the rest of her life. This decision had to fall on me to protect my wife from herself.

The second point was to protect myself. I could play this scenario out in my mind for eternity. Did I do the right thing for my daughter, or could we have had just a little bit longer together? I didn't want the rest of my life to be haunted by this thought, so I put my faith in God that when I saw the right signs and decided to act, that this was meant to be, and the timing was right. I was willing and able to own this for my family.

A few hours later, around 10 p.m., Emilia's oxygenation levels dropped into the 60's and held there for what seemed like forever, though probably only really a few minutes. The RT's and nurses rushed in to try and see what they could do to help, and nothing was working to get her oxygenation levels back up even to the high 70's and low 80's where they had for the past few hours. Something wasn't right. I was watching my daughter slowly slip away. I realized that even if we did make it to the morning lab results, at what cost would this be to Emilia? I couldn't bear to watch her suffer anymore. After watching them all do everything they could for Emilia to help her breathe more comfortably over the next few minutes, I jumped out of my seat and said, "Stop! it's time!" I looked over at Felicia and said, "It's time!" I could see the sadness on her face. I could see her wanting to scream "NO!" to me. I looked at her again and said emphatically, "This is it!" She reluctantly agreed and nodded. We turned to Raina and the other people and the room and said, "We're ready." We asked them to call the priest back to give Emilia her final rights and help us prepare to send our baby off to watch over us in heaven.

The Journals: Day 38

Day 38: 4/21/20

- I love you
- Daily Scripture Theme - do something outrageous. My Thoughts - I read this to you out loud and recorded it with you, your mom, and I all together. It was hard not to break down...I thought this might be the last day overall. God is outrageous and full of surprises. Every minute with you has been full of surprises and joys. Highs and Lows. Love and Optimism. Scared and Afraid. It's been a journey I will never forget and has profoundly changed everything about me to the core (more on this to come).
- By the time the morning came, your vitals had stabilized from the traumas of the past few days but the damage had clearly been done. Your Mom and I had a decision to make. It is the hardest conversation I've ever even thought to consider.
- You are still fighting and going strong...you won't ever quit. You make me so proud. You truly live your life fearless and will never throw in the towel. Because of this...I can't make that decision for you. Your mom and I talked and agreed to let you fight on until it was absolutely clear what the outcome would be. Even if there was

the smallest glimmer of hope, I knew I would never forgive myself if I didn't let you go for it.

- That's what we are learning parenting is...we can't do it for you. We have to watch you succeed or fail on your own while we sit on the sidelines cheering you on with love and unwavering support. I can't / we can't make this decision for you. We won't let you be in pain, but we also won't stop you if you want to keep trying.

- We made the call to fight on today, but we have a plan in place for tomorrow if you aren't showing progress in the next 24 hours. I won't watch you be in pain that can't be overcome.

- Today was such a blessing. It's a BEAUTIFUL spring day outside. God...you would love to be out in the yard playing or us the tennis courts with teaching you new shots. There are so many things that I'll never get to do, but TODAY is a blessing I won't forgot.

- Your mom and I spent all day holding your hand, reading you books, talking about the amazing times we have so far already. Crying about what we'll miss most and what we won't be able to see you achieve. It was memories that I will never forgot and YOU gave this to us. We love you so much.

- How many people get to spend time with their daughter and do all the last things they've dreamed. That is a unique experience I'll cherish forever.

- Your Mom and I will be fine, but forever changed.

- No one can take away this time we've had. I will MAKE SURE the world knows your story and doesn't forget. I VOW this to you here and now.

- I will live my live in your honor. I will demonstrate your strength in how you lived and fought. I will never give up just like you showed me how to do. They are going to need to drag me from the field beaten and bloodied and not on my own power before they would see me quit. You'll never see anything unleashed like the new me now that it is infused with your strength and power.

- As I'm writing this... 5:16 p.m. alarm and Sia Alive went off. I got to play it again for you and tell you how strong and powerful you are. If you have a miracle in you...let's see it baby. Tonight is the night!!!

- Your Mom and I Face-Timed your immediate family members so they could say a personal goodbye. You are so loved. My biggest regret is not being able to show you off to the whole family and rest of the world. You literally would have taken this world by storm with your strength and adorable cuteness.

- So...the hospital won't let us all stay together tonight because of coronavirus rules as you are "stable" and even though we are planning on tomorrow making the call based off of your lab results overnight. Really sucks. I wanted your mom to be the one that guides you through the night, and we'll all be back together again in the morning.... assuming you don't make a miraculous turn around. I sent her home to get cleaned up and grab some clothes for tomorrow. I'm here all alone with you and this is the most scared I think I've ever been. I'm worried that I won't be able here with you if you pass away from something bad happening tonight. I'm also terrified that I won't be there physically to support you and your mom through this. This is really cruel. It makes me want to puke.
- I have to sit at home, alone, and without you, on most likely, the last night of your life. What kind of a sick world is this.
- The Nurses have muted all the noises in your room as your sats are so low and would be triggering alarms all the time. Those quiet times with just you and I in your room are magical. No nurses, de-sats, binging or bonging, blood gases, labs, x-rays, poking or prodding, etc. Just you, me, the ventilator breathing noise, and my thoughts. I'll cherish those times forever. I need more peaceful time like this is my life of just sitting and thinking.
- Your nurses made a little heartbeat recording for us all to remember you should you pass away. Listening to your heartbeat in a quiet room is so relaxing.
- I love you

The NICU Marathon: Emilia Finishes Her Race (Day 38/39)

I have NO IDEA how to start writing this last section of Emilia's marathon here on Earth. A big part of me doesn't want to even put these final words on paper because it will mean she really is gone. How does one summon the courage to write about watching their child's slow journey toward taking their last breath on this Earth? I have been writing (and crying) every morning for the past few months as I've sat in my office and typed Emilia's story and the impact she has had on our family's life. We've written about all the ups and downs, highs and lows, and everything in between. It has been a crazy journey to write and share. Personally, I have gotten really good at keeping a rhythm of writing Emilia's story every day for the past few months. It was nice to feel that connection with her on some level each day as I sat down to type in my office. Every morning, I look up at the photos of Emilia on the wall in my office, read her little "Though She Be but Little She is Fierce" picture next to her name, see the painting that I had gotten made for Felicia for Mother's Day of a mommy and daddy lion holding their little lioness cub, and just start typing away. Last week was Christmas and New Year's Eve of 2020. They were another pair of our first holidays that we are missing without Emilia by our side this year. We've gone through Easter, Mother's Day, Father's Day, Halloween, Thanksgiving, and now Christmas and New Year's without our precious daughter by our side. The only one we have left now is her 1st birthday on March 15, 2021. I have no idea how we are going to get through that one. I hope to present to her this finished first draft manuscript of her life and story as my gift to her. On Christmas Eve, I wrote the last few pages of the previous section about how we got to this last day of Emilia's marathon. Something inside of me screamed to stop and take a break. I can't get this wrong! I can't fail my daughter while sharing her finest hour and a memory that is single-handedly the worst AND best night of my life. I had to get my mind right and finish this race in a way that was representative of the strength and courage that my daughter displayed at the end of her race. So, I took the week off to get my thoughts together, to reflect on this past year, to think about Emilia, and to get ready to finish this race strong. Here I sit, back in my office, and ready to cry my eyes out as I write these last beautiful 7 hours of my daughter's life. I hope and pray that I make her proud.

Here we go…

After I jumped up and said, "It's time," around 10 p.m., on April 21st, the next few hours were a bit of a blur of activity and special moments that I will do my best to share here with you all. Our nurse, Raina, and the Nurse Practitioner for the night got to work getting everything prepared for us to spend our last few hours together as a family. The plan was to have one last kangaroo session with Emilia, and then we would extubate her and slowly let her pass away. I don't know what I thought was going to happen; I've never been a part of a situation like this in my life. I've never seen a person slowly expire before, let alone my daughter. I remember asking Raina and the NP to walk us through what normally happens with other patients once they've been extubated. They said, "It's hard to tell as every patient is different, but usually within 30 minutes to an hour, the patient slowly passes away until their heart stops beating." In my mind, I envisioned this was going to be a tender few hours of hugging, crying, holding, and loving our daughter. Then, they would extubate her, and within 15 to 30 minutes, it would all be over, and Emilia would finally be pain-free and in a better place. I couldn't have been more wrong. Little did I know that I was about to witness, over the next 7 hours of my life, what would come to be the most beautiful and courageous acts of strength, love, and endurance than I could ever imagine in my wildest dreams from both my wife and daughter. This was truly a night that will redefine all of our lives forevermore.

Raina, the RT's, and NP's got the room rearranged to pull the recliner over near the isolate, moved all of Emilia's strings, medicine, IV bags, and ventilator tubes around to make sure Emilia would still have the support of the respirator and pain relief while we held her. We asked for them to call the priest again to come back and administer Emilia's final rights. They made the call and we were told he would be there in a few hours. Around 11:15 p.m., I reached into Emilia's isolate to pick up my daughter and cradle her in my arms for what would be the last time while she was alive. I slowly handed her over to Felicia, who was waiting to receive her in the recliner to begin their final kangaroo session together. Remember all the times we had previously talked about the magical and legendary kangaroo sessions earlier of Felicia and Emilia? Those two were handmade for each other by God to snuggle together. They just fit together like a perfect lock and a key set made in heaven. It had been since right before Emilia's last unexpected surgery that Felicia and Emilia had conducted their last kangaroo session. Emilia's body had been in such a critical and traumatic state for the past five days that it had made taking her out of her isolate a huge risk that we weren't willing to take. Here we were. Their final kangaroo was all set to begin.

After we got Emilia all situated and comfortable in Felicia's arms, I sat down next to them on a tiny stool and held Emilia's hand as Felicia cradled her to her chest. The nurses all left the room to give us some private time. We cried and cried and cried some more. We read Emilia the daily scripture reflection from our Trusting God Day by Day book and cried some more. I read her a few more jokes out of my "Dad Jokes" book...and cried some more. Then, all of a sudden, Emilia's oxygenation sats started to rebound from the mid-60's up to the high 70's and low 80's. She was breathing a little easier again on her own. For the first time in days, Emilia looked like she was finally at peace in her mother's arms, and it was helping her to feel and breathe better. She had been stuck in that isolate, swollen, in pain, and on her back for days. Being where she belonged, back in her mother's arms, provided much-needed relief for her. Felicia looked at me and said something like, "See? This is working. We don't have to do this!" As much as I wanted to believe that, we both knew that wasn't true. I so wish that had been true. I wish more than anything in the world that we could stop this process of saying goodbye to our daughter that we had already set in motion. There is nothing more in this world than I would have wanted than to believe that. Sadly, that was not the case.

It did feel better to know that Emilia's suffering had been lessened. All she ever really needed was her mom's love and support in this world. The love that those two shared as they held each other was so powerful that I'm not surprised it could have generated that kind of lift to Emilia's body and spirits. We sat there for the next few hours crying and holding Emilia until around 1 a.m., when the priest eventually knocked on the door. He sat down next to our recliner to pray with us and administer Emilia's final rights. He was such a kind, old man. I remember writing in my journal that I don't understand how these doctors, nurses, and priests do this stuff. How could walking into a room with so much emotion, love, pain, sadness, gratitude, and despair be their regular Tuesday night? This is life-defining, once-in-a-lifetime stuff for 99% of this world. For these saints, this is their every day. I can't imagine (there it is again) being a witness to an event like this and the feelings and emotions they must experience.

The priest left, and we spent the next 15 minutes again by ourselves in the room with Emilia. Around 1:30 a.m., I got up and walked out of the room to call for Raina to let her know we were ready. The NP, Raina, and RT's came back into the room to begin the extubating process. After a few minutes, they had removed Emilia's ventilation tubes, taken off the tape of her face, and wheeled back her ventilator jet. For the first time since Emilia had been born, she was breathing air without a tube, and we could finally see our daughter's whole face without all that equipment. She was so beautiful. Felicia held Emilia tighter against her chest, and we began to wait for whenever the moment would come when Emilia took her last breath. I looked up at the NP and asked, "How long again can she breathe without the vent?" She said, "It depends. Could be minutes or an hour even." I thought, "AN HOUR? How is that even possible?" Raina and the NP left us alone again in the room and said they would be right outside and to ask for them if we needed anything or had any questions. Of course, I had questions. "How will we know when she has passed?" They said that they would come in and check her heartbeat and let us know. We cried and cried. Felicia held Emilia tight to her chest, and I stroked her tiny little hand. Emilia looked so peaceful and happy in her mother's arms. About 30 minutes later, I got up and went to the door to grab Raina. "Is she gone?" I asked. The NP came in and checked Emilia's heartbeat. Still 100 BPM. What? "My daughter is the strongest person I've ever met. How is she doing this?" I was baffled. She and Felicia were radiating strength back and forth, and neither one wanted to let go. The NP left the room, and I went back to hold Emilia's hand on the stool next to the recliner that Felicia was in. I sat there for another 20 minutes holding Emilia's hand and then got back up to go call for Raina and the NP. They came back in, "Still 80 BPM," she said. I couldn't help but wonder if we were doing the wrong thing. I thought, "How is Emilia doing this? She was so banged up, kidney's failing, heart rate irregular, and oxygenation in the low 60's WITH a breathing tube." I truly couldn't comprehend what I was witnessing. I went over to the other side of the room, grabbed the couch, and slid it right next to the recliner to give myself an easier way to see Emilia and hold her little hand. Around 3 a.m., almost an hour and a half since we started, I called Raina and the NP in again. She checked her heart rate and said, "Still 50 BPM." My daughter is the strongest person I've ever met and the personification of the new family motto, never quit.

Meanwhile, watching Felicia, I understood where Emilia got her strength and endurance. Felicia had been sitting in this recliner for 5 hours straight, clutching Emilia to her chest since we began this process back at 10 p.m. the night before. Felicia was showing the true definition of never quit as well in her actions. She was never going to let Emilia go. Their combined strength was incredible to watch. As for me, I started to slowly drift off to sleep, holding my daughter's hand from the couch. I don't know how or why. My body just gave out from exhaustion from the past few days of not eating well, the stress, and lack of sleep. I really can't explain it. I just collapsed. It is crystal clear where Emilia gets her real strength and endurance from..., and it isn't me. Felicia never blinked an eye through this entire process. She held on to our daughter with every bit of strength she had left to be there for Emilia and make her last few moments here on Earth peaceful and pain-free. Maybe part of me knew that my partner in life had this part of our journey. That is what partnerships are for, after all. We have to compliment each other with our own strengths and weaknesses. I was able to use my powers of quick action and decision-making to bear the mental brunt of owning that I'm the one that set us down this path that we are at in this exact moment. Felicia was using her superpowers of endurance, strength, and focus to step in and be the nurturing rock that Emilia needs as she leaves this world. Maybe, that is why my brain let me shut down for a few minutes because I knew my partner had my back and was there for our child.

Around 5:10 a.m., seven long hours after this final leg of our marathon began, a gentle tap on my shoulder woke me as I laid on the couch next to Felicia and Emilia's recliner. I sprung up from the couch, literally not even knowing that I had fallen asleep. Felicia had woken me up and let me know that Emilia's heart had officially stopped, and she had passed. The NP and Raina were sitting in front of Felicia's recliner after they had just checked to confirm. It was finally over. Emilia's marathon had come to an end, and she had truly gone out in the style and grace that only a baby that was born into a thunderstorm and had grown up overnight could have shown. From the moment that Emilia first entered this world, she faced incredible odds of even surviving her first few minutes, let alone 39 days. Every obstacle, challenge, and setback that was thrown at her spurred her on. Nothing was going to stop her, and she was never going to quit or give up on her marathon and shot at life. She was crossing that finish line on her own terms. As I looked at her peaceful little body being held by her mother at this moment, I could never have been a more proud father. Not too many people get to meet their hero in life. Luckily for me, I just had, and I'll never forget what I just witnessed. Speaking of heroes, Felicia had sat in that recliner, holding our daughter and doing the unthinkable of watching her child's life slowly fade away for 7 hours straight. It's remarkable what the love of a child can allow a human being to endure. Felicia is my hero as well. I will be forever grateful that she took on the heavy load of this final journey with our daughter and was there for her in ways I could never have come close to achieving.

For the first time in 39 days, a sense of calm and peace filled the room. It was a bizarre feeling, given what we had all just gone through. Deep down, I knew that I had just witnessed a miracle of some sort that I will never be able to truly describe. Watching Emilia and Felicia's last kangaroo session is the stuff of legends. I'm surrounded by two of the strongest women that have ever lived, and I couldn't have been more proud that I got the privilege to be in their lives in some capacity. We had all been through so much since this journey began on March 15th, and I know that each member of this family gave everything they could to try to stay together for a chance to live as a family in this world. No one on Team Sears held anything back. There were absolutely ZERO regrets; only love and peace filled my mind as this epic journey concluded.

The Journals: Day 39

Day 39: 4/22/20

- I LOVE YOU SO MUCH!!!
- Dad Joke of the Day - What happens when you get hit by a rental car…it hertz.
- Daily Scripture Theme - "there's peace in no." My Thoughts - Your Mom and I read this to you while she was holding you during your final hours. I think the biggest thing I can take from this is our decision to end your battle. We said no to you and there is peace in

that. Some might question our decision, but they aren't your parents. They didn't see who you were and what was going on with you. They didn't see your pain, discomfort, and struggles to come in the future even if you did miraculously make it through all of this. We said no to you in the most selfless act I've ever made in my life. I knew you wouldn't quit (which is why I love you so much and you are my role model…more on that to come).

- I don't even know where to begin today as so many things happened.
- Let's start with 10:30 p.m. on 4/21. Your mom and I were together with a few of your nurses who were looking after you. I don't know what changed but your blood pressure started dropping a little and then your oxygenation started sating WAY lower than it ever has before and you were on 100% oxygen. I don't know what had changed because the whole day you were so stable in your extremely critical state. We were hoping and praying you could maintain until 4 a.m. the next day for your lab tests to see if your kidneys had started to recover…. we never made it.
- I'm not sure why (and I don't think I'll ever really know) but I jumped up and said it's time when your oxygenation sats dropped so low in the 60's for over a minute. It was kind of out of nowhere but I think my dad instincts just kicked in and said I can't let you keep doing this to yourself. From there, it was all a blur.
- Around 11:15 I picked you up out of your isolate and carried you over to your mother waiting in a chair to kangaroo with you. It was incredibly emotional and we cried forever it felt like. The care team left us alone all together and we just sat there thinking about you, talking about your life, reading you some dad jokes, reading the daily scripture and discussing, etc.
- You started to do so well on your vitals…you just needed your mother.
- You 2 looked so perfect together…like you were literally made for each other. I can't even describe what I'm saying. It was like a lock and a key. It just all fit so perfectly together.
- For the first time in 5 days, it started to look like you and I could see you were comfortable. You were so tired and exhausted from them poking you all the time for IV's and blood gases. You just wanted your mom and to rest. It was so clear.
- Around 1:00 a.m., the chaplain came in to read you your final blessings. He was the same old guy from the night before for the baptism. He was sweet and kind. I have no idea how these people do what they do.

- Around 1:30 a.m. we called in Reyna, the NP, and the RT to extubate you while your mom was holding you. We were all ready to send you to a better place where you could be pain free, grow, and heal.
- They extubated you…. we cried and cried. Your mom kept holding you tightly and I held your little hand. The Nurse Practitioner told us it might be minutes to an hour for you to pass.
- Again, you looked so peaceful being held by your mom and we could finally see your full face again without all the tubes and tape. I could tell you were happy.
- After about 30 minutes, I walked out of the room to go talk to the nurses as I had no idea what was going on…were you alive, gone, etc.????
- The nurses came in to check your heartbeat…you were still around 100 BPM. I was dumbfounded. How could this be? How could my little girl be so strong? Was I doing the right thing? This was so confusing.
- Another 20 minutes pass and we still hadn't heard anything. I called in a nurse again. 80 BPM now. Oh my god…why did we not talk about this before. We were told an hour max. Are you really THIS strong??? Was this the right decision???
- Around 3 a.m. I couldn't keep my eyes open any longer. I feel asleep holding your hand on a couch I had pulled up to be next to you and your mom. You were still holding strong. The nurse came in again and I was awoken. Still 50 BPM.
- I'm so exhausted. I haven't slept for days, hadn't eaten, I was out of energy…I fell asleep next to you and your mother.
- Finally - Around 5:10 a.m. I get a tap on my shoulder from your mom and I spring out of my slumber. The nurses are finally let us know your heart stopped beating. Over 4 HOURS after we extubated you. In that moment the decision we made couldn't have been clearer. YOU WOULD HAVE NEVER GIVEN UP NO MATTER WHAT THE CONSEQUENCES. We had made the right call for you as you were too strong to give up yourself. It was the hardest thing I've ever had to be a part of.
- While hard, it was so beautiful to watch. I've never been more at peace in my life than looking at you and being held closely by your mother and seeing you at ease. You had gone through hell the past 5 days and this finally gave you some relief.
- I have NO idea how your mom did what she did. She sat in a chair for 7+ hours holding you so tightly and never moved. Here's something to know about your mom…she normally pees like every hour. It's

always drove me crazy. She didn't today. I know where you get your strength and endurance from. It certainly isn't the little bitch that passed out on a couch. It is your mother...you 2 are both my role models. I'm glad she was there to share that moment with you.

- Reyna came in as we got cleaned up and she dressed you up in a gown and we took a few photos.
- You looked beautiful and at the same time you looked like you had just endured so much. Another reminder that we were making the right decision.
- We cleaned up the room and packed up. What a surreal moment. This had been our home for 35 days. We had stuff everywhere. It felt like we were packing up our house.
- I walked all of our things to the car with a little red wagon. As I walked through the hospital alone and passed the guards we saw every day...they said..." going home??? Congratulations!" I didn't know what to say. I just nodded and kept walking. I can't remember if I was embarrassed, scared, tired, or what. It was just so weird.
- I walked back in to the room, grabbed your mom who was holding you by the window, kissed you goodbye, and got the hell out of that place. While I loved our time at Riley, I couldn't take being there another second. Reyna offered to make us some mementos and we said we'd come by tomorrow to pick them up.
- Driving home - I called my mom and told her your story. It is so clear that I'm going to spendthrift rest of my life living up to you.
- We got home in a daze...everything was blurry and crazy. We were so tired. WE SLEPT.
- We woke up around 12 and cried and cried together over how much we missed you.
- We pretty much spent the rest of the day on and off crying all the time.
- Eventually I thought to myself, this isn't how you would want us to live. Emilia wouldn't live this way. Emilia just DID. When she was confronted with an obstacle...you just kept on going and didn't think twice about it. Emilia would keep on pushing through.
- I made your mom watch my stupid DarrenDaily. I thought...this is so dumb for me to care about these things but it turned out to be a great message. Ironically it was about how to keep on fighting in times of crisis. It was like you made the video for us. 1 step at a time...1 step at a time.
- I got us up and cleaned up. Forced us to eat. We then made a vow to finish your book and live every day like Emilia would.

- We walked outside…it was the most amazing spring day. You were shining down on us telling us it was okay.
- YOU ARE MY ROLE MODEL!!!!
- Your Mom and I opened up the most expensive and special bottle of wine we owned and had been saving for 8 years. It was incredible. We talked about you and all of the things we loved and missed. I told your mom that I've always struggled my whole life to understand my WHY. I've always been talented and successful but it was empty. It was just me forcing myself to do it for I have no idea. That has always bugged me. I then read a book, ironically during your ICU stay, that had talked about knowing your why and how important that is as motivation to develop new habits that will compound overtime to make an impact on yourself. One of the things they discussed was know you're WHY. The example they gave was why would you cross a tightrope to a burning skyscraper to save what was on the other side. When you know that…you know your why. Before I met you, I had no why. That is what I've been missing my whole life. Knowing what you've survived and went through and how you would never quit…you gave me the example that I will live the rest of my life by to honor your name. YOU ARE MY WHY. Being your role model and living up to your strength will make it so easy for me to do what I need to do to better my life for myself and our family. It will Never be a struggle to muster up the courage or strength to do the stuff I hate because how could I let you down. All I have to think is what would Quinn do…and it is so easy.
- Your mom and I took a walk together. We agreed to call this our "Emilia Walk" that we would take every night and talk to each other about you, life, etc.
- NO ONE WILL EVER FORGET YOU…I WILL NOT LET THAT HAPPEN.
- We told the world of your passing on Facebook. It was painful but I'm glad we did. We told your story and it was beautiful.
- We were flooded with condolences and sadness. It is funny when people say I'm so sorry for your loss. The truth is, don't feel sorry for me at all. It was an honor to know my hero and role model in this physical world for 37 days. I'm not sure how you can change that saying but I'll try to remember that the rest of my life.
- We finally slept.
- I LOVE YOU SO MUCH

The NICU Marathon: After the Race and Heading Home

I've never personally run in a real sanctioned marathon or half marathon in my life; however, I've watched Felicia do it many times and know the drill of the race finishing process well. Once the runners cross the finish line and they stop running, it's like their bodies and minds realize all the trauma and pain of what they just went through, and they just want to give out. They stumble to grab a drink, pick up a banana, and go to the section near the finish line with all the friends and families waiting. They take a few photos to document their experience for memories, put their medal around their neck as a souvenir, and just sit on the ground and start thinking about what the hell just happened and how much their body and mind just endured. Eventually, they snap out of that post-race fog and slowly start to come back to reality. They realize they need to go find and grab all their stuff, somehow stumble to the car, and head home to take a nap, eat, or whatever they need to recover.

That's exactly what I felt after the longest night of my life had finally ended.

Raina cleaned up Emilia, put her in a little white dress that people donate for situations like this, offered to take some photos, and put together a few keepsakes in a box for us to take home. Felicia and I held our lifeless child in our arms as Raina captured a final few photos for us to have together as a family. Felicia kept cradling Emilia as I cleaned up all the stuff in our room. We had been living in this place for 39 days, so there was a lot to clean up. All the cards, mementos that the nurses save and turn into little crafts, blankets, clothes, pillows, etc., needed to be packed up. I packed everything into one of the little red wagon carts that Riley Hospital for Children has everywhere and headed to the parking garage to load up the car. At Riley's, usually, whenever you see a family with their wagon packed and leaving the hospital, it is a joyous occasion. It is something to be celebrated as you take all your stuff in that little red wagon, walk through the lobby, and out to your car in the garage. I had dreamt about this day since the moment we arrived, but obviously, we were missing the most important part of what I had hoped to walk out of Riley with. Never in my wildest dreams did I think that I would be leaving that building without my daughter someday. It had never really occurred to me as a possibility before this exact moment.

As I walked by the front desk in the lobby, I passed by one of the security guards that I had become something of good acquaintances with at this point. He was a strong, middle-aged, black man that engaged me often in dialogue beyond the normal security screening after he had seen me come through a few times wearing my NICU badge during his shift a few weeks back. As I was making my way through the metal detector one day, he shared, "Just so you know, I once had a son in the NICU long ago as well. It was a bad situation. I mean BAD! I'm happy to report that he is 30 years old and doing great. There's hope." From that moment on, I made it a point to stop and say hi whenever I saw him working the security entrance as he was such a nice guy. On this day, he happened to be working the front security in the lobby and saw me walking by with my cart full of all of our stuff. He looked at me with a smile and said, "Going home? That's great news!" I didn't have the heart to tell him what had just happened less than 30 minutes prior to this upstairs in our hospital room. I just smiled slightly back, put my head down, staring at the floor, and kept walking on my way to the garage. That one hurt a lot.

I unloaded all the stuff into the car and headed back to our room up on 4 West. As I walked in, Felicia was still holding and rocking Emilia as she stared out the window in our room. I asked her if she was ready to go? She told me she didn't want to leave without Emilia. She wouldn't let her go. Eventually, we placed Emilia back in her isolate wearing the little white dress that the nurses had put her in after they got her cleaned up. We stared at her and held her hand for another five to ten minutes, and asked Raina, "What do we do now?" Raina said we could leave her in this room, and they would call our funeral home and arrange for her to be picked up. That is what we did.

Eventually, Felicia and I reluctantly left our once lively but now empty NICU room, with our daughter lying peacefully in her isolate, wearing her little white dress. It was about 7 a.m. at this point. We headed down the elevator and toward the parking garage, got in our cars (we had driven separately the night before because we had planned to still switch out again), and for the last time, rolled out of the Riley parking garage. This was not the way I planned to leave this place. On my drive home, I called my mom to give her an update, share the story of Emilia's incredible final few hours, and how much strength she showed us all. I cried my eyes out again the entire drive home as I listened to my mom and recapped the whole previous night. We got into our house, threw all the stuff on our table in the breakfast nook, stumbled to our bedroom, and collapsed into our bed.

AuthorHouse™
1663 Liberty Drive
Bloomington, IN 47403
www.authorhouse.com
Phone: 833-262-8899

Published by AuthorHouse 08/19/2021

ISBN: 978-1-6655-3528-1 (sc)
ISBN: 978-1-6655-3527-4 (e)

Library of Congress Control Number: 2021916986

Editor - Tonya Fahari
Cover Illustrator - Rafael Caro

Print information available on the last page.

This book is printed on acid-free paper.

I CAN'T IMAGINE

EMILIA QUINN SEARS
AND CHRIS SEARS

authorHOUSE

PART II

Chris' Story

CHAPTER 4

The Atomic Bomb Theory (Days 39 – 121)

When we lost Emilia, it was like a metaphorical atomic bomb went off in our world. Everything changed in an instant, and our current reality was blown to pieces before our eyes. The entire life plan Felicia and I had been working toward for the past 15 years since we met came to a crashing halt; it evaporated into thin air during one seven-hour marathon kangaroo session that resulted in our daughter taking her last breath here on Earth. For the past 39 days, we had been living life on the edge. We were teetering between the life we had carefully planned and the harsh reality of the life that we had been dealt. I would never allow myself to think of an alternate reality where Emilia wasn't with us in this world. How could I? That would be violating an important part of the Stockdale Paradox by giving up the crucial element of unwavering hope that we will always prevail and make it home someday. We had been solely focused on keeping our dreams alive and getting our daughter home safe and sound up until this point. Every ounce of energy was dedicated to this goal. Long gone were the carefree days of that last dinner with friends, on March 13th, where we were smiling and laughing, planning baby showers and nurseries, and talking about baby playdates with all of our friends' newborns that were sure to be Emilia's besties. We had been holding on to the rails for dear life and doing everything to maintain the life Felicia and I had painstakingly dreamed, designed, and been building together since we started dating back in 2006 at Purdue University. Those dreams were to be filled with healthy and happy children, thriving careers, family, travel, and exploration. Unfortunately, in an instant, that reality vanished and no longer existed.

What do you do when your world is suddenly blown up, and you are left staring at the rubble that was your previous hopes and dreams? This is a position and a question I could never have imagined (there it is again) pondering 39 days before April 22nd, 2020. However, this was our new reality, like it or not. After we lost Emilia, and after the dust settled on all the immediate post-death activities, like funerals, picking out headstones, hosting family in town, etc., Felicia and I both sought professional counseling to help us make sense of all that we had been experiencing. In one of my session's with my therapist, Loretta, months removed from Emilia's final heroic days and hours and after countless hours of thought, reflection, writing, and reading, I started to layout to her a theory that I had been working on in my head that I was beginning to call my Atomic Bomb Theory. The Atomic Bomb Theory was my answer to the question, "What do you do after your whole world, all your hopes and dreams, and life as you know it, is blown up in an instant?" It was as follows...

Atomic Bomb Theory - When an atomic bomb falls on your city and everything you know is gone in an instant, what do you do next after the fog lifts and you snap back to reality while coming to terms with what just actually occurred in your life? It is at this moment that I believe you have four paths in which you can take your life following the aftermath of the blast. All are valid. None are wrong. While we didn't have the power to choose what happened to us, I believe we do still have the power to choose where we go from here, what actions we take, and what world we want to recreate from the ashes of our misery and pain. The Atomic Bomb Theory was my way of taking back control and choosing how I wanted to live my new, unwanted, and unplanned life.

The four paths of life following the blast were as follows:

Option 1 - Sit in the rubble and stay locked in that moment forever.

Your city was destroyed, and you are resigned to this reality for the rest of eternity. This is your fate and where you belong. Who you were no longer exists, and you don't have any strength or fight left in you to try to rebuild in any way, shape, or form. You want nothing more than to just sit in the rubble, think of all you have lost, and slowly let your spirit leave this Earth.

Option 2 - Run away.

Abandon the ruins of your destroyed city and go seek a new life where nobody knows your name, your story, what you've been through, and what you've seen. Lock away the memories deep down inside and hope to never have to address them again as you try to pretend your past didn't happen.

Option 3 - Rebuild the old city. FAST.

As soon as you come back to reality and the daze has worn off, scramble to put all the pieces of your previous world back together again as quickly as you can. Rebuild your old life from memory as quickly as possible. Remember where all the old buildings were, what they looked like, how the streets were planned out, etc. Replant the same trees, parks, and flowers. Try everything you can to restore order or what you knew as order the day before that bomb destroyed your city out of nowhere. Get your life back and pick back up from exactly where you left off before the blast.

Option 4 - Think, Reflect, Imagine and Rebuild a Whole New World.

Sit in the rubble of your previous life. Process what had just happened. Use as much time as necessary to think, reflect, and embrace what just happened to you. Use this pain and suffering that you did not ask for, nor want, as a blank canvas in front of you to redefine your life in a way that you never knew could exist before. Take the lessons and use them to reimagine a whole new world that you never thought was possible, given the constraints of your previous life and paradigms before the blast hit. When ready, get to work on building your new city with the purpose and clarity that was missing in your previous existence.

IMPORTANT NOTE FOR ALL OPTIONS – No matter which option you choose, we always have to remember that a new path was/is built on destruction, death, pain, and suffering. You will never escape that the blast happened, destroyed your whole city, and left it in pieces. At the end of the day, your new world and its foundation will be built on the ashes of your previous life, no matter what path you choose. Think of it as the ground that the twin towers once stood on in New York City. If you lived through that, you would never forget what stood there before September 11th, 2001. You'll never be able to look at that piece of real estate the same way when you see what it has become today. Sure, we rebuilt an even bigger and better building in its place, but survivors will never forget what used to stand on that hallowed ground and all the memories, pain, and suffering that terrible day and tragedy brought on their lives. Over time, people far removed from the original event will have some vague idea of what happened prior to this new building's construction, but that memory won't be the same. Survivors of a tragedy, on the other hand, will never forget what stood in that space before and how this new building came to be in existence. Such is the circle of life. Our whole world, in some ways, is built on other's pain and suffering, and we don't even realize it most of the time.

After Emilia passed away and the metaphorical atomic bomb exploded in our lives, everything inside of me wanted to go with option two and abandon my old world behind and start a new one elsewhere. I wanted to run away as fast and as far as I could. I wanted to take Felicia, pack up our stuff, go somewhere for an indefinite period of time, and be on an island far away from our previous lives where no one knew us. I wanted so badly to just leave the rubble behind, run away, and never come back until I was mentally ready to take on this cruel world again. I begged Felicia to do this with me, or at least to let me do it myself if she didn't want to come. I didn't want to be around people that we knew and who knew what had happened to our family. I didn't want to have to talk about my daughter and explain why she wasn't with us anymore. I didn't want to have to respond to all the love, support, gifts, donations, and cards that were being sent by people to our door every day. I didn't want to answer the phone, respond to texts, Facebook messages, etc. I JUST WANTED TO BE LEFT ALONE!

As I'm writing this, I noticed all the I's in these past few sentences. Clearly, I was being selfish and only thinking of what I needed. What I really needed to do was to remember what this was all about, Emilia! I needed to remember all the strength, courage, and fight she showed us all during her short life. I needed to prove to her that I could be half the person that she was and the dad that she would be proud to point out to her friends in heaven as they looked down on us. I remember writing this short little poem, if you want to call it that, in my journal the day after we lost Emilia that I called "Never Quit."

Never Quit: We have to keep moving for you...

- It's so hard to get out of bed...what would Emilia do?
- It's so hard to eat...what would Emilia do?

- It's so hard to respond to all the messages from friends and family... what would Emilia do?
- I don't want to write...what would Emilia do?
- I don't want to work out...what would Emilia do?
- I don't want to call the funeral home and cemetery...what would Emilia do?
- I don't want to update the world on your next steps...what would Emilia do?
- I don't want to answer the phone...what would Emilia do?
- It's so easy to just give up. How did you not give up? How were you so strong? How were you able to endure what you did? Why couldn't I protect you. How could I stop you from trying?
- I wrote.
- I ate
- Your Mom and I took a walk.
- I answered messages.
- I updated the world.
- I took care of the funeral stuff.
- We kept moving for you

I still look at this poem every morning before I sit down to write, and it is just as powerful now as it was when I first wrote it. It always takes me back to that feeling of nothingness that I felt when we got home from the hospital after Emilia's final hours. It reminds me of all the pain that Emilia endured, that Felicia and I endured, and the pain of loss that we continue to endure today. Most importantly, it reminds me of my why. It gives me the motivation and desire to keep fighting every single day and to go about my life with the never-quit attitude that I watched my daughter personify in all that she did while on this Earth. In the few days and weeks after Emilia's passing, I didn't know which path my new life was going to take me at this moment. The only thing I definitely ruled out was option one (sit and die) pretty quickly. I wasn't going to let this pain we had been dealt beat my family and me. I didn't want this to define who we were for the rest of our lives.

After weeks and months of forcing myself to just keep moving for my daughter and remembering my why, the path forward ultimately found me. That path forward would become Option four, reimagining my world and rebuilding bigger and better than ever before with purpose and Emilia by my side. I was going to take this pain and suffering that we had been given and use this as an opportunity for growth and "bouncing forward," as Sheryl Sandberg says in her book, Option B, about her own personal tragedy. Luckily for me, I am

Emilia Quinn Sears and Chris Sears

blessed to have an amazingly generous employer, Salesforce, that provided me with up to six months of full paid bereavement leave. Their generosity allowed me the time I needed to process what had just happened to my family, discover the truths and the lessons that I was seeking to uncover, and provide the chance to redefine my life and lay the foundation to begin to build my new city. I don't know that the second half of this story would even have been possible had Salesforce not given me this opportunity and time away from the grind of daily work and life to stop, reflect, and process what had just happened to myself and my family. I don't know that this book would even exist without their support and compassion. Oftentimes, I feel like most of us are forced into option three (scramble to put all the pieces back in place) by necessity. Life doesn't stop for most of us, and we feel like we don't even have the chance to take option four. I was blessed to have this time, and I was going to do everything I could not to squander it for myself and my daughter. I didn't know how or what that actually meant, but I was going to do everything I could to figure that out.

So, I set out on a journey that began a few days after my daughter's death and which I'm still happily on today. I didn't know where it would take my family and me, and truthfully still don't, but that is what makes life fun. With Emilia powering my thoughts and actions, providing me with the motivation and strength needed, I decided to face this thing head-on and see what kind of new city we could build together.

The next section of our story is a look into how my new city came to be. We'll start with the events immediately following the blast of Emilia's death and the immediate aftermath. From there, we'll wander through the rubble left by the blast together as we come across life lessons and new knowledge that I acquired as I learned, reflected, and tried to begin living my life again. We'll then begin to pour the foundation of the new city that was forged while wandering through the rubble. Finally, we'll finish our story with a tour of the new city and a vision for the future that is currently under construction and rising slowly from the ashes of my previous life.

ATOMIC BOMB THEORY - The Blast and Immediate Aftermath - (Day 39-42)

I want to start this next section of the book with a quote from a book I read along this journey called *Hiroshima* by the author John Hersey. Hiroshima is a story of 6 survivors and their unique personal stories that begin when the literal atom bomb struck their city. The story begins with the day of the blast, follows them throughout the rest of their lives, details how their new post-blast lives took shape, and how this singular event shaped so much of who they would become in dramatically different ways.

At this point in our story, where I had just lost Emilia, I want to particularly focus on a passage here from one of the survivors' experiences immediately after the bomb destroyed the city.

"He was the only person making his way into the city; he met hundreds and hundreds who were fleeing, and every one of them seemed to be hurt in some way. The eyebrows of some were burned off and skin hung from their faces and hands. Others, because of pain, held their arms up as if carrying something in both hands. Some were vomiting as they walked. Many were naked or in shreds of clothing. On some undressed bodies, the burns had made patterns—of undershirt straps and suspenders and, on the skin of some women (since white repelled the heat from the bomb and dark clothes absorbed it and conducted it to the skin), the shapes of flowers they had had on their kimonos. Many, although injured themselves, supported relatives who were worse off. Almost all had their heads bowed, looked straight ahead, were silent, and showed no expression whatsoever."
— John Hersey, <u>Hiroshima</u>

"Almost all had their heads bowed, looked straight ahead, were silent, and showed no expression whatsoever"…

That particular line spoke to me deeply. It reminds me of the nothingness that I felt that morning after we lost Emilia. We had gotten back from the hospital around 7:30 a.m., and our bodies had given out from exhaustion as we crumpled into our bed. We awoke sometime around noon on 4/22/20. Nothingness is the only way I can describe what I felt when Felicia and I awoke in our home that afternoon. Our bodies and minds were exhausted, but that didn't matter. Both of us were silent, and we just sat staring at the wall in our bedroom. We didn't talk to each other or even look at each other. We were both in our own little worlds. I think Felicia was crying, but I honestly don't remember. I don't know what she was thinking about at the time, but I know all I could feel and think was nothingness. Nothing mattered. I had no emotions left to give. I had no idea how to process what just happened or what we experienced. I wasn't hungry. I wasn't tired. I wasn't in pain. I wasn't angry. I wasn't confused. I wasn't anything! I didn't have a single thought or emotion in my mind.

After sitting in bed and staring at the wall for what felt like an hour, my mind briefly switched on, and I decided to turn on the TV in our room. A new show that I had been really excited about for the past few weeks, called The Last Dance, had just aired its first episode that previous Sunday (4/19/20). If you don't know, The Last Dance is a ten-part ESPN documentary about Michael Jordan and the Bulls teams he led to 6 titles back in the 1990s. I had recorded it in hopes of catching some of it at some point in the future but obviously hadn't had a second to think about TV since we had been dealing with so much going on with Emilia and her post-surgery nightmare at the hospital. I decided to start the show. I turned it on and stared at the TV. I don't remember a single word that was said. I don't even remember if I was looking at the TV or not. After about 15 minutes, realizing that I wasn't even aware that the show was playing, I turned the TV off again. Nothingness. I couldn't even find a distraction to put my attention toward. The only thing in my head was nothingness.

Eventually, the one thought that popped into my head was about Emilia. I started to think about all the strength and courage that I had just witnessed from her during her last few hours of life here on this Earth. I thought to myself, "This isn't the way that Emilia would want us to live our lives." I told Felicia that we need to get up and get moving. To where? I have no idea, but I figured we had to do something. I immediately leaned on the habits that I had been trying to do every day back in the NICU to give me some sense of direction. On a normal morning, the first thing I watch is a little five-minute daily mentoring video with this guy named Darren Hardy. That has been something I have done for the past four years. So, I figured I'd watch the DarrenDaily clip and have Felicia watch with me. She wasn't into it, but she sat through it as I played it on my phone while in bed next to her. I don't remember the exact message, but it was something about resilience and how to keep fighting in times of crisis. It is like our Emilia had hand-picked this to be the message we were receiving that morning.

After watching the video, I forced myself to get out of bed, go get cleaned up, and make some food for Felicia and me. Eating is seriously the last thing that I cared about at that moment, but I forced myself to choke something down and tried my best to get Felicia to eat something as well. It was in these first few hours after we awoke that I vowed to finish writing this book for Emilia to tell her story. When we had originally begun our journaling back on March 15th, the idea was to compile all of our daily logs for Emilia's eyes only so she could one day read back through her story and what we had all experienced. I had mentioned to Felicia an idea along the way to one day turn these journals into a book or something for other NICU parents as a guide to help them someday as they embarked on their own journey. However, that idea to turn all the journals into a book was just an idea at this point. The goal was always to get Emilia home and document her journey to share with her when she was old enough to read it. Now that we had lost her, I thought we owed it to her to write this book and tell her story to the world. A story about her strength, courage, fight, and never quit attitude that we had just witnessed. I had no idea how to write a book or what content would be covered in it. I just knew that we had to finish this story for her. I didn't want my daughter's name to be lost to time and only live in her parent's memory. Felicia and I agreed to keep journaling every day about our individual experiences, at least until Emilia's original due date of 7/13/20. We would figure out the next steps with the book after that if it made sense. For now, the goal was just to write to our daughter.

Somehow, a few hours after we awoke, I got Felicia to agree to go take a walk with me outside. With all the sadness and pain we were experiencing, we had forgotten that it was officially spring in Indiana. Springtime is everyone's favorite time of year in the Midwest. The weather is perfect, the plants and flowers are blooming, and the grass is turning green. It was a perfectly sunny and 70-degree day outside on this particular afternoon. These are the kinds of days you dream about in the Midwest, as we only get a handful a year. It really felt like Emilia had a hand in this beautiful weather. She was doing everything she could to keep her parents' spirits up as we grappled with our new reality. Thank you, Emilia!

Felicia and I decided on that walk, just a few hours after losing our daughter, to try our best to take a walk every day around the 5:16 p.m. time frame, which was Emilia's birth time back on 3/15/20. We decided to call this our daily "Emilia Walk." The goal was to get out of the house, talk about our daughter, and remember her presence and importance in our family. I'm happy to say that we were able to successfully keep this daily tradition alive and well for many, many months to come. These nightly walks were hard at first, just like everything was, but they eventually became fundamental to Felicia and me staying connected as a family with our daughter and to each other. A lot of important conversations, sharing, and crying happened on these walks that we will get into later in the story. As for today, this was our first walk, and it was as hard as you can imagine. I don't really remember much at all from this first walk other than the weather and that we made it out of our house and back home somehow.

As we got back to the house and walked up the stairs from our driveway to our patio, I got the idea to open up our favorite and most cherished bottle of wine that we owned from our collection, have a glass at the patio table, enjoy the weather and sunshine, and hopefully talk a little about life and our daughter. Felicia agreed. Opening up this bottle of wine was actually a really big deal. Felicia and I loved wine. Wine was something that had been a big part of a lot of our travels together. Whether it was trips to Napa / Sonoma, Italy, France, Spain, Portugal, and even Canadian Wine Country (Niagara on the Lake, which is amazing if you've never been), wine was always a big part of destinations and experiences that we choose when going on a vacation. We loved exploring vineyards around the world and experiencing their unique wines, cultures, tastes, and traditions. Throughout our travels, we had always brought back a few of our favorite bottles from each location to add to our small private collection. That collection had been steadily growing over the years that we had been together. The more we traveled, the more the wine collection of our favorites from our travels grew. The funny thing is, the wine that we were collecting (in my head) had become off-limits for us to actually consume. Maybe, on truly special occasions, I would let my guard down and Felicia would convince me to open up a particular bottle. It had happened two or three times before over the past decade where I let my guard down and agreed to open up one of these cherished trip souvenirs. The sad thing is that I honestly don't even remember what the event was that was so important now for us to open one of these bottles. The running joke had become that there really is no occasion special enough that would actually get me to open one of these bottles of wine. My aversion to drinking anything in our collection had become almost comical, and Felicia had basically resigned to the fact that we were never going to drink any of them. She was probably right.

These wines represented much more than just wine to me. These wines had become souvenirs of cherished memories that Felicia and I had experienced together. We've had some amazing adventures over the years, traveling all over the place and experiencing the world together. When I looked at these wines, I remembered those precious moments of looking at how happy my wife was when she was exploring a vineyard, talking about new cultures, laughing, and enjoying incredible wine and food. Each bottle and label had its own story of why we bought it, when we bought it, what that vineyard was like, and the tastings and experiences we had shared together. To me, those bottles were truly priceless. How could I ever bring myself to literally drink my priceless memories? It would have to be an event that I would never forget if we were to drink any of them that would equal the value and importance that those wines already meant to me.

Out of all the wines in our collection, one was always at the very top of that pyramid. It was a pinot noir from a vineyard named Lynmar Estates in the Russian River Valley region of Sonoma, CA. That particular trip out to Sonoma was a friend's trip celebrating the 30th birthday of one of my best friends and college roommates, Samir.

Talk about an amazing trip! A group of 8 of us were to take part in this adventure, and we had rented out a secluded house up in the mountains near Santa Rosa to serve as our home base. To get to the house, we had to drive for 20 minutes up a winding mountain road. Every morning we would travel down from our Airbnb rental after a night of hot tubs, food, wine, and friends and head back down to 4-5 wineries to experience all of Napa and Sonoma. We had a great time. One of our trip mates, Sam, had recommended this amazing winery called Lynmar Estates that he visited on a past trip. He said they have some amazing pinot noirs, which just so happen to be Felicia and my favorites, so we couldn't wait to check it out. We all decided to make this one of our stops. We arrived at Lynmar and immediately could tell that the vineyard and ambiance were incredible. It felt very country chic. They had these trails all over the place that you could hike around while taking in the view of the rolling hills of the vineyard or just hang out in their beautiful gardens near the tasting room. Of course, the wine was incredible as well. On this trip, the group had developed a bit of an impromptu tradition of one couple buying a bottle of their favorite wine at each vineyard we visited, and we would all drink it before we left and set out for the next vineyard. So someone bought their favorite wine, and we all spent some time enjoying it while hanging out in their outdoor gardens/drinking area before departing. Before we left, Felicia and I decided we had to buy a bottle of their 2012 pinot noir that we had tried in the tasting room and take home for our collection. We brought it home, and in the cabinet it went, securing the top spot in our hierarchy in the current wine collection (I had ranked our favorite wines in the cabinet in order so we would remember). The Lynmar Pinot Noir had remained the #1 spot for the subsequent six years since that trip, and no wine we had encountered or purchased in any of our travels had come close to topping it at this point.

I share all this to let you know the importance of this wine and this memory to us. If you asked me 39 days before this particular day if I ever thought that wine would actually be drunk someday, I would have emphatically said, "Hell no!" However, today was a day that we had just lost our daughter. Today was a day that I will truly never forget for the rest of my life. Our previous life had been blown to smithereens. The shit that mattered before no longer mattered. Just hours earlier, all I could think of was nothingness as I awoke just a few hours after my daughter had just passed away in my wife's arms. A stupid bottle of wine that mattered so much before meant absolutely nothing to me at all at this point. All that mattered to me was my daughter, my wife, and living in this moment. It's crazy how much life can change in an instant. One day, an item can have so much importance and value, and the next, it is just another random item. Our worldview paradigm had dramatically shifted before our eyes in less than a 24-hour period.

As we sat at the patio table and drank our most cherished bottle of wine from our collection, our minds were still reeling from that marathon kangaroo session in our NICU room at Riley's just 12 hours earlier. The sun was shining down on us, and you could feel the warmth of the beautiful spring afternoon. It really felt like Emilia was there with us, doing everything she could to keep our spirits up. As we sat there, I remember telling Felicia about one of the books I had just finished while we were in the NICU, called *The Compound Effect* by the author Darren Hardy. If you remember back to our time in the NICU before everything went off the rails, this is the book that I was reading next to Emilia when we decided on never-quit as my personal brand. A quick reminder about what this book is about. The compound effect is the accumulation of tiny little actions over time that, if done every day, compound into powerful habits over time that produce magical outcomes that you would have never dreamed possible. It sounds easy in theory, but doing those little daily activities to form lasting habits is really hard. For that reason, so many people miss out on the compound effect that comes after months and years of doing the same little simple actions every day. Darren states that because it is so hard to will yourself to do these little things every day, the only thing that can push you through those hard times when you want to quit is falling back on your why. What is your why? To me, your why is the central reason for your existence. It is your mission, your purpose, your why! Darren says, "Your why is the reason you would walk across a wooden plank between 2 rooftops, without thinking twice, to get to what is waiting on the other side."

I started to share with Felicia the whole "why" concept as we sat on the patio and drank our favorite bottle of wine. The whole idea of your why really stuck with me after I read the book back in the NICU and had made me reflect a lot about my own personal why over the previous few weeks. I went on to tell her that I lived my entire life not really knowing my why until the day I met Emilia. Before Emilia, there was absolutely nothing in my life that would make me walk across two rooftops without at least considering the outcome and trying to find alternatives. I say that lovingly to all the other important people, activities, and things in my life. I had never had anything in my life that would drive me to act without giving it a second thought, let alone risk my life crossing two rooftops on a wooden plank. Upon reflecting further, I told Felicia the fact that I had never had a real why in my life was one of the reasons I felt I had never truly achieved all that I was capable of in life. Don't get me wrong, I've certainly had a lot of success in my life, but it was always achieved out of sheer grit and determination. I lacked the passion and excitement that was needed to stick with anything over a truly long period of sustained effort in order to achieve that exponential growth of the compound effect in my life. Everything that I could point to in my life up to this point was soulless achievements that were driven by what society dictated to me as important. If I had to distill down the essence of my why prior to Emilia, it was my OCD around not letting tasks that I started go unfinished. It would drive me insane, and still does, to see things out of place and not completed. I like order and consistency in life, I guess. Something inside of me would never let me quit until whatever I was working on was finished, no matter how much I hated or loathed what I was doing. Order and consistency...what a boring-ass why! Then, I met Emilia, and now I truly understood what a real why is supposed to be.

I want to make one thing clear. My newfound "why" wasn't just my daughter's existence. My why was striving to be as strong and courageous as she was in the way she lived her short life. Her never-quit attitude and ability to endure provided me an inspiring blueprint to follow on how I should and could live my life as well. If a little baby that was born in a thunderstorm and had every obstacle thrown her way could keep fighting and never give up, I sure as hell could do that each and every day of my life no matter what task I asked myself to take on. I made a vow in my journal on this day that I will do everything I can to spread the story of Emilia Quinn Sears and her enduring courage and strength for the rest of my life. THEY WILL NEVER FORGET YOUR NAME! It is kind of ironic. Most parents are supposed to be their children's role models. I was somehow blessed to have a daughter that was my role model, my hero, and the why powering everything I do for the rest of my life.

We went back inside the house after a few hours of talking and crying on the patio while drinking our previously untouchable Lynmar Estates 2012 pinot noir. The rest of the day was a bit of a blur. We notified the world of our daughter's passing via Facebook and crumpled back into our bed to sleep through our first official night as parents that had lost a child.

We awoke the morning of April 23rd to nothingness again. For 40-ish days, our lives had been pure chaos with constant running to and from the NICU, stressing over our daughter's tenuous situation, managing life, trying to return to work, etc. We had been a blur of activity and action. On this day, everything was quiet in our house; we had nothing to do, no child to tend to, and nothing mattered anymore. Friends and family didn't matter, work didn't matter, and life didn't matter. The only thing that Felicia and I could think about was each other and missing our daughter. This was the morning that I wrote my Never Quit poem inspired by my daughter that I mentioned at the beginning of this chapter. I'll redo it again here because I like it, it inspires me, and why not?

NEVER QUIT
We have to keep moving for you…

- It's so hard to get out of bed…what would Emilia do?
- It's so hard to eat…what would Emilia do?
- It's so hard to respond to all the messages from friends and family… what would Emilia do?
- I don't want to write…what would Emilia do?
- I don't want to work out…what would Emilia do?
- I don't want to call the funeral home and cemetery…what would Emilia do?
- I don't want to update the world on your next steps…what would Emilia do?
- I don't want to answer the phone…what would Emilia do?
- It's so easy to just give up. How did you not give up? How were you so strong? How were you able to endure what you did? Why couldn't I protect you. How could I stop you from trying?
- I wrote.
- I ate
- Your Mom and I took a walk.
- I answered messages.
- I updated the world.
- I took care of the funeral stuff.

We kept moving for you.

Just the small act of getting out of bed, writing this passage in my journal, reading a little bit of a book, and exercising on this day felt like pulling an elephant up a mountain. Every bit of my body wanted to sit motionless in the rubble and destruction that the atomic bomb had left in our lives less than 36 hours prior. I can honestly say the only thing that got me moving on this day was the searing imprint on my mind of my daughter's courage and strength that she had demonstrated to me over her short life (better known as my why). Everything inside of me wanted to give up, lay in bed, stare at the wall, and ask how God could do this to my family? I definitely did all of those things on this day; however, with the help of Emilia, I was eventually able to summon the strength to get up, get changed, and get to work on whatever it was that needed to be done to keep our life moving.

I told Felicia I was heading back over to Riley's Hospital for Children to pick up some of the memorial items that Emilia's nurses had prepared (things like hand molds, feet molds, and the recording they made of her heartbeat). I got in the car and drove back to the place where we had just lost our daughter only 36 hours before. As I pulled into the same garage that we had come and gone from so many times, everything just felt a little different. I wasn't here as a parent to a patient. Now I was just another dude visiting a hospital. This place had felt like our second home before we lost Emilia, and now it made me want to puke at the sight of this parking garage. As I got to the front desk, I asked them to buzz the NICU and let them know that I'm here to pick up the rest of Emilia's things. They said someone would be down shortly. I went over to the big open seating area in the main lobby to wait. As I walked by the security guard station on my way to the lobby sitting area, I saw my old security guard friend, who had been all smiles while wishing me luck a few days before, as I pulled my little red wagon full of stuff out to my car. He didn't realize that I had just cleaned out the hospital room because Emilia had passed away, not because it was her time to go home. I still didn't have the heart to correct him on what was really going on. We exchanged some pleasantries, and I continued over to the lobby area to sit and wait. Jessica, one of Emilia's favorite nurses, came down with the few boxes of things that I was there to pick up. We hugged and she handed me the items. I said thank you and ran out of the building as fast as I could without drawing attention. As I was leaving, my security guard friend said, "I sincerely hope to never see you again." I couldn't agree more with him.

As I was walking back to my car and entered the garage, I ran into the father of another NICU baby that was two doors down from Emilia, almost our entire stay while at Riley. Their family name was the McGrew's. I only know this because every room had the last name on a little plaque outside the door. Even though our families had seen each other in passing every day on the NICU floor, I honestly don't think we had ever said a word to each other. They appeared to be a 30-something couple like Felicia and me that looked like a lot of our other friend couples. Who knows, in another life, maybe we would have actually been friends. Even though we had never spoken a word to each other, they knew of us just like we knew of them. I have no idea what their child's situation was or what had specifically brought them to the NICU, but they were clearly in a serious situation as well and were going to be in the NICU for a long stay, just like us. There was an understood and unspoken bond that united both of our families as we all went through the most trying situation in our lives. Even though we didn't "know" each other, we understood what we were each going through.

As I walked by the father of the McGrew baby in the garage that morning, he saw me carrying these boxes full of mementos. We said, "Hey," and nodded to each other as we passed. That little two-second interaction has stuck in my mind until this day. I often wonder what the McGrew family thought about not seeing the Sears name on the room two doors down after the previous morning? What did they think happened? Did they already know when he saw me that morning? Did their baby survive? I know if I was in his position and our situations had been reversed, I would have been devastated to see him walking out of the parking garage that day, knowing all the pain and suffering he must have been going through at that very moment. I also would have been so thankful that it wasn't my life and circumstances as well. If I had to guess, they probably never gave more than a few seconds of thought. He and his wife probably mentioned it to each other once, saying something along the lines of, "I wonder what happened to the Sears family, and I'm praying for them." That is exactly what I would have done as well. I would have then turned my focus back to my life, said a tiny thank you that it wasn't my family and me, and never given it much of a thought after that.

It's a funny thing about the atomic bomb business; most people don't want to actually sit and imagine what it must be like to experience the atomic bomb that just went off in someone else's world. We are more likely just to be happy that we didn't have to go through something like that in our own lives. We give it maybe 30 seconds of thought, say "I can't imagine," and go back to our lives because that is all that really matters to us. We are the most important people in our own universe and rarely spend any time thinking about others. We leave people to sit in their own rubble and figure out their own problems. I'm not saying that it is wrong or bad. It just is. One of the key discoveries in my own life since losing my daughter is understanding how bad we are at truly empathizing with and understanding one another. How truly selfish we all are in our lives and how little time we spend actually imagining life from another person's perspective. It was a revelation in my life when I realized how much of a selfish jerk I had been, over the course of my own life, toward others going through their own atomic bomb events. We live our lives with the "what you see is all there is" bias, as Daniel Kahneman would say in his book, Thinking Fast and Slow. We stay in our own little bubbles, and we are the center of our own little universes. We can do so much better. We'll touch on this topic more later in the story.

As I returned back home from my trip to Riley's, I walked into the house and told Felicia that I wanted to post on Facebook about Emilia's passing. Felicia was too distraught to even really care and told me to do whatever I wanted. I thought it was important to share our love for Emilia, her fight and courage, and make our universe aware of the atomic blast that had just hit our family. I know that I didn't really want to see anyone, per se, but I didn't want to shun people's thoughts and prayers for Emilia and our family. I wanted to get the word out. The only outlet and forum that I knew to use was Facebook. For all the hate and crap people talk about social networks and how they make society miserable, there is a lot of good that can come from them as well, and this is one of those instances. The last thing in this moment that I wanted to do was to explain to my friends and family over and over again what had happened to our beautiful daughter and relive the nightmare that we were going through each day. This platform gave us the ability to share something deeply personal, give others the chance to let us know they are thinking about and praying for our family, and still give each other the space and privacy that are so important in trying times like this.

Also, in addition to the above, I wanted to reach out and ask our network of friends and family to do us a favor as well to honor our daughter. We asked that in lieu of sending flowers and cards, they donate to raise money for Emilia's care team and all the nurses and doctors back in the NICU at Riley's Hospital for Children. Back when we were still in the NICU and in keeping with rule number two of the NICU of always say thank you, Felicia and I had devised a plan to try and do something special for her care team each and every month that Emilia was in the NICU to keep their spirits up and show our appreciation for all of their tireless work and dedication to our daughter. Unfortunately, we never got an opportunity to even do our first month's gift due to all that happened. We were just in the beginning stages of talking through some ideas when the second surgery hit, and all hell broke loose in our world. I thought this would be a good opportunity to make good on that idea and see if others wanted to help us out to contribute to this goal. In my mind, I was hoping to raise maybe $1,000 or something that Felicia and I could match to get some nice personalized gifts for a few of the nurses on Emilia's care team. That isn't what happened at all. Within hours we had hit $1,000. Within the next few days, $3,000. By the time it was all said and done about a week later, we had raised and were able to contribute over $7,500 to Emilia's care team and the NICU back at Riley. With all the pain and suffering that we were going through, this small act of love and kindness by a lot of our close friends and family really helped provide a sense of joy for Felicia and me. It really felt good to give back to people that meant so much to our family and our daughter. Emilia's care team are mainly the people that ever truly got to know her in person. They had become like family to us, and it felt good to do something small to show our gratitude.

From the $7,500 we raised, we gave $5,000 to the Riley Foundation to use on some ongoing projects for the 4 West side of the NICU. We figured that would cover the broader staff of the NICU that we had some limited interaction with as we didn't have enough to do a personalized gift for the whole staff. With the other $2,500, we bought some special gifts for some of our favorite doctors and nurses that we had talked about in the earlier parts of our story.

For Emily, Staci, and Lori, we bought some new Dansko shoes. I had never heard of Dansko shoes before being in a hospital for 40 straight days, but apparently, they are all the rage amongst the nurses. From what I've been told, they are super comfortable clog-like shoes that help to keep their feet feeling good while they are on them for 12 hours straight each day. Lori, Staci, and Emily all rocked their Dansko's every day with pride, and we had multiple conversations about them during our time in the NICU. These shoes are kind of hard to miss as they look like fancy crocs or something. The crazy thing is that they are super expensive. I couldn't believe it when they first told us how much they were. Felicia and I thought there was no better gift that we could think of than that to show our appreciation. For what it is worth, I think they look hideous, but no one cares about that.

We got Dr. Osa some of his favorite shoes as well, Chuck Taylor Allstars. Dr. Osa is a cool cat. That dude had style and a youthful take on his fashion. Specifically, Felicia and I always marveled at the strong shoe game he displayed every day. He seemed to really love rocking Chuck Taylor's with no shoelaces all the time. I still haven't figured this out yet and probably never will, but doctors are the only ones that wear regular clothes in the hospital. Everyone else is in scrubs, but not the doctors. I never really understood why. Because of this, we got to see a little more of their personalities through the clothes they wore. Dr. Osa clearly had a sense of style all his own. We figured that since he really loved his Chuck Taylor's, we'd help feed his addiction and let him have some fun with a gift card to go buy some more and keep rocking them at the office.

For Raina, Sara, Allison, and Jessica, we got gift cards to a day spa downtown in Indianapolis, so they could go pamper themselves and relax at some point in the future. These nurses work so hard and are so selfless that we thought it was important for them to have some of their own self-care time to rejuvenate. It really felt good to be able to do that for all the nurses and doctors that supported Emilia in her time at Riley. It especially felt great to do something special for some of our favorite people that we will remember for the rest of our lives and who helped give our daughter a chance at life.

Is This What They Mean by a Paradigm Shift?

Back to the ongoing nightmare that was our life. April 23rd was another beautiful spring day, and the grass was beginning to grow faster and faster as it usually does in late April with spring in full swing. I decided I'd try to go and do something I've done 1,000 times before and mow my yard. We have a beautiful yard and property that we are blessed to call our home. It is the reason we bought this house eight years prior. It is so unique and awesome. Felicia and I envisioned a life filled with children playing in our gigantic yard and having a blast. Even though we live close to the downtown area in Indianapolis, our property feels like a park in itself. Our house sits high up on a hill, overlooking a gigantic front yard, with no neighbors to our right or across the street because a creek runs through it all. It is a densely wooded, large, and secluded property that is very rare to have so close to the city. We loved this yard from the moment we looked at the house and put an offer in almost instantly after seeing the place. It was our forever home, and we couldn't wait to start a family here someday. Even though this property is amazing, the landscaping and upkeep is a lot of work and a labor of love that I happily take on each and every spring, summer, and fall. I generally spend at least four hours a week mowing, pulling weeds, hedge trimming, cutting back vines, mulching, etc. It is a lot of work, but I've always done it with some level of joy and satisfaction over the years.

As I fired up the mower, put my AirPods in, and started cutting my backyard, which butts up to the actual neighborhood we live in, I couldn't help but start thinking, "Why the hell am I doing this? This didn't matter at all anymore!"

I had always envisioned Emilia and her siblings playing in this yard. That reality had evaporated when the bomb dropped on us a few days prior. Our future children were the reasons that we bought this home in the first place. They were the reasons that I subconsciously spent so many hours over the years meticulously maintaining the property. This was always all for them, and now that was no longer possible. I started to cry as I mowed my yard. It really hurt.

As I was cutting the back yard, I saw a little girl (maybe around two years old) chasing her little puppy down a sidewalk that comes slightly downhill and dead-ends at our property. Her mother slowly walked behind her with a smile on her face, making sure she didn't hurt herself as she ran downhill on the sidewalk after the puppy. You could see all the joy and happiness on the little girl's face as she chased that tiny puppy and giggled. Behind her, I could see her mother smiling and loving watching her little girl slowly chasing after a puppy and having a blast with these little joys in life. However, as I was mowing my yard and watching this scene from across the street, all I could see was the world that I wanted for myself and Emilia that could never happen now.

Prior to meeting Emilia, I was not a huge baby or kid person. Don't get me wrong, I wanted kids, of course, but I never really found little kids or babies cute and adorable like the rest of the world seemed to. Felicia always made fun of me because, as I mentioned earlier, I could never pass a puppy or dog anywhere in the world without smiling, making a stupid googly-eyed face at it, speaking in baby talk to the dog, and asking the owner if I can pet it. Little known fact, German people apparently don't like strangers to pet their dogs. It is a big no-no over there and a lesson I learned the hard way on one of our trips abroad when some German lady acted like I had just said the f-word in church as I leaned over to try and pet her dog while we were walking out in a town one day. Dogs were adorable to me and always made me smile. I couldn't resist them. Babies, on the other hand...meh. That was until I met Emilia, of course. She was the most beautiful little baby I had ever seen. I swear that I'm not just saying that because I'm her dad. I promise you that if I had an ugly baby, I wouldn't mind expressing that to other people. Of course, I wouldn't say that to my baby or anything, but you get the point. Either way, for some reason, my attitude toward all children and babies had shifted a little bit, and now they all seemed just a little cuter. As this adorable little girl ran down the sidewalk, she reminded me of the life I wouldn't have now but so badly wanted. I somehow cried my way through the rest of the cutting of the yard, put the mower away, and went back into the house.

Felicia and I tried another nightly Emilia walk around 5:16 p.m. These walks were so hard the first few days but also so necessary for each of us in our own way. On this particular night, Felicia and I were walking, and she was uncontrollably crying next to me as we made our way down a street in our neighborhood. You could visibly see and feel the pain, sadness, and suffering in her eyes and face as she walked in the sunlight that early evening. We all know what it is like to walk next to someone that is publicly crying. We feel a little embarrassed and want to do everything we can to make it stop because people will think we are the assholes making our walking buddy cry. Obviously, given the state of our life, Felicia could give two shits what anybody thought of her as she walked by them crying. I doubt she even realized people were passing by her. She was in her own world of sorrow and pain. Probably the last thing on her mind was how random strangers perceived her as we walked. As we passed by neighbor after neighbor on this beautiful spring day, it seemed like the entire damn neighborhood was out for an early evening walk that night. I couldn't help but feel the tiniest bit embarrassed as I could feel the stares we were getting as people passed us, particularly the stares I was getting. I'm sure they were wondering how horrible of a husband I must be to make my wife break down crying as we are walking outside on a beautiful spring day. And to silently walk next to her without even pretending like I cared; I must be a monster. That is all I could think as Felicia's crying continued for the entire 30-minute walk. I didn't dare say anything to her about it, obviously; that would have truly been me being a monster.

That walking experience got me thinking as we returned home and as I was journaling to Emilia. That experience brought me back to something I had learned in one of my favorite books I've ever read, called *The 7 Habits of Highly Effective People* by Dr. Stephen Covey. This book is a classic. One of the things that Dr. Covey talks about in the opening sections of the book is about paradigms and the unique and limited lens through which each person typically views the world. As Daniel Kahneman would say again, "What you see is all there is." Most people typically only view the world through what they know and are pretty closed off from imagining any other scenario other than the obvious ones our societal paradigms are instructing us to see. In order to truly "seek first to understand" anyone else, Dr. Covey encourages us to focus on being open to shifting our paradigms to allow us to be more open to seeing the world through other people's lenses and all the possible scenarios that may be playing out that our lived experiences might not illustrate at first glance. In doing this, we can "seek first to understand before seeking to be understood ourselves," which is habit number five.

Well, talk about a paradigm-shifting experience in my own life. How many people would see a crying woman walking next to a man and assume that the man is an asshole and the woman is a victim that needs saving? I know that is what I would be thinking. I wonder how many people's first thoughts, upon seeing Felicia crying, would be, "That woman probably just lost her daughter tragically two days prior, and this couple is trying their best to keep moving and fighting together." Who would think that? I dare you to find one person you know that wouldn't have judged Felicia and me that day as just a dysfunctional couple that was embarrassing themselves on display for all to see. When what you see is all there is, you are missing a lot in this world. There are endless ways and angles to look at any situation, problem, life event, relationship, etc. All you have to do is stop, listen, and be open to questioning and challenging the world as you know it. This lesson is something that I've tried to take to heart and will try to never forget for the rest of my life.

As we got back from our walk, Felicia's mother and other close family members had arrived at our house from their flight from Texas to be here for the funeral and to support Felicia over the next few days. I was glad they were there so I could shift my focus over to the task of writing Emilia's eulogy that I had agreed to take on. Emilia's funeral would be the following morning, around midday. I was running out of time, and this eulogy needed to be great. I couldn't let her down. It would be my finest honor and duty to tell Emilia's story to the world. You don't get second chances to eulogize your daughter. This wasn't something that I wanted to half-ass because that isn't what Emilia would have done or deserved. Everything she did, she gave it her all. This eulogy had to represent that as well because, at the end of the day, this was about Emilia. This was her story, her life, and her meaning as seen through her father's eyes. It had to be perfect because Emilia was perfect. I don't love public speaking. Who does? However, I wasn't scared of this particular public speaking activity at all. The only thing I was terrified of was not doing a good enough job to explain who Emilia was and how she was the bravest, most courageous, and strong human being I've ever seen with my own eyes.

As I sat down to write, the ideas flooded into my mind. I wanted to say so many things, but I couldn't figure out where to start. I just kept thinking and thinking and thinking, but nothing seemed to be manifesting onto paper that I could use the following day. I started writing a few things, and it just wasn't working for whatever reason. I decided to give myself a break and to start fresh again in the morning during my daily reflection time to really work through all the thoughts swirling in my mind. I went to bed and started dreaming about the eulogy. I started to dream about what I wanted to say and how I would present this speech. I started dreaming about what Emilia would be proud to hear. My mind was swirling as I laid half asleep in my bed. All of a sudden, I wrote the speech in my half-asleep mind. As if out of nowhere, the words came to me, and I knew exactly what I wanted to say. I replayed it in my head over and over and over again, trying to commit it to memory so when I woke up in the morning, I would not forget all the beautiful thoughts that were swirling around in my head as I laid there in the middle of the night. Around 2 a.m. I grew concerned that I wasn't going to remember all of this by the time I awoke, so I sat up, grabbed my phone, opened my Evernote app, and just started typing it all out as fast as I could. I spent the next hour or so hammering away at getting the whole speech out of my mind and into my notes so I could just look at it in the morning to proofread and revise. I was so relieved and glad I did that. I felt that Emilia would be proud of what I had just written, and I was proud to be able to deliver it. I felt at ease and finally was able to go back to sleep.

As I fell back asleep, I began to have a terrifying dream about being back in the NICU. Specifically, it felt like it was a redo of the prior Saturday night when Emilia was being X-rayed, poked and prodded, and administered every drug imaginable as we fought to get her blood pressure stabilized after her last surgery. My dream wasn't that exact scenario, though. It was something a little different. This time, just like before, I was sleeping next to Emilia's isolate as the nurses and doctors kept coming in and out of the dark hospital room where the only light was coming through the door from the hallway. They were all wearing their pandemic full-body PPE uniforms, so I couldn't really see their faces as I cracked open my eyes from the recliner. I would wake up delirious and see them all huddled around Emilia, talking amongst themselves and furiously working on trying to save her. They would leave, I would fall asleep, and the same thing would happen over and over again throughout the night. I swear, it felt like it was so real. It really felt like I was back in the NICU with my daughter in my mind. As I awoke from the dream in a cold sweat, I was kind of panicked. I started to wonder if that was some weird alternate reality, perhaps, one where we didn't make the call to end Emilia's life a few days prior, and I was seeing her suffering play out as what would have been. I had no idea what I had just experienced, but I know it was terrifying and comforting at the same time to feel like I was still with my daughter somewhere in this universe. Maybe it was just the post-traumatic stress from going through what we had just gone through. Who knows?

We woke up the morning of Emilia's funeral. What a surreal sentence to even type. I had only been a father for approximately 40 days, and I was already burying my first child. I've heard a variation of this quote many times in my life before and felt it so true to include here: "Mothers are not supposed to bury their children. It goes against nature. When a mother loses her young, the world slips off its axis and spins out of control. The universe mourns knowing it has gone against the circle of life; children should bury their mothers, not the other way around." This is not how it was supposed to happen.

We got ready to leave for the funeral home for the viewing and service. Even though Emilia was baptized as a Catholic, we couldn't have her funeral in the church because the coronavirus pandemic had literally shut down the church, and no one was allowed in. We also couldn't have more than ten people total at her service at the funeral home either due to the ongoing pandemic. I was actually okay with this one since the last thing I wanted to do was to have to be around a bunch of people at that moment. We live-streamed the funeral so everyone else could tune in if they wanted to say their goodbyes to Emilia and watch the service. Our small group of in-person guests at the funeral home was to be my two grandmothers, my sister, my mom and dad, Felicia's mom, aunt, sister, and cousin Becca. I realize that is actually 11 people, but the funeral home luckily gave us a pass on this one and allowed it.

Felicia and I arrived separately from everyone else so we could have some time alone with our daughter and place a few of her mementos from her hospital room around her casket. As we walked into the large showing room, there was this tiny little casket, surrounded by flowers, about 50 yards away from us at the other wall with a little kneeling bench in front of it. As Felicia and I slowly approached, we both started crying. When we finally made it all the way to her casket, Felicia collapsed onto the little kneeling bench as she stared over Emilia's tiny body. She broke down crying. I don't think she moved from that little kneeling bench for the next 30 minutes or so until the actual service started. This was the first time we had seen Emilia since we had left her with Raina after our last marathon kangaroo session a few nights prior. I placed some mementos around her casket. Emilia's little lioness stuffed animals that had protected her in her hospital room and her little foot and hand moldings laid near her.

After that, I did my best to comfort my wife, who was crying inconsolably as she looked over Emilia's tiny casket. I don't think Felicia knew that I was even next to her at that moment. The two most important women in my life were united again, and that was all that really mattered. After a while, our select family members started to arrive and slowly approached Felicia and me as we stayed by Emilia's casket. They hugged me and knelt next to Felicia, trying to comfort her as she sobbed while never lifting her gaze from our daughter. I stepped back from that whole area and stood next to my sister, who I could tell was afraid to approach Emilia's casket. I'm not the best comforter in this world; it is something I really suck at and wish I could do better. At this moment, I knew Felicia needed far more comforting than my limited skill set could provide, so I stepped back and let her mom take my spot next to her as she knelt. Ironically, this was the first time that most of our closest family members, besides my parents, actually got to look at Emilia in person. I wish they would have gotten to see how beautiful she was without all the battle scars from her last few days, even though she still looked beautiful in her casket as well.

After we all cried, hugged, and comforted Felicia, we took our places for the service. The priest presiding over the service came from my childhood church, St. Mark's, which was situated right next to the funeral home. He gracefully and eloquently delivered Emilia's funeral opening remarks. The whole time he was talking, all I could think about was the eulogy. I wasn't nervous, but I knew that I couldn't mess this up for Emilia. I was more focused on this than probably anything that I've ever done in my life. This is, and will always be, the most important presentation that I will ever give in my life. Usually, I only ever get nervous when I'm speaking publicly about a topic that I didn't know very well, and I feel like I'm thinking the whole time instead of feeling. Luckily for me, there was nothing that I knew better in this world than my daughter and what I had just witnessed the past 40 days as she fought for her life at Riley's Hospital for Children. I only wanted to do my absolute best to make sure everyone in that room knew who Emilia was, how she lived her life, understood why she was my hero, and most importantly, that she never quit on her chance at life. I wanted everyone to know that it was her parents that had to make that call to end her suffering and not Emilia as she fought until her last breath. When the time came, the priest signaled for me to come forward to deliver Emilia's eulogy. I walked up to the podium, grabbed a tissue, and started reading from the speech I had written at 2 a.m. that morning.

I started the speech off by letting everyone know that they shouldn't feel sorry for our family. We didn't want to hear that. We weren't sorry that we got 39 amazing days with our beautiful daughter. If anything, we were blessed that we even got that long together. I truly meant that and still mean that to this day. If you asked me to relive this whole experience all over again, I would do it without hesitation every day for the rest of my life if it means I get to spend another day next to my daughter. I then went on to talk about finding my why in Emilia. The way she lived her life every second of every day is something unforgettable and will always propel me forward in life to do my very best while living for both of us. Finally, I publicly committed to writing and finishing this very book someday so others will know the story of Emilia Quinn Sears, understand her remarkable life, and prevent her name from becoming lost to history as an unknown preemie baby that died during a pandemic without ever getting to meet her family. I finished the speech by reading my journal entry about our final kangaroo session that I had written after witnessing the most incredible expression of love and connection between Emilia and Felicia during Emilia's last night here on Earth. I'm glad I shared that intimate look into our lives publicly with the world. I wanted them to know that Emilia didn't ever give up and that it was her parents who pulled her out of the game. I wanted them to feel what I felt while watching Felicia and Emilia as they held onto each other until her last breath. I wanted everyone to know why I called my daughter my hero and my why.

I finished my speech, returned to my seat, and sat down next to Felicia. She grabbed my hand, and I saw in her eyes that she was proud of what I had just done for our daughter. I was also proud of what I had just done for our daughter. For the first time in my life, after giving a public speech, I don't think I had any doubts about my performance. I felt at ease and almost good about what I had been able to do for my child. It felt good to make sure the world knew who she was in the eyes of her father.

I honestly don't remember much of the rest of the funeral. Felicia read some final remarks of her own. Then we all got up, cried, hugged, and departed for the cemetery to place Emilia in her final resting place. We got to the cemetery, the priest said a few more things, and then a few of our family members read some of their own comments about Emilia. We all cried a little more, hugged again, took a few mementos, and then departed back home to our house.

The only thing I remember about the burial was the relief that this was all finally over and that we had made it through the day. The only experience that I can compare it to was our wedding day in that so much build-up and anxiety led up to the event that it was overwhelming to your emotions. Finally, once the event was over, you could relax and let your guard down a little. However, in the wedding scenario, you're rewarded with an incredible time at the reception with friends and family afterward. In this scenario, the next activity is back to nothingness in a world without your daughter. That tiny moment of relief, though, is how we both felt as we got back into our car and headed home. We felt relieved to be past this moment so we could go back to feeling depressed and sad at home by ourselves, away from the world.

As we got back to our house, our nine guests that were able to attend the funeral came over to share a meal and be there to support Felicia and me. We played some board games with everyone. That was especially meaningful because that is an activity that Felicia and her family loved to do when we were all together. It was the first time in which we did something that had a little bit of joy in it since we lost Emilia, and it felt like we were honoring Emilia a little bit by showing her what family life would have been like maybe someday for her in an alternate universe where we hadn't lost her. We ended that day by taking another nightly Emilia walk together and thinking about our daughter that we had just buried earlier that day.

As we laid down to sleep that night, I had another dream similar to the night before. I was back in the NICU with Emilia as her condition worsened. Once again, I was back in my recliner, fighting off sleep in the middle of the night as nurses and doctors were coming in and out of the room, huddling around Emilia's isolate. This time, the tension in the room was palpable, and the whole scene felt even direr. This time, it felt like Emilia was slipping away, and there weren't any options left for the doctors to medically intervene. I could hear them talking. I was terrified as I watched my daughter slowly slip away, questioning how I can keep letting her do this to herself?

Then, all of a sudden, I sprang up in bed, looked around, and started frantically asking Felicia, "Where's Emilia? Where's Emilia?" I was so confused as to where I even was at the moment. I really thought I was in the hospital room. After a minute or so, I finally snapped out of it and back to reality, realizing that we were at home in our bedroom. Felicia was calmly putting her hand on me, speaking very softly and slowly, and telling me that Emilia is gone and we are at home. I laid back down and tried to fall back asleep as my heart was pounding.

I'm still convinced to this day that those dreams on back-to-back nights were showing me the alternate reality that could have played out if we had chosen NOT to pull Emilia from the game when we did. I'm convinced that this was someone or something showing me that we made the right decision a few days prior. What I was living in my dreams was a visualization of what was in store for my family; another two days of pain and suffering for our daughter as she slowly slipped away. I don't know if alternate realities exist or not, but I truly felt like that is what I was being shown in my dreams.

The Journals: Days 40-42

Day 40: 4/23/20

- I love you
- Dad Joke of the Day: Did you hear about the 2 radios that got married? The reception was fantastic.
- Daily Scripture Theme: Like a Child. My Thoughts - Holy shit. They nailed this one. It was all about how children love unconditionally, try hard, want to experience everything, and how we can model our life this way. Clearly, you are my role model from this day and for the rest of my life. I've learned so much from you. I have my why. I will honor you with living every day the way that you would, with unending love, energy, and fight.
- Is this really only day 2. It feels like 2 months. How is this even possible to have time go this slow?
- We have to keep moving for you.
- It's so hard to get out of bed…what would Emilia do?
- It's so hard to eat…what would Emilia do?
- It's so hard to respond to all the messages from friends and family… what would Emilia do?
- I don't want to write…what would Emilia do?
- I don't want to work out…what would Emilia do?
- I don't want to call the funeral home and cemetery…what would Emilia do?
- I don't want to update the world on your next steps…what would Emilia do?
- I don't want to answer the phone…what would Emilia do?
- It's so easy to just give up. How did you not give up? How were you so strong? How were you able to endure what you did? Why couldn't I protect you? How could I stop you from trying?
- I wrote.
- I ate
- Your mom and I took a walk.
- I answered messages.
- I updated the world.
- I took care of the funeral stuff.
- Your Grandma and Grandpa came by to drop off food. That was nice to talk and feel a little normal for a while.

- I went back to Riley's to pick up some of your memorial stuff they prepared for us. It felt so weird being there again and so familiar at the same time.

- I ran into the amazing guard I always saw every day going through security. He had always been so nice and treated me so well. He said "I hope I never see you again." He was an amazing person. He told me one time that his 28-year-old son was a micro preemie and that "It was ugly" and there is hope. He was so supportive.

- I ran into the McGrew's on my way out. The McGrew's were your next-door neighbor for 30+ days. He said "What's up man?" I just said hey…I didn't have the heart to tell him. They still have their own battle to fight. I pray that they're okay.

- I talked to my dad about some feelings I had about how he was handling all of this. I was worried and confused. I know my dad loves me and I love him. Sometimes it doesn't feel that way as we've never really expressed a lot of emotion toward each other in our lives. Now that you made me a Father and I learned what that means, I wanted to tell him why I needed to understand how he didn't have the same pain and sorrow for me that I have for you? We were able to talk about it. It was a struggle. I told him that you're my role model and one day I hope he can say the same thing about me. I just want to live my life to the fullest to honor you. I promise I will do that every day. I'm doing it now as I'm writing all of this. I don't want to do this at all, but what would Emilia do?

- I posted on Facebook to send donations to us so we can do something special for the nurses at Riley that took such amazing care of you during your time there. Within an hour we had $1,000. I can't wait to share with them when we are done.

- I typed this…it was really hard to do and took hours.

- Tomorrow I have to type your eulogy and I don't know how I'm going to do that…. Is this your Eulogy?

- I got my haircut today (even though no places are open because of the pandemic lockdown). Marta is a saint for helping me and allowing me to come to her home for the haircut. I just didn't want to look like an asshole for you as we sent you off from this world tomorrow at your funeral.

- Felicia's friend Ellen made us an amazing Spotify playlist and we listened to it together until 2 a.m. It was really nice.

- I love you so much.

Day 41: 4/24/30

- I love you
- Dad Joke of the Day - Did you hear about the population of Dublin? It's Dublin
- Daily Scripture Theme: Fight off Stagnation. My Thoughts - Another great and timely message. Be proactive and do things with intention. When you find something you don't want to do (which is everything right now), you just have to do it. It may not seem like much, but each step forward will lead you to something you never knew was possible. With how much you fought…I'd be ashamed to stagnate and waste God's blessings.
- It's another beautiful spring day today. Thank you so much Emilia, I enjoy this time outside thinking about you and avoiding stagnation.
- I cut the grass today. As I was cutting it, I couldn't help to think why am I doing this? I wanted more than anything to be able to play with you in our beautiful and big yard someday. You would have loved it. I had to stop myself and remind myself again of my why. That why is and will always still be you. I need to keep this yard pristine so you can enjoy it wherever you are. When I think of it like that, it's pretty easy to keep mowing.
- Your mom is struggling a lot right now and I'm worried about her. I can't get her to eat and she is in a constant state of depression. I can't seem to find any way to pull her out of this and it hurts me to see this. I'd love your advice on this one? You were so much like your mother…I could already tell. You both had endurance I've never seen before. I'm worried her endurance around being in pain will be a catastrophe for us all.
- Our nightly Emilia walks have really helped. I think I need to keep pushing this one as it will build on itself eventually and make a little impact every day to help us through.
- Grandma Genie is on her way today. I'm hoping that will help your mom as well.
- I MISS YOU SO MUCH!!!!
- I woke up in the middle of the night and thought I was still in the NICU. I thought you were right next to me and it felt so real. When I realized I was at home, it was so sad because I knew you weren't there. Those nights in the NICU may have been a nightmare, people coming in and out of the room all night, flashing lights, bonging, etc. I'd take all that every night for eternity if it means I'd get to still see you another day.

- We've now already raised $2,000 toward your nurses' gifts and my company will double whatever the end total is. I can't wait to do something amazing for them in your honor. You would have loved meeting them and having them in your lives as you got older. They cared so much about you.
- God…it is so hard writing this stuff as I can't stop crying.
- I have to write your eulogy tonight. What kind of a nightmare is this????? No parent should ever have to do this! I'm dreading it so much but "What would Emilia Do?" Keeps ringing in my ears. I'll get it done and make it great.
- I love you.

Day 42: 4/25/20

- I love you
- Dad Joke of the Day - What did Cinderella say when her photos didn't arrive? Someday my prints will come.
- Daily Scripture Theme - There's Only One You Really Need. My Thoughts - Today is the second hardest day of my life…your funeral. It is hard to believe that we'll get through this, but God gives us strength to keep doing what we need to do. I need to live my life the way you would have lived and just keep moving forward step by step. Your memory and spirit is my why. I'll get through this.
- I wrote your eulogy at 2 a.m. this morning. I couldn't stop all the thoughts swimming in my head so I woke up and just started writing. I want to make sure I do my absolute best for you so I'm going to rewrite and practice this morning. I still can't believe I'm having to do this.
- It happened again…2 nights in a row now. I woke up in the middle of the night after dreaming I was asleep in the NICU. We were talking about your care with your nurses and could feel you were slowly fading. I woke up and was asking where you were to your mom? Your mom kept telling me you were gone and for some reason my mind couldn't understand it???? It felt so real. She told me it was Saturday and you left us Wednesday. I just repeated that out loud over and over as it wasn't computing in my head. Finally, it clicked after like 3 minutes of confusion. Then I was even more sad, and now just confused as to why this is happening to me over and over? Is this some alternate universe where we didn't make the decision to

end your battle? Is this me living out the experience we would have had? That's pretty torturous if that is the case.

- We are heading to your funeral. Why is this happening??? I want to be present and remember this whole day, but I also just want it over truthfully. I want all of these people out of our house. I want to be alone with your mom.

- I saw a commercial today for a lawnmower where a Dad was cutting the yard and his daughter saw him from the window, grabbed a baseball glove, and came outside. Then they were throwing a ball in the yard. I wanted that so bad for us.

- It's another gorgeous spring day...thank you

- We got to your funeral and saw you. It was overwhelming at first. To see your tiny little baby in that tiny little casket.

- You looked beautiful. It was so clear that you had your mother's looks. I hadn't seen you in a few days and I was so worried about how you'd look given your state we left you in on Wednesday night. You looked like our baby again!!! I'll forever remember you that way vs. Wed night.

- Your mom never left your side until the service. She sat in front of you and cried while everyone hugged her. You 2 are just so made for each other.

- I set out all of your mementos, shelties, and lions around your casket.

- I'm so relieved that we could only have 10 people there and live stream it to others. I needed all of my strength for your eulogy.

- Father gave an amazing service.

- Finally, it was time for me to speak. I had worked really hard on your eulogy because I wanted to make you proud of me. I wanted to show you my promise that I would always live like Emilia and never quit. I normally hate public speaking, but I wasn't scared.

- I gave you the speech of my life and I have no regrets. It was what you deserved. I'll continue to work like that through you for the rest of my life. Thank you for your strength to get through it.

- Your mother spoke beautiful words about you as well. I'm so excited to finish this book together for you. It will be a true mashup of all of our talents combined together. It will help so many people and keep your memory alive at the same time.

- On to the cemetery - Your little final resting place is in the area with a bunch of other little baby infant angels. The priest spoke eloquently again.

- All of your family that was able to be present spoke, except your Grandpa. They all shared beautiful thoughts, poems, and words.

God, I wish they all could have gotten to know you better. You would have LOVED your family so much, and they would have loved you as well.

- I'm out of energy and just want to go home. I'm the sprinter remember...I tire easily. I'm so jealous of you and your mom has endurance as a superpower. It's so admirable.
- I just want some wine, tacos, and time alone.
- We got home and spent the rest of the day with family in love, smiles, and happiness. It was really nice to not feel sad for a change.
- We played some board games late into the night. Your mom's family loves playing board games...you would have had so much fun at our Christmas' down in San Antonio every year.
- Your EULOGY:
    - Thank you all for being here today, and Thank You all so much for the love and support you're shown to Emilia, myself, and Felicia over these past few weeks.
    - I've never in a million years dreamed that I'd be eulogizing my own daughter, but here we are and it is pretty surreal. We still can't believe she's gone. We thought with all of our hearts that she was going to make it home safe and sound, but God had a different plan.
    - First and foremost, I want to make it clear that I don't want anyone to feel sorry for Felicia and I. Emilia gave us 39 beautiful days together. Felicia and I will be forever grateful for the time that we had with our little miracle baby. Focusing on feeling sorry for ourselves is not how we want to choose to move forward from today.
    - I wanted to start off by saying a few words about Emilia. Even though we only got to know her in this world for 39 days, I don't think I've known a person better in my life. She was feisty, courageous, loving, a fighter, ADORABLE, and most importantly never quit. She had to endure so much. EVERY challenge or obstacle that was ever thrown her way; she took them head on without a second thought and just kept pushing forward.
    - Because we had a lot of time in the NICU to ourselves, I spent a lot of that time reading and writing. One of the books I read was called the "Compound Effect." It's a story about how little consistent actions each day can turn into habits, and those habits over time compound to have powerful results.

o   In one section of the book it talked about to maintain a habit it is essential to have a powerful "why" behind all you do. The why is that driving force that whenever you want to give up compels you to keep moving forward. If you have a why...everything else is easy.

o   They described a true why as that thing that would make you walk across a tightrope, in between 2 skyscrapers, to rescue someone on the other side from a burning building. Basically...something you don't even have to think twice about because the why is so strong.

o   I started to think about that as I was reading. I kept pondering what was my "Why"? I've always tried hard my whole life and done the right things, but it was always such a struggle and took so much energy to create positive habits and momentum.

o   It finally dawned on me that I've never had a why before I met Emilia. That why wasn't necessarily her physical person, but who she was and how she lived her life each day. Her courage, fight, and never quit attitude is inspirational and something that makes me so proud of her to call her my daughter. Watching her battle each and every day and wondering where she got that energy and that never quit attitude was remarkable to see. She never asked for this, but she never once felt sorry for herself, quit, or gave up. Ultimately, her Mom and Dad had to make her quit to protect herself from undue pain...even then she still wouldn't give up. She's already become my role model and the most amazing person I've ever met in my life. I'm the proudest dad in the world. I vow to live the rest of my life trying to live up to her incredible standards, and make her proud to call me her dad when we get to meet again someday.

o   In keeping with making you proud of us...your Mom and I have decided to write a book to you based on our daily experiences since this journey began. We plan to publish this and give this to other NICU parents as a guide to help them in their own journey's. We won't stop writing and will make you proud.

o   Here is my journal entry from her last day Wed...read day 39.

•   I love you.

Atomic Bomb Theory: Lessons from the Rubble - Living, Learning, Thinking, and Growing (Days 43-118)

IMPORTANT NOTE as it pertains to this next section of the book and its correlation to the journals. Up until this point in our journey, the remembering self and experiencing self look into my family's journey has been pretty linear and a direct corollary to the journals as they were happening in chronological order. As we got further and further removed from Emilia's funeral and continued journaling to our daughter, our lives were anything but linear. We were truly living one day at a time and had no idea what we were doing, what lessons we would learn, or where life would take us from here.

One thing I learned about grief is that it is anything but linear and follows its own timeline uniquely for each person. The lessons that were learned during this period of my life weren't following some sort of a process or timeline like we had experienced in the first half of the story. Due to this, all the thinking, reflection, learning, and events that took place as I sat in the rubble of my life happened all over the place and in totally random orders over the next few months of my life. This next section will look at my life as I aimlessly wandered through the rubble and share those stories and lessons that occurred during this period of my life. With that said, the journals will officially end here as it relates to our story to not confuse the reader. Please visit, www.clubany.org/icantimagine-journals, if you would like to read the complete journals in chronological order as they written.

We'll resume the story by picking up where we left off right after the funeral. From there, the rest of the stories will begin to come from any time over the next four to six months after Emilia passed away.

Lessons from the Rubble - Reference Points Matter!

The funeral was over, and Emilia was in her final resting place. Our first day of our new normal without our daughter officially began. It is hard to describe those first few weeks after we lost Emilia and what our lives were like at this time. I think the best way I could describe it would be a state of confusion. Our days were filled with nothing to do, nowhere to go, and sadly no one else to care about other than ourselves. I think what hurt the most was that Felicia and I were back to being a childless couple again. We had spent the first eight years of our marriage as a childless couple and had been incredibly happy. We explored the world, ate at fancy restaurants, went to dinner parties with friends, had season tickets to the local playhouse and sports teams, and built and sustained successful careers. Life before Emilia wasn't bad by any means. However, now we had a taste of what life is like with our beautiful child. Having it stripped away and going back to being the childless couple seemed impossible and something that neither of us wanted.

All of those things we used to do and care about were utterly meaningless to us, and to a large extent, still are as I'm writing this today. We couldn't go back to that life because we were supposed to be caring for our first newborn child and all the wonderful craziness that entails. Instead, we were waking up without anything to do and with no direction in life. Both Felicia and I had taken an extended leave of absence from our jobs, so we literally had no tasks or activities that either of us had to complete each day other than eating food and staying alive. Each day was a battle to just get out of bed and keep moving. For what, we had no idea. The only thing I knew was that we had to keep moving for our daughter. A part of me wanted to go and do everything I could in Emilia's name and become a Tasmanian devil of activity. Another part of me wanted to sit in bed all day, watch TV, be miserable, ask why this happened to us, and disappear from the world. I think that the hardest part of the fallout after the blast is deciding what happens now? Most of us are always so busy in our everyday lives. Urgent and important tasks drive our days and activities. We have so much on our to-do lists, and we are a flurry of activity. When the whole world stops, and nothing is urgent or important anymore, you finally wonder and ask the question, "What now?"

My only answer at this time was to channel my why (Emilia's never quit attitude) and force myself to keep moving. Every day I set a goal to read for a minimum of 30 minutes, write Emilia's journal entry for 30 minutes, and exercise for 30 minutes. I didn't know what the end vision was at all from these activities. I had no goals. After all, what the hell was a goal anymore anyway? So, each day I read, wrote, and exercised. Once those activities were completed, the rest of the day was mine to do whatever it was that came my way. In the early days after losing Emilia, that extra time was filled with misery, pain, broken dreams, crying, anger, depression, and helping a wife that was crippled with grief. I also started responding back to a lot of the cards, gifts, and messages that we had received from friends and family. I sent thank you messages for people that had been giving and were still giving to Emilia's Care Team back at Riley. Felicia and I took our nightly Emilia walks where we talked, didn't talk, cried, or expressed our anger and sadness.

One of the early days after the funeral and with Felicia's family still in town, we all drove the hour or so down from Indianapolis to my parents' lake house in southern Indiana to spend the day. It was still late April, so the water was too cold to swim, but the weather was beautiful, and we could take the boat out and spend a little time in nature. That was really the first time that Felicia and I left our house for anything of substance besides the funeral. If you grew up in the Midwest, you know how amazing summer lake life can be. Summers at my friend's lake houses were some of my absolute favorite memories as a kid. Tubing, jet skiing, water skiing, bonfires, grilling out, smores, sunburns, floating out in the water, etc. There's just something magical about being in southern Indiana surrounded by rolling hills, nature, trees, and splashing around in a warm lake late into the long summer days. I had always been so jealous of my friends that were blessed enough to have their own lake houses in their families. It was always such a treat whenever we would get to go down and hang out at their places for the day or weekend. I always had a dream of getting my own lake house someday if I ever was blessed enough to afford a second home on a lake. I envisioned my own children and their friends having the time of their lives out there all summer just like we used to. Luckily for me, my parents helped me out and decided to purchase their own lake house seven years or so years before Emilia was born, so I didn't have to someday. My parents have put a ton of time and energy into remodeling and reconstructing their amazing retreat. That lake house is everything I could have imagined buying myself someday, and I'm so happy that it is in our family.

However, the fun I had as an adult going down there just wasn't the same as it was when I was a kid. That's because lake houses are really for the kids, in my opinion. The adults really just sit around drinking beer, wine, and cocktails while grilling out all day. There isn't anything wrong with that, but I can technically do that back in Indianapolis with my friends without having to pack an overnight bag and driving an hour to accomplish that. All the actual fun happens out on the water. I realized long ago that I couldn't wait to bring my own children down here someday to experience that magical summer lake life together. As strange as it sounds, there are really only two experiences in life that I had ever dreamed about doing with my children. The first is playing and teaching them tennis and the second is playing out on a lake in the summer. If I get a chance to do those two things with my children someday, my dreams as a parent will have been fulfilled, I thought. I had been waiting for years for Emilia to get here to experience fun moments and memories down at the lake, playing with her cousins and grandparents. Going back down there for the first time that season, childless again, hurt a ton. I couldn't get this thought out of my mind the whole day we were down there.

As we drove back to Indianapolis after departing the lake that evening, Felicia and her family were in her car, and I was alone in my car with all of the stuff we brought down for the day trip. I had completed my writing and exercise before we left that morning, but not my reading for the day, so I decided to put on the audiobook I had been about halfway through listening to while back in the NICU. It was a book called The Hard Things About Hard Things by the author, Ben Horowitz. Ben Horowitz is the co-founder of an influential venture capital firm in Silicon Valley called Andreessen Horowitz. He is also a former CEO and entrepreneur of his own businesses prior to launching the VC firm. This book was about the hard things that no one really likes to talk about in the startup world and building a business, all the bad things that can happen, how much it sucks sometimes to be the leader, and how hard it really is to run a business and have to make those tough calls that only a CEO can make. Ben talks a lot about the taboo things like having to fire friends, poaching competitors, knowing when to cash in, and making the hard and necessary decisions that inevitably will happen as a leader of a company. On this particular drive back, the section in the book was discussing a time when Ben's business, LoudCloud, was on the verge of collapse, and he was stuck in a no-win situation. They had no more runway (money) left, and he needed urgent help and some form of outside intervention to keep everything from going under and having to close up shop. They were down to their final hours in business if he didn't execute a plan to bring them back from the brink. His options were to sell at a loss, close up shop and lay off a bunch of people, or find a way to secure financing to take the company public in the middle of a stock market collapse. He was staring at no good options, and the fate of his company, all of his employees, and their families hinged on him making the right call of which direction to go. He went on to say, this is the definition of being a CEO and a leader. Are you able to make a hard decision and own it when there are no good options in front of you? Can you handle that wearing on your conscience if you are wrong? People will question you, but you can't doubt yourself. That is the definition of a leader, making a decision that no one else wants to make and living with the consequences.

I couldn't help but immediately stop the book when I heard him finish this section as I drove by myself on the way back from the lake. My mind was racing, and I was fuming over what I had just heard. Let me explain. Prior to meeting Emilia, I've spent my whole adult working life dreaming and working toward one day being a successful owner of a startup business like Ben Horowitz and being in the position that he was talking about in his whole book. I've studied, learned, listened, and tried to build multiple companies. That was my dream, and I knew one day I would make it a reality. Hearing these words from Ben in the past, I would have been inspired by the grit and determination Ben was describing as he lived life on the edge, narrowly making it out to see his business come back from the brink of destruction. I would have eaten up his description of what it takes to be a real leader, holding the success and failure of so many people's lives in their hands, weighing the options, making a decision, and not being scared to own the consequences, good or bad. However, hearing this now, as I'm driving back home less than a week after losing my daughter, I couldn't give two shits about all this stuff anymore.

I couldn't help but think about how meaningless that whole section of the book, and the book in general, truly was. Do you think having to make a decision that impacts a couple hundred family's ability to pay their mortgage is hard? "Try making the call to take your own daughter's life!" I thought. I almost started laughing and crying at the same time, thinking of the irony of Ben's words as they rattled around in my mind. If that is the hardest decision a leader of a business has to make someday, I feel happy for them. Taking your own daughter's life is the real "hard things about hard things" discussion that I wanted to have in my own mind. Weighing the options of taking her out of the game or letting her fight while watching her body deteriorate as she is in excruciating pain was indescribable. For the rest of my life, I will look at photos of Emilia and wonder if I did the right thing or not. Was there a miracle to be had? Why did I pull her out of the game when I sat next to her isolate the day before, making a promise to her and her mother that I would never do that? I was willing to accept the personal consequences of shame from her care team and having to watch her excruciating pain and suffering to give her a chance at a miracle and life. However, I lied to my daughter, and I will forever have to live with knowing this and owning my decision to pull her from the fight when the possibility of a miracle still existed in theory. That is the real-life "hard things about hard things."

I didn't know this at the time that I was listening to Ben's book, as I wouldn't stumble upon this answer until later in my journey when I came across a book called *Thinking, Fast and Slow* by world-renowned economist Daniel Kahneman. It was then that I realized I was living and experiencing something that Kahneman called "Bernoulli's Error" at this very moment as my reference points had dramatically changed almost overnight.

Here is a brief description of the problem and Kahneman's explanation: In 1738, Swiss scientist Daniel Bernoulli explored the relationship between psychological value or desirability of money (utility) and its correlation to the actual amount of money. Bernoulli concluded that utility is a logarithmic function of wealth: the psychological response to a change of wealth is inversely proportional to the initial amount of wealth. For, a gift of $10 has the same utility to someone who already has $100 as a gift of $20 to someone whose current wealth is $200. Bernoulli's theory assumes that the utility of wealth is what makes people more or less happy. However, as psychology has shown, the experience of happiness is determined by the recent change in wealth relative to the different states of wealth that define the reference point. Basically, Bernoulli's Error is that he disregarded the reference point of where you began before predicting the utility of an amount of additional wealth. $10 isn't the same to a millionaire as it is to someone that only has $10 to their name. The moral of the story, Bernoulli's error, according to Kahneman, is that his theory lacked a reference point. The value (utility) of anything is largely dependent upon someone's current situation.

Well, my current situation was not Ben Horowitz's situation. I would have given anything to have to make the "hard things about hard things" decisions he was describing in his book. Less than two months ago, his book, experiences, and lessons would have carried an immense amount of weight in my mind as these were the kinds of things that were seemingly important to me at the time. Within two short months, my reference point went from thinking how hard it must be to start and build a company to how do I get out of bed each day knowing that I took my own daughter's life?

Reference points matter. Where people are in their lives and what is important to them in each new day matters. We have to strive to meet people where they are on their own journey in life. One huge lesson I took out of my own journey and experience was to seek first to understand where each unique person is on their own journey before trying to impart your own wisdom and knowledge onto them. I think at our core, we all understand that we should listen with empathy to the people we encounter each and every day. However, listening with empathy is really hard, and I would guess that 99% of us don't do this that well, if at all even. We are so caught up in our own lives and worlds, and we rarely look past our biases and our own reference points. Prior to Emilia, I had gotten into the habit of immediately judging people based on my own experiences and biases without even giving them the slightest chance to understand where they are in life and what brought them to this very moment. I used to use this thing called the DISC profile all the time in my previous life. The DISC profile is a personality assessment that I had become very well versed in and leveraged all the time as a leader of my team, hiring people, coaching employees, and honestly evaluating almost anyone I met in my everyday life. I used that DISC profile like my bible and lumped everyone into these four categories as if it was a hard fact and could never be changed. I like to think of it as almost the business world's version of the sorting hat in Harry Potter.

This is just who people are in my mind. D's are dominant, task orientated, selfish, get-shit done types who are also bad listeners. I's were super social, influencers, a people's person, but a bit disorganized and lacked follow-through and initiative. S's were the steady relaters that got along with everyone, were great team players, super agreeable, but hated conflict, and were bad at expressing emotion or challenging things. C's were the analytical engineer types. They loved tasks, were super detail orientated, asked a lot of questions but were slow, stubborn, and resistant to change. Everyone I met fit into these categories. I would look to define and sort them quickly, so I knew how to act toward them or work with them. From that initial classification, that is who they were and would stay forever in my mind.

This is how I lived my life before all of this happened to my family, in nicely defined categories. This is how I thought life worked. I assumed the chaos of life could be structured into order and be somehow understood and organized by our feeble minds. However, these days and with my new reference points of life, I was finding out that assessment couldn't be further from the truth. We are all in such a fast-paced, go-go-go mindset trying to get our agenda's done that we forget what this is all really about. We are quick to judge and categorize people instantly, and I was no different. We talk a lot, do a lot, complain a lot, and think the universe revolves around us. What we don't do is listen with empathy, understand people's individual journeys, and try to truly support one another in how each of us uniquely would want to be treated. People can change. Life can change. Our worlds can change. There is an infinite number of ways in which to view the world.

As this story goes on, I will come back to this topic later and a lot of other lessons I learned while sitting in the rubble of my destroyed city. On this particular day, this lesson of always remembering that people's starting reference points matter hit me really hard. Knowing that someone else in this world thought the hardest thing in their life was having to make a decision about their business, so much so that they wrote a book about it. On the other hand, there are people in this world having to make decisions as to whether their children live or die, and they might also write a book about it, just like I am right now. In another person's world, I can't even imagine (there it is again) what they are going through that may be even worse, and they will write a book about that someday. The point is, everyone has a story to tell, and they all should be heard, listened to with empathy, and embraced for their unique personal stories. We don't have to compare, rationalize, argue, offer guidance, or relate and share our own similar stories. JUST SHUT UP AND LISTEN!

As we arrived back at our house late that night from being down at the lake all day, we laid down to go to bed, and I had another dream. This time it was different. There was no chaos in the room. No hushed, secret talk with all the nurses and doctors huddled around Emilia. No one looked panicked. Everyone seemed to be calm and at peace. I remember seeing a dark object standing in the light of the doorway. I wrote in my journal the next morning, "Was that the grim reaper, holy spirit, or something else like it?" It felt like the fight was finally over, and Emilia was being called to heaven. We were now almost four days past Emilia's passing, and this was my third and final dream about being back in the NICU. I couldn't help but to think that this truly was the alternate universe ending that I was watching unfold had I not made the decision on that Tuesday night to end my daughter's suffering. I still to this day think that God, Emilia, or someone, was showing me the "other" option that would have played out had we let Emilia fight to the end. As dumb as this sounds, I think that was real, and it has provided me with a ton of comfort knowing that I ultimately did the right thing for Emilia in helping to end her suffering and pain when we did. I still think about that decision a lot, but not in a bad way or with any anger with myself, but with sadness that I even had to make that call for our family. I would never wish that on anyone. At least I know I'm qualified to be a CEO now, per Ben Horowitz.

Lessons from the Rubble – Restless, Wanting to Run Away, and Missing the NICU

Felicia's family left and flew back down to San Antonio a few days after the funeral, and for the first time since the day Emilia passed away, Felicia and I were back to being just us again in our home. All alone without our child. We were back to being the childless couple once again and living our new normal. Right after a tragedy strikes, your support network rushes in to rally around you and help in any and every way they can, if you're one of the lucky ones. You are surrounded by a flurry of activity and people. So many things are going on that it makes it a little easier to mute the immense sadness and void that is left in your heart and mind from your loss. The first week or so after we lost Emilia, this was our life. People were living in our house, a funeral and burial to coordinate, messaging to the world, people bringing food and gifts, responding to messages from friends and family, etc. Eventually, all that stops, and people go back to their own lives. I don't blame them. What are they supposed to do? Sure, people still come by and check-in regularly, but the constant barrage of support slowly fades, and the families are left to really begin the battle of grief, anxiety, depression, and questioning on their own. There is only so much family and friends can do. Eventually, you have to take the training wheels off and begin your journey toward whatever direction your future holds. That is where we were at this point in our journey. We had to figure out how to make it through each day on our own and what that path would be.

I've always been a doer. I run a million miles an hour at all times, and I'm a flurry of activity. Hell, Felicia and I accomplish more on our vacations than most people do in 6 months of their actual day jobs. Within just a few short days of having nothing to do but sit in my sadness, I was already becoming extremely restless. Everything inside of me wanted to revert to my default mode, where I would just keep doing more stuff until everything else works itself out. Instead, my new life was to wake up, work out, read for a few hours, write my journal for Emilia, and then have nothing else to do the rest of the day. This was a life I didn't know or understand. I didn't know how to stop moving and do nothing. I didn't know how to live an unscripted life where I could do whatever I wanted, whenever I wanted. Worst of all, I started to recognize that I didn't know how to be sad. I noticed I was having a lot of trouble even letting myself be intentionally sad, upset, angry, or cry in those moments when I wasn't forcing myself to do something. I don't know what it was, but I avoided it like the plague. I was struggling to embrace the pain that I knew I was experiencing. I was trying to drown it all out of my mind with things to do. I would clean the house, reorganize a room, do a ton of yard work, re-stain the patio table, etc. I was trying to find anything and everything I could to avoid having to stop and sit in the rubble that the atomic bomb had created in my life.

On the other side of the house, Felicia was ONLY existing in that intensely sad state that I was struggling to achieve in my own life. She was living every moment of her day existing as if the blast had just happened over and over again. I would wake up every morning to her crying and holding a little stuffed animal that we had gotten for Emilia at one point when she was a newborn. That morning cry lasted for months, and I don't even remember exactly when it finally stopped. I would get back from a run, and she was crying on the couch. I would come to find her when it was time to try and get her to eat something, and she was crying. I would sometimes have to come to check on her in the shower as I heard her crying all the way across the house and would get worried. We would take our nightly Emilia walk, and she would cry the whole time. We were in two different worlds. I was trying everything I could to run away from the rubble, and Felicia was chaining herself to the only tree still left standing in our blown-up city.

I begged and pleaded with her to run away with me, go to Hawaii to live on the North Shore of Oahu, and remove ourselves from our previous life and all the reminders of what we were going through. The North Shore was a special place to us. I figured if there was anywhere I could get her to say yes to, it would be the North Shore of Oahu. Felicia loves beaches; they're her happy place. I love adventure and exploration on vacations. The North Shore is a match made in heaven for our personal goals and needs for fun and relaxation. We had visited there and rented an Airbnb house right on the beach one year and had an amazing time. The North Shore is just an incredible place. All the beauty of Hawaii with the secluded feeling of living in the country. There is still tons to do and explore in nature as well. You can drive from beautiful beach to beautiful beach all day long, and it never gets old. If there was a place to disappear to, this was it. Pandemic be damned, I didn't care if they made me quarantine on a private beach. That sounded like heaven to me at the time.

Felicia wouldn't budge. She told me it was fine if I went by myself, but there was no way I could do that to her. I couldn't leave her to go through this alone, and I also needed her to help me through all of this as well. I had already had one of the amazing women in my life taken from me recently. I wasn't about to voluntarily leave the other one. I was stuck in Indianapolis with my restless existence.

Looking back on it, being prevented from running away by the pandemic and Felicia forcing me to embrace the rubble head-on was actually the best thing for me as it forced me to feel, stop, learn, think, and ultimately regain my curiosity for life. That would ultimately prove to be the catalyst that would help me to reimagine the new world that I was going to create with the help of my daughter and the strength and support from God. Much more on this portion of the journey is to come later in the story.

So there I was, stuck at home, unable to run away, with no work to distract me, and running out of home projects to keep me occupied. I was trapped and had no way out other than to sit in the rubble and embrace my new reality head-on. Surprisingly, I found myself really missing the chaos of the NICU more and more each passing day. That place had become my safe space and my happy place. Even with all the trauma and pain that it brought, I would have rather been there at this very moment than anywhere else in the world. I would live that life for the rest of my existence if it meant that I got to be with Emilia every day. It is amazing how adaptable the human mind and body can become. It can normalize itself to almost any circumstance or environment, no matter how crazy or traumatic. Even though it had only been 39 days, the NICU had become our new normal. It was our new job, if you will. I actually remember saying those exact words to Felicia the first day we came back to the NICU at IU Methodist after being released from being a patient. As we pulled into the parking garage early that morning, it felt like we were walking into our first day at our new job. We had our lunches, backpacks, snacks, laptops, and a change of clothes. We were trying to figure out where it's best to park, how to get past security, etc. Basically every first-day job experience I've ever had.

During our time at Riley, we woke up every morning, drove to the hospital, said hi to the security guards, ate there, worked there, socialized with the nurses and doctors there, sometimes slept and showered there, and most importantly, that was our de facto nursery. That had become my happy place because that is where Emilia was. It was where I learned from Dr. Osa and all of Emilia's nurses so many things about modern medicine that I had never imagined. It is where I read and wrote every day and started the journey of this book. Most importantly, it is where I got to watch my daughter grow and see her eyes open for the first time. It was evident the first moment that I met her that for the rest of my life, wherever she was would feel like home for me.

Even with all the trauma and pain that the NICU brings, eventually, it normalizes. I remember telling one of the nurses one time, "The worst noise in the world is the sound that stupid alarm makes when Emilia's oxygenation sats would dip below the 92% oxygenation threshold." It's so stressful. A moment of panic would take over as I stared at the board, waiting for the next few seconds to see whether the numbers would either get worse or better and if I needed to jump up and run for a nurse to come into the room to address the situation. I then followed that up with the comment to the nurse, "on the other hand, the absolute best sound in the world was the alarm that would go off when Emilia's oxygenation sats were high and above the 96% threshold set on the monitors. I could listen and watch that all day." Obviously, it was the same sound, and I was kidding, but not really.

I've never experienced PTSD or read enough about it to have an educated thought here about it. I've always associated PTSD with the military because that is where it is used so often to describe the battle within after the war ends that so many brave soldiers go through in their minds. However, I wonder if what I was feeling was somewhat similar to how a lot of soldiers feel after they leave the battlefield? I wonder if all the noises, sights, sounds, and smells that scared the shit out of them in the moment, become something that they miss back when they are in a safe space at home. I can't even imagine (there it is again) what it must be like to have guns and bombs going off all around you at all times and fearing that your life may end at any moment. However, I can imagine all the bings, bongs, and alarms from the medical equipment in my daughter's hospital room that went off all day long and fearing that we could lose her at any moment. Eventually, those noises normalize to us, and they just become the background noise to our lives. We figure out which ones are really serious and which ones aren't that big of a deal. I would look up, see what is happening, let my brain decide if I should act or not, and go back to peacefully reading most of the time.

When I would think about those noises and feelings the first few weeks back in our safe home, I honestly missed them because they brought a sense of comfort to me and reminded me of happier times when I was an actual dad. If I had to guess, soldiers probably think of those war noises, sights, and smells and miss their brothers and sisters they fought with, their work, and the adventure of a lifetime that they were unknowingly on as well. Even though those noises, sights, and smells are torturous, they provide comfort and joy at the same time.

Lessons from the Rubble – Marriage, Going in Different Directions, and Emilia Walks to the Rescue

As I already mentioned, shortly after losing Emilia, Felicia and I both sought professional help to work through the thoughts and emotions we were both experiencing. I went to a therapist named Loretta, whom I still speak with every week, and I'm thankful for all of our conversations and support over the past year. Felicia started going to a grief counselor provided by Riley's Hospital for Children, named Elizabeth, whom she still speaks with every week as well.

It took about two weeks or so after we lost Emilia for Felicia to be connected to her therapist and schedule their first appointment. I remember desperately waiting for that initial appointment to occur for my own relief as well because there was nothing I could do to help provide the comfort Felicia needed at this time in our journey. I tried everything in my ability to help, but as I quickly learned, nobody has the skills or training needed to help their partner deal with the loss of a child.

I remember, after one of her first sessions with Elizabeth, she got off the phone, entered our bedroom, and I asked, "How did that go? Did you learn anything that would help?" Felicia said it was helpful and that Elizabeth really was there just to let her talk and listen, so she didn't learn much. She did say something that stuck with me enough to write about it here in this story. She told me that Elizabeth shared a metaphor about what grief is like that I found interesting. Elizabeth told Felicia that, "Grief is like shoving a pillow into a jar. Grief is the pillow, and it will never shrink; however, the jar will get bigger over time." At this point in our journey, Felicia's jar was the size of a can of baby food, basically non-existent. She was shoving a pillow into a tiny mason jar that Tinkerbell wouldn't even want to call home. For me, that metaphor was powerful because it reminded me that even though Felicia and I were experiencing the same loss and had the same pillow of grief, our jars were going to grow at our own unique pace, and I had to always keep that in mind as this journey continued.

We all know that marriage can be so hard sometimes. However, throw losing a child into the mix, and that is a volatile concoction that has been the end of many a great pairing. A 1985 study by Teresa Rando on bereaved parents showed a divorce rate between 80-90% of the time. I don't know if this is true or not, but I can certainly believe it after going through what we experienced. At the time we lost Emilia, I had only known of two couples that had lost a child in my life. One was my aunt and uncle, who are still married today and managed to stay together after a lot of ups and downs. The other was a former coworker of mine who was a work acquaintance that I didn't know that well at all. Even though my former coworker and I weren't really that close, I knew him well enough to know that within a year or so of losing their child, he and his wife, whom he shared three or four other kids with and had been married to for a long time, had separated.

Within two weeks of losing Emilia, I learned of another couple that I came across that had also lost a child. I was out in my yard doing some yard work when the new neighbor hollered at me from behind her fence. She introduced herself as Kristen and let me know that they had just moved in a few weeks ago and wanted to say hi. We talked for a few minutes to get to know each other, and she shared that she and her husband had recently moved to Indianapolis because her son needed specialized treatment at Riley's Hospital for Children about a year or two prior. She went on to tell me that, unfortunately, her son lost his battle, but she decided to remain in Indianapolis here with her two daughters.

What were the chances of this one? A new neighbor that had spent a ton of time at Riley and had also lost a child recently as well? I mentioned this before, but you have to always be watching out for the omens in life. This stuff doesn't just happen for no reason.

My new neighbor, Kristen, and I continued chatting, and I felt compelled to share my own story about Emilia and what we were going through just a week or two prior to this first meeting. I really wasn't ready to share Emilia's story with random strangers, but Kristen and I had that uncommon commonality of losing a child at Riley's Hospital for Children experience that strikes up an instant connection and deep understanding of someone, even if they are just a new connection. As I shared my family's story of our time in the NICU with Emilia, I could tell how devastating it was for her to hear, and I could feel her heart sink hearing what Felicia and I were going through. I'm sure it brought up so many memories of her own experience that she probably tries not to think about unless circumstances like this pop up.

I'm starting to understand that deep empathy of my own when I hear stories today about people I know who just lost a child. It has only happened once, but my mind immediately goes back to the days I'm writing about now and all the pain and horror that accompanies it. I would give anything to take that pain away from that couple, but I know there is nothing I can do.

As Kristen and I continued our unexpectedly deep conversation for a first-time neighbor encounter, I came to learn that she actually moved to this particular house because she and her husband had separated recently, and this was now her new home as a divorcee. Hearing that immediately struck a nerve and sent shivers down my back. I wondered if this was going to be Felicia and my fate two years from now? My new neighbor Kristen and I said our goodbyes as I walked up the hill back to our house. All I could think was, "Shit. There it is. 2 out of 3 ended in divorce." I was terrified that this was our fate.

After meeting Kristen and hearing her story, it got me thinking about my former coworker that I knew had lost an infant child and how long his relationship lasted before they crumbled. I creepily jumped on Facebook and went back to look through all of his old posts from the past few years to try and see when all of a sudden his wife stopped appearing in them, and his new girlfriend started popping up. It appeared to be about a year and a half later after losing his daughter. I thought, "Kristen and her husband lasted two years. My coworker and his wife lasted a year and a half." I was starting to get really scared.

Felicia is and will always be the romantic love of my life. There is no one else in this world that I could ever imagine (there it is again) doing this life thing with. I was determined not to become another statistic and to not let this be our fate as a couple. We were going to be one of the couples that had a happy ending after the loss of a child. All I could think is that we would be disrespecting the memory of our daughter if I let our marriage crumble. I couldn't let Emilia down. My strategy to keep us together was our nightly Emilia walks. Rain or shine, hell or high water, we were taking that damn walk every night. I had to find a way to keep us connected at some level as we slowly drifted apart during our own grieving processes.

As the first few days and weeks passed after we lost Emilia, it became more and more abundantly clear to both Felicia and I that our grief jars were growing at dramatically different paces. I don't want this to sound like this was a competition or something, as it wasn't. I wasn't "winning" the grief game vs. my wife. I'd have to be a psychopath or something to gamify the grief battle over losing our daughter. I don't even know if my grief jar growing bigger and faster was even a good thing, to be honest. Who's to say that sitting in the rubble for a longer period of time, keeping your jar small, and feeling all the feels isn't the better path forward? Maybe Felicia's process was better, and I should have spent more time intentionally crying and feeling sad. I have no idea, and I'm not a grief expert. I think the most important lesson I could learn from this experience was that grief is a personal journey, and there is no path, process, or linear trajectory to turn to in order to move forward. I can only write about what I saw and felt on my side of the equation in this marriage and in this story, which is what I will focus on here.

Personally, I was having a lot of trouble intentionally feeling sad, as I mentioned before. I remember being on a road trip back down to my parents' lake house by myself one day a few weeks after losing Emilia and trying to create an environment to feel intentionally sad. I was all alone in my car, the windows down, driving through the Indiana cornfields on a backcountry road, and I thought, "I want to feel sad right now." I don't know why, but I knew that I needed to embrace the pain in this moment of solitude in my car. So I turned on some sad music, tried to listen intently, think of Emilia and how much I missed her, and how much my life really sucked at that moment.

After about 5 minutes, I gave up. I thought, "What is wrong with me? Why can't I do this?" I felt broken or something. Felicia can't stop crying all day long. Her immense sadness is clearly the only thought in her mind from the moment she wakes up until the moment she goes to sleep every day. I knew I was sad too, but why couldn't I express it? To be clear, it's not like I didn't cry a little every day as well. I was just more Chris about it than Felicia. Chris is a very habitual being. I'm very task-driven and direct for the most part in my everyday life. I woke up and wrote to Emilia in my office, where I would cry almost every morning as I wrote what was on my mind and shared it with my daughter in my words. Once I was done, I tried to turn the sadness switch off and get back to living my miserable reality without my daughter. Felicia, on the other hand, looked like she was perpetually stuck in sadness quicksand. She was sitting in that rubble all day long, didn't want to talk to anyone, see anyone, would barely eat, and was constantly crying. My problem was trying to balance what was keeping me going and not forgetting that there are 2 of us grieving in this process. I may have been able to turn off my sadness in one room of our house, but just down the hall, there was someone who was in their own deep dark space that I couldn't pretend didn't exist. I couldn't avoid the dark rain clouds constantly hanging over my wife's head all day, every day.

We were going in two different directions, and I could feel us slowly pulling apart. The best story I can provide to illustrate the delta that was emerging between us was, as Felicia puts it, her "gigantic tsunami waves of emotion" that would spontaneously overtake her at any given moment throughout the day. I realized how far apart we were drifting when I was accidentally swept up in her tsunami wave one morning, about a month after Emilia had passed.

One morning, I got up, wrote to Emilia and cried in my office, read one of my books, and then went for a 45-minute run. I had a great run that morning. I was really moving at an awesome pace, and I could feel that my body was slowly getting stronger and stronger from all the exercise that I had been forcing myself to do each day. I could feel the progress, and it was nice to feel a sense of accomplishment for a change over the searing sense of loss that I normally felt all the time. As I walked back into the house with my headphones blasting and covered in sweat, I walked into the kitchen to get some water and grab a yogurt out of the fridge. After chugging some water for a minute, I opened up the yogurt and put my AirPods back in their case for charging. As I took my first bite of yogurt, I turned the corner from the kitchen and entered the living room, where Felicia was sitting on her usual spot on the couch and immersed in a massive crying spell. She was sobbing uncontrollably and almost hyperventilating. She was in a dark place at that moment. Sadly for both of us, these events would happen regularly. This was the textbook illustration of the gigantic tsunami waves of emotion that would rush over her in an instant and consume her entire being, seemingly out of nowhere.

I can't begin to describe to you how hard this was for me as well on so many levels. I was getting ready to enjoy a bite of yogurt after feeling accomplished from an awesome run. My mental state was, for a brief moment of time, at an eight when most of the time I was living at a 4 in this terrible new reality of ours. I turn the corner in the safety of my house, and out of nowhere, I'm thrust into an environment where someone I love is at a negative five. Somehow, I have to figure out how to shift from an eight to a negative five in the manner of an instant with a mouthful of yogurt and covered in sweat. We literally existed in two different worlds in the same house.

At that exact moment, it was so easy to see how the divorce rate could be 80-90% for couples that had lost a child. Managing your own grief jar is hard enough; however, when you are married, it's never just about you anymore. You can't run the same race at different paces and expect to have that person still in your life when the dust clears after all of this. After all, grief isn't a finite game. It's a life sentence and an infinite game, if you will. There is no finish line for grieving. I will always grieve the loss of my daughter for the rest of my life, as will Felicia. Marriage, on the other hand, isn't a life sentence. We have the ability to get out of that through a divorce. Marriage requires sacrifice, and if I was going to share the rest of my life with Felicia, I had to make sure to stay at her pace in this race, or I was going to lose her.

Emilia walks to the rescue…sort of.

As time slowly and excruciatingly crept along after we lost Emilia, it was crystal clear that the rate at which Felicia and my grief jars were growing was slowly becoming more and more of a concern each day. Let me be clear, at no point in this journey did a thought ever cross my mind that I didn't want the rest of my life plan to involve Felicia. However, I could feel those thoughts beginning to creep into my mind on a distant horizon, and they seemed to be getting closer and closer as each day passed us by on this new journey as bereaved parents. It was something I could never have imagined (there it is again) before we lost Emilia. Not in my wildest dreams could I have imagined that this is where our relationship and marriage would be just six months prior when Felicia told me we were expecting our first child. The more that delta between us grew, the more our daily lives started to diverge into completely different worlds. I was doing what I was doing, and she was doing what she was doing. We were both respecting each other's space and trying our best to do what we could to process all that we were going through individually.

We occasionally would come and sit with each other throughout the day, and most of the time, those conversations ended in pure frustration and anger on both of our parts. I'm ashamed to admit this, but I'm an awful listener. The reason I'm ashamed to admit it is because I know how important listening is in relation to being a great friend, partner, coworker, husband, or basically any human relationship. If you can master listening and empathy, you will have conquered 90% of how to be the best human you can be. This skill is something I aspire to master someday, but I still am nowhere near even what I would consider being a proficient level. Personally, I love problem-solving, helping people, and collaboratively finding a solution. That is what I've always excelled at and what brings me the most joy in life. However, just sitting and listening with empathy when no problem is trying to be solved is a freaking mystery to me at this point. This is a skill that I've been working on improving for years and years and have been slowly making progress, but my skills were nowhere near where they needed to be yet to deal with what Felicia and I were experiencing. My biggest problem is I just can't just shut up. I tend to want to try and help solve something, and most of the time, people just want to be heard. I'll touch on lessons learned around listening with empathy later in the story, but what you should know at this point is that my lack of empathetic listening skills was becoming a huge problem in our marriage.

The same scene played out like the movie *Groundhog Day* over and over with Felicia and me each day. I would walk into a room she was in, mainly the living room, most days. She would be crying, looking incredibly sad, or in the midst of a new tsunami. I'd ask if she wants to talk about it? She would start saying something. I'd listen until she stopped, and then I'd begin to try to provide some advice. She would tell me to stop and that she didn't want my "help." I would get frustrated, try to apologize, and rephrase what I was saying to try and make the point more understandable. She would tell me not to worry about it and then shut down. I would try again to reset the conversation. She would get more frustrated, continue to tell me not to worry about it, and slowly go back into her shell. We would both walk away from the situation worse than when we started.

This seemed like EVERY SINGLE INTERACTION OF EVERY SINGLE DAY! It was so frustrating on my end. I'm sure that the feeling was mutual for her as well. She was just looking for me to listen and wanted no help or advice. I, on the other hand, could only see that my wife was in pain and wanting to do anything I could to be the hero and help her solve her problem. Our interactions were leaving us both in a worse state of mind.

The only time we ever seemed to be able to connect on any level was during our Emilia walk time each night. As crazy as this sounds, I think our Emilia walks are the only reason we are still married to this day and didn't end up as just another divorce statistic of bereaved parents. As much as each one of our lives individually sucked at this time, we found a way to connect through our walks each night in doing something together. In retrospect, it sounds like a no-brainer and that every bereaved couple should do something similar. I tell you what, though, this was not an easy habit to stick to or maintain. These walks were painstakingly hard at first. I already shared one story earlier about the paradigm-shifting experience I was seeing in action on one of our first few walks where Felicia was sobbing, and our neighbors were staring at me like I was a wife beater or something. Then there were times when we would argue, with the same pattern I described above, as Felicia would try to open up about something and I would mess it up, and then we would both just silently walk next to each other without saying a word until we returned back to our house.

These Emilia walks didn't just help us to stay connected as a couple, they also got us out and interacting with the world and helped us to dip our toes into the waters of talking to people again. About a week after losing Emilia, we were on a walk one night where we officially ran into the first person in our life that wasn't a close family member since losing our daughter. It was our neighbor named Justin that lived down the street. Justin is a great person, but someone that I would consider to be a good acquaintance. We see each other here and there, have fun in neighborhood activities with other families, etc. We know each other's families, but I'd hardly consider us to be close friends. On this particular night, he was out walking his two-year-old daughter, Ophelia, in a stroller. We happened to see each other as we began to cross over a bridge that passes over the creek that runs through our neighborhood. When we saw Justin coming, we knew there was no way to avoid the interaction as we were on a bridge and couldn't change directions. We all waved to each other when we realized that this encounter was unavoidable. Justin stopped his stroller as he got to us, and we began to chat.

I could tell how uncomfortable Felicia was with seeing his daughter, Ophelia, staring up at her from the stroller. Felicia didn't want anything to do with this conversation, and I could tell by her expressions. I was uncomfortable myself as I wasn't really in the mood to shoot the shit with really anyone at this point in my life, let alone fringe acquaintances.

Justin and I said hello and exchanged some pleasantries. We talked about how things were going for him as he is an RN and had been dealing with all the coronavirus stuff at work. After a few minutes of nervous, awkward chatter, Justin said, "I'm so sorry for your loss." I was caught off guard because I honestly didn't even know that he knew. I forgot we were friends on Facebook. Facebook can be a powerful tool. I told him we appreciated it and then said how much of a blessing Emilia was to us and mumbled some other meaningless words. We awkwardly ended the conversation and continued on with our walks in separate directions.

I can't begin to tell you how painful it was for Felicia to see Justin and his daughter out on a walk, a reminder of what our family could never have. It hurt me as well to see a father and daughter together, living a "normal" existence. However, these situations were going to happen in life, and without an Emilia walk, this may never have happened if our marriage situation and distance between us had worsened. These walks got us out into the world and forced us to deal with life together like we always had.

Those first few weeks were especially tough, seeing all the young families out playing with their children. We passed by couple after couple walking their happy families and children around and enjoying life. After each stroller passed by us, I would always glance over at Felicia and could see the pained look on her face. It was like each stroller was a reminder of what she no longer had in her life, and it hurt so bad. Sometimes we would talk about it and all the emotions (anger, sadness, jealousy) that the situation brought. Most of the time, we just stayed silent, knowing what the other was silently thinking.

Eventually, the walks became a little bit easier and something we both started to look forward to. It allowed us time to share some things that we were each going through, get some sunshine, force ourselves to face the world, and deal with all the little triggers that accompanied being around other people. A few times, I even convinced Felicia to turn the Emilia walk into an Emilia run. Felicia was always the runner of the family, and it is something she immensely enjoyed pre-Emilia. With me running and working out every day as a part of my own recovery plan, I thought this would be a great way to connect our worlds together.

It did not go very well. Felicia ran with me a few times, but they always ended in her breaking down in tears and frustration mid-run and telling me to just keep going without her. She told me that the act of her body allowing her to run again and seemingly function normally made her so frustrated. She would start crying, trying to understand how her body could handle physical activity and be okay, but not work for Emilia and carry her safely to term. I can't imagine (there it is again) what she must have been wrestling with in her mind. I don't want to even speculate because I'm sure the words that I would choose would do a disservice to what she was grappling with in these moments. Needless to say, I abandoned the run idea after a few tries, and we went back to just walking.

On one particular Emilia walk, about a month and a half removed from Emilia's passing, Felicia and I started the conversation that I had wanted to have for a while now. As we were beginning our walk and had gotten about ¼ mile away from our house, I sheepishly asked Felicia if she was ready to have a conversation about having more children someday. I didn't know what I expected to hear from her as the words left my mouth. The searing pain of losing Emilia was still there for both of us. Things weren't great in our relationship either, and I honestly wasn't fully ready yet at this point in time to even visualize what this process might become. However, because of the daily journaling and reflection, I had been thinking and writing a lot about this topic in the days leading up to this particular walk.

I remember writing about the corollaries between a promotion from an individual contributor to a leader at work and being promoted from a husband to dad in life. I shared with Felicia that I felt like I had been stripped of my promotion to dad, and it hurt so much. I don't know if you have ever experienced a big promotion at work where you went from an individual contributor and moved into a leadership role. I've been lucky enough to have that happen to me a few times in my professional life thus far. Those moments are rare, and so much time and effort go into getting the opportunity to turn that dream into a reality. The shift in roles from contributor to leader is incredibly challenging, and it isn't for everyone. Not everyone is cut out to be a leader. To be clear, I'm not saying that being an individual contributor is bad in any way either. However, they are two different jobs, two different skill sets, and two different mentalities. Making that shift from an individual contributor to a leader in a company takes years of hard work, consistent success, discipline, additional education and training, anxiety, competition, and politicking, to acquire the trust you need from leadership to work toward that big day when you finally hear, "Congratulations on being promoted to your new role as a leader in the organization." The feeling is indescribable when you realize that all of your hard work has paid off and that you are ready to embark on a new journey of leading people versus just worrying about yourself. You are now responsible for the fates of everyone that reports to you, and that is not to be taken lightly. However, even with the years of the build-up and work to get to that moment, you never really know if you have what it takes (or if you even really wanted it in the first place) until you are in that role and staring at a room filled with your new team as you introduce yourself and begin to set the foundation needed to forge a successful path forward as a group.

That is how I felt when Emilia gave me my big life promotion, elevating me from husband to my new title and role of dad. Felicia and I had started our trying for a child journey almost three years before Emilia was born. Just like the work promotion, there is a lot of hard work and planning that goes into preparing to bring your first child into this world. From the getting pregnant phase to being pregnant, getting the nursery ready, to the delivery room, each phase brings a whole new challenge and new elements to learn and check off all in preparation for that day when the doctor delivers your child and tells you, "Congratulations Mom and Dad. It's a girl." Once you get that promotion, there is no turning back. The life and development of that little child is now in your hands whether you are ready or not.

Like the promotion to a leadership role at work, this is not to be taken lightly. The big difference between work and life promotions is, with work, they can strip that title and leadership role from you and fire you at any moment. With life, no one can take that title and promotion of dad (in theory) from you once you bring a child into this world. Sadly for me, I felt like I had been fired from my new role as dad to Emilia. Those 39 days with her were magical and changed my perspective on life. I knew in my heart that I was still a dad (the noun), but I didn't have anyone to be a dad (the verb) to anymore. I definitely knew that I wasn't that married dude without a kid anymore, but I also knew that I wasn't a dad in the traditional sense either. I was stuck in a weird limbo world that I wouldn't wish upon anyone.

It was and still is very confusing to reconcile what my role truly was/is. I really struggled with this after Emilia passed and still do to this day. Is someone really a dad if they have no one to dad? Dad's didn't have time to do what I was doing every day because they are, you know, busy being a dad to a newborn. On the other hand, I certainly was no longer someone who had never been a dad either. All the stuff I used to find fun and important no longer provided any joy. I was trapped in two worlds without an identity.

If I asked someone that was previously in a leadership role and now back to an individual contributor if they were still a leader, the answer would be a resounding no. If you don't have anyone to lead, you aren't a leader. With that logic in mind, what really is a dad? Is dad a state of mind, a verb and action you perform, both, or neither? I have no idea.

As I was trying to figure this out for myself, I got a peek into how the rest of the world may view the answer to this topic, and I didn't love what I discovered. Days after Emilia's funeral was over, I found out how my employer, Salesforce's, stance on this very topic as my temporary bereavement leave had come to an end.

Salesforce is truly a special company in how it cares for its employees and goes above and beyond to treat them like human beings. They have some of the most innovative and generous policies in the world on a lot of things, and parental leave benefits are certainly tops among them. Salesforce provides six months of paid paternity leave for parents to bond with their children that can be taken at any time over the 12 months after the birth of your child. As we talked about before, this is incredibly generous, and I wouldn't have been able to even sit in this rubble, learn the lessons I learned, to even pick the option to reimagine my life and write this book without their generosity. I do NOT want this to sound like an attack on them, as it was an honest mistake. However, after Emilia passed away and my quick bereavement leave ended, I figured I would be able to keep on my paternity leave as I still had four months left to use before it expired. It turns out that wasn't the case, apparently, as I was no longer able to "bond" with my child because she wasn't there anymore, as the leave management company put it. The company that manages Salesforce's leave policies made me file for a switch from paternity leave to an extended bereavement leave of absence after I informed them of Emilia's passing. The amount of time off and pay benefits were still the same, but I was labeled as something different than a dad and had to jump through a bunch of hoops to switch my leave of absence in the system with the leave administrator. I know this doesn't really matter in the grand scheme of things, but it mattered to me. This was confirmation of how society saw me now. I was no longer a dad because I had no one to father.

To make matters worse for me on this topic, Father's Day came less than two months after we lost Emilia. I refused to celebrate. I told Felicia that I didn't want any gifts, and I didn't want anyone to make a fuss about it either. In my opinion, Father's Day isn't about fathers celebrating being fathers (the state of mind); it is about children celebrating their fathers and all they do for them in their lives (dad the verb). I didn't have any children to celebrate all that I did for them in this world, so I didn't want to take part in this holiday. I wasn't a dad, the verb. Everyone wished me a Happy Father's Day and told me that Emilia is smiling down on me. They tried to cheer me up and make me feel like I was still a dad, the verb. They told me that, "Just because Emilia isn't here, it doesn't change the fact that you are a dad." I couldn't disagree more. Yes, I had fathered a child, but I wasn't a dad at that moment. I spent my Father's Day crying at my daughter's grave, talking to my child about how much I missed her and being able to be a dad, the verb, to her. I hated that day and vowed not to go back there again the next Father's Day. Fathers aren't supposed to visit their children at a cemetery on Father's Day. The cemetery was filled with people that day, but it was mostly filled with children visiting their fathers, not the other way around.

Before we had Emilia, I wasn't really sure I wanted more than just one child. I always joked that if Felicia wanted to have another child, we could always adopt a 17-and-a-half-year-old and let them live with us for six months and then tell them they are on their own once they hit 18. I honestly didn't know if I wanted more children, and Felicia felt the same way. It wasn't that we were opposed to the idea, we just didn't know anything about parenting and didn't want to commit to more than one when we decided to start trying for children. I still felt this way all the way up until the moment that I met Emilia in that delivery room. However, she changed me that day. As soon as I saw her and watched her for a few days fighting for her chance at life, I told Felicia that I want all the babies and to get ready. There wasn't a doubt in my mind that I wanted to grow our family, and Felicia felt the same. Even though this declarative statement from both of us was just a few months ago, I didn't know if Felicia still felt the same way now.

This brings us full circle back to Felicia's answer on our Emilia walk on this day, where I mustered up the courage to ask the future children question. I don't remember her saying much other than she isn't ready to talk about that yet, but we can talk about it again when she feels more ready. I immediately smiled because she didn't dismiss the idea off-hand. I took this as a huge win, put my head down, didn't say anything else, and we kept on with our walk. I'm jumping ahead a little in the story, but as time passed and weeks turned to months, the topic was brought up time and time again on these nightly Emilia walks. I don't remember exactly when the scales tipped in my favor, but eventually, Felicia and I came to the decision to try for a sibling to Emilia. This was an exciting and terrifying new chapter that we were about to embark on (much more to come later in the story).

The moral of the story, without our Emilia walks, I don't think any of where my life is today would have been possible. Our paths were going in such different directions; it truly felt like we were walking on the edge of a cliff, and at any moment, our marriage could have collapsed had we not found a way to stay aligned. These Emilia walks kept us connected, and a lot of big life decisions and discussions occurred during these moments together. I can imagine that I could easily be writing this story and detailing how our marriage ultimately fell apart, led to us getting a divorce, and trying to move on with our own fresh starts in life. I think Emilia had a lot to do with keeping her parents together even after she passed away, and I'm forever grateful for her support.

Lessons from the Rubble - Grief Awareness and Learning the Platinum Rule

A few weeks after Emilia's passing, and once I got past the feeling of nothingness and decided to keep moving like Emilia would have wanted, my natural instincts of keeping things in order started to eventually kick in. I hate clutter and disorganization in my life. Seeing all the boxes, flowers, food, unread cards, texts, emails, and Facebook notifications was beginning to drive me insane. I think the thing that drives me the craziest is seeing that little unread message number next to a text, email, or app icon. As everything started to pile up, I felt compelled to try and do my best to manage this process and restore some semblance of order in our lives. As I looked over at my wife sobbing in bed, I knew that she could give zero shits about any of that stuff, and this was my own personal problem that had to be addressed if I wanted it done.

Side note, Felicia is one of those people that has over 10,000 unread emails in her inbox on her phone. Just typing that line makes me want to have a panic attack. In normal times she can deal with clutter in all areas of her life minus the two or three she cares about most, in which she's extremely organized. I mention this for context to say that in these moments, we were the furthest from "normal" times in our life, so I'm sure you can imagine that she literally couldn't have cared less about everything that I'm typing right now.

I decided to take my first stab at responding to some of the text messages from friends and family to let them know we appreciated them thinking about and praying for our family. The stock text I started to use was something like, "Thank you so much for the thoughts and prayers. While we are obviously devastated, we also feel really blessed to have been able to get to meet Emilia and share 39 days with her as she was the most amazing miracle." I really meant that, and it wasn't just me trying to put on a brave face or something. Hell, I even stated at the very beginning of my eulogy for Emilia, "Don't feel sorry for us!" These weren't just words to me; it is really how I felt inside, but I could see how people may not have believed that was how I was really feeling given all that we were going through.

One of our good friends, Bryan, replied back to my response, "You don't have to be a superhero. It's okay to feel pain and cry." This line hit me hard and stopped me dead in my tracks! I honestly didn't know how to respond back or even if I wanted to at all. I couldn't tell if I was pissed or proud that I had people in my world willing to challenge me at such a vulnerable time in my life. It really made me think, so much so that I still remember it to this day. I can without a doubt say that there isn't a single other response that I received from my reply to anyone else that I can remember right now, but I remember this one from Bryan. This one really got me thinking in so many ways. I started to question, why was this so impactful to me? Was I lying to myself somehow? Was I running away from the pain and sadness or something? Was there something wrong with me? I wasn't trying to be a superhero. I was just trying to honor my daughter's memory and her never-quit attitude. What did people want me to do? Collapse and crawl into a hole? Cry all day? Is that better than trying to stay positive and keep moving?

I think in some regards, Bryan was right, and I appreciate him challenging me upon reflection. We eventually talked about this in person, and I told him the same thing. As we will talk about later in the book, one of the key discoveries that I made during this journey is that life is all about trying our best to maintain balance. Bryan's comments reminded me that I wasn't being balanced at this moment at all. While I certainly didn't need to sit around crying all day long, I did need to spend a lot more time embracing the pain, sadness, emptiness, and loneliness that was thrust upon me after losing Emilia. I couldn't run away from this. I couldn't use positive thinking to somehow pretend like nothing happened. I couldn't pretend that the pain didn't exist. If I was going to honor Emilia the way I intended, I needed to sit in that rubble for as long as I could take it until I had reimagined what "never quit" and "living for two" really meant.

As the mail and packages kept piling up, I slowly began to hate mail time every single day. Every time I saw the mailman drop off a bunch of packages and cards, I knew what I was in for. It was like death by 1,000 papercuts. Every piece of mail, card, gift, keepsake, etc., was another reminder of Emilia and brought me right back to the NICU in my mind as I watched my wife cradle our dead child in her arms while I cleared out the room of all of our stuff. Mail time each day began to feel like another groundhog day where I had to relive my daughter's passing over and over again. I'd spend all day clearing out the inbox, texts, cards, breaking down the boxes and taking them to the trash, etc. I'd put everything away and in its place, lock it away in my mind, and then a fresh batch would arrive the next day that would force me to do it all over again. It felt like torture to me. Felicia felt differently. She deeply appreciated each little keepsake that arrived from friends and family with Emilia's name on it. While I'm glad it was giving her solace, it was giving me pain.

Not only was the constant barrage of gifts and messages forcing me to relive my daughter's passing each day, but it also started to make me feel like a charity case. If there is one thing in my world that I am not, it's a charity case. Don't get me wrong; there is nothing wrong with the act of giving. Giving is one of the most deeply gratifying things we can do as humans and a necessary part of this world. I'm proud to call myself a giver and do so as often as I can. However, charity, in my mind, meant helplessness. Charity is what you do for someone that can't do for themselves. That's the opposite of how I would describe myself. I'm fiercely independent, a problem solver, and a creative thinker. I challenge and question everything. If there is a problem to tackle, I'm all over it and will find the resources and people to help if needed. I certainly don't need some hero to come in and take it all off my plate.

Sadly, I was even starting to get frustrated at my own mom, who was still coming over every night to bring food for Felicia and me weeks removed from Emilia's passing. I kept telling her that I was okay and didn't need any more food. I'm a big boy and can take care of myself and my family. My mom is an amazing woman who also happens to be an amazing chef as well. I'm really lucky to be surrounded by such amazing women in my life, my Mom chief among them. She also knows me well enough to know that I don't need help. Hell, when I was 7, I banned her from doing my laundry because she wasn't "doing it right." She gladly accepted. This is the person she birthed, raised, and knew my fiercely independent nature all too well. I don't accept help willingly and would rather solve my own problems as that is how I learn. However, she also knew that I was in deep pain for the first time in my life, and she was just trying to do anything she could to help. Cooking is a unique gift of hers, and she knows that her cooking, in particular, brings me happiness as I have a complicated diet and don't really trust anyone to cook for me other than Felicia and my Mother. I appreciated that and didn't want to take it away from her.

Luckily for both of us, I was in the middle of reading a book at this exact moment called *The Go-Giver*, in which I would learn a powerful lesson that I could apply to my growing receiving dilemma from my mom and everyone else. *The Go-Giver* is a short story about the power of giving and how it can change the world. It had been recommended to me by my boss earlier in the year. I was consuming books like it was my job at this point, and *The Go-Giver* just happened to be on the docket during this particular week. The following is what I learned.

The five laws of giving, as laid out in The Go-Giver, are as follows:

1). Your true worth is determined by how much more you give in value than take in payment.

2). The law of compensation - If you want more success, find more people to serve.

3). The law of influence - Your influence is determined by how abundantly you place other people's interests first.

4). The law of authenticity - The most valuable gift you have to offer is yourself.

5). The law of reciprocity - You have to be open to receiving to complete the cycle of giving.

As I finished up reading about the final law of giving, the law of reciprocity, it hit me really hard. I started to reflect and write in my journal about why I hated mail time so much. Why was I getting mad at my mom for wanting to come over with food every night? I was turning away help from anyone and everyone, and I didn't know why. I proudly call myself a giver and will happily give unprovoked all day, every day. However, at this moment, I realized that if I truly wanted to call myself a giver, I had to be open to receive and welcome the support from everyone else. I needed to let others complete the cycle of giving themselves when I was in need of support this time. This is how giving works. It isn't a one-way street. After reflecting on this, I called my mom and told her about my revelation around reciprocity and the 5th law of giving. I asked her to continue to come over every night to bring food for as long as she would like. She happily agreed, and I could tell it made her smile even through the phone.

The funny thing about grief is that no one manages it or deals with it the same. Two people can be going through the exact same tragedy and processing it in completely different ways. There really is no right answer on how to handle this as a friend or loved one because you truly have no idea how each person is processing their own pain, let alone what will bring them comfort. One day, about a month after Emilia's passing, I was over at my parents' house and talking with my sister as we sat in my parent's family room. We were catching up on life and talking about all that I had been experiencing since Emilia's funeral. I started to tell her about my atomic bomb theory, still in its early stages at this point, and talking about the concept of post-traumatic growth that I had been hearing from different books I was reading. After listening for a few minutes, she recommended a book called *Option B* by Sheryl Sandberg, the famous COO at Facebook. My sister thought some of the concepts I was expressing frustration and curiosity about might find a friend in this book.

Option B, I would come to find out, is about Sheryl Sandberg's own personal atomic bomb that went off when her husband unexpectedly died while working out in a gym on vacation in Mexico with friends. She describes dealing with her own fallout while navigating friends, family, work, etc. The book then goes on to talk about how pain can sometimes leave a gift, how people can learn resilience and even "bounce forward" from terrible life events and tragedies that strike out of the blue. It sounds like a familiar story, right?

To be honest, I wasn't really into reading books about pain, tragedy, and loss. I had actually been trying to avoid them as I wasn't really interested in going down that rabbit hole yet in my mind. I was still actively trying to stay away from imagining other people's traumatic stories as I still couldn't process my own at this point in the journey. I was really into reading books about core values, culture, deep-thinking, philosophy, questioning, religion, business, psychology, etc. I told my sister, "Cool. I'll check it out. Thanks for the suggestion." I had no intention of reading this book after I left my parent's house that day. Luckily for me, my sister is another one of those amazing women in my life, and she went ahead and ordered it on Amazon that day without me knowing. The book arrived at my house a few days after our conversation. As I opened the package and saw the book, I laughed and thought, "Why not?"

I started on the book later that day just to see what it was all about. It was during the first few chapters that I first heard Sheryl use the term "The Platinum Rule," which I had never heard of before and instantly resonated with as I thought nailed the dilemma I was experiencing at the time with all the gifts, cards, food, etc. So what is "The Platinum Rule" exactly? Well, to understand the Platinum Rule, we first need to discuss something we've all heard in the Golden Rule. Quick reminder, the golden rule is, "Treat others as you would like to be treated." That rule is great and all, but it is kind of selfish in nature. Just look at the words, "treat others the way you want to be treated." The golden rule asks that you think of yourself first and then decide on how you want to interact with others. It is the most basic form of logic to apply to human interaction. It certainly works because you wouldn't want to harm yourself, so you don't harm others.

Unfortunately, Golden Rule logic doesn't really translate well when it comes to dealing with individuals grieving or going through a traumatic experience. How are you supposed to know how you would want to be treated if you've never been through the same experience? Understanding someone else's pain, suffering, and grief requires next-level human understanding, listening, and empathy. It requires us to go far beyond thinking of ourselves and focus all of our attention on the bereaved individual. This is where "the Platinum Rule" comes in to save the day.

The Platinum Rule is "treating others the way they want to be treated." It's a subtle but transformational change from the Golden Rule. Changing the "you" to "they" changes everything. The last thing any grieving person wants to do is to try and make you feel good or bad about whether you helped them or not. The sad truth is, they don't care about you at this moment in their life. The Platinum Rule, unlike the Golden Rule, puts the grieving person first. You may not know what they are going through or be able to imagine the reality they are experiencing, but you know them and what might be good for them in this difficult moment. The Platinum Rule requires a friend or family member to think about the person going through a tragedy, deeply consider how they might be processing this, and what might bring them some relief based on their personalities. A great example of how to apply the Platinum Rule thinking would be the topic we discussed earlier when Felicia and I were both processing mail time each day. Because Felicia is a naturally emotional person and enjoys feeling emotions, her friends and family should send her sentimental items like mementos and cards. I, on the other hand, am a problem solver, a doer, and a task-driven, independent person that hates disorganization. If you were using the Platinum Rule on me, an idea might be to send me something to keep my mind occupied, like a plant to figure out how to take care of, volunteer to come over and help me do some landscaping to keep my yard in order to free up more time for Felicia, or take me to a tennis court and force me to play. What you don't want to do for me is give me more things that I don't need and add clutter to my life. Sending me more unwanted things and adding clutter is Golden Rule thinking, in my opinion, from the sender. They are thinking, "What would make me feel better at this moment?" And then they do that.

The Platinum Rule has become my new go-to on how to relate to others in every aspect of my life. It is the key to unlock the fifth habit from *The 7 Habits of Highly Effective People*, where we seek first to understand, then we might actually make the desired impact in our loved ones' lives that we seek when dealing with a tragic situation. If we used a little more Platinum Rule thinking the next time before we sent anything to a loved one experiencing a loss or trauma, we might realize that all that person really needs is someone to send a text or leave a voicemail to check in and say they love them and no need to respond unless you just need someone to listen to you as we know you have a million things on your mind. The simple act of letting them know they are loved and not having the burden to respond could mean everything. Plus, we could all save a little money by not buying that 100th piece of jewelry or that Harry and David gift basket that 95% will get thrown out, etc.

Lessons from the Rubble – Stories of Post-Traumatic "Firsts" (Lessons in Re-Engaging with Society - Extended Family, Friends, Strangers, and Tennis)

Within the first few months after losing Emilia, I slowly started to reemerge into the world and began partaking in more "normal" activities with family and friends. Felicia, for the most part, continued to isolate herself at home as she just wasn't ready to fully re-engage in the world at any level. It really sucked (and often hurt) not to have her with me as I embarked on trying to figure out how to interact with people again when all I could think about was Emilia. Felicia is my forever comfort blanket. She is my better half. Half is the keyword there because without her by my side, it felt like half of me was missing as I was embarking on these new firsts in my life. I wasn't going to push her to do something she was uncomfortable with as everyone has their own grieving process, so I started reemerging alone into the world and braving this by myself. Maybe it was my past struggles with panic attacks and learning how to overcome them by diving headfirst into what scares me, maybe I was trying to be the superhero like Bryan said, maybe I just wanted to prove to myself that I could do it, or maybe it was the spirit of Emilia in me pushing me to never quit. I honestly don't know what was propelling me forward at this moment in my life. Nevertheless, I did, and I'll spend the rest of this chapter walking through a few of my "firsts" that I experienced while sitting in the rubble period of my life.

Firsts with Tennis - Learning How to Answer "The Question"

I've touched on this a few times in our story, but tennis has been my lifelong sporting obsession. I started playing when I was four or five years old. I was winning city championships in my National Junior Tennis League programs not long after that, played and trained all day long in the summers as a kid, was #1 singles on my high school team my senior year, and won intramural championships in college. Since college, I've continued to play competitively in USTA leagues, where the winning and fun have continued, and I have no plans of stopping for the rest of my life. If anything, my love for tennis has only grown as I've gotten older. It is my outlet for fun, competition, exercise, challenge, and escape from my day-to-day life. It motivates me to work out harder in the gym every day to stay in shape to play at a decent level. Most of all, tennis is something I was desperately hoping to enjoy with Emilia and my other future children someday. I always imagined it would be "our thing."

Since Emilia's birth, tennis had taken a huge back seat to everything else going on in my life (and rightfully so). Courts started to shut down due to the pandemic in late February, Emilia was born in mid-March and passed away in late April, and now it was late May. It had been about three months since I had last picked up a racquet or even thought about tennis. There had been a long gap post-college when tennis had left my life because I had become primarily focused on "my career" and making money, my tennis playing network had shrunk, etc. Luckily, in my late twenties, I reconnected with my first sports love, and we have been inseparable ever since. At this very moment in my life, this was the longest I'd gone in over seven years without playing the game. I'm used to normally playing at least two to three times a week on average. To put it mildly, tennis was an important part of my life pre-February, 2020.

However, I wasn't sure if I was ready to play again or not. I didn't know how I was going to be able to focus on playing a stupid game again when all I could think about was my daughter and the searing pain from losing her that permeated my every thought. I was honestly scared to learn if tennis, like everything else, would ever be the same again. Losing your daughter puts a lot in perspective. While tennis was important to me, was it really that important? Also, most of my tennis friends were literally just that, "tennis friends." I don't hang out with a lot of them outside of when we are playing, and I've always preferred it that way. Don't get me wrong, a lot of these people are amazing people that I would love to hang out with outside of tennis, but for some reason, I've never really been keen on mixing those two worlds. I really didn't want to bring my personal life into this arena. Tennis is my forever escape from all the other aspects of my life. Put me on a court, and all the other distractions in life disappear. I can play for hours and hours without even knowing the outside world exists. It never gets old. I don't look at my phone, watch the clock, worry about to-do's, discuss politics, religion, life, etc. I literally am in my own little world that is focused on competition, exercise, and trying to improve shot by shot. I was worried that this would no longer be true now, given what was going on in my world. Nothing was separated anymore for me. Everything was all Emilia all the time.

Late in May, one of the guys on my USTA league team, Alex, texted me to see if I wanted to join him at the park down the street for a doubles match. I knew that Alex was aware of what was going on in my life, so I didn't want this all to be super awkward. I stared at his text invitation for what felt like hours before I just decided, "What the hell. Let's give it a try!" A few days later, Alex and I met up at the courts with a couple of his other friends he had invited, Kent and Bert. I barely knew either of them, and I don't think I had played with them before, so that was a relief. I wouldn't have to answer any questions about Emilia or how Felicia and I were doing. We all said our hellos and started warming up. Alex briefly asked me how I was doing, and I said something like, "It's been tough." We nodded, and I think he understood that I just wanted to play and not talk about it, so that is what we did. For the next couple of hours, I felt a little bit of normal Chris begin to return. Though the immense sadness would occasionally overwhelm me in between points, while I was swinging the racquet and running around the court, I didn't think about much else other than playing tennis. It was so nice to not be the sad dude that just lost his daughter for once and be able to be in my own little tennis bubble with people that didn't know me well enough that I had to talk about this aspect of my life. We were there for tennis and tennis only. This was exactly what I needed and wanted in this experience.

After we finished playing, we all said our goodbyes, and I took the short walk back to my house, which is just down the street from the courts. I had officially played tennis again for the first time after losing my daughter and made it through the experience. It was the exact escape I needed at this moment. I had proven to myself that tennis can still hold some value in my life, and I was ready to keep playing more.

Over the next few months, I slowly started to play more and more regularly again. Since a lot of the leagues I normally played in were shut down due to the pandemic, I found a few local informal challenge ladders to start participating in instead. Those were amazing! I barely knew anyone, for the most part, so all I had to do was play tennis and just be another competitor. I never had to address any conversations about Emilia, and I could use it as the escape from my regular life that I've always used tennis as prior to all of this.

Meeting all these new random people did have one unintended side effect. It taught me how to meet new random people again, how to talk about my life, and how to talk about Emilia to strangers. Specifically, it taught me how to address the question, "So, do you have any children?" At any other point in my life, this would have been such an innocent question, one that I would have never even given a second thought about if someone asked. It is about as commonplace as, "What do you do for a living?" or "Are you married?" when you are first meeting someone at my age. Sadly for me, this question wasn't innocent banter anymore. It was a fully loaded question that actually brought an insane amount of stress and anxiety when it was brought up during changeovers in between games.

The first time this happened, I was playing in one of these new challenge ladders matches against someone that was basically a stranger. We had just finished our first set, and we were both grabbing a drink of water before starting our next set. As we were chatting, we were talking about COVID, what we did for a living, etc. And then, the dreaded "So, do you have any children?" question was asked. I froze and didn't know how to address it. I wasn't really expecting it, and I had no idea how to respond.

A part of me wanted to tell him everything about our experience and my amazing daughter, but I was worried that would be too intense. A part of me wanted to say I don't really feel like answering this question and just getting back to the match. A part of me wanted to say, "No," because I technically didn't have any living children, but I thought that wouldn't be fair to Emilia because she is certainly my child, and I'm so proud of her.

After thinking about it for ten seconds, I said something like, "Well, that's actually kind of complicated." I then proceeded to tell the entire story about Emilia being born early, our fight in the NICU, how amazing she is, tragically losing her, and sharing all the graphic details in between. It was like someone had thought they just turned on a kitchen faucet only to realize it was actually a fire hydrant. I went on and on for about five minutes, not holding much, if anything, back. Halfway through, I think I realized that was a little too much, but I couldn't help myself. It just kept coming out of me. This was my life; I was proud of my daughter and wanted to talk about her.

After I was done sharing, I could tell that I had shocked the poor guy as he wasn't expecting that. He looked at me with his eyes facing the ground and his head sunken and said, "I'm so sorry. I can't imagine what you are going through." I thanked him, and we awkwardly ended our chat and got back to playing the next set.

Over the course of the next few months, this question came up a handful of other times with new players I met. Slowly but surely, I stopped getting overwhelmed by the question and started to find a way to talk about Emilia, share our story, and not make it overwhelming for the other person. It was like Goldie Locks and her porridge. It gradually developed from sharing way too much to sharing a little too much to sharing just the right amount of information where all parties could leave satisfied with the response. The final refined approach that I had perfected to this all-important question went something like this, "Yes, I have a daughter. She was born super premature, about four months before her due date. She battled with everything she had for 40 days in the NICU, and tragically lost her fight due to complications from an unexpected surgery."

That 20-second "elevator pitch" shared enough for me to feel happy that they understand that I do have a daughter, and I'm proud of her. They also can get an understanding of the journey that we went through together. That satisfied my need to talk about Emilia, and it gives them a short enough description where they don't have to feel incredibly awkward with me sharing too many graphic details. If they want to know more, they can ask, and I'm happy to keep going. If they don't, they can say, "I can't imagine. I'm sorry for your loss!" and we can get back to playing.

As weird as this sounds, all these tennis chats were incredibly important training for me as I made my way back into the world and learned how to talk about my daughter that was fair to her and myself. I never wanted to hide

Emilia from the world like she was a deep dark family secret. If I was going to "live for two," I couldn't neglect to talk about the other individual in that equation. It is my duty to share her story with everyone that will listen and live my life with the inspiration she bestowed on me. As crazy as this sounds, playing tennis again helped me to find our voice.

Don't Take Things for Granted!

I'm time-jumping a few months into the future from these other stories to late September 2020 because I wanted to share a father-daughter tennis moment that brought me to tears to illustrate how much it hurt knowing that I would never get to share tennis with my daughter. Months down the road from where we currently are in the story (May/June 2020), I was back to playing some tournament tennis down in Evansville, Indiana, for the Southern Indiana Open in September 2020. I had just won my first match of the day, against a 20-year-old college player, and was recovering and eating before I had to play my next match a few hours later against an 18-year-old kid (I may have been a little ambitious on this one as I'm getting a little old for this).

The first match was brutal, and I barely escaped with a win in the third set tie-breaker. We beat the crap out of each other in the hot summer early morning. My body was wrecked; I was dehydrated and hurting all over. I needed all the time and rest I could get to recover if I had any chance of winning the next match (which I sadly didn't).

To get out of the heat, stretch, eat, and cool down, I drove over to a nearby indoor court facility where I hung out on the upper balcony by myself as I ate some food, got some A/C, and stretched while waiting for my next match. This upper balcony overlooked all the indoor courts, so you could see everyone playing below you across the whole facility. Since it was summertime, most of the courts were empty except for one doubles match with some old-timers playing.

As I sat there doing my best to get my mind right for the next match, out walked a dad and his two young daughters onto the court with a hopper full of balls. One of the two girls looked like she was 10 or 11, and the other looked like she was 5. The little, tiny five-year-old girl took out her racquet, sat on the bench in between courts, and watched with excitement as her dad and big sister started doing some hitting drills out on the court.

242

The dad was feeding balls and coaching the older daughter while they were rallying back and forth and doing drills. She was pretty good and hitting solid shots all over the court as her dad guided her on shot selection. You could tell that they do this regularly, and her training was something that they all took seriously.

After about 15 minutes of hitting and drills with the older daughter, the dad called the younger daughter in to feed her some balls while her sister took a rest and got some water. It was like a WWF wrestler just got tagged into a match to come and help out their partner. This little girl came sprinting off the bench and skipped out to the service line to await instructions from her dad. She was so excited to play. He started to feed her a few balls and instructed her to rally back and forth with him. I was expecting her to struggle at that age, but I was blown away by how well she was doing.

They hit back and forth for about 20-25 shots straight as they played a little game of mini tennis in the service box. Mini-tennis, if you don't know, is when you play tennis on a condensed court with the service line acting as the baseline. You don't have to hit it hard. All you have to do is get to the ball and hit touch shots to get it back over the net and keep it inside the service line. It is a great game to learn how to rally and play as you can focus on footwork, racquet preparation, touch, and feel, etc.

This little girl was a natural. She would get to each ball quickly, tap it over the net back to her dad with a nice controlled swing, and then run back to the middle of the service box and await the return from her dad. They were in a great rhythm, and I couldn't help from looking on from my perch up on the balcony. After a few minutes of watching in amazement at the little girl's skill and excitement, I pulled out my phone and started recording. I began to cry. All I could think about was little Emilia running around that court, excited to play with me, just like this happy little girl was with her dad. This was my fatherhood dream. It hurt so bad to watch, yet I loved every minute of it. The little girl barely missed a shot as she rallied back and forth with her dad for about 5 minutes or so until it was time for her big sister to come back in and work on her game again. When her time was up, she skipped back over to the bench with the biggest smile on her face and her eyes wide open as she watched her big sis start hitting again.

I was bawling my eyes out as I sat back down on the balcony at a table to eat. I sent the video to Felicia. I hope the father of those two girls understands how blessed he is to be able to do that with his daughters and never takes that for granted. This is a great lesson for us all. Whenever I find myself complaining about stupid crap (like my leg hurting while I'm running on a treadmill, for example), I remember moments like this and the paradigm shift that could be someone else's life (like a former runner that became a paraplegic who would probably give anything just to be able to run again).

DON'T TAKE THIS STUFF FOR GRANTED!

Firsts with Friends

A Kaleidoscope of Experiences

The first time I remember actually seeing anyone other than our immediate families was a month or so after Emilia had passed away. Felicia and I got up the nerve to invite two of our couple-friends, Mark and Bryan and Dustin and Amanda, over for some socially distant wine and conversation on our patio sometime in late May. Felicia and I were both pretty apprehensive about this one as we weren't sure if we were ready to be social again. Prior to this event, our only time even seeing anyone we knew outside of family was about a week after she had passed away when we ran into Justin, and his daughter on one of our nightly Emilia walks about a week after she had passed away. That was a five-minute encounter with a random acquaintance, and it was still hard. Were we really ready for an entire evening with close friends that knew us so well? It felt like we were in this in-between stage where we weren't quite ready to fully engage with the world, but we also didn't want to just sit at home by ourselves all the time either. So, I thought a safe evening with good friends in our own home might do us both a little good, and Felicia reluctantly agreed. She told me, "I'll give it a try, but if I feel like I want to leave and go back inside, I will." I told her that was totally understandable.

I was actually pretty nervous, as I'm sure Mark, Bryan, Dustin, and Amanda were as well. What were we going to talk about? Our past conversations would always revolve around wine, traveling, work, food, etc. None of that mattered to Felicia and me anymore. I knew that I didn't want to burden anyone with what was actually going on in our life now or how awful and depressing each day was for us either. On the other hand, I can't imagine (there it is again) what they thought as they got in the car and drove over to our house that evening. I've never been in a situation where I was supposed to play the role of a friend having the first get-together with another friend after a recent tragedy in their life. That has to be an incredibly tough position for them to assume as well. I know that if the roles were reversed, I would have been terrified of not knowing what to expect. I would have been worried about what to say right off the bat. Do we talk about it? Do we not talk about it? What would make them feel best? Do we talk about our lives and what is going on for us? Will that be offensive? Do we talk about the stuff we used to talk about? After all, we didn't invite all of them over to grieve together. We were there to have fun together, whatever that meant at this point in our lives. It's a difficult spot for everyone, and I really appreciate all of them braving this awkward dance with us in retrospect.

Mark and Bryan arrived first, about 15 minutes before Dustin and Amanda. After exchanging some socially distant air hugs, we sat down at the patio table, poured a glass of wine, and started catching up. None of us said anything about Emilia. I don't remember what we even spoke about (probably Covid and quarantine or something). Felicia kind of blankly stared down at our patio table, didn't make a ton of eye contact and hardly spoke. I was doing my best to smile, laugh, and act like my old self, but the conversation felt a little forced with an underlying sense of, "Should we talk about it or not?"

Dustin and Amanda arrived and walked up onto our patio from the driveway. We all exchanged a few more air hugs and poured them a glass of wine as they joined the table. After a few minutes, Amanda, bless her heart, finally said, "We don't all have to pretend like nothing happened. You two are going through something terrible, so if you'd like to talk about it, we are here to talk about it." That is why we all love Amanda. She's never afraid to just say what everyone's thinking and open it up for discussion. That blunt comment officially broke the ice, and you could feel the elephant slowly get up and walk out of the room. I was so relieved.

So many crazy things had happened in our lives since we all last saw each other back in early February for a dinner party that Mark and Bryan had hosted. We wanted to talk about our daughter, how amazing she was, and how much we miss her. We wanted to share her photos and stories from the NICU with our friends. Thanks to Amanda, and a good amount of wine, the conversation started flowing, and the rest of the night was filled with friends sharing real feelings, opening up, and being vulnerable about all kinds of topics that aren't normally discussed at a patio wine hangout. Felicia even started opening up and sharing, which was so amazing to see. It felt really good to see a glimpse of the woman that I married as she slowly re-emerged from her shell out on the patio that night. The fact that she stayed out there with us late into the evening before retreating back inside was a huge win in my book.

At one point during the evening, the conversation shifted to talking about grief awareness, or lack thereof, in our world today. Felicia and I were sharing some of our newly minted thoughts and observations on the topic around, as a society, how truly bad we are at this one. We shared how people always seem to feel the need to make other people's stories about themselves so they can appear empathetic and relatable. The problem with an empathetic approach, it is almost impossible to truly empathize with someone else's story as it is so rare that your experiences were truly the same. What we were finding people doing with us was trying to draw corollaries to their own experiences in an attempt to make us feel better. Really, all that was doing was making them feel better and showing that they understood what we were going through.

Amanda chimed in with a comment that I loved during this exchange. She compared people's individual lived experiences to that of a kaleidoscope. The moment I heard her say the word kaleidoscope, I immediately thought, "Nailed It!" We all have our own stories to tell, and each deserves to be heard and embraced for the unique journeys that they are. We don't need to empathize. We just need to listen.

To be fair, my grief awareness toolbox, prior to our experience, was embarrassingly empty. In my daily writing and reflection, I was starting to realize and explore how awful and unsupportive I had been with some of my own close friends and family going through trauma and personal loss. As I reflected on this, I was becoming almost disgusted with myself at how badly I mismanaged my interactions with my own friends in some of their most vulnerable life moments. One great example of where I fell spectacularly short was in engaging with my military friends returning from deployment. I don't think I've ever even asked them about their time serving abroad, and I definitely didn't give them a forum to express themselves, share their stories, and be vulnerable upon their return from such a traumatic and life-changing experience. I did the Golden Rule thing. I thought to myself, what would I want out of this interaction and made the assumption that they didn't want to talk about it. I assumed that they were the same person as when they left and would basically want to forget about the war that they had just returned from and put that in the past and resume their lives. I made no effort to learn about their new experiences, understand how they had changed their life, and learn about the new paradigms that were evolving based on their unique journey. I'm so ashamed of that behavior. Mostly, I'm sad that I missed out on some important stories and life lessons I could have heard if I would have just asked and listened.

As we wrapped up the evening with the group, I remember Bryan sharing a final thought about how nice it is to be around friends who are willing to share deeply and be truly vulnerable with each other. I could not have agreed more with this sentiment. I heard a saying once, "When times are good, your friends know you. When times are bad, you know your friends." I think this perfectly summed up this night. I'm happy to say that this group of people must be real friends because they weren't afraid to continue knowing Felicia and me when times were bad in our life. They stepped up and walked right through that door, which I'm sure was very scary. Our first return to life around others couldn't have gone any better. It gave Felicia and I hope for the future that we might possibly still be able to incorporate Emilia with who we were before all this happened. Not only could we incorporate her, but we had a real chance at developing even deeper connections with our friends and family if we were open to sharing together and listening to each other and our individual kaleidoscopes of experiences.

I May Look Okay…But I'm Not Okay

One of my lifelong best friends, Adam, was back in town, visiting from his home in Florida, sometime in early July. To put my relationship with Adam in context, my mom, dad, and sister are probably the only people in this world that know me better than Adam. We've been best friends since age five when we met on the pee-wee baseball diamond and have had an incredibly close connection ever since. We are two peas in a pod. He is the only person in this world that might be as competitive as I am. At any point in time, we can turn the most mundane activities into a battle for who can be the best, and it never gets old no matter how much we age.

Together, we've been through damn near everything life can throw at us, and we've always stayed close. Whether it was separating during high school when his family got a divorce and sent him to like six different schools over four years, to me moving off to college, to crippling drug addictions that almost took his life, to living together in a one-bedroom apartment in South Bend, Indiana when we both wanted to kill each other as Adam fought to regain his footing and overcome his past life, to moving to Florida and starting a whole new chapter of rebuilding his own world, we've been through it all together,

247

and somehow we've always been able to stay the exact same in our friendship. To put it mildly, Adam and I have been through some shit together.

Since Adam moved to Florida about a decade ago, we only see each other once or twice a year, but we make the most of it whenever we are able to be together. Normally, the second we reunite, it feels like nothing has changed no matter how much older we get or what is going on in our lives. On this particular occasion, however, things were completely different than the last time we last saw each other six months prior, back in December of 2019, for the Colts-Bucs game we went to see down in Tampa. I certainly wasn't the same person that he had seen back in December when I was so pumped to officially tell him we were expecting our first child. We were both incredibly excited and full of hope back then. Since that time, I felt like I had aged about 15 years, and I could hardly even recognize myself anymore as my life was changing at lightning speed.

He was only going to be in town for a weekend visit, so we thought it would be a great idea to meet up for a quick trip down to my parent's lake house to take the boat out for some fun and sun. Adam brought his fiancé, Rachel, and we had all hoped that Felicia would make it out to hang with us all as a couple. Unfortunately, she still wasn't really ready for activities like a day at the lake, so I met up with Adam and Rachel solo.

When I arrived at the lake house, Adam and Rachel were already there, having arrived a few minutes before me. From the moment I arrived, this visit felt different than any of our past interactions. Firstly, I didn't have Felicia with me, which was totally out of the norm. Secondly, as I pulled into the driveway, I was on a video chat talking to my therapist of all people. It is hard to explain how weird it is for me to even write that last sentence. Before Emilia, the thought of me ever having a therapist was almost laughable to me. I was way more likely to have a psychic (which I did) than a therapist. I've never really seen a ton of value in a therapist in my life. I figured any mental problems I needed to solve, I could figure it out on my own and usually did. If I needed help from an outside voice, I'd watch a video, read a book, listen to a podcast, etc. However, here we are. This is a whole new world and a whole new Chris. Loretta and I spoke every Saturday at 10 a.m. and had been since Emilia had passed away. This just happened to be the same time that Adam and I had agreed to meet up at the lake house, so I figured I would do double duty as I drove down from Indianapolis with the intention of wrapping up the call before they arrived. I figured I would have a few minutes to chat alone before Adam and Rachel got there, but, of course, Adam had to beat me down there.

As I pulled in, I hurriedly hugged Adam and Rachel, let them into the house, told them I was going to finish the rest of my therapy session down by the water and that I'd be back up to the house in 15 minutes. I ran down to the dock, far away from the house, to finish the conversation as privately as possible. As Loretta and I finished up our session, I walked back up the stairs from the dock to the balcony on the back of the house where Adam and Rachel were waiting. Keep in mind, at this point in time in my journey, I was about three months removed from Emilia's passing. I had been working really hard to reflect on my life and who I wanted to be since my daughter had passed. I was slowly starting to emerge from the rubble of the blast, and the blueprints of my new city were taking shape. I say this to put into context that, while I was no longer feeling nothingness like I was back on April 23rd, I definitely still wasn't okay yet at this point and had no idea exactly where my life was headed.

We hugged again once I got back to the house, and I think Adam seemed a bit relieved to see that I was somewhat looking and acting like my old self. After a few minutes of catching up, talking about Emilia and this whole journey, and hearing about what was going on in their lives, we got straight into Adam and Chris mode. Before I knew it, we were having a diving contest off the dock to see who could dive the furthest out in the water and measuring it with a noodle floaty to mark where we landed. I don't think you could make a more Adam and Chris game than that. Somehow a few random dives off the dock slowly escalated into a fierce competition where we had to enlist Rachel to be the judge to ensure no one was cheating and the winner was fair. That is the perfect scenario to illustrate our relationship. The best part is that I know we both love every minute of it, and it never gets old, even if we are both in our mid-30s.

The rest of the day, we hung out, had a few drinks, took the boat out, and played more stupid games. As we were winding down the day, hanging out in the water one last time before we headed out to the cars and back up to Indy, Adam said something like, "It's good to see that you are doing okay." I remember responding to him, "I may look okay, but I'm not okay." I was still struggling every moment of every day, desperately missing Emilia and crying every morning as I wrote in my journal to her. I was still struggling to make it out of bed each day just to finish the stupid reading, writing, and exercising activities I had self-imposed on myself to keep me moving. I was still struggling to find a way to muster up the courage to make it out of my house and down to the lake house to see my best friend while leaving my grieving wife at home alone. I was still struggling to answer and return phone calls from other close friends that I had been putting off for weeks because I knew what we were going to talk about, and I didn't have the strength to do it. I was still struggling to keep my marriage alive and worrying about if all of this was going to break us at the end of the day. I was still struggling to understand why this happened to us and how I was going to live for two every day to honor Emilia. Quite honestly, I was still struggling a lot. I may have been able to hide it well to one of my best friends that I had known for 30 years, but sadly, I was no longer the Chris that he once knew. I don't know if that change would be good or bad in the long run, but I know that I wasn't the same person and never would be again. I was in the process of rebuilding my city, and it was still TBD on what that would end up looking like. The only thing I knew for certain was that my new city wouldn't look anything like it had before.

Life Sprinters vs. Marathoners

We've touched on this a few times earlier in our story, but I'll throw this out here as a quick reminder again. When we first found out we were pregnant with Emilia, we learned within a matter of months that four of our closest friends were also expecting around the same time. Two of Felicia's really close friends, Katie and Ashley, were both expecting their first children with their husbands. We found out that we were all having girls, and Felicia, Ashley, and Katie were all pumped to have each other together on this new journey of us all embarking on parenthood for the first time.

At the same time, two of my close friends, Rob and Samir, also found out they were both expecting their first children as well that would be due in the late summer / early fall with their wives. It was about to be a baby bonanza of firstborn children, and we all couldn't wait. Emilia was always supposed to be the first one born of this whole group, and then the next four would follow almost monthly through late summer and early fall of 2020.

Well, that whole dream quickly went out the window when we lost Emilia. Felicia couldn't bear to see Facebook photos documenting the pregnancies, announcements, or baby shower invitations from her close friends Ashley and Katie. It broke her a little more every single time she saw an event occurring that we knew we would never have the ability to share with our Emilia. It was like the ultimate slap in the face to Felicia. She wanted nothing to do with any of it, and I completely understood where she was coming from. I, on the other hand, had a different approach whenever these events and situations came up.

I thought about how amazing my time was with Emilia and how special it felt to be a dad. This made me want to be there for my friends as they embarked on their own journeys. I figured that I would rather take the supportive role than feel sorrow, anger, and resentment for myself.

When the invites came for Rob and Samir's baby showers, I reluctantly accepted. Don't get me wrong, this wasn't an easy, "Oh yeah!" like you would hear from the Kool-Aid Man as he burst through the wall. This was a reluctant "yes," like I was the cowardly lion in the Wizard of Oz. It wasn't easy to muster up the courage, and I tried to think of every excuse possible to get out of both events before reluctantly dragging myself to the respective parties when the time came.

At the end of the day, I'm so glad I did. Rob's diaper party was to be first on the agenda as his little daughter, Basil, was due a few months before Samir's son, Jay. It is Rob's diaper party that we will focus on first as it happened first chronologically and was also the first time that I really had any interaction with complete strangers in a social setting since Emilia had passed away. This event occurred in July, around the time that I was slowly starting to emerge from the rubble and just after completing the journaling project to Emilia.

Here's to the Marathoners in our Lives:

One of Rob's best friends, Tom, had coordinated a get-together to celebrate Rob's little bundle of joy that was set to arrive sometime in late summer 2020. The event was taking place at another mutual friend's house, Dan, where we were going to have a few drinks, share some funny Rob stories, and then eventually head out to dinner somewhere while his wife, Molly, was hosting their baby shower back at their house.

As I arrived, I said hello and congratulations to Rob, dropped off the diaper box on the little pyramid that was beginning to form from other party attendees, grabbed a drink, and took a seat while everyone was chatting and catching up. I was really nervous. I was most nervous about taking any attention away from Rob and his special day celebrating his impending induction into fatherhood. I didn't want to make this about me, Emilia, and the recent tragedy in my life in any way. I truthfully was hoping not to even speak about Emilia as I didn't want to ruin the vibe.

Besides Rob, I really only knew a handful of other people at this get-together outside of some high school buddies that we shared in Tom, Dan, and Brian. To my knowledge, no one else really knew anything about what was going on in my life, and I was happy not to talk about it in this setting. I can't imagine (there it is again) how awkward this must have been for Rob at this moment, knowing that we were there to celebrate his first child while I was mourning the loss of my own.

Somehow I had lucked out as the only open seat that was available happened to be right next to Rob, who was really the only person I wanted to see if I was being honest. I'm so glad that chair was available because within no time after I sat down, Rob and I started catching up like old times, and I quickly felt okay and at ease. The nervousness of the day began to subside as Rob and I started chatting more. Rob has always had a way of making me feel comfortable and safe.

Rob and I have been best of friends since we were in grade school, just like Adam in our previous story. Rob was probably my first and original comfort blanket before I met Felicia. He and I were inseparable from about 7th grade, all the way through high school (while Adam was out bouncing around from school to school and raising hell). Rob was my safety net, and I was his. Everywhere we went, we were together for the most part. We even ended up going to Purdue together and were roommates for the first year and a half until Rob decided that he wasn't digging his experience there and chose to move back to Indianapolis, ultimately deciding to join the military. As we've gotten older, life has caused us to drift apart a bit. However, whenever he and I see each other, it all comes flooding back, and we are right back to where we left off in our school days.

As we talked, I felt genuinely happy for Rob, and I couldn't wait to hear all about his pregnancy journey as well as all the things he was excited about with fatherhood. I was really glad that I made it out there for him, even if it was hard.

After we had some good catch-up time together, I was left to fend for myself with the rest of the people at the party, which is when I really found myself starting to struggle a little. I now had to socialize and carry on a conversation, mostly with people I didn't know and had never met in my life. As I sat and listened to all the conversations going on around me, I felt like I was living in a different universe than everyone else. The conversations were about the most trivial things like alcohol and food, a lot of complaining about life and marriage, what was happening in the world, some jokes about how tough parenting is, etc.

Every once in a while, I would try to put on a smile and engage in the dialogue, but mostly I was just listening and observing what was going on around me and all the little conversations taking place. It was beginning to disgust me, to be honest. I'm sure no one there would have ever had any idea, but that is all I could think about at this moment. I thought, "Is this really all there is? Are these really the people I want to call friends? Is this what people talk about in real life?" It all seemed so meaningless. How could people not see how special this world was and why did they choose to be so miserable every day?

I don't want this to sound bad at all, as all of these people were very nice; I was just living on a different planet these days. My paradigms on life had shifted dramatically. I was living and seeing with a completely different set of eyes, ears, and reference points. I'm 99% sure that prior to the atomic bomb going off in my life, I wouldn't have thought twice about what I was experiencing and writing about now. At this moment, sitting in this circle of chairs out in Dan's garage, all I could think was how much I didn't want this lack of a larger perspective on life to have any place in my new city that was beginning to rise from the ashes. I didn't want people walking around my new city that didn't understand what life is all about, what is truly important to them, who they are, what they value, etc. I may have been okay with these paradigms in the past and even happily participated in them myself. However, that was not to be going forward as I had changed to my core.

When I got home that night, Felicia asked me how everything went. I told her it was great to see Rob, I ended up spending a lot of quality time with him, and we had some great conversations. I was so excited for him and his upcoming journey. I also told her about how hard it was for me to connect with everyone else and how frustrating it was, having to listen to a lot of the other conversations around me. If anyone would understand, I knew Felicia would.

She told me that she had recently been talking with her grief counselor, Elizabeth, about this exact topic and how they were discussing the difference between life sprinters versus marathoners. I loved this concept, and it immediately flooded my mind with new thoughts to explore. I thought it really nailed exactly how I was feeling and what I was experiencing at Rob's diaper party.

We all have marathoners and sprinters in our lives, and each brings its own unique value. One is neither better or worse than the other. To be a marathoner, you need strength, endurance, stamina, and the ability to pace yourself physically and mentally over the long haul. It requires discipline, sustainability, thoughtful action, and a plan. To be a sprinter, you need strength, speed, aggression, explosion, courage to push the limits, and a killer edge to attack a situation in an incredible burst of energy that is over before you know it.

In my opinion, life is a marathon with some "sprinting time trials" in between. Don't get me wrong, there is nothing wrong with either as they are both a necessary part of living a balanced life. No one should always be a sprinter or vice versa. Too much of anything is a bad thing. Balance must be maintained in order to truly live life to the fullest. No one is confined to only one thing in life as it is always lived on a spectrum that changes based on each unique situation. In one person's life, you may be a sprinter to them. Like, say a co-worker that was paired up on a project that you both crushed together. In another person's life, you may be that marathoner that is in it for the long haul no matter what life throws at us, like Adam in our previous story.

Both sprinters and marathoners can bring extreme value to our lives. I can name 500 sprinters that I've been around in my life that have had a huge impact on me at any given moment of time. You need people in your life for both events to help you get the most out of life and maintain balance in your universe.

At this moment, I realized that most of the people at that party, outside of Rob, were life sprinters in my world. Not only were they sprinters, but they were also sprinting in the wrong direction from the path my life was going. That was the disconnect I felt as I sat in the circle of chairs in Dan's garage that day. At the same time, I found myself so thankful for Rob, who is a marathoner in my life, as he will always be with me no matter where either of our journeys takes us individually. We have a connection deeper than just one thing and genuinely care about each other's lives even if we aren't in them every single day anymore.

It made me very grateful for a lot of other marathoners in my life as well as the ones to come. From the original marathoners of best friends in grade school, Adam, Kevin, Mike, and Rob, to the marathoners I picked up in college, Samir, Newcomb, Snow, Yoder, Baker, and Mark, to career marathoners I've met, April, Amanda, Nash, and Ryan, and to my new marathon crew of my business partners, Trieu, Nichol, and Blake, I'm so grateful for all of them in my life. I don't know where I would be without any of them. So here's to the marathoners in our lives. I know Emilia would love you all so much because she was the ultimate marathoner.

The Power and Beauty of Life Sprinters

I couldn't end this section of the story without talking about Samir's diaper party as well as a really touching moment that happened with a life sprinter I met while attending baby Jay's shower. This conversation with this complete stranger is the perfect illustration of the power and impact that life sprinters can have as well in your life, and I can't wait to share it with everyone.

First off, Samir and Sarah's baby shower extravaganza was an incredibly fun day! I can't believe I just typed those words. However, Samir and Sarah are the ultimate host and hostess and always know how to throw a great party, even if it is a baby shower. I knew this was going to be something I didn't want to miss, and boy did they deliver.

Samir and Sarah live in Chicago, which is about a three-hour drive from Indianapolis, where we live. We only get to see each other sporadically these days, but our time together is always epic and a ton of fun. This one was to be no different. Baby Lakhani's shower was not just the traditional baby shower for the women while the dudes had a diaper party, and everyone went home after a few hours. This was an all-day affair of drinking, eating, games, and unique settings for both guys and girls. It had more of the feel of an elaborate cocktail and dinner party with close friends than anything like a traditional baby shower that most people are used to. I would expect nothing less from Samir and Sarah as they are the ultimate givers in life. They love to make people happy and have a great time together.

The day's activities were as follows. We started out with a nice little private brunch at a rooftop restaurant somewhere in Chicago. From there, we would all go hang out on the patio at Samir's sister's condo for a few hours as we drank, played games, and talked before heading out later for dinner. Finally, the evening would wrap up at another swanky rooftop bar and restaurant on a Chicago skyscraper somewhere with an amazing view of the city where we would drink, eat, and talk around a fire pit until our old asses couldn't handle any more fun for the day.

By the time baby Jay's shower had arrived in September, I was already deep into rebuilding my new city and much better equipped to handle a full day affair of this magnitude with good friends and strangers, unlike back in July for Rob's diaper party. Thank God for that prior training because this one would have broken me if Emilia and I hadn't been prepping together for months prior.

It was an amazing day, and I was once again so happy to be there for Samir to celebrate the coming birth of his little son Jay. Samir is an amazing friend and another person that I would proudly label a marathoner in my life. I wouldn't have missed this event for the world. With that said, this story isn't actually another story about the power of life marathoners again. This story is a shout-out to the value that life sprinters can bring and why they should be embraced and cherished as well.

Our story begins at the final event of the day-long baby shower at a rooftop bar and restaurant on top of a Chicago skyscraper. We arrived at the restaurant, and all took our seats around the fire pit outside on the roof. As the drinks and food began to flow, we all sat around talking and sharing stories. I ended up sitting next to a total stranger for most of the night around this fire pit. I had never seen or met this guy before, so I had no idea who he was or his correlation to Samir and Sarah's life at this point. Ironically, the whole day I had observed him buzzing around each new venue of the baby shower, engaging everyone with a genuine curiosity that I rarely ever witness from most people. He was incredibly social and seemed like he was best friends with everyone at the party. His boundless energy stood out so much that at one point, while we were at the brunch, I asked Samir who that guy was because I was shocked I had never met him before as he seemed like best friends with everyone there. Samir told me that it was their wedding photographer whom they had met a few years back before they got married. Samir said that he and Sarah had become great friends with him and his wife over the past few years.

As we ordered more and more food and drinks and as the night went on, I finally had a chance to witness up close this guy's genuine curiosity and desire to learn about any and everyone that came across his path. I watched him pepper seemingly total strangers with question after question and carry on conversations as if they had known each other since they were kids. After about an hour of observing this and loving every minute of what I was observing, especially being a curious person myself, I asked him, "You seem to love learning about everyone, which is amazing. I'm genuinely curious to learn more about you if you don't mind sharing?"

That small question started a chain of events that would ultimately leave me in tears of joy in the bathroom about an hour later. It was kind of funny at first because he seemed genuinely surprised that I asked that of him, as if that doesn't happen often. I could tell that he is so used to learning about others that it was almost awkward and out of character to even consider talking about himself. However, he seemed to like the question and began sharing some details about his life.

For the next 15 minutes or so, he talked about all kinds of things. He shared that he and his wife were Columbian and had immigrated to the US at some point in the past 15 years. They loved living in America and all the opportunities that it brought to their lives. He stated that he was forever fascinated by everyone he meets and loves to learn about all of their stories, which is why he asked so many questions. He told me that he was a photographer and that he loved what he did as he got to meet so many new and interesting people while having the opportunity to build a business doing what he loved. He then started talking about how he and his wife were getting to the point where they were wanting to shift their lives away from their business focus and move toward starting a family someday. He went on to say that he was in his early 40's and had loved every minute of what they did and their current lives today, but they were just beginning to really think about this whole kid thing as the next evolution of their marriage. He shared that they were still a little on the fence, but he thinks that is where they were heading.

He then stopped talking and asked, "Do you have any children?" I paused, gathered myself, and deployed my elevator pitch answer that I had learned through my time on the tennis court earlier in the summer. I told him, "Yes, I have a daughter, and she was actually born earlier this year, back in March, about four months premature. She fought with everything she had in the NICU for 39 days and unfortunately passed away due to complications from an emergency surgery." As I finished my refined elevator pitch, his eyes widened, and he looked at me like a deer in headlights. I could see the sadness on his face. However, what came out of his mouth next shocked me to my core. His next words weren't, "I can't imagine," like most people say, so they can get out of this shit storm they just accidentally walked into. Instead, his next words were, "Would you mind telling me about her?"

I was blown away. A random stranger wanted to learn about my amazing daughter and my family's painful journey. I thought, "Hell yes!" and I opened up the floodgates to my world. We spent the next 30 minutes talking about Emilia and her amazing story, how strong she was, how she was my hero, etc.

It just started flowing out of me, and I couldn't stop. I was so happy he asked and wanted to listen to me talk about my daughter.

After I was done sharing our story, he stood up as he was almost in tears, grabbed me, hugged me, and said he was so happy to have met me tonight. I was really happy to have met him as well, and I thanked him for listening and for being a great person.

I told him I was feeling a little overwhelmed, in a good way, as I could feel the tears starting to come in the back of my own eyes and said I was going to run to the bathroom. I got to the bathroom and broke down in tears of happiness.

Never in a million years could I have imagined (there it is again) crying tears of joy in the bathroom at a swanky rooftop bar in Chicago before I met Emilia, and we embarked on this journey together. This was mind-blowing to me. I'm not an emotional person, and I had probably cried a handful of times before I met Emilia. Now, I damn near cry every day in some fashion. Hell, I'm crying right now as I'm writing these words and telling this story.

This guy was the definition of the ultimate life sprinter and the power that they can bring. I probably will never meet him again, and that is okay. We shared a powerful moment together that I get to share with the world and hopefully help someone else, which is still important. So here's to the life sprinters that you meet at a rooftop bar, whose name you can't even remember, and who cause you to end up crying tears of joy in a bathroom.

Firsts with Family - We Want to Talk About Emilia, Everyone Has a Story, and Remember the Why

Intro to My Family...

I want to preface this section of the book by stating that I have an amazing extended family that has been pivotal in shaping who I am today and who my children will become in the future. We are a large, loud, and fun family who care deeply about each other and have always been extremely close and active in each other's lives. Specifically, my mother comes from a family of eight in a traditional Catholic, Italian-American upbringing. My great grandparents were first-generation immigrants from Sicily and Calabria who started a famous Italian restaurant in Indianapolis back in the early 1900s. The restaurant, Iaria's Italian Restaurant (Iaria being my mother's maiden name,) is still around today and is currently run by the fourth generation of other parts of my family. We are like you would imagine any other Italian-American family to be. We yell a lot, eat a lot, talk with our hands a lot, get pretty passionate about almost anything, overly share our opinions, and are sometimes a little too involved in everyone else's lives. If you've seen *My Big Fat Greek Wedding*, we're kind of like that, but far less intense. I'd call it more like My Big Fat Greek Wedding Light.

My aunts and uncles, in particular, have been like older brothers and sisters to my sister and me since we were born. My mother is the oldest of the bunch and is 15 years older than the youngest, Jeff. Therefore, she naturally had the first children, who in turn weren't really much younger than her youngest siblings. To put things in perspective, my youngest aunts and uncles are only like five to ten years older than my sister (who was the firstborn child), so there was never a huge age gap between us. They really felt like they were more of a hybrid between aunt/uncle and older sibling as they spent so much time with us growing up. To put things in perspective, my sister, who is the aunt to Emilia, is 39 years older than her. My aunts and uncles were closer in age to my sister and me than they were even to my mom, who was their actual sister. They've all had a huge impact on our lives. My aunts, Kristie, Sandy, and Joanna, all spent their summers babysitting us while they were in high school and college. Hell, I still get a puffed-out chest when I tell people about how cool it was that I got to go up to the upper room floors of my Aunt Joanna's sorority when I was in 6th grade and slept there overnight. They had to yell, "Man on the floor" every time I came up the stairs. "Damn right!" I thought I was super cool.

My absolute favorite memories were the times when my Aunt Kristie and Joanna would take my sister and me shopping after Thanksgiving and Christmas as they went hunting for all the best deals in the holiday shopping frenzy of big box stores and malls of the '90s. It was a blast. Let me be clear, I didn't care so much about the shopping as the competition of the event. This was a dog-eat-dog, battle royal event like no other in society at the time. You either got what you came for, or you went home an empty-handed loser. This was my sweet spot and the ultimate way to leverage my super competitive spirit, and my aunts knew it. They would use me as their personal retriever dog to get what they wanted most. They would draw out where I needed to go in the store, let me weasel my way to the front of the line next to the gates using my cute face and tiny body, and then let me unleash the Kraken on all the unsuspecting other shoppers that didn't know what was about to hit them when the gates were opened.

As soon as the gates opened and the shopping frenzy began, I'd sprint off using my quickness and tiny body to dodge and weave around all the old ladies and out-of-shape parents, to get to where my aunts told me to go. Once there, I'd grab what we needed and camp out until my aunts met me to load up the cart or sometimes flatbed. I never lost! It made waking up at 4:30 a.m. so worth it, and I loved every minute of it.

By the end of those long shopping days, they would have their carts and flatbeds full of crap to check out of multiple stores. I have no idea what they did with all of that stuff, and I really didn't care. I just know it was a blast, and I loved spending that time with my aunts. Those are some of my favorite childhood memories, specifically my time with our Aunt Kristie, whom we tragically lost in the past few years. She was the most amazing, selfless, and giving person you will ever have the privilege to meet, and I miss her so much.

Those eight kids have gone on to produce 13 grandchildren and now eight great-grandchildren so far (soon to be growing to ten). All of us roll up to the matriarch of the family that we affectionately call "Big Momma" (my grandmother, Carolyn Feltz Iaria Bundy). Big Momma's name is ironic because she is actually only five feet tall and probably 100 pounds, if I had to guess. She is the furthest thing from a "Big Momma" in stature, but she is a "Big Momma" in that you dare not cross her or otherwise you will get a strongly worded talking, email, or even letter in the mail expressing her disappointment and encouraging you to get back on the right track!!! She is fiercely religious. She is the definition of a leader and who we all take our cues from on how to live a life driven by core values and unshakable faith. Words honestly can't really even describe how amazing she is and the incredible life she has led, but I will try to do it justice in a section later in the book that is dedicated to her and our big finishing section after entering my new city.

I know my Grandma Sears is probably reading this right now and saying, "What about all the Sears and me?" Don't worry, grandma, I have my own section dedicated to how amazing you are and all that you've meant to my life. To all the other Sears, my father's side of the family, you all are amazing as well. The Sears' have been instrumental in shaping who I am today, and I love them all very much. Unfortunately for me, the majority of that side of my family is scattered all over the country, and my sister and I rarely got to spend the kind of time with them like we did with my mother's family. Due to this, when Emilia passed away, none of my Sears family, besides Grandma Sears, were physically around in Indianapolis to have any stories to share in this book.

Now that you all have a quick intro into my immediate extended family, on with the story…

We Want to Talk About Emilia!

The first time I remember really seeing the majority of my entire extended family was in early June 2020 for my oldest niece's (Sarah) 10th birthday party hosted over at my parent's house.

Quick context on my immediate family structure, I have one older sister named Kristin. She has lived abroad and all over the world (Thailand, China, and Germany) for the past eight years with my brother-in-law and her three beautiful children (Sarah, Michael, and Katie). Those three little ones are amazing, and I'm so proud to call them my nieces and nephew. Sadly for me, I hardly get to see them other than summers when my sister takes an extended leave back in the states and stays at my parents' house for a couple of months. Sarah is ten now and has lived abroad since she was two. Michael (seven) and Katie (three) have spent the majority of their whole lives in other countries outside the US for the most part. They are all becoming amazing young people, and I can't wait to see them continue to evolve into their teens and early adulthood.

This year was a little different…way different actually. In March of 2020, just before the pandemic really took hold in Europe, my sister evacuated her family back to the states to ride out the pandemic for a few months at our parents' house vs. being stuck abroad. They made it out of Germany a day before the travel ban went into place as Europe and the US went on lockdown. For us, that meant that Sarah and Katie would get to have the rare birthday celebration in the states with their family for a change. Katie's birthday is in April, so we had to do the weird pandemic special drive-by celebration thing for her because social distancing and the lockdown were still in place to flatten the curve. Fortunately for Sarah, by the time June came around, the curve had been flattened, and the panic of the pandemic was calming down a little bit, so most people were feeling more comfortable with outdoor group gatherings.

So that is what we did. For the first time in months, the whole immediate family came together over at my mom and dad's to celebrate my niece Sarah's tenth birthday and enjoy a beautiful Midwest summer day out in the backyard as we socially distanced ourselves. Other than my parents and sister and the brief 30-minute drive-by at my niece Katie's drive-by celebration when we left the NICU really fast, popped down to wave hi, and then immediately headed back, I hadn't really seen any of my family since Emilia was born. For the most part, because of the pandemic, no one in my immediate family had any face-to-face contact with Felicia or me as we went through the most traumatic experience of our lives. They all sent messages of encouragement regularly, followed along on the NicView camera, and did their best to help us grieve after she passed but hadn't really actually seen us. So here we were, all together again in June of 2020 and only a few months removed from Emilia's passing. I was extremely nervous to attend this event. I didn't want to take away from Sarah's big day, and this was supposed to be a celebration. I also didn't want to be overwhelmed with answering questions about how Felicia and I were doing. Finally, I definitely didn't know if I could process normal life chit-chat about current events like the state of the pandemic, wearing masks, George Floyd protests, etc. My thoughts were still 95% consumed by the pain of losing Emilia at this point, and I had little capacity for anything else. Felicia still wasn't ready for this type of activity in any way, shape, or form, so she respectfully declined the invite. I went by myself while missing my better half as I braved the world again without her or my daughter.

I arrived at my parents' house, walked in, hugged my mom and dad, gave Sarah a happy birthday greeting, and that was it really to my surprise. Everyone was buzzing around me, kids were laughing and chasing each other around the house, and people were at the dining room table or outside patio-table eating and chatting. It felt like a totally normal family get-together, like nothing had ever happened. I'm sure, like me, they were all worried about bringing anything up if I had to guess. My Uncle Jeff stopped me in the kitchen and asked how we were doing and said that they loved us. I think I remember my Aunt Lisa did something similar as well. For the most part, it was business as usual in our family, and they left me to myself.

To be fair, no one knows how to handle these types of things, so I don't know what is good or bad in this situation. Did I want to talk about Emilia? Yes! Did I want to talk about Emilia in a big group setting? Probably not at this point. Did they want to talk about Emilia? Probably; however, I can imagine they were likely afraid that it would be scary and traumatic for me, which I totally understand. It's the giant elephant in the room during every first interaction you have with someone you knew after a traumatic event happened. When do you talk or not talk about it? The problem is, as we discussed earlier, this is all Golden Rule thinking at the end of the day. When you project your feelings and how you would like to be treated first, this is what you get, and I was just as guilty as anyone else. I wasn't talking about Emilia either, and that was due to my own insecurity and Golden Rule thinking. The only thing that I knew for sure was that not talking about Emilia wasn't good for anyone either.

It wasn't until I was back home in my safe space, journaling in my office, that I realized what I let happen on this day with my family. I was guilty of using Golden Rule thinking to protect myself to the detriment of my daughter's memory. I quickly realized and regretted how poorly I was treating my own daughter at this moment. Me not talking and sharing all the amazing moments and details of Emilia's life was not acceptable. That was the epitome of Golden Rule Thinking on my part. If I don't talk about Emilia...who will? This world will only take their cues from me, and I had to stop thinking about myself and my insecurities and remember that this is about Emilia and no one else (which is platinum rule thinking).

So much had happened in our lives in the past few months, and it was all bottled up. I was literally a different person, going through the hardest moment of my life, and had a ton to share. My daughter is the most incredible human I've ever met. Why wouldn't I want to tell the world about her whenever I had the chance? One of the other things that hurt me while reflecting back was not seeing pictures of my daughter all over my parent's house that day. I saw picture after picture of their three other beautiful grandchildren, but none of the newest edition to the family in Emilia. She was just as special as any other grandchild, arguably more, but had no representation in her grandparents' home. When we don't talk about these things, it hurts even more. Emilia isn't some deep, dark, secret that our family needs to keep hidden away. Emilia is the most courageous, strong, and amazing person that has probably ever graced our family and deserves to be championed.

SHUT UP AND LISTEN!

As my niece's birthday party continued, I found myself sitting at the kitchen table next to Big Momma, eating a plate of food I had grabbed from the buffet spread in the kitchen. I quietly sat there, listened, and took in all the conversations going on around me. I don't remember talking much at all, which is highly unlike me as I usually never shut up. As I sat and took it all in, I started to see that same Golden Rule thinking in action all around me in conversations I was hearing. The most egregious examples began when the conversation shifted to the George Floyd racial protests that were in full swing at this point all over the country. This was and still is a highly emotionally charged topic, and the opinions were flying fast and furious from around the room.

I don't want any of this next portion to sound rude to my family at all because I love all of them dearly, but I'm just sharing my thoughts in stories that shaped my new city, and this is one that stood out along the way. I hope they all forgive me for writing this, especially my Aunt Joanna. Also, please keep in mind my state of mind at this point in my life as well. My grief jar was 95% stuffed full of pillow still while processing my daughter's death, and I had little room for anything else, much less opinionated debates and thoughts around race riots. I was seeing my family at a celebratory event for the first time after my daughter passed away and had spent the past two months of my life basically in isolation reading, writing, thinking, and exercising as I tried to process my life and existence. I was hypersensitive to these types of things and was beginning to learn to listen with empathy given what I had experienced myself in having an atomic bomb dropped on my life. Bottom line, I was seeing the world through a different lens than probably anyone else in the room at this moment, which is why I thought it important to share this story here.

I sat and listened to everyone share their opinions about the protests and watched as the debate turned a little more animated. Opinions and thoughts were flying all over the room from a bunch of white, middle-class, middle-aged men and women. Then my Aunt Joanna chimed in with her thoughts on the whole situation that was unfolding in our country.

For reference, my Aunt Joanna is one of the sweetest and nicest people that you will ever meet. There isn't a single bone in her body that would wish ill will upon anyone. She is the ultimate giver and a great person. She is also incredibly smart and talented, which she demonstrates as a successful practicing lawyer here in Indianapolis.

With all that said, with only good intentions in her heart, my aunt began to share her thoughts on the situation unfolding and how she understood what Black Men and Women were experiencing and feeling like they were living by a separate set of rules because as a woman in the legal profession she had been subjected to a lot of harassment and obstacles along her journey to get to where she is today. She continued that she had been a victim in her own right, but you didn't hear her complaining, or something to that effect.

I think her point was to say that we all have obstacles to overcome, and we should embrace them head-on and stop complaining. It isn't a bad thought at all and largely makes sense. My issue with her statement, at that moment, was how she came to that conclusion. By drawing on her own lived experience to then project a feeling onto someone else was where I was seeing the problem of Golden Rule Thinking rearing its ugly head. All I could think was, "What in the world did the struggles of being a white female lawyer have to do with being a black man that was racially profiled by police?"

I get that both are traumatic experiences, and I appreciated her telling her story, but that is her story. That correlation has nothing to do with understanding what it must be like to be worried that getting pulled over by the police could end in your life being taken for no reason. I'm not saying that is what happens, but that is clearly how people of color, specifically black men, were expressing how they feel. At the end of the day, perception is all that really matters, and we should hear their stories and be open to receiving them for the unique views that they bring.

The truth was that there was not a single person in that room on this day that should have had any opinion about how a black man may feel during interactions with police because...WE AREN'T BLACK MEN! We have never lived that experience and have no way to understand or empathize with what they may or may not be going through, how they feel, and how that shapes their lived experiences. No one in that room has any idea what that would be like or not if we were honest. We may try to understand by drawing corollaries to our own life as my aunt had just done, but that is only to help us feel better...not the people that are trying to express their pain and have their stories heard.

With my new paradigm's on life and Platinum Rule thinking hat on, I was seeing this scenario play out all over the place in interactions I was encountering as I rebuilt my new city. As humans, we have such a strong desire to understand and will pull from any of our experiences to try and have it all make sense in our minds. In doing this, we inadvertently discount the actual person's lived experience in the process and somehow end up unintentionally making it all about ourselves.

I personally experienced this myself a few times when talking to people about the NICU with some work colleagues before we lost Emilia. They told me, "Oh yeah, I was in the NICU for a couple of weeks with my child, so I get how scary it can be. "UH...NO, YOU DON'T!!!" What you experienced was your healthy 35-week-old child receiving free child care for a few weeks. Felicia and I had life or death every minute. That is like someone that won a CYO fourth grade basketball league telling Michael Jordan they understand what he is going through in the last two minutes of game seven of the NBA finals. No you don't! That is absurd to even utter out loud, yet we all do it all time.

None of this is to discount my aunt's own lived experience either because her story matters as well, which is ultimately my point. Just like you don't know what it is like to have a child fighting for their life in the NICU, I don't know what it is like to be a black man in America or a white woman lawyer fighting to gain acceptance in a male dominated industry.

Using Platinum Rule thinking, I should have said to my aunt at this moment, "Aunt Jo, I'm so sorry you went through that experience, and I'd love to hear more about your journey." I honestly would love to hear my aunt's story as I can't imagine (there it is again) all that she went through to become the successful professional that she has become in a male-dominated industry like the legal sector. I'm sure I could learn an immense amount from her around perseverance and overcoming biases. Her story deserves to be told, and I'm happy to listen.

Unfortunately, at this moment, she was equating her powerful story and lived experience to something that had nothing to do with her to try and help it make sense in her own mind. I'm not judging because we all do it. My ears were open to noticing these little occurrences more now, and the lack of Platinum Rule thinking most of us rarely exercise in our lives. We all think of ourselves first, then draw our corollaries to make sense based on what we know, and then tell the traumatized people we get what they are going through and offer our unsolicited advice. We have it backwards. We should just shut up and listen. We should be embracing all stories and letting them be heard.

This lesson applies to this very book and story as well. Losing a child in the NICU is not the same as having a miscarriage, or stillbirth, or having your two-year-old die in a drowning accident. Those are all very different situations and come with a completely different set of emotions and lived experiences. I would be doing anyone reading this book a disservice to say that this story will help them if they've ever suffered a stillbirth, miscarriage, or pregnancy loss. They are different and my family's story is unique to only us. I don't have any other deep insights on life other than what I've personally experienced.

I recently had a close life marathoner of mine, who I won't mention by name for privacy's sake, confide in me about a couple of tragic miscarriages that he and his wife had recently had around the same time as we were going through our loss with Emilia. He went on to tell me that, "This is nothing to the magnitude of what you experienced, and I don't really want to throw that on you." I felt so bad when I heard him say that to me as a loss is a loss. Pain is pain. Tragedies hurt no matter if you had a scud missile hit your city or an atomic bomb that blew everything to pieces. What he's going through was hard as well, and his story deserved to be heard and listened to. How much you suffered vs. someone else isn't a competition, and I hate that we all think that one person's trauma and pain out-trumps another's. We all have stories to tell, we all have pain and suffering, and we all deserve to be heard.

Sorry, Aunt Jo, for sharing that story. I hope you aren't pissed reading this as I love you dearly.

My psyche couldn't take hearing about George Floyd, and everyone's hot takes anymore, so I got up from the dining room table and walked over to the family room where all the little kids were running around and playing with toys and video games. This scene was a lot more fun than the one I had just left back in the dining room. They were all so happy, having a blast with each other.

My little three-year-old niece, Katie, went running by me chasing a balloon that she was playing with by herself. As she popped it up in the air over and over while giggling, I joined in the fun. The next time she popped it up, I jumped in and hit it back in the air before it reached her little hands. Every time she was just about to catch it, I would jump in and hit it back into the air from seemingly out of nowhere. She looked confused at first every time the balloon would mysteriously not make it to her hands as expected. Then she slowly realized what was happening and looked up at me, smiling, giggling, and realizing that she now had a playmate. We ended up playing with this balloon over and over again for the next 15 minutes, and every time I kept her from catching it, she couldn't stop smiling and laughing. It was really adorable watching her reactions and all the fun she was having with a stupid little balloon.

Somewhere along the way of playing this game with her, my mind went to Emilia and the realization that I'll never be able to do this exact same thing with her. I almost started to cry as I realized how much I was going to miss out on all these basic little joys of life that I won't ever get to do with her. That was really hard. Once I felt that wave of emotion coming over me, I was ready to call it a day. I slowly started to say my goodbyes to everyone and made my way out of the event as quietly as I had come in.

Lessons from the Rubble - Hitting Rock Bottom

Wait…Did my Grandma Just Yell at Me??? Always Remember the Why!

The final story about my family I want to share from my lessons learned while sitting in the rubble occurred during the Fourth of July weekend in 2020. We were almost three months into wandering through the rubble and the early stages of reimagining what my new city would look like after losing Emilia. The journaling for Emilia was entering the home stretch as her original due date was July 13th, 2020, and was to be our last entry. This was about the time when I hit rock bottom and started to feel more lost than ever before.

For a few weeks leading up to this event, I was starting to feel like I had my life somewhat back on the right path, felt a direction and purpose again, and I was beginning to draw up the blueprints on what this reimagined city might look like. However, it wouldn't be too long before I was brought back down to the reality that I was still very much still lost and wandering around the rubble of my old city and nowhere near fully ready to depart. Life has a way of keeping you in check like that. Just as soon as you feel like you have this whole thing figured out, life will smack you right in the face and remind you that you don't know anything. My metaphorical slap down happened around this time when I was once again back down at my parent's lake house to celebrate my father's birthday with the rest of my family on the Fourth of July weekend.

The majority of my immediate family had made it down to spend the day together, playing out in the water, grilling out, and going tubing out on the lake. There really is nothing better than lake life in the warm Midwestern summers. For me, I was back down there once again, alone and missing my wife and daughter. I was getting really sick and tired of feeling like I was living a separate life from my wife, whom I could only ever convince to really come out of our house on our nightly Emilia walks these days. Answering the question, "Where's Felicia?" started to hurt more and more every time I was asked. At first, I was okay with it and understood she needed space. By this point in our journey, I was wondering if we would ever be in the same room again with anyone other than each other outside of our home. At this point, whenever I would get the where's Felicia question, I would always respond with some bullshit answer about how she wasn't feeling up to it yet. They would always nod and respond, "We totally understand, and she needs time to heal." The truth is, Felicia and I were basically living separate lives at this point outside of the nightly Emilia walks. So, if I were to answer honestly, I would have said, "Felicia and I are struggling. I'm worried about her and our marriage as I have no idea if we are going to survive. I really miss my wife!"

Back at our house, I was on an island most of the day stuck in my mind and hammering away on whatever book I was reading or stupid arbitrary goals I had set around playing tennis, trying to run a 6-minute mile, rebuilding my side business, etc. I had come so far in this journey only to feel like I was hitting a brick wall of life again. I found myself asking, "What am I doing all this for?" I was stuck in this rut and didn't even know it. I thought I was making a lot of progress. I was learning and reading more than ever. My core values were becoming more and more clear every day in my mind. I was in better shape than I'd ever been in my life and was destroying people on the tennis court. Then, before I knew it, life dealt me a curveball that I would have never seen coming. I got metaphorically smacked in the face by Grandma Sears that day down at the lake.

I was in a shitty mood from the moment I woke up that morning. I went through the motions and did my reading, writing, and exercise as quickly as I could to try and get out the door and make the hour and 15-minute drive down to the lake house from Indianapolis. Just days before this July 4th weekend, Felicia and I had gotten into probably the worst fight I think we've had in our marriage. IT WAS BAD! It all stemmed from a miscommunication around how to handle some framed photos of Emilia that Felicia had purchased and wanted to put up in the house.

It all started sometime back in late May. Felicia had come to me one day and said she wanted to order a bunch of framed photos of Emilia from this website called Mixtiles. Mixtiles would take these photos and turn them into these little 9x9 photos that we could stick on the wall to create a collage of sorts. "Of course," I said. I loved the idea and being reminded of Emilia. We had keepsakes all over the place that I looked at constantly to remind me of her as often as possible. I thought that a few new pictures sounded like a great edition. Little did I know that "a few photos" was actually 40 of these little 9x9 MixTiles. I was expecting three or four and clearly completely misunderstood what Felicia was trying to do with this project. When she said, "All over the house," she really meant all over the house.

The Mixtiles arrived in late June, and Felicia came flying into my office smiling, holding this huge box, and ready to show me all the photos of Emilia and strategize where to put them in the house. She opened up the box and started pulling out photo after photo after photo of our daughter. It seemed like this box was filled with a never-ending collection of 9x9 photos of my dead daughter. I don't know what it was, but seeing all of these photos of Emilia suddenly triggered me, and I started to feel like I was going to have a panic attack or something.

I'd had trouble looking at photos and watching videos of Emilia ever since she passed. Every time I would open my phone and look at them, I would just start crying my eyes out. Those photos hurt me deep down to my core whenever I would see them. In reflecting back, I had honestly been avoiding them as much as possible to avoid that painful feeling. The only time I really would look at her pictures and videos is when I would visit her at the cemetery once a week and cry my eyes out. Even then, it still took all of my strength to open up the photos app on my phone and hit play on one of the hundreds of videos I took back in the NICU. Most weeks, I would only be able to make it through 2-3 minutes before I had to close my phone and refocus back on the gravestone. After each visit, I would lock her photos away on my phone and get back to grinding away on rebuilding my city. Don't get me wrong, we had keepsakes everywhere around the house, and I loved seeing those every day. Those keepsakes reminded me of my hero and gave me the energy to keep going. However, looking at her actual pictures seemed to suck the life out of me and reminded me of everything I had lost.

As Felicia pulled out more and more photos from the MixTiles box, I started to freeze up. Some were of Emilia when she was in her most traumatic states and in visible pain during her last few days. Some were even of us holding her immediately after she had passed away. Seeing these traumatic photos come to life in a 9x9 little Mixtile sent me into turtle mode or something. I froze, visualizing my future of seeing these triggering images all over my house, every day, in every room. It felt like I had been hit by a ton of bricks as she pulled out more and more photos and laid them on the ground. It was like this box of 9x9 photos was never-ending.

All I could think was, "My house is my safe space and not supposed to be a 24/7 trigger of the most traumatic event I've ever experienced in my life." I asked Felicia to stop and told her, "I didn't realize that when you said you wanted to get a few photos of Emilia, you meant 40!" She said, "So? What's your problem?" I said, "I don't really want to look at pictures of some of the most traumatic moments of my life and times when our daughter looked like she was in incredible pain in every room of my house that I walk in!" I continued, "I'm just not ready for this yet. I'm so sorry. I didn't realize that this is what you had in mind."

Felicia looked devastated. She had a smile on her face and some excitement in her eyes for the first time in weeks, and I had just crushed her heart. I was only thinking about me and not her at that moment. You see, while I struggled to look at photos of Emilia, Felicia loved looking at photos and videos of Emilia all day. This had become something of her favorite pastime. She would spend time every morning staring at them and crying. I guess that was her way of grieving and connecting with Emilia. To me, that seemed so bizarre as I didn't understand why she wanted to be reminded of that pain all the time. My way to connect with my daughter was to channel her never-quit attitude every day, get to work, and never stop moving. No one way is right in managing grief, obviously. She did her thing, and I did mine. That was until these photos arrived, and we were at a crossroads of sorts.

To no surprise, this disconnect between us turned into a massive fight. Felicia insisted that I couldn't tell her where she could and couldn't look at pictures of our daughter. I would counter that I had literally given everything I had to help her on this journey, done everything imaginable to make her feel safe and protected, and asked for literally nothing in return to support me at any point in my own grieving. I was asking this one time for her to respect what I was feeling at this moment, as seeing all these photos was causing a lot of pain for me, and I couldn't bear the thought of seeing them around our home in every single room I walked into.

We were at an impasse, and it turned uglier and uglier over the next hour or so as we battled harder and harder. The screaming and name-calling grew louder and louder. By the time we reached our conclusion, Felicia was a crying mess, and I was red in the face, about as angry as I feel like I've ever been. We both retreated to our own areas of the house, and she continued to cry as I sat on my office floor in silence, staring at the box of photos while wondering why I couldn't get over this and feeling awful at how I just made Felicia feel. We could barely look at each other for days after this one.

I felt so bad for reacting the way I had! I tried to fix it. I went through all the little MixTiles and pulled out seven or so of the ones that I could tolerate from happier times in the NICU. I then, in a show of compromise, put them up on a wall and arranged a little collage of sorts in the office / Emilia's nursery with a lot of her other pictures and memorabilia from our time with her. I called Felicia in to show her, and she couldn't have cared less. Felicia was so pissed that a few days later, she came to me and told me that she decided she needed some time to herself and was going to book a flight to go back to Texas to be with her mom and family for a while. I was heartbroken, angry, and afraid that my marriage was falling apart. I had driven my wife away from me to the point that she needed space and left me by myself back in Indianapolis with our dog and a home with no Emilia.

All of these events happened a few days before this July Fourth weekend where I was feeling more alone and lost than ever before. I was miserable, frustrated, angry, and going through the motions of life as I slogged through the rubble. Once again, I was by myself as I made my way down to the lake house, missing my better half and safety blanket in Felicia. By the time I arrived at the lake, I could feel I was a little off and just in an angry and mean spirit. I said hi to a few people, grabbed a glass of wine, and headed out to the upper balcony deck, where I sat down at a table with my mom and both grandmothers on either side of me. A lot of people were out on the deck, watching the kids down on the dock and making sure they were staying safe while playing in the water. That is when the moment happened that I truly realized I had lost my way and that I needed a wake-up call. I honestly don't really remember exactly what I said specifically to set this off, but I know I had tried to make some snarky comment about my dad, trying to poke fun at him about one of his many quirks.

Quick background about my dad. Everyone always rags on him, in a fun way, because he is a very unique, one-of-a-kind cat. We all know he secretly enjoys it because it makes him special and the center of attention. To paint the picture that is Dale Sears. He is the kind of guy that will show up whistling some '70s Led Zeppelin song from his hippie pot-smoking days while attempting his patented Dale Spin, while holding some bougie cocktail that he won't stop talking about and trying to get everyone to taste, all the while rocking a Mexican poncho or something silly that he got on vacation somewhere, and sharing stories about his new machete that he just bought that is out in the garage, and he can't wait to use on God knows what. I'm not making any of that up. He does all of these things. That said, all of that makes him sound kind of cool, which he definitely can be. However, he is like a walking contradiction which is what makes him such an easy target. He is a successful businessman, who wears khaki shorts as he goes on a run or bike ride, stares at himself at every mirror he passes to make sure he still looks good and has more quirky things he does or says than almost anyone you will ever meet (except maybe his son). The best way I can describe him is like a metrosexual meets a lumbersexual meets an engineering nerd meets a Bear Grylls wannabe. It's a lot to take sometimes, but in a fun way, and we all love him. He adds a certain je ne sais quoi to all of our lives, which just wouldn't be the same without him. However, because of all the weirdness, he is the easiest target to make a joke about, and we all do it regularly with love.

On this particular day, I must have pushed my commentary on my father too far as I said some dumb snarky joke about one of my dad's many quirks, and then all of a sudden, I heard someone near me snapback, call me out, and start to get upset. I turned, a bit startled, to come and realize that it was my Grandma Sears of all people who started to get upset at me and began to publicly admonish me in front of everyone out on the deck! She was super angry at me for saying something about one of her children, and she had every right to put me in my place. I was mortified and can't tell you how taken aback I was when I realized that she was angry at me. Never, not even in my wildest imagination, would I ever have thought Grandma Sears would yell at me at any point in my life for many reasons. First off, she is the kindest, most loving, and caring person you will ever meet. She would do anything for anyone to make them feel special and loved. She has always done that for me my entire life. Second off, I honestly don't think I've ever made her mad at me at any point in my life that I can remember.

I hate to say this, as it is pure speculation, and apologies to all of my cousins and sister for this comment, but I have to be my grandma's favorite grand or great-grandchild. I don't have any specifics as to why, but we've always just had a great connection, and I can feel her pride in me whenever we are around each other. I'm also the only grandchild or great-grandchild in Indianapolis, so I get a lot more time with her than any of my other cousins or siblings. Maybe she makes all her other grandkids feel the same way and I just don't see it. If I'm wrong, so be it, but I stand by my statement here.

Knowing this, to say that I was surprised at her reaction that day would be the understatement of the century. However, reflecting back, I totally deserved it, and she was 100% right in publicly calling me out. It was my dad's birthday, and I was being a little jerk, acting out with inappropriate comments filled with anger and pain from my own situation. Most of the time, when taking a dig at my dad, you could always tell it was lighthearted and just for fun. However, if I'm honest, deep down on this day, I knew that my comments weren't of the lighthearted and fun variety. I was trying to be a jerk when I opened my mouth. I was in pain, missing my wife, angry at myself, miserable without my daughter, and more lost than ever before while wandering through the rubble of my life. My words and actions were beginning to reflect how I felt inside. I knew my dad wouldn't care, as that is who he is, and I took advantage of it. It was at this moment that I knew that I had officially hit rock bottom. I was making mean, snarky comments to my dad on his birthday while my pissed-off wife was in Texas fuming at me. I was all alone braving this world without the two women that I loved the most. I was angry, sad, in pain, not dealing with my emotions well, and now even making my sweet grandma mad at me for talking shit about one of her kids right in front of her. If that doesn't say rock bottom, I don't know what else could.

As I drove back from the lake that next day while replaying that scene with Grandma Sears over and over in my mind, I was trying to figure out where I had lost my way on this journey. Then it hit me. I had forgotten my why! I had forgotten what all of this was all about. I had forgotten why I was working so hard to learn, think, reflect, and grow every day. I had forgotten about Emilia. I had forgotten that this was about channeling her never-quit attitude, picking up the baton to finish her marathon and "live for two" like I had promised her in her eulogy only a few months before. This was about honoring the most special person I had ever met and doing my best to make her proud to smile down from heaven and call me her dad.

That following morning, I decided that I wasn't going to let myself slip again. I wrote down at the top of my journal the Never Quit poem, my core values, and my why so I would be forced to look at it every single morning as I sat down to type in my journal. I vowed that I was going to make sure that I made it to Emilia's grave at least once a week to talk with her, spend some quality time, let her know how things were going, and do my best to visualize how we were going to "live for two" in the week ahead. I went on reminderband.com (those little rubber reminder bracelets) and made some little rubber bands to put around my wrist with "Remember the Why" and Emilia's name on it to make sure that I had this reminder with me at all times. I wasn't going to let myself get sidetracked ever again or forget what this was all about. I felt more ready than ever to get back at it, finish journaling over the next two weeks, and get to work on writing the second half of this story.

Atomic Bomb Theory - Setting the Foundation (Days 118-121)

Finding God, My Core Values, Purpose, and Finishing Emilia's Marathon

When we first found out that we were pregnant with Emilia, back in October of 2019, Felicia immediately asked me to get really involved in learning about this pregnancy and all that it would entail for both of us. She encouraged me to buy a few books and research all about what she and Emilia would be going through. I didn't do any of that. I said, "Sure thing," and kept on keeping on like normal.

One day, a few weeks into Felicia's pregnancy with Emilia, Felicia knew that I wasn't really taking it as seriously as she had asked and offered a compromise. She said, "At least download this Daddy app that will show where we are in the pregnancy, progress on how Emilia is growing, and tips on how to make things easier for yourself and your partner." I reluctantly agreed, downloaded the app, and paid the $5 or whatever it was on the App Store right then and there. That seemed to appease Felicia enough, and we got back to living our lives as we waited on our first child to arrive.

Every morning the app would send a push notification about how big Emilia was, how many days to go until her due date, and any pregnancy milestones to be aware of. I rarely looked at it. Maybe once or twice a week or something, I would pop in for 20 seconds and look it over. The only thing that I really liked about the app was the countdown of how many days we had left to the due date. It was a visual reminder for me of how much time I had left to get the nursery done, stuff bought for the house, basement fixed up, etc.

The day that Emilia was born, I remember being in the Mother/Baby room at the hospital with Felicia, pulling up the app, and seeing "121 days to go until your daughter arrives" at the top. The NICU team tells you from day one, "Expect to be in here at least until your original due date," to set proper expectations for parents. So that number, 121 days, was burned into my memory from the start. 121 days was the length of this marathon that we had to run to get Emilia home safe and sound. The thought of 121 days seemed like climbing Mount Everest. At that very moment, we were still reeling from the trauma of the trip to the ER, the delivery, and now our little bundle of joy fighting for every breath in the NICU. I was thinking, "How in the hell are we going to do this for 121 days?"

Well, we are now at day 119 of this journey. The finish line was fast approaching. We had all run this marathon together, and it was almost unfathomable to believe all the joy, sadness, pain, love, excitement, heartache, and everything else that we had endured as a family since March 15th, 2020, when this all began. Unfortunately, as you all know, this story wasn't the triumphant and happy ending that I had originally set my mind on. However, that didn't mean that Emilia's due date no longer held any significance to Felicia or me. July 13th, 2020, would officially mark the end of our marathon, and it would finally be time to put this chapter of our life behind us.

As our marathon was concluding and I reflected back on our journey, I realized that the foundation for my grand new city had been slowly taking shape since the day that Emilia had passed away, and I didn't even know it. My whole life had changed, and I was no longer the same person that anyone knew before she was born. In this next section of the book, we will take a look at how the building blocks of our new city began to take shape and create the foundations that would be necessary to support our new masterpiece that was now ready for construction.

Finding God

Earlier I touched on my relationship with God prior to meeting Emilia, but I'll go into more detail here. If this was a Facebook profile and you were looking at my relationship status with God, it would read, "It's complicated." It wasn't complicated because I had some deep, profound thoughts that conflicted with how the universe came to be or something actually important like that. It was complicated only because of how much pain and suffering organized religion has inflicted on our world as I've watched humans go to wars, terrorize, fight, and kill over the right to claim that their God or religion was superior to all others.

At my core, I'm a pacifist. I don't want anyone or anything to experience hurt or pain. I've never once even physically hit someone out of anger. That isn't to say that I've never been angry, as I have a terrible temper. When it comes to going beyond just words, I could never imagine (there it is again) actually physically hurting someone and inflicting pain and suffering with my body. With that said, seeing how religion (and God in turn) could bring so much violence, suffering, and conflict into this world never made sense to me. How could Muslims want to kill Christians in the name of God in a despicable act like the 9/11 Twin Tower attacks? How does that make any sense? Christians were no better in my mind either as they have done their fair share of killing in God's name as well, as has every other religion in the history of humanity at one point or another. The more I observed all the walking contradictions of humanity, our thoughts on God and who is right or wrong, etc., the more I stepped further away from the fray and called it all bullshit from the sidelines.

What really solidified my views on God and religion was the conflict it created in my own home growing up with the never-ending battle over the importance of religion between my mother and father. My mother is devotedly Catholic, carries her faith with pride, and is a rule follower. My father is a questioner, a rule-breaker, and a challenger in all aspects of life. He won't accept surface-level answers on God and religion that words like "I have faith" bring and seems to satisfy my mother. That led to his never-ending probing and prodding of my mother and her beliefs as he tried to "prove his point" on how flawed and irrational religion appears. My mother would fight back with faith as the defense, and the conversation would forever go round and round in circles. This went on for my entire childhood and probably still goes on in their household to this day.

I think the best way I can illustrate the lifelong impasse on religion between my mom and dad is with this fun story. I was in high school, and my sister was already off to college. We were all sitting down for dinner at the dining room table one evening, which we did every night. Everyone was eating their food and talking. Somehow, the conversation shifts to something about religion and my dad challenging some dogma of the Catholic faith which happened regularly. Normally these conversations would naturally run their course and end in my parents agreeing to disagree. This time, before you knew it, I heard my mom say, "Fine, Dale. We just won't be together in the afterlife, and I've accepted that." What?! I feel like a record scratch would be appropriate here if there was sound. I can't stop laughing as I'm writing this, thinking of how in the hell this was a topic of conversation at dinner on a random weeknight with your impressionable teenage son sitting there.

I want to be clear, my parents were and still are amazing parents, but we all have flaws. They will be the first to admit that communication around God and religion has been a life-long tug of war between the two of them. Marriage is hard, and this is just their cross to bear, so to speak. On the flip side, they've given my sister and me incredible examples of other great core values and virtues that helped shape who we are today. Chief among them is that they never gave up on each other. No matter their differences or life challenges, they are still together and going strong after over 40 years of marriage. I definitely don't want to make this sound like I had a shitty childhood or anything. That couldn't be further from the truth. However, religion, in particular, was an area that I would not grade them highly.

To further cement my growing hatred of religion, I attended a Catholic school for my whole childhood. While the community of people was amazing, and I loved the education I received, these environments only made my relationship with religion and God even more complicated and confusing. I heard their messages and teachings every day in church or religion class. Then I saw or heard of these same "religious leaders" often being walking contradictions in their personal lives and how they conducted themselves once school was out. It further made me think that this is all a bunch of bullshit, and I wanted nothing to do with it.

After high school, when I was finally free to make my own choices on God and religion outside of my parents' house, I never went back to church willingly ever again. I completely shunned it and never looked back. Besides going to mass on Christmas and Easter to appease my mom, I don't think I ever willingly walked into a church on my own. Check that, I did go a few times with my Grandma when I was in my late twenties when I was experiencing crazy bad panic attacks, and I thought a few trips to church would "cure me." Shockingly it didn't. As a matter of fact, it probably made my relationship with religion even worse because I had a panic attack at mass both times I went. Before I knew it, the thought of attending church became its own trigger toward my next panic attack, which made it even easier to stay away.

Luckily for me, Felicia didn't care one way or another about religion, and it has never been a source of conflict in our relationship. We have always been in lockstep surrounding religion which is really all that mattered to me. We had talked a few times about "going back to church" once we had kids to help instill good core values and provide a stable community for them, but that was about it. It wasn't about God, spirituality, connection to something deeper, or anything like that. Just a community of "good" people that we could be around to help provide good examples for our kids.

If you haven't noticed, I've only been rambling on about religion and hypocritical humans at this point and have barely even mentioned what this is all about, GOD! The reason being that is all I knew for most of my life pre-Emilia. I had no relationship with God or even had more than a few conversations with him/her/it (pick your pronoun), which didn't consist of me praying for something out of desperation when I, or someone close to me, needed help. The point is, I've never had a relationship with God or anything even close to it. To put it bluntly, it was non-existent. I knew all there is to know about religion and the church, but hardly anything about God. I've always known that this world and all the beings in it were far too complicated and amazing for there not to be some higher entity out there that helped to design all of this. That was about the gist of my relationship and understanding of God up until the moment I met Emilia, and we began our marathon together.

The day all that began to change was 3/15/2020, when I first laid eyes on my daughter. My crazy journey of finding God on this marathon actually began with the gift of a tiny little book from Felicia's good friend, Ashley, and her husband, Nick. Ashley is one of those close friends I mentioned before that was also pregnant, expecting their daughter a few months after Emilia. Ashley and Nick heard about Emilia's unexpected entrance into this world and wanted to do whatever they could to help us. They stopped by and dropped off a few things for us while we were running back and forth from the hospital to be with Emilia. One of the items they brought was a book called, *Trusting God Day by Day*, by Joyce Meyer. It is a book of 365 devotionals and reflections that you can read each day and spend some time with God. On the inside cover of the book, they wrote this note, "Felicia + Chris, not every single day feels super relevant, but this book really helped Nick and me find strength and faith (in both each other and God) when our world felt very dark and uncertain. We are praying for the health of your little family and hope this book can fortify you in the weeks to come. Love Ashley + Nick." They marked the day March 15th in the book with a little stick-on post-it note.

Ashley and Nick are amazing friends and definite life marathoners for Felicia and me as a couple. I knew that they had some of their own personal struggles in the past that I won't get into here. I thought if this helped them, why not try? I was desperate for anything I could find to try and help us get through each day back at the NICU as Emilia fought for her life. Felicia and I picked up the book together, read the first daily devotional of March 16th, 2020, and shared our thoughts together.

I guess we liked it enough to keep trying it, so we brought the book to the NICU to have it there each morning when one of us arrived. Whoever had the morning shift would take a photo and send it to whoever was at home so they could read it to start their day as well with the daily reflection. As you will see in my journals, this became the first thing that I read every day and what I started out each journal entry with, besides the dad joke.

It was this small act from Nick and Ashley that ultimately set my course and helped put Felicia and me on a journey of re-discovering God in our own lives as we were running this race. I can't tell you how important this book has become in my life. It was a game-changer and not because of the content or anything, but because it got me talking to God for the first time in my life. Over a decade of daily religion classes didn't do that, but this little book and Emilia did.

As I read the passage each day and wrote my own thoughts in my journal, it turned out that God and I had a lot to talk about together. I didn't even realize it at first, but I was talking to God for the first time in my life and then writing down our conversations to share with Emilia. How stupid could I be? The answer to the question, "How do you find God?" was literally with me the whole time. Instead of trying to listen to what everyone else had to say about God, religion, or faith, I just needed to use my own voice and speak with him/her/it myself. It was mind-blowing to me. If you want to find God, just use the most precious gift that God gave humanity, our consciousness, and our ability to think, and you will find God will always be there and ready to chat about whatever you wish.

This reminds me of a story I heard in an audiobook once called *The Ultimate Jim Rohn Library*. This is a great self-help and motivational audiobook from one of the pioneers in the personal growth industry. The whole book was filled with great philosophies and wisdom on how to better yourself and achieve all that you dream of. However, one section really stood out to me and has stuck with me since hearing it. It also happened to be the last thing that Jim left the audience with before concluding the book. In his finishing section, Jim mentions that he hadn't talked much, if at all, about the role that God played throughout all of his teachings and philosophies on how to be our best selves. Because of that, he wanted to end his talk discussing God as He is a ginormous piece of the puzzle and deserves to be recognized. His words and story really hit home for me, given my new journey with God in this very moment of my life.

Jim's story was as follows, "Life is a two-way street. I think God will do his part if we do our part. During this program, we've spoken mostly about our part of the equation. There is a story about a man that came across a rock pile and in two years turned it into a fabulous garden. People came from everywhere to see it. One day a man came by and saw the garden and thought it was fabulous, but he wanted to make sure the gardener didn't take all the credit. He had this deep feeling inside that a lot of people leave God out when showing off what they've created. So he toured the garden and then had a chance to meet the gardener. When he shook his hand, he said, "Mr. Gardner, you and the good Lord together have made this beautiful garden." The gardener understood his message and his point, so he replied, "I think that is true. If it wasn't for the sunshine and the rain, the miracle of the soil and seasons, there would be no garden at all." He then continued, "But you should have seen this place a couple of years ago when God had it all to himself."

This message really hit home for me. God is us, and we are God. There are so many things that we can't control in this world. Emilia's story is a perfect example of this. There are elements like the seasons, weather, violence, suffering, pain, joy, and happiness, which only God knows the reason for. The world is full of random events that have no rhyme or reason to our mere mortal minds. We will go mad trying to understand this grand design and unlock God's code in our short existence on this Earth if we dare try. However, that doesn't mean we are helpless in this equation. God may have created a world full of seemingly random things that only He/She/It can understand. That said, God didn't leave us empty-handed on our quest. He/She/It endowed us with a magic key to unlock any door of our choosing. That magic key is our ability to use our minds, create our own thoughts, and bring a bit of our own flair and personality to this world. Using this key, our thoughts, and cognitive abilities, we can talk with God anytime we choose and create together. We can then go and try to manifest our conversations and ideas by unleashing our creativity onto this world to do our small part to contribute to the mission that is humanity.

To accomplish this, all we have to do is stop and think. That is it! It's really that simple and mind-blowing at the same time. Just stop and think, and you will find God! That thought rocked my world. Sadly for the majority of us, I bet the amount of time we spend using our most precious gift of thinking, questioning, and talking with God is probably less than 10 minutes a month if any time at all. I was no different until this journey was thrust upon me, and I came to the realization that I was building my garden my whole life without my most trusted business partner, God. When we started to team up together on this journey, magical things started to happen in my life that only God and now Emilia can truly comprehend.

Over the past year, I've read that little book that Ashley and Nick gave us and then written a reflection each morning. That reflection is my "God and Chris" time where we talk about life, and then I write down my findings and thoughts on how I can build a better garden for myself, my family, and as many other humans as I can help. God and I have talked about a lot over this past year as we had a ton to catch up on after 35 years of backlogged topics that we needed to discuss together. Some of my favorite topics we've discussed were my core values, marriage, life, work, and, most importantly, Emilia. I can't fathom where I would be today without these daily chats as they slowly built and set into motion this new city that was taking shape. Thank you, Ashley and Nick, for the gift of that small seed you provided to Felicia and me to help start us on our journey to grow our new beautiful gardens with God in our life.

Finding My Core Values:

One of the main topics God and I discussed while I sat in the rubble of my blown-up universe was my core values. Who was Chris Sears? How did I honestly want to live out the rest of my time here on Earth? God and I discussed what I truly valued in life, who I wanted to be, and the lasting impact I wanted to leave when I'm gone. These daily conversations with God slowly changed my life and helped to construct the strong foundation that would be needed to allow my new city to rise up in all its glory.

After a few weeks, I ran out of my own questions that God and I could discuss, but I didn't want our conversations to stop. I quickly learned that if I was going to talk to God every day, I would need to come with some new ideas so we could have a robust dialogue each and every morning. To feed the flames of our new fire, I turned all the reading I had been doing into a knowledge quest of sorts about all different types of topics and values I wanted to explore further. These books filled my head with new thoughts and questions to bring back to God every morning. Two books, in particular, really caught my attention and sparked a ton of questions and thoughts that I wanted to explore deeper with God. Those two books were *7 Habits of Highly Effective People*, by Stephen Covey and *A Man's Search for Meaning*, by Viktor Frankl.

You've probably heard of both of them as they are regularly listed in the ten most influential books of all time. If you haven't, here is a brief overview of each:

The 7 Habits of Highly Effective People is a book first published in 1989 that is a business and self-help book. The author, Stephen Covey, presents an approach to being effective in attaining goals by aligning oneself to what he calls "true north" principles based on universal and timeless character ethics. Covey argues against what he calls the personality ethic, which is prevalent in many modern self-help books. The character ethic is based on aligning one's values with so-called universal and timeless principles. In doing this, Covey distinguishes between principles and values. He sees principles as external natural laws and values as internal and subjective. Our values govern our behavior, while principles ultimately determine the consequences. Covey presents his teachings in a series of habits, manifesting as a progression from dependence through independence to interdependence.

A Man's Search for Meaning is a 1946 book by Viktor Frankl chronicling his experiences as a prisoner in Nazi concentration camps during World War II. In the book, Frankl describes his psychotherapeutic method, which involves identifying a purpose in life to feel positive about, and then immersively imagining that outcome. According to Frankl, the way a prisoner imagined the future affected his longevity. The book intends to answer the question, "How was everyday life in a concentration camp reflected in the mind of the average prisoner?" Part one constitutes Frankl's analysis of his experiences in the concentration camps, while part two introduces his ideas of meaning and his theory called Logotherapy (meaning therapy).

These two books have had a profound effect on my life. They laid the foundation for learning the importance of truly understanding my core values, putting them first in every aspect of my life, and thus finding my life's purpose so I can feel fulfilled no matter what circumstances this world throws at me.

Let's start with *The 7 Habits of Highly Effective People*, my reflections and most profound insights that I received from this book, and how they related to my views on the importance of core values.

After months of deep conversations with God, we came to the agreement that core values are everything in life. They're really all that we have as humans. If you don't know your core values, you don't know yourself. Your core values are the manifestations of the actions you bring to the world every single day. They are your North Star and compass that guide how you work, play, love, and approach every other interaction you have in this world. They guide everything we do and say, or at least they should.

In *The 7 Habits*, Dr. Covey spends a lot of time talking about the importance of paradigms, our unique takes on how we view the world. He compares paradigms to a map. I like to think of a map as an analogy for your life's purpose. If you are looking at the wrong life map (wrong purpose), then it doesn't matter where you are going or how you get there, so the impact of living your core values is lessened. However, once you are on the right map, that is when core values can become a game-changer and a lightning rod to propel you forward in the direction you seek.

Everyone's core values are different, unique, and deeply personal, which is the beauty of it all. They are what gives your existence meaning and what defines "you" to the world. No one's core values are the same, nor should they be. Your core values can only be crafted in your mind after serious thought and reflection (i.e., conversations with God). No one can control who you and God decide that you want to be! Core values are deeply personal, and a lot of God time should go into crafting and cultivating them over your lifetime as they are ever-evolving. In essence, I like to think of core values as the fertilizer to the rock garden we talked about in the previous section. God will provide you with all the infrastructure in the soil, sun, and rain. You plant the seeds of your purpose, and your core values are the fertilizer you lay every day to help you transform your pile of rocks into a beautiful garden.

None of this information was earth-shattering to me because we all know this stuff. The problem is that 99% of us don't live this stuff. I'd bet $100 to everyone reading this book right now that if I asked you to rattle off all of your unique core values that guide your life in all you do in the next 30 seconds, you wouldn't be able to. Go ahead and try right now. I'll wait. Okay, done? I'm willing to bet that almost no one reading this book can successfully complete this exercise if they are honest with themselves (unless deceit is one of your core values, and then I'm cool with it, and you do you). However, If you were one of those rare humans able to do this in 30 seconds or less, then I want to meet you and join you on your journey because you are the type of person I want in my tribe. I will also gladly pay you that $100 because it will be worth the investment knowing that I'm in for an adventure with someone that knows where they are going. I can almost guarantee you that I will get back that $100 tenfold in value as we join up on this mission together. Seriously, give me a call if you were successfully able to do this so I can send you your $100 and meet you. I can't wait for the conversation to hear about your core values. My email address is cmsears8384@gmail.com, and my phone number is (317)432-0728. I look forward to hearing from you!

To be fair, there is no way in hell that I would have been able to do this 33-second exercise before my own experience with Emilia, the atomic blast, and my time searching in the rubble. Hell, I'm still not sure if I could do it now, and I've been staring at my core values at the top of my journal to Emilia every day for a year straight.

Sure, in my previous life, I could have rattled off a few things pretty quickly if you pressed me. It would have gone something like this, "Uh…I guess…. Uh….grit, fall in love with the process, grind, discipline equals freedom, do the things you hate the most first, extreme ownership, radical candor, fail fast, etc. I don't know. How does that sound?"

I'm guessing a lot of you reading were the same as me, and that is okay. All these ideas I just rattled off weren't my real core values. They were all ideas and philosophies that I've stolen from other people's core values and how they live their lives every day. I'll gladly admit that I stole them from countless hours of listening to podcasts like How I Built This, where entrepreneurs candidly discuss their personal journeys of how they started their companies, all the struggles and triumphs, and lessons learned to create the success that they achieved. Or from my daily mentoring videos from Darren Hardy, where he shares his thoughts and reflections to help jumpstart your day to "Be the Exception." Or from what my teachers in grade school, high school, and college taught me. Or from what the Catholic Church says is right. Or from whatever other thing I was doing, listening to, reading, or consuming every day to try and "better myself" over the course of my lifetime.

The point is, none of those core values were actually my own. I liked the idea of them in theory, but I had never taken them out on a true test drive in my life to see if they were a real fit. If you challenged me on what percentage of my life I lived based on those values I listed above, I would have to admit it would be less than 10% at best. Honestly, after reflecting on those values and discussing them with God, I found out that I didn't even want to live my life that way 100% of the time, as that sounds miserable. Who the hell wants to wake up every day, look in the mirror, and say to themselves, "time to grind" or, "do the things you hate the most first?" That really doesn't sound like a ton of fun to me! That sounds like a workaholic that is helping others to achieve their goals. That is exactly who I was before God and I began crafting my core values.

Now that God and I had solidified and mutually agreed on what my core values were and the critical role they play in all of our lives, the next impactful and transformational insight that I got from *The 7 Habits of Highly Effective People* was the concept of always striving to "put first things first" which happens to be habit number three. Per Stephen Covey, "Putting first things first means organizing and executing your life around your most important priorities. It is living and being driven by the principles you value most, not by the agendas and forces surrounding you."

Basically, it is the practice of actually using your core values to determine the activities that you value most and prioritize those activities every single day. Once again, this isn't groundbreaking new scientific research that will blow your mind or something. It is actually quite the opposite. This is a tale as old as time and common knowledge that almost everyone knows and understands. So don't let other people's agendas usurp our own values in how we live each day. I get it!

Of course, we all know this, but hardly anyone really does this every day and in all of their actions. This single act of literally putting first things first every day is probably the most challenging thing we can do in our lives because it requires us to say no to society's agendas, values, and norms. I mean, come on, who doesn't dream of being able to prioritize the things that they value most every day?

Whether it is learning, exercise, playing, sports, family time, or even work, we all have those activities that we say, "If I only had more time, I would do X." The problem we all run into is that other people's urgent and important tasks get in the way, and we push our non-urgent but important activities to the side. We say, "I'll get to the gym right after I get done responding to all these work emails," or, "I'll pick up that book when I have an hour of free time after shuttling kids to and from soccer games all day." Unfortunately, when the time comes to finally pick up the book, lace up the shoes, or sit down at the piano, we say we are exhausted and just don't have any more energy to do what we said we value most.

It is a sad reality, but one that we all know too well. That conflict between living our true core values and who we are versus living someone else's core values is the source of so many people's panic and anxiety that is becoming all the more common in this world today. I know this feeling all too well as I lived for years of my life with crippling panic attacks that seemingly came from nowhere and slowly took control of my whole life. It wasn't until I discovered this source of conflict and made environmental changes that I was able to finally turn the corner and regain my life back from the anxiety.

We can't deny the realities of this world we live in, but that doesn't mean we have to forsake ourselves and what we value in that process, either. Everyone matters in this world, and they deserve the right to live a life of fulfillment and purpose. Let's say, for example, you value family, learning, and health as core values. What if you woke up a little earlier to make it to the gym first thing in the morning, followed by listening to an audiobook on the way back, and then made a family breakfast for your kids each morning to talk about their day ahead? That is the concept of always putting first things first. Put your own core value-driven activities first each and every day and then fill in the rest of the day with all the other rat-race urgent and important tasks that we do like work, social media, chores, politics, responding to messages, etc. Do you think that may be a better way to live your life? I certainly did, and putting first things first in my life every single day has had an unbelievably profound effect on the trajectory of my life.

Living this lifestyle requires the following three things:

1. A paradigm shift to get on the right life map
2. Understanding and defining your core values
3. Putting activities first in your life that honor those values before anything else

That's it! Nothing more to it than that.

With all that said, I had my right map, "living for two," and now I needed to lock in my core values in order to continue my new quest and begin the construction of my new city. The following is what God and I came up with on who Chris Sears says he TRULY values in his life and how he wants to live each and every day as he strives to put first things first in all that he does.

Quick disclaimer - I will spend the next few pages listing off my core values and providing a brief description of what each means to me. One final note before jumping into this exercise, I'm writing this as of 2/28/2021. These are my core values and thoughts as of right here and now. It is my belief, after about a year of going back and forth on this topic with God, that core values can and should change as we evolve in life. These aren't like The Ten Commandments, where they are etched in stone and never to be altered for eternity. I like to think of core values more like the constitution of the United States of America, which is a living, breathing document that can change and evolve over time.

That said, what I am about to list off are my values as of this moment and are subject to edit and change at any moment, assuming thoughtful consideration and reflection with God before I make that kind of change. In thinking this way, I've kind of built a bit of a backdoor into my core values, with one of them being "learn every day." Because learning every day is one of my core values, I can't pretend that I have any idea what I'm about to experience or learn during the rest of my time here on Earth that might dramatically shift my views on certain topics and actions or how I want to live my life.

So, if I'm going to live up to the one sentence that I want others to remember me by, that I live each day of my life guided by my core values, I can't in my right mind say that these are the end-all and be all right here today because I will have violated the "learn every day" core value. That is my logic, and I'm sticking to it. Convince me otherwise as I'm open to the challenge, which is another of my core values you will learn below.

On with the show. Chris Sears' Core Values (in no particular order) as of 2/28/21…

1. NEVER QUIT (AKA "The Emilia Rule") - I've dubbed this one "The Emilia Rule" because it is inspired by the strength, courage, and fight that I saw reflected in her every single minute of her life. No matter what challenges were thrown at her, she took it head-on, never thought about giving up, and always searched for a way forward. It is hard to describe to someone that wasn't there to watch her journey in person, but you could just tell how focused she was on life and was never going to give up on her dreams of having a chance in this world no matter what obstacle was thrown her way. It was the most inspiring thing I have or will ever witness in my life, and I will never forget it, which is why it is on this list. To be clear, committing to never quit doesn't mean you should keep banging your head against a wall even when you know that you can't get through. Never quit means to endure. It means to never stop trying to find a way to have a chance at this life and make the most of what you are given. Never quit reminds me that this is all about the journey and to never give up on yourself no matter what as you will be missing out on a chance at the most beautiful experience we could ever imagine, and that is called humanity.

2. BALANCE - To me, life is all about the never-ending quest of constantly striving to find and obtain balance in our existence. If I was ranking my core values in order, balance would be first on the list as I feel that everything stems from striving to maintain balance in all that we do. Humans are complex. Our bodies and minds are almost inconceivably complicated. We have so many dimensions to our existence like work, love, health, divinity,

family, play, and community, just to name a few. Each dimension of life has a polarity, meaning an extreme to both sides. If we are using running as an example, Usain Bolt is on one extreme pole as the fastest sprinter in this world, running the 100-meter dash in mind-blowing 9.58 seconds. I ran track in high school (not well), and I think my best time was like 11.5 seconds or something like that, and I wouldn't call myself slow. Usain Bolt is on a whole other universe than everyone else. On the other end of the pole is someone like Eliud Kipchoge, who is the only marathoner in the world to run 26.2 miles IN UNDER TWO HOURS!!!! This dude maintained a 4-minute, 35-second-per-mile pace for 26.2 miles! I've been trying my hardest to run one mile as fast as I can all year, and the best I've been able to do is 5 minutes and 35 seconds. Think about that...MY BEST is still a minute PER MILE off of this dude's AVERAGE for 26 miles. That is crazy on both sides and something to be marveled at for what a human can accomplish if they dedicate their life to something. I'm glad there are people in this world like Usain and Eliud, but that isn't for me. The amount of time and sacrifice it takes for those two men to achieve what they've done is inconceivable. I literally can't imagine (there it is again) what their lives must be like in order to achieve something like these out-of-this-world outcomes. They've most likely had to make extreme sacrifices in every other area of their existence to achieve such remarkable feats. Sadly, a lot of super achievers like Usain and Eliud, who are at the extremes poles of life, often feel like they are lost once their quest is over and they've achieved what they set out to conquer. I've heard all kinds of similar stories like this from Olympians, chess players, professional athletes, movie stars, music, business, astronauts, etc....the list goes on and on. Their entire existence and identities are wrapped up in this one thing or goal, and everything else inevitably falls to shit. It's a story as old as time and repeats over and over and over again. If you've ever followed the life of Tiger Woods, you know what I've been talking about. Imbalanced people seeking perfection in one area of life become like robots of some sort and lose touch with what it means to be human due to neglect of everything else. This is my theory why they have such EPIC flameouts once they reach the heights of their existence. Life also has a rhythm to it. If you go to one end of the extreme, the swing back will be just as far. Again, see Tiger Woods if you are looking for an example. That is not how I want to live my life. My ideal world is running pretty far and pretty fast while trying to get a little better each and every day with a limited time I have to dedicate to ALL the activities I want to do. I'd love to be 80% proficient in each area of my life or something, i.e., running 4 miles in 30 minutes. That is a pretty solid time and achievement that pushes me but doesn't require me to dedicate my life to it to achieve. That is what balance is to me. In my mind, being human means experiencing it ALL and trying our best to keep everything going in harmony at once. We need all these dimensions to be our happiest (whatever that means) selves. The concept of balance reminds me of that halftime show of the dudes that try to keep all the spinning plates going at once. It is awesome to watch them try because we all know it won't last forever, and we can't wait to see one of them finally fall, and then the rest come tumbling down one by one afterward. How we live our lives is no different than the spinning plates halftime show, in my opinion. We try our best to keep ALL the plates going for as long as possible. Inevitably, as you add more and more plates, it becomes impossible to keep them all spinning well, and they eventually will all come crashing down and break into a million pieces. We aren't gods and don't have all the secrets to the world to keep everything going faster and faster all the time. It is evitable we fail because we are mere mortals with limited time here on this Earth. Striving for pure balance may seem like a fool's errand to a lot of people as it is impossible to obtain, which I agree. To me, it is the quest for balance that is the fun because you will never win, and there is always something to get better at. We all know that it is possible if you forgo everything in this world and focus on just trying to spin one plate, that you can become a Usain Bolt, Eliud Kipchoge, or a Tiger Woods. There is a "Tiger Woods" in every area of life somewhere. Why try to be like everyone else? Does anyone know who the Tiger Woods of balance is? It doesn't exist because it is an infinite game with no set rules, unlike golf. I'd rather go after trying to achieve the impossible and progress it for the next generation than waste all of my existence on trying to be the best at something others have already conquered. While I know I will never truly be 100% "balanced" in all areas of my life, the fun to me is trying! Give it a go and see what happens, and you will be better off in the long run, in my opinion. Your plates will crash all the time, but the trick is to fall back on the first rule and NEVER QUIT. The more you try, the closer you'll get.

3. GIVE MORE THAN I TAKE - Humans are social creatures; we are here on this Earth to help our fellow humans to do our best to survive, thrive, and pass on our genes to the next generation to do the same. Our family, friends, and all the people we interact with during our lifetime are REALLY what this is all about. Because of this, at our core, I believe that we are GIVERS by nature as we want our species to survive and thrive. Takers are the exact opposite. They suck the life out of humanity and leave it worse off than they got. I can tell you one thing with certainty; people don't want to be around other people that are takers in life. At our evolutionary core, I think that we instinctively know that takers aren't here to progress humanity, and we do our best to avoid them at all cost once they've been discovered and outed to the rest of the tribe. One of my favorite books I read on this journey was called

The Go-Giver that we touched on previously. Quick refresher, it is a short story about the power of giving and the impact that it can have on your life and those around you when you focus on putting giving at your core. It details the five laws of giving as shown through the journey of a young businessman named Joe and the people he meets along the way as examples of each law. The first "Law of Giving" and my personal favorite is as follows – "Your true worth is determined by how much more value you give than take in return." I want to make an important note here. This isn't to say that you shouldn't take anything. It just implies you have to give more than you take. For us to grow, we have to take sometimes, but if we always strive to give more than we take, it will create more for everyone. Your legacy is wrapped up in the people that you interact with, what you write down, what you learn, what you create, and how you help others to find their path. My goal, and hopefully yours as well, is to do my part to leave the people I come across better off than they would have been without me. That is a mission that I can get behind and why it makes this list.

4. PLAY – "All work and no play makes Jack a dull boy!" Have some damn fun, and don't be so serious all the time. Again, we are social creatures, and we express ourselves through play and creativity with our fellow humans. It is a necessary and critical element to our balance equation. All too often, playtime gets left by the wayside and is looked down upon by adults in our uber-productive and business-driven world. Well, that won't be my life as I'm on a mission for balance in all dimensions of my existence. I will find time to play and express myself, whether it be on a tennis court, in a boardroom, writing this book, or hanging with my wife and children. WE WILL BE MAKING TIME TO PLAY AND ENJOY LIFE!

5. CHALLENGE EVERYTHING - If you know me, you know that this is the one core value that I have always truly lived every single day for as long as I can remember. I love to challenge everything! I have the classic last-born kid syndrome. I will push every boundary and try to break every rule. Since I was a little kid, I have been challenging everyone in my world with my actions and never-ending questions on why the world works a certain way. It started with my parents and family, then my teachers and friends in school, then Felicia, and finally, I added my coworkers into the fun as well. People don't always love it. Just an example, I don't think Felicia had ever yelled at anyone before she met me. She's just not that kind of person. Eventually, she loses her patience with my constant need to challenge everything. I've made more peaceful and calm people end conversations with me saying, "I just can't anymore with you," than you can even imagine. Most people would feel bad

about that, but for me, it is like a badge of honor. Questioning and challenging the world is what makes things fun for me. Challenging assumptions and pushing boundaries is the first step to unlocking your creativity and opening your mind to all the possibilities that it can create. If you aren't challenging the status quo, you aren't doing it right. I think this way in all areas of my life and in any project that I take on. Striving for constant improvement invigorates me and keeps my blood pumping every day.

6. DON'T DO IT ALONE: Questioning everything, always challenging the world, etc., is a very selfish activity. I'm taking people's energy, stamina, and mental capacity to focus on my questions and problems. If I keep doing this all the time, eventually, I will run out of people to annoy and will be left on an island questioning a volleyball like Tom Hanks in Castaway. That isn't living in balance or giving more than I take. So, to counteract this, I've included "don't do it alone" into my core values to always remind myself to be the best human I can be and to pull back when I take things too far and push people to their limits. I need this included to always remind myself to pick and choose the right spots to engage and to always remember that everyone has their own story to tell, a question to ask, and a problem to solve. I need to give more than I take by listening and being there to help them in any way I can. If I'm truly going to do great things in this world and carry on my daughter's legacy, then I certainly won't be able to achieve this all by myself. "Don't do it alone" is included in my core values to stop me from being the worst version of myself.

7. HUMILITY – If you are reading this and have known me for a long time, you are probably laughing when you see this word included in my core values. Humility and Chris Sears go together like lamb and tuna fish (hopefully, you are a Big Daddy fan and understand that one). I can hear my friends saying, "This is the dude that always thinks he is right about everything and will do and say anything to win an argument no matter what the cost. I'm calling bullshit on this one!" Well, touché and you're right. Humility is a new addition to the list and is a result of being humbled over the past year. Over this time, I've realized a few really important lessons. Firstly, I'm a finite player in an infinite game. I read this book by Simon Sinek called *Infinite Games*, and I loved every minute of it. Sinek's main hypothesis is that there are finite games, like golf, chess, etc., that have rules and can be mastered and won if you dedicate enough time and effort. Then there are infinite games that have no winner and no defined rules like business, marriage, and life itself. Infinite games can not be won or lost. They go on in perpetuity, but that doesn't mean you shouldn't play them. Infinite games require you to have a

different mindset, to realize that you aren't in control of the outcomes, and to focus on being the best person you can be to achieve goals while you are blessed enough to be here on this Earth. Well, losing Emilia was the ultimate humbling act and realization that life is one of those infinite games for me. It made me realize how little control I had in my life and that I had to adjust my mindset and be open to seeing things differently if I was going to survive and thrive. The second big lesson was my never-ending quest to learn something new every day. I've learned more in this past year than I have in my entire life up to this point, and it kind of blows my mind sometimes thinking about it. The more I learn, the more I realize that I don't know anything, which is more than okay. There is more knowledge in this world than I could ever imagine (there it is again), but I aspire to consume as much as I can for the rest of my life. I'm hooked on learning as a lifestyle. My new motto is that I don't know anything, and I can't wait to find out. As I stated above, core values can change and grow as you change and grow. This past year humbled me to my core, and I'm living every day knowing that I don't know anything and that this is an infinite game, and I'm just trying to do my part to progress our species while I'm here on this Earth.

8. LEARN SOMETHING NEW EVERY DAY: This one is pretty self-explanatory, and I just touched on this above. What I would like to add here is the importance of learning to the whole thesis of this book and the "I can't imagine" equation. My theory is that in order for you to imagine, you have to be able to bring a question to work through in your mind with God. You can't bring any new questions if you are only using what you always already know to be true. You will run out of things to talk about, and in turn, your imagination will run dry. All this can be counteracted by constantly making learning a part of your everyday life. Listen to a podcast, watch a documentary, read a book, listen to an audiobook, explore YouTube, type a search in google, and go read the answers on Wikipedia, etc. The possibilities of how you can learn in this modern world are endless at this point, and all can be found in the palm of your hand in an instant. All you have to do is be willing to seek it out and find it. I had a huge AHA moment while reading the book Sapiens along this journey that I wanted to share here. The author was talking about his theories on why Europe rose to become the dominant player in the modern world seemingly out of nowhere when it would have made much more logical sense for this world to be dominated by Asia and Africa, which had been the home to all thought leadership and ancient civilizations. His theory was pretty simple. Those ancient Asian cultures looked within to grow and stopped searching for new knowledge. The Europeans, on the other hand, realized that they don't know anything and set out on quests all over

the world to seek out new knowledge and bring it back to their people. This thought blew my mind as I reflected on it one day in my personal journal. I thought, "Man…those European explorers were literally willing to risk their own lives and leave their families behind on the HOPE that they would sail around the world, with no promises of success, and MAYBE be able to bring one new piece of knowledge back to their people. They were willing to risk EVERYTHING and years of their lives in search of new knowledge. Then I looked at this modern world only to realize that we are too lazy to even look at our phones or computers where everything we could ever imagine can be found in an instant." That wasn't going to be me anymore. I'd always valued learning, but I rarely searched for my OWN knowledge around exploring what really interested me. Most of my past learning was dictated by others in formal school or workplace settings. Well, that ended on 3/15/20, and I'm never going back.

9. Currently Under Consideration with God – "I Don't Run for Trains." I wanted to include this one in here quickly just for fun and to illustrate that our core values should always be a living and breathing thing that evolves over time as we grow and change. "I don't run for trains" is currently "under review" between God and me as we are talking through it slowly to see if it makes the cut or not. The reason that it isn't fully "on the list" is that I haven't really started to implement it in my everyday life in all that I do. It is more of a theory or a philosophy to me at this point that I need to work through in practice and make sure that it fits who I want to be. Core values have to be implemented every single day for them to really be true. If not, they are just thoughts from other people. This "under review" time is like buying a new pair of jeans that are still sitting in your closet and haven't made it to the regular wardrobe rotation yet, if you know what I mean. You like the jeans, decided to buy them, but just haven't found the right application or occasion to really break them out and see if they truly fit you and the vibe you are going for. We all have tons of items of clothes like this in our wardrobes. We have the regular rotational outfits that fit us like a glove and represent who we are. Then we have the items of clothes that could carve out a place in the regular rotation, but you just don't know yet until you break them out and wear them in the world. Until this happens, they are theoretically clothes that represent you. That is "I don't run for trains" at this point to me. I've bought the concept, but it is still on the shelf in my core values closet and not in the regular rotation just yet. Still to be determined if it fits me or not. So what does this saying even mean? "I don't run for trains" is actually a quote from Nasim Talib in his book *The Black Swan*. This story is an amazing adventure, and I encourage anyone reading this to check it out as well. Warning and

buyer beware, as *The Black Swan* is a dangerous book to read if you are only reading one or two books a year on your learning diet. It is intense and needs to be watered down by a lot of other ideas for the concepts to truly resonate, in my opinion. It would be like if you only had one drink of alcohol a year and decided to make that choice Absinthe, Everclear, or Moonshine. I imagine that would probably give most people an aversion to alcohol. Or worse, maybe they like it and began to drink Everclear all day which is just as bad. The Black Swan needs to be slowly sipped and balanced out with a healthy dose of way less heavy content and counter views for the meaning to truly resonate. With that disclaimer in mind, Talib finished off The Black Swan with this "I Don't Run for Trains" as one of his final thoughts and what it means to him. Here is Talib's explanation on the concept, "Snub your destiny. I have taught myself to resist running to keep on schedule. This may seem a very small piece of advice, but it registered. In refusing to run to catch trains, I have felt the true value of elegance and aesthetics in behavior, a sense of being in control of my time, my schedule, and my life. Missing a train is only painful if you run after it! Likewise, not matching the idea of success others expect from you is only painful if that's what you are seeking. You stand above the rat race and the pecking order, not outside of it if you do so by choice." I loved this quote and have reflected on it a lot over the past year or so, given all that has happened in my life. If you miss the train, so what? There will always be another, and maybe you will end up sitting next to the person that will become the love of your life or some other marathoner with whom you will be forever. Life is random as hell, which is basically what the book is about. We have no idea what is coming next, and it is stupid to even try to believe we do. If you had told me a year ago that I would be over 400 pages into writing a book that was dedicated to my daughter that passed away in the middle of a pandemic, I would have said you're insane! Firstly, I'm not a writer. Secondly, my daughter died? What the hell happened? And thirdly, what the hell is a pandemic? No one could have predicted my life other than maybe God or whatever hirer power this whole universe runs on. To think about all that I've missed trying to catch the right trains and stay on schedule in life infuriates me now. I'm done running on someone else's time and agenda. To me, "I don't run for trains" means that I'm not going to let anyone else's core values trump my core values in any activity that I do for the rest of my life. Life works in mysterious ways, and sometimes missing that train is the best thing that can happen for us as it just wasn't meant to be for whatever reason. You have to be open to seeing these omens and embracing them when they enter your life. Most of us try to spend all of our time trying to bend life to our will, which truly is a fool's errand as we will lose every single time. So embrace it with open arms. Keep your mind sharp and be open to receiving. Don't run for trains! Still

TBD on whether or not this makes the cut in the future or not. God nd I are leaning toward an emphatic YES!

So there you have it. These eight values officially define Chris Sears circa 2/28/2021. If you see me out and about and living my life without adhering to these values, please call me out. I welcome the challenge. I also now know that I'm humble enough to welcome new knowledge from outsiders as I've discovered that I don't have this all figured and never will. The irony of life is that it is hard to live the way you say you want to live. It sounds so easy in theory, but in actuality, it is the hardest thing we can imagine. That's the true "hard things about hard things," if you will.

It is so easy to let one of your spinning plates fall and not even realize it was close to running out of steam. However, you can't even play the infinite game of life until you've paid the admission fee of first knowing yourself to your core, understanding your values, defining them and what they mean to you, and then trying your best to constantly improve and keep them all spinning together in harmony and balance at once. Core values are your compass, and you can't go through life without regularly checking that you are still going in the right direction, or you will end up lost and alone.

For the first time in my life, I can safely say that I am going in the right direction, and it feels really good, despite all that I've endured over the past year. This is my own beautiful garden, created out of a rock pile that God gave me, and I want to keep it surviving and thriving for myself and my daughter.

Finding Purpose and Finishing Emilia's Marathon

My New Life's Purpose: "Living for Two"

I had mentioned another book in the previous section that had a profound impact on my life called, *A Man's Search for Meaning by Viktor Frankl.* Specifically, it provided the catalyst to ask deep questions about my own purpose and life mission.

Over the course of my time sitting in the rubble and crafting my core values with God, I began to develop a deep love of humanity (and all things living, for that matter) as I realized how truly remarkable we all are as individuals and as a species. Our existence is a miracle, and what we are able to do is nothing less than spectacular. As my core values started to take shape, I began a quest to learn as much as I could about humans in general. I studied how we think, why we do what we do, how our bodies work, our evolution as a species, how civilizations came to be, the importance of culture, and stories of how other remarkable humans expressed their own core values while overcoming some of the harshest conditions you can imagine.

One of the stories I found to be an example of the ultimate expression of core values was *A Man's Search for Meaning* by Viktor Frankl. As previously stated, this is a story chronicling Frankl's experiences as a prisoner in Nazi concentration camps during World War II and his psychotherapeutic method, which involved identifying a purpose in life to feel positive about and then immersively imagining that outcome. I'm not going to go into details of the story as we all have learned how truly horrifying this experience must have been for these poor souls that were thrust into this existence and subjected to all of the worst things and conditions we can create as humans. What I do want to briefly touch on is the importance of this story in helping to understand how much having meaning in your life can truly matter. Frankl was tortured, beaten, and starved, but he didn't allow the circumstances thrust upon him to dictate who he was in his own mind. It didn't matter what they did to him; no one could touch his soul unless he let them. Despite the horrific circumstances, he stuck to who he wanted to be and figured out a way to live that existence, even in the face of unbelievable circumstances. His core values literally saved his life because they gave him meaning and a purpose. If that doesn't push you to this way of living, then I don't know what else can.

In the second half of the book, Frankl goes on to talk about his post-concentration camp life and mission that centered around his continued work as a therapist. This was when he developed a technique called Logotherapy, also known as meaning therapy. Basically, it is a therapeutic method to help individuals find their purpose or meaning in life. It is used to overcome struggles and get back on the right paradigm or map to resume their lives and living with a purpose.

Frankl's words and inspiring story helped me to further explore some deeper conversations with God around my own purpose and meaning in life. Those conversations ultimately led me to discover my own meaning in life and come up with my life's mission that I like to call "living for two."

What exactly is "living for two"?

Emilia's physical time here on Earth was cut dramatically shorter than anyone could have ever imagined or would have wished for her or my family. However, that doesn't mean that what she stood for and how she lived her life can't continue to have a far-reaching impact that reverberates throughout the world someday. I feel it is my duty to pick up where she left off and to tell my daughter's story and the impact she made on me, as demonstrated through my actions every single day.

How "living for two" works:

This book is a direct reflection of how I'm demonstrating the "living for two" mission in my everyday existence. I've spent every morning for the past year typing for Emilia before heading off to the metaphorical train station to catch all the other speeding trains of my life that could easily distract me from our mission like my day job, the remodeling projects going on in my house, politics, the pandemic, Felicia's complicated new pregnancy, etc. I have a duty to make sure that her story is told that I'm truly practicing what I preach and "living for two" in all that I do.

My core values aren't just mine alone; Emilia had a huge impact in crafting and shaping them over the past year, so much so that I now like to think of them as our shared core values.

This project and the daily act of writing this book allow me to express all of Emilia's and my shared core values into this world. For example, I Can't Imagine provides balance to Emilia and me by being able to connect with God through our daily reflections on life, connect with each other by relieving our story through words, and a forum to express our creativity. It allows us to laugh, play, cry, and use our unique voice to tell our story to the world. It shows that we can endure and will never quit on life no matter what hardships and roadblocks are thrown in our path. It is giving more than we take by dedicating countless hours of time to getting this all out on paper in hopes of helping another family out there that may be experiencing what we tragically went through. It is challenging ourselves to do something that we've never done before, which is to become a writer and produce a work of art in our shared memoir. It is not doing this alone and having the support of Emilia, my mom, Felicia, my sister, and so many other friends, co-workers, and family members that have listened to me talk about our vision for this book and encouraged me to keep writing and telling our story. It is being humbled to my core knowing that writing this story wouldn't even be possible without having to go through the unspeakable tragedy of losing my firstborn child.

And finally, how striving to consistently learn, grow, and hear new voices in our life ultimately provided the fuel for Emilia and me to start to ask our own big questions in life and find our own voice to be able to share with others in this world and make our own permanent dent on the human experience.

This book is what "living for two" is all about. This is a work of art that was co-created by and with my daughter by my side each and every day. I'm sure every father naturally worries if they will be able to find that connection to their child and leave a lasting legacy through them. I know I certainly did. Even with all that Emilia and I have endured together, through this mission and work like this, I feel more connected to her than I ever could have imagined the first time I learned I was having a child. If I lose my way someday and I let that connection fade, this book will serve as my forever reminder to get me back on track and "living for two" in all that I do.

Finishing Emilia's NICU Marathon

As we got closer and closer to July 13th, Emilia's original due date, it felt like our metaphorical NICU marathon and journey was truly coming to an end. By this point in our journey and after months of wandering aimlessly through rubble since the initial blast back on 4/22/20, I was feeling more and more prepared to kick off construction on my new city. We now had a rock-solid foundation in place, and we were all set to begin construction on something truly amazing. All that was left was to finish the race and break through that finish line tape before we could get to work on our new life's mission.

Somewhat ironically, throughout this whole quest through the rubble, I had become somewhat of a decent runner. This is something I've never thought I would ever be (or want to be) before this whole journey began. Remember, Felicia is the marathoner of the family. I was the family sprinter. Somehow I found myself regularly running 3-5 miles every day at a pretty decent 7-minute-30-second-per-mile pace. I was beginning to feel physically stronger than I ever had before. The daily routine of never missing a workout was starting to add up, and my body could really feel it.

While I may have been improving and getting stronger, the idea of ever running an actual marathon was still a pipe dream and not on my radar in any way. I was running to run. I had no goals other than to challenge my mind, my body, to set a good example for my daughter, and to have a little fun. That was my only agenda.

On my daily runs, I never went much longer than 5 miles. A few times, I had made it to 6 or 7 miles. On one occasion, I actually did 9.5 miles back in early June, which blew my mind because I've hated distance running my whole life. I never ran anything close to that before in my entire life. That particular run started out with the goal to run to downtown Indianapolis and then back, which would have been roughly about 6 or 7 miles. When I got to just east of downtown (about 3.5 miles into the run), I felt good and thought I'd run straight through the downtown area, which was another 2-or-3-mile stretch. Before I knew it, I found myself running by Riley's Hospital for Children, which is about 6.5 miles away from our house. When I hit the hospital, I thought I should just keep heading east for as long as I could before I wanted to stop. Eventually, I was clear in the middle of a little neighborhood called Haughville on the near west side of downtown and had run 9.5 miles straight from our house, through the city, and almost 3 miles past it. I was spent and realized that I didn't have the energy to run all the way back home, so I called Felicia and asked her to come pick me up. It was kind of fun, but also something I wasn't really too excited to keep trying because, again, balance is my core value, and running longer and longer wasn't on the docket for a balanced life agenda. I was happy to maintain running 3 to 5 miles and slowly try to get faster and faster at that distance. That was having positive effects on my life, and that was good enough for me.

However, something magically happened out of the blue on July 12th, 2020, a day before Emilia's original due date.

We were only one day away from completing our journaling experiment for Emilia that had begun back on March 15th, 2020. As that all-important end date inched closer and closer, it began to feel very bittersweet for Felicia and me. On the one hand, we were devastated that we weren't going to be bringing Emilia home on this day, which is what we originally had thought this day would hold. On the other hand, all that pain and sorrow didn't change the fact that we had been writing to Emilia for almost four straight months every day, and it felt like we had really achieved something of note that we all could feel proud about.

Writing to our daughter every day was a labor of love and forever changed our lives in a lot of ways. It really wasn't easy, especially for two people that weren't "writers" before this crazy journey began. There were certainly many days where I had to dig really deep to find the strength to sit down and write to Emilia. However, it was so worth it. Writing provided us a channel to allow us to stay connected to our daughter in some way even though she was no longer physically with us. I didn't want my Emilia time to end, but I also knew this couldn't go on forever in this form. Ending our journaling to Emilia felt almost bittersweet. I wanted it to end, and at the same time, I didn't.

So, on July 12th, 2020, the day before we finished the journaling project to Emilia, it was a beautiful Sunday summer morning and a perfect, sunny, and 75 degrees outside. Felicia's mother and sister were back in town, staying at our house to make sure they were there for her and me to help mark this July 13th date together as a family, as it was a pretty emotional date for us all. I decided to make my work for the day another run. I threw on my running shoes and air pods and set up for a quick normal 3-to-5-mile run on one of my normal routes, around the park, down to the Pensie trail, loop over to Arlington Ave, and eventually back to our place. This route is about 3.5 miles or so, and I had run it countless times over the past few months. That workout was supposed to be nothing more than the normal 3-to-5-mile route, and get back to the house to be there for Felicia and help prepare for the big day that was to come tomorrow.

It started off like every other run. I was jamming to my music, moving at a good pace, and my legs felt strong. The weather was just perfect and felt amazing. The sun was shining bright, not a cloud in the sky, and I was fully present and enjoying the moment.

While on my normal planned route, I rounded around the park near our house, about a mile from our house. At this point, normally, I would have turned left when I hit Michigan St (on the south end of the park) and headed back west over to Ritter to make my way down to the Pensie trail to continue the run. This route keeps me in my neighborhood and in areas, I feel comfortable and know well. It is my go-to safe run. For reasons unknown to me on this day, when I hit the south end of the park where I normally turn left, I decided to turn right down Michigan St. When you turn right at this point of the park, that marks the beginning of leaving my neighborhood and sets you on a direct course towards downtown Indianapolis about 3.5 miles away. I only ever turned this way when I wanted to extend my "normal" run an extra mile or two, which is what I guess I decided I was going to do because I was feeling good and enjoying the weather.

As I deviated from my original plan and began running east down Michigan St. toward downtown Indianapolis, I was loving how the sun felt and how energizing the light breeze was on my face. This was just perfect running weather. As I got to a point on Michigan St. where I would normally need to turn to start to make my way back to Irvington and complete my "extended" 5-mile run, I just decided to keep going for whatever reason, knowing that this meant I was setting out for a longer run than I had originally intended. I was feeling really good, and I thought, "Why not? I'll maybe do 6 miles today and make my turn when I hit Woodruff Place or something to loop back home."

This journey was starting to feel a lot like that 9.5-mile run I had run about a month prior to this date.

When I got to Woodruff Place, just east of downtown Indianapolis and about 3 miles from my house, I again said, "Why not? Let's make it 7 miles and loop back when I get to College Avenue or something." College Avenue really marks the entrance of the Downtown Indianapolis area from where I was running from.

As I got to College Avenue, I remembered my last long run where I kept running down Michigan, and I went so far that I ran past Riley's Hospital for Children. I thought to myself, "Let's go visit Emilia," and just kept running across downtown Indianapolis toward the hospital. Riley's is actually located on Michigan Avenue, which is ironically the same street where our house sits roughly 6.5 miles to the East. It is literally a dead straight shot from our house on the same road.

When I got to Riley Ave and Michigan, which is about 6.5 miles into the run, I turned right down Riley Ave and started to make my way toward the Simon Family Tower that Emilia spent the majority of her 39 days in on this Earth. As I got closer and closer to the building, I felt a wave of emotion begin to wash over me. I felt goosebumps from my head to my toes, and that choked-up feeling in the back of my throat like a cry is coming on. When I got right next to the building, I looked up at 4 West (Emilia's floor), and I started to cry, thinking about how much I missed my daughter and how much I didn't want this to be our life. I didn't want to have to be the dad that runs by the hospital that his infant daughter died at. I started to think, "Why is this my life? Why am I doing this right now?"

Moments later, as I kept my body moving and my legs slowly pumping in a light jog, I felt a wave of happiness hit my face. I looked up again and started smiling and waving to Emilia. I thought, "Stop feeling sad for yourself and let your daughter feel proud of her dad by letting her know you were okay, strong, and can endure just like she did." I was imagining that she was smiling down and showing all her little friends how cool her dad was and the stuff he was able to do.

It was an incredibly emotional moment that I was not planning for at all when I left my house that morning. Again, the real emotional day was supposed to be the following day on July 1ˢᵗ, 2020.

As I slowly ran by the rest of the Simon Family Tower and started to make my turn back toward my house, I thought to myself, "I'm going to run all the way back and finish this half-marathon today for Emilia!"

So that is what I did. This time, unlike a month before, I didn't call Felicia to come pick me up. I challenged myself to complete this half marathon come hell or high water. I channeled my daughter's strength and courage and said I'm not quitting until I hit 13.1 miles. I just kept on running and running and running until I made it back to Irvington and hit 13.1 miles on my running tracker app. Ironically, it turns out that to Riley's Hospital for Children and back to my house is almost exactly the length of a half marathon. Who knew?

Talk about mysterious omens that life can bring! Keep your mind open to seeing them as they are subtle but there for a reason. I was meant to run this route on this day. This was destiny and out of my control. It felt like I was called to do that on that day by a higher power, and I'm glad it happened. I haven't run that far since, and I don't have any plans to do it again. I have no idea how people run those distances and beyond for fun.

Just to prove that I had no intentions of doing this originally, I actually had a freaking tennis match scheduled for that evening in which I ended up playing a two and a half hour three-set match against a really hard opponent and actually lost (which was a rarity over the past year). No way in hell would I have ever planned to run a half marathon and then gone on to play a tennis match as well. I'm not a psychopath, which is what I'd have to be for this to have been a reality.

This particular day was definitely unbalanced when it came to my fitness, but that was okay as I was running for two on this day and I guess had to go pick her up from Riley and carry her back home to complete her race and make it home for good to see her actual nursery for the first time. As the weeks and months passed since that July 12ᵗʰ, 2020 day and this whole journey became more and more clear, I could feel God and Emilia pushing me to finish her race. I didn't know what it meant at the time, but I figured it out eventually, and that is what I'm going to share in the next section, the dramatic finishing act of our story.

July 13th, 2020, finally arrived, and it was an incredibly emotional day, as one could imagine. It wasn't supposed to be this way, but here we were. We ended this whole journey with a visit to Emilia's grave with Felicia, her mom, and her sister, Sarah. We arrived in separate cars and brought a bunch of gifts and flowers to decorate Emilia's grave. We spent some time together crying and missing our daughter.

Eventually, I decided that I was ready to depart, and Felicia said she was going to stay behind for a few more minutes. As I was walking away from Emilia's grave and back to my car, I saw another young mother on the other side of the infant circle arrive with flowers in hand, presumably for her child. I didn't think much of it as I drove off and left Felicia with her mom and sister.

Later that day, when we were all back together at home, Felicia asked me if I saw that woman that had arrived on the other side of the infant circle as I was leaving? She said the lady saw her crying and felt compelled to come over to sit with her and learn about Emilia. Apparently, as they talked, this young mother shared that she had lost her own child just a little over a year ago as well. She said that she and her husband recently had just given birth to their newest addition to their family and called it her "rainbow baby." She wanted to let Felicia know that there was still hope in this world and that she was there for her if she ever needed to talk. They exchanged numbers, and both departed the cemetery. Felicia thought it was so nice of her to come over and sit and share at that moment.

Again, be open to seeing the omens in this world. I had never heard the term rainbow baby before, so I did what everyone in the world would do. I Googled it. It turns out a rainbow baby is a name coined for a healthy baby born after losing a baby due to miscarriage, infant loss, stillbirth, or neonatal death. The name comes from the idea of a rainbow appearing in the sky after a storm or after a dark and turbulent time. Felicia and I had just started to talk about trying for a sibling to Emilia again recently on our Emilia walks, but we really hadn't made a decision yet. We had wanted to wait until after July 13th passed before really thinking about whether or not we wanted to try again. What a perfect message, at the perfect time for Felicia. Life sprinters sometimes come out of nowhere when you need them most to give you that little, tiny boost of energy to go forward. Well, I don't know if it was God or

Emilia that brought this lady over to Felicia that day, but thank you. (STAY TUNED TO FIND OUT WHY)

The Journals: Days 118-121

Day 118: 7/10/20

- I love you
- Dad Joke of the Day: How did Egyptians select the next pharaoh? It was a pyramid scheme.
- Daily Scripture Theme: God is with you. My Thoughts – "God gives you the strength and courage you need to fight through your struggles and tackle your biggest fears and challenges." I'm really torn on this message. I think God provides us the opportunity and the ability to understand ourselves, learn, and improve to fight and be courageous. Just saying that God GIVES us that ability could be misconstrued so dramatically that people are blindly willing to fight wars, kill others, etc., all in God's name because he gives them courage to fight and be brave. I don't disagree with the message that God is with us. He is with us to help us discover ourselves, but it is our own thinking and learning that will bring us to the decisions to be brave and courageous and not blindly following someone else.
- The Universe Message: "Whether it's praise, love, criticism, money, time, space, power, punishment, sorrow, laughter, care, pain, or pleasure...the more you give, the more you will receive." My Thoughts: Since we met and lost you, I feel like I've experienced every possible human emotion in a very short time span. Every time my negative thoughts have had an extended stay...the rest of me has felt like overall crap. Whenever I focus on learning, growing, positive messages, listening, understanding, etc...my mind, body, and universe feel in harmony. Without a doubt, I will stay focused on this path as much as possible. If I feel myself slipping, I will set some daily reminders like writing and reflecting to quickly counteract hopefully. I'd rather put more of this positivity into the universe than negativity.
- 3 Days to Go!!! - This is so bittersweet to me. This should be some exciting times for our family. They only thing I'm really excited about it wrapping up this project at this point.

- Remembering Self vs. Experiencing Self. I recently came across this concept of our 2 selves, our remembering self and our experiencing self. The studies concluded that our experiencing self is pretty indifferent in the moment to what is actually going on in our reality. What we REMEMBER, the story we tell ourselves, is actually the most important things for our minds. We love to tell stories as humans...it helps us to make sense of what happened to us. As it turns out, when we are remembering, we really only tend to focus on Beginnings, Peaks, and Endings of everything we experience. Duration really doesn't seem to matter much, and time apparently really has no impact. Endings in particular are critical to how we judge an experience apparently. If it is a positive ending, then we typically remember the whole experience in a much more positive light. This made me think of our time together and how our time ended together in particular. In retrospect, I'm so grateful for the shared experience we all had when you passed away. We had 5 amazing days together as a family where we finally got to all physically be together, got to cherish you, talk to you, talk about you, hold your hand, baptize you, read to you, etc. All of this culminated in a miraculous final 7 plus hours where you and your Mom held each other while you slowly passed away. It was one of the most amazing and emotional experiences of my life. Something I will never forget. I'm so grateful that we got to share those moments together. It really does help my remembering self to look back at our incredibly traumatic experience a little more favorably. It helps me to remember that while your time with us was so short, it doesn't mean that you didn't leave a forever positive lasting memory in our minds. I love telling this story to people because it is a powerful, positive, and happy ending to a story that was so sad and traumatic for all of us. When I think back on my experiencing self in the NICU and how that truly was, it was full of anxiety, scariness, questions, worry, fear, panic, boredom, tiredness, etc. That was the true day-to-day experience that we all lived through. However, I don't remember those things at all. I remember being so excited you were born and thriving, getting to see you every day, talking to your nurses and meeting our new medical family, learning about neonatal care, watching you grow, and then getting to say a beautiful goodbye on our terms. Just the beginning, the peaks, and the ending.
- I love you

Day 119: 7/11/20

- I love you
- Dad Joke of the Day: My Wife Emailed Me our wedding photos, but I can't seem to open any of the files. I always have trouble with emotional attachments.
- Daily Scripture Theme: You were created for adventure. My Thoughts - I am a giver. I'm opened for God to send me wherever he sees fit. I'm ready for our next adventure. Whether that be writing this book, having more children, starting a new business, etc. I'm fully ready, confident, and here to serve. I can't wait to see what the future holds.
- The Universe Message: "The more good you find in another, the more good you will find in yourself." My Thoughts - This is so true. Lately, I've been finding on my daily runs through the neighborhood that I'm waving and truly acknowledging everyone I see and meet (not just that polite nod or something). I mean EVERYONE...it has been weird. I'm stopping to talk to my neighbors when I see them and introduce myself. Same thing with people I encounter in my day-to-day life like at the grocery store, meeting a new person for a tennis match, etc. It's so not like me, but has been pretty rewarding for all involved, I think. Just seeing people for people, letting them talk and listening, and truly caring about others has made a remarkable difference in my feelings toward the world and myself. Sadly, the inverse can be totally true as well unfortunately. The worse you see in everyone, the more you feel miserable yourself. Your mind is really powerful...use it for good.
- I can't wait to get to writing on your first section of the book once this process is complete. By the end of this month, I want to have a first rough draft of the book completed. I'm so excited about this next chapter to come and getting your story out to the world.
- Baby wrangler...please help your mother stay chill about having another child and give her patience through this process. She's all in on having another sibling for you and that is exciting. The problem is I fear is that she is SOLELY focused on this right now and is not doing it 100% for the right reasons. She loved you so much that she is now putting a ton of pressure on herself to get pregnant as quickly as possible and it is stressing her out a lot. I don't want her to want another child as a way to heal herself and fill a missing part of her. I want her to want another child to ADD to her life and re-found strength. This all needs to be natural and a PART of the healing

process…NOT the whole healing process. Please watch over her, help us, and protect your siblings as we go through this process. I know you won't let us down. We love you so much.

- I've always been so amazed at the fathers I've seen in my life that appears to just do it all right. They are spiritual, successful in business, in shape, great family person, respectful of everyone they meet, amazing mentors to their children, patient and kind, etc. I've always seen them and thought I have no idea how they keep it all together and how in the hell am I going to do this once we have our own child. The truth is that I've always wanted children but was never really in a rush to have them because I was worried that I didn't know myself good enough yet to be fully selfless and devote my life to them. Even after waiting until my mid-30s to have you…I still didn't really feel "READY" per se. I thought I'll do what I always do and figure it out as it comes and adjust my life accordingly. That plan has always seemed to work out well for me in the past, but I knew that I wasn't going to be one of "those dads" that I referred to in the beginning of this reflection. I was okay with that. Maybe someday I'd get there but it was a far off and distant dream of 10-15 years down the road at the earliest. And then I met you and we went through this whole process together. I've sped my life up by 10-15 years in the past 4 months it feels like. I feel like a whole new person. I feel like my personal self is in total harmony. I've learned a way to live my life that is sustainable and has a purpose for all aspects truly founded in principles and values I hope to bring to the world. I feel like I'm really ready to be "that Dad" for your future siblings. I owe that all to you. My beautiful first born baby girl. You've changed my life in more ways than I could ever put into words. While I wish I was able to show you in person, I know that you will be with me every step of the journey to come until we can see each other again someday. They say that your life truly changes when you become a parent. I can unequivocally say that I'm finally becoming that person I've always hoped to be, and I owe that all to you. I love you so much.
- I love you.

Day 120: 7/12/20

- I love you
- Dad Joke of the Day: I was going to tell you a chemistry joke…But I didn't think I would get a reaction.

- Daily Scripture Theme: The Stepping Stones to Your Success. My Thoughts - This passage was about failure and how you have to fail before you can succeed. For years I've always said the words that I like to FAIL FAST as a bit of a mantra. Meaning, try something new and if it is going to fail, figure it out and move on to the next idea as quickly as you can. Recently, I've been convinced that this mantra needs to really be LEARN fast and not FAIL fast. Every time we fail at something, we learn an extremely valuable lesson (good or bad). Those lessons are then applied to the next test, the one after that, etc. The ONLY way to truly get where we want to get is to learn as fast as we can until we hit that breakthrough we seek. If we look at everything as a learning event and combine that with the NEVER QUIT (Emilia Rule) then eventually you will do something amazing and it will compound on itself in the long run. So basically, start and try something new, keeping learning, and never quit...you will eventually figure out what God has put us on this Earth to do.

- The Universe Message: "What if everything was not only working out just fine, but today, as things are, you're actually way ahead of plan?". My Thoughts - Lol. We are so short sided sometimes as people and forget to take in the whole big picture. The last few years doesn't make up our entire life or set a precursor for what is to come. It is a funny trick our mind plays on us as a bit of a recency bias. If I stop to think about how far I've come in life, all the things I've accomplished, how happy I and in my marriage, and excited about what is to come. I start to realize I've lived a pretty amazing and blessed life. I've seen areas of the world I've never dreamed, achieved successes I my life that I wished for when I was younger, etc. I'm pretty blessed and I can't wait to see what the future holds. Your mom, you, and I still have a LONG journey ahead of us with many wonderful events and things to see and do together. Sometimes, as Ferris Bueller (God I wish you could have seen this movie) would say... "Life moves pretty fast, If you don't stop to look around once in a while you could miss it."

- 1 more day to go...just 1,000 bittersweet thoughts all through my head. On Mach 15th, tomorrow was etched in all of our minds as the ending to the amazing and awful experience where we got to bring you home. Even though our journey started off in a crazy place... it would have a happy ending. July 13th was like the top of Mount Everest off in the distance. It was the final tape of the marathon. We weren't supposed to think about it ever. Remember that is the goal, but keep that far off in the distance as it would be too overwhelming and distracting for us all as we needed to focus on the harsh day 2 day truths in front of us. Well here we are, we have almost finished the race and I have no idea what to make of any of this anymore. Still have no idea what all this was about. I'm not sure if I will ever truly know. I was watching my stupid favorite trashy TV show that I love (Below Deck…which you would have loved as well I think), and one of the deck hands was talking about his 10 year anniversary of sobriety. He went into more detail about his story and said that he actually started that journey in rehab with his mother. Then he started crying as he talked about how he had to leave her behind to stay sober and she ultimate passed away from her addictions. He then said, I have to keep going for her…she gives me the power to move forward in my journey and to stay sober. He didn't say it but I could hear it in his voice. His Mom's death turned into his why and completely changed his life. 10 years later it still hurts enough to cry on television but that "power" as he put it was still burned into his brain and he will never forget it. Sadly, that is how I feel our journey is wrapping up as. Your mom and I are leaving this without you physically here with us but we are also forever changed because of you at the same time.

- You grandma and aunt are in town to be here with your Mom as we come closer toward to your original due date. I keep hearing your mom and her family talk about you as if you are still here with us and musing about how you would have been in the future. It is all done with love, joy, and happiness. It truly brings a smile to my face to hear as your mom isn't sad while talking about you. It feels good to hear your name and people talking about you just like any other child. I'm thankful for that and for your Mom's brief reprieve from sadness.
- I love you.

Day 121: 7/13/20

- I love you
- Dad Joke of the Day: Just read a book about the history of glue…I couldn't put it down.
- Daily Scripture Theme: You're Not Stuck, You're Going Through. My Thoughts - Going "THROUGH" something means that we are in the process of learning and growing. Going through something could be a good or bad event. It is ultimately up to you if you want to go through it by processing it, growing from it, and applying it

to your life going forward. That is what going through means. Not every will find meaning in their journey's unless they focus on it. Unfortunately for us, we have been going "through" a difficult event these past few months where a LOT of growth has happened for us all. I've been going through a ton with this process and I'm blessed to have been given this time by my employer to fully immerse myself in the process. I've never learned more, felt more, balanced more, tried harder, thought more, loved more, etc than I have these past few months. While I'm no where near through this journey and still have a long way to go, I feel like the deeper meaning is starting to take hold in all of us that will empower us all as we go through the rest of our lives. Would I trade these learning and new found growth for you… in a heartbeat. Sadly, this is all that I have left of you ins the growth, faith, strength, and knowledge gained during this time. I'll treasure that for ever because if I don't…it is like I'll have lost you twice.

- The Universe Message: "No one in your shoes could have done better than you've done, with where you began, what you had, and all you've been through. No One". My Thoughts - This has been a long journey, a tiring journey, and a challenging journey. I'm truly grateful that God gave this burden to myself and Felicia and not someone else. I wouldn't wish this on my worst enemy. As I write this, I had to stop and go help your mother as she was loudly sobbing across the house and needed comforting. This is hard and no one should have to go through this process. It is brutal, painful, lonely, etc. However, as I've learned, extreme's do happen unfortunately and are a part of life. Because that is a fact that can't change, someone has to go through this. If it had to be someone, I'm glad God choose this incredibly strong and resilient family. You were the strongest person I've ever met, closely followed by your mother, and then maybe a distant 3rd for myself. This strong family of lions will not be broken by this…I swear it. If someone has to go through crap like this, then let it be us.

- We are finally here. …July 13th. A date that will forever be burned into my mind. It was supposed to be the best day of our lives when we find out you were coming last November. Sadly, it is whatever this is.

- Yesterday, I'm not sure what happened, but I went out for a normal run 3-5 miles but just felt compelled to keep going. It was such a beautiful and a perfect day for a long run. Before I knew it, I was 6 miles in and getting closer and closer to Riley's Hospital for Children (where you lived all your days) and decided it would be a nice moment to run by your old room. As I started to turn toward the main entrance and got closer and closer, my breathing started to get really heavy and fast. I started to run a little faster. Then I started to talk to you in my head. I realized I was doing this to show off for you a little. To show you how strong your Dad has become and to give you a peace of mind that this won't break me and you don't need to worry. It was pretty emotional for me as I looked up and could see that 4th floor window of your room that I spent so much time looking out. Your home for the 39 days you were with us. As I made a loop around the hospital, I thought to myself that I'm just going to finish out a half marathon today no matter what. So that is what I did, 13.1 miles later, I got back to our house and was exhausted. I've never run anywhere close to that far in my life before (9.5 miles was my previous longest run). I thought it was pretty representative of this whole process overall and how far I'd come. I've always been "in shape" but never anything like that. Plus…I've always been a sprinter as well. I loved playing sports all the time. I love competition and getting quick results. I'm impatient and get frustrated by a lack of quick feedback on performance so I can improve. If you knew me before this whole process, running a mini marathon was the last thing you would think I would have done and I wouldn't even have contemplated it. I would laugh at your Mom when she would ask me if I wanted to do the next one with her. I wasn't (and still not) a "marathon" runner. That is your mother and you. You 2 can endure the pain, the suffering, the boredom, etc of a meaningless run for distance. I was the dude on the sidelines drinking an Aperol spritz (literally) and cheering her on as she went out and did her thing. You have to have a particular mindset to be a marathon runner and that wasn't me at all and will probably never be me even if I run a marathon someday. The longest I had ever run in my life before we had you was probably 4 miles, if I had to guess. I enjoy a quick and fast 2-mile run and get on with my day. But there I was, finishing up 13.1 miles on a beautiful Sunday in July for no reason at all. It wasn't even a real "race" or something. It was literally just me, you, and an audio book out running around Indianapolis. That run about sums up the changes in me through this process and how you have pushed me to another level to be the best person I can be. Did I do it for you? Did I do it for me? The truth is…I don't know, but I JUST WISH YOU WERE HERE TO SEE IT AND BE A PART OF IT.

- What was this journey all about? I can say with certainty that I have no idea.
- Today, as we were visiting your gravesite, a woman around your mother's age pulled up on the other side of the infant circle,

presumably to visit her own child. Your Mom and I had driven separately, and I needed to head back home as your Grandparents (my parents) were coming over for dinner to join us all to talk about you. Your mom, her sister, and her mom all stayed behind for a few more minutes to say goodbye. As I left, your mother was still sobbing, and your grandma was consoling her on the ground next to your headstone. Later that night, your Mom shared with me a story about the other woman that I saw on the other side of the circle as I was leaving. Apparently, she saw your Mom crying and felt compelled to come over to introduce herself and sit with your Mom and her family. It turns out that she was there to visit her son that she lost a little over a year before you passed away. She just wanted to let your Mom know that she was there for her and could tell what she was going through. She shared that she actually just recently gave birth a few months ago to a healthy child that she called her (Rainbow Baby). Your Mom and her exchanged numbers and they have been texting back and forth already. 2 things come to mind in this story. 1 - no one really has any idea what we are going through unless they have experienced this kind of loss themselves. When you get a chance to encounter someone in this tragic club…it is your duty to try and help them out, acknowledge their pain, and offer to be there to listen if they need it. I'm grateful that this nice woman stepped up and selflessly gave her time to try and help your mother. I could tell it really helped her and she was truly touched when she was telling me the story later when she got home. I just finished reading a book called Give and Take by Adam Grant today as well. It was all about the importance of being a giver and the positive impacts it can have on your life and the lives of others you encounter. At one part in the book, he talks about uncommon connections and how they can bring people closer to each other. The losing a child club is about as uncommon of a connection as you can ever find. For that reason, I vow to always give selflessly to this community for the rest of my life. That's what you would want, that is what you deserve, and that is why I'm writing this book. I want to help as many people as I can that are going through the pain and loss we are fighting through today. If our words and experiences can help one person or couple…it will all be worth it. 2 - there is light at the end of the tunnel. This is the first time I've heard the words "Rainbow Child" but I get the concept. The fact that this lady and her husband were able to battle through this dark chapter in their life and can still experience joy and happiness of a healthy child gives me hope that we can do this as well. We are so excited and ready to welcome another amazing brother or sister to join you and this family. We can use all the help we can get from the "baby wrangler" we've heard so much about from Margo. After all, the NEVER QUIT rule is named the "Emilia Rule" for a reason. You wouldn't give up…and we certainly won't either.

- I LOVE YOU SO MUCH

PART III

Rebuilding our New City with Purpose and Together

CHAPTER 5

Tour of the New City and Construction Projects! Slowly Building on the Foundation

By July 14th, 2020, I was feeling stronger, smarter, and more balanced than I ever had before in my life. The compound effect of all the daily thinking, writing, learning, reflection, and action was really starting to add up. All the slow day-by-day changes were beginning to manifest themselves in everything I was doing, and changes were starting to be more visible.

We had just been through four straight months of the craziest roller coaster you could even imagine and somehow found a way through. We had finally hit the finish line, and I was left sitting there thinking, "What next? What do I do now?" I knew I was supposed to be "living for two," but I didn't fully know what that actually meant or where I was supposed to apply this new mission in my life.

All I knew is that during the darkest and scariest moments of my life, I had somehow unearthed my why (Emilia), my mission ("live for two"), and my compass (core values), which would be the basis for the foundation of our new city. Even though the groundwork had been laid, I still didn't have the blueprints, building designs, or even know what building I really wanted to start construction on first. I didn't know exactly when that map would reveal itself, so I figured I'd keep plugging away with the daily habits and the foundational elements that brought me here in the first place, which were daily learning, reflection, thinking, and action.

As I continued to build on the foundation and lay new bricks day by day, God slowly started to reveal the blueprints and key projects that would need my attention first. Over the next few pages, we will take a look at some of the new buildings that have begun to emerge or are currently under construction in our newly reimagined city and how they came to be.

LET THE TOUR BEGIN!

Emilia Tower: The Soul of the City

The first building I set out to complete was what I'm calling Emilia Tower. Emilia Tower was to be built directly on the intersection of The Why Boulevard and Never Quit Avenue while overlooking Living for Two Central Park. It was to be the most beautiful building in the city, the shiny building on top of the hill for all the world to see, the tallest skyscraper in the world, and the soul of our city.

Emilia Tower was the construction of this book. This was to be the masterpiece in my new city, and I knew I had to get this construction started and finished before turning my attention to anything else. Emilia's story, enduring spirit, and never-quit attitude had to be heard throughout the world, and I couldn't wait to build on the journals and write the story around them that would become this book.

We broke ground on Emilia Plaza on July 14th, 2020. I had every intention of having this work of art completed and ready for visitors by August, 2020. I really thought that I could get this whole tower finished in just half of a month. What an absolute idiot, but an incredibly valuable lesson to learn right out of the gate after our marathon ended. I just described Emilia Tower as the shiny skyscraper and most magnificent piece of architecture known throughout the world; you don't build those overnight, it turns out. I guess that is that eternal optimist in me at its finest!

Looking back, my plan was simple. I'd spend a few days re-reading my journals to proofread them, clean up some grammar, pull out some themes and lessons to build an outline for the story, and then get to work on writing the stories around the journals of our experiences. I figured, by the end of July, I would have the first draft of Emilia's book ready to send off to a publisher, and Emilia Tower would be open for business for the world to see. After all, I wasn't back to working full time yet or anything, so I knew I had the time.

The "planning fallacy" from *Thinking Fast and Slow* was in FULL EFFECT on this majestic skyscraper, and I didn't even know what was about to hit me. If the planning fallacy is a new concept for you, the basic gist of it is that human beings are astonishingly bad at estimating how long it will take to complete tasks. As recounted in Kahneman's book, one study found that the typical homeowner expected their home improvement projects to cost about $19,000. The average actual cost? $39,000. Despite ample available information, 90% of high-speed railroad projects have missed budget and passenger estimates, with an average overestimation of passengers of about 100% and underestimation of budget of at about 50%. I suppose before I dove into the construction of Emilia tower, I could have enlisted the help of the "outside view" that Kahneman talks about in the book as well and consulted a few actual authors to get some advice and guidance on what to expect, read up on how to write a book, figured out the average time it takes people to write a novel, etc. Well, I didn't. I just took my why and started laying bricks and figured I'd be done in no time. I fell right into the planning fallacy head first.

My original vision was only to write roughly 30-50 pages for the "remembering self" stories to wrap around the journals at most. I'd then slap a bow on this beautiful tower, schedule a ribbon-cutting ceremony, and open the doors to share with the world. To figure out how long this would hypothetically take me, I spent 30 minutes on Google learning how Stephen King and Maya Angelou write each day and thought, "I can do that." Their process was pretty easy; write 5-6 pages a day, proofread it, shut it down to recharge, have a glass of wine and dinner, get a good night's sleep, and then wake up and do it all over again the next morning. Easy peasy. I could write five to six pages a day. Hell, I'm only planning on writing 30 to 50 pages anyway, which puts me at six to ten days max.

I was so confident that I could get this beautiful building done by the end of July that I emailed my boss and the leave administrator and said that I was ready to come back to work on the first Monday of August, which was August 3rd, 2020. August 3rd also happens to be my birthday. I thought that would be perfect timing, and I figured that I had left myself tons of time to finish my signature building before embarking on these other new projects. Also, I was ready to get back to work. This had been the longest absence of work in my adult life. Work is an important part of the balance equation, and I was ready for the challenge. I wasn't afraid of that big scary monster at all anymore after all the searching and learning I had just done the past few months. I had spent months up in the metaphorical mountains of my mind, and I was ready to get back down to the valley to get to work on applying what I had learned. I felt extremely prepared for re-entry into the rest of society. I was feeling stronger than I ever had in my life, and I was ready to get out there and start "living for two" in everything that I did. That meant my day job as well.

On July 14th, I got to work on proofreading the 121 days of journal entries. I worked for five hours that first day until my brain felt like it was going to explode. I looked up at the page number and saw that I was only on day 15 of the journals and had 106 more to go. "Uh oh! Okay, new plan, I'll get this proofreading stuff done in a week, and then really get to work on the writing, and still have this done by the end of July."

I tried my hardest and worked my butt off every day, but when August 3rd came around along with my return to work, I still had like three pages of journals left to just proofread! It wasn't all bad news, though, I suppose. As I had been slowly re-reading and re-living the whole experience with my journals, I was able to take a new look at our journey and all that had happened to us since March 15th. The stories and lessons were popping out all over the place as I re-read my own life day by day. I was constantly crying when I sat down to read and re-live each entry. The journals were zooming me back in time. I was amassing this amazing outline of a story and topics that I wanted to share, and I was even more motivated to get to work on this project. I knew I had the blueprints for an amazing skyscraper that I wanted to build, and I couldn't wait to begin.

After I returned to work, I shifted my expectations on the project. I decided not to set a goal date to get this building finished or pressure myself to do more than lay one brick day by day. What I did instead was double down on my core values and leverage them to find the motivation for me to continue writing each and every day even after I returned to work.

How did I do this? I thought about all the giving I would be doing by sharing Emilia's story with the world. I thought about how I could challenge myself to find time to carve out an additional 30 minutes before every workday on top of my normal reading, writing, and exercise. I thought about the never-quit mentality and how I couldn't let this project fail. Framing the project in this manner gave me all the added motivation necessary to find that extra one hour each morning before starting my day job to keep working on the tower. This is why core values are so important!

They are your first line of defense in your battle against yourself. You have to have that North Star to keep you going when you want to give up. This stuff really works. If it ever doesn't, that is when you bring in the nuclear option, which is calling on your why. If your core values break down and your mind is no longer responding, you have to call in your why as the safety net to catch you and keep you going. Spend some time reflecting on why you are really doing all of this and then get back up and keep laying each brick one day at a time.

So here I am, almost nine months later and after writing and working on this project every single day since July 14th, still not fully finished with this beautiful building. To be honest, I wouldn't have it any other way. As it would turn out, our story wasn't completed yet anyway, and there was still so much more to learn and experience to help me create the building that would be the heart of the city.

This building wasn't supposed to be finished first. It might not ever be truly finished. Maybe I will turn it into something like the Sagrada Familia in Barcelona that has been under perpetual construction for the past 100 years. Masterpieces don't happen overnight. However, I did set my sights on at least having a first rough draft of a manuscript to present to Emilia by her 1st birthday (3/15/2021), and I'm more motivated than ever to do just that. Just for note, I'm writing this sentence as of 3/2/2021, and we are so close to the big finish.

Rainbow Baby Plaza: Hope for the Future

The next shiny new building that we broke ground on would come to be known as Rainbow Baby Plaza.

On our nightly Emilia walks, the talk of trying for a sibling for Emilia slowly started to matriculate into our discussions more and more. Over time, it became clear that Felicia wanted to try to grow our family again, but it was really a matter of figuring out the right timing. In late June, Felicia officially let me know that she was ready to start trying for baby #2 sometime in late July after Emilia's original due date, July 13th, had passed.

We wanted to do this right and be as safe and cautious as possible. So, before we began work on construction, we consulted an expert project manager over at our second home, Riley's Hospital for Children, and the high-risk OB area, where we met Dr. Scifres. Dr. Scifres walked us through all the information about what we know that may have caused Emilia's preterm birth, options of how we can monitor these things closer, and what preventative actions were available to us should we indeed get successfully pregnant again. In summary, we still have no actual idea why Emilia was born early. All we really have are hypotheses to explore, and the main guesses were around an incompetent cervix. That is what we all agreed would be the focus on prevention going forward should we successfully get pregnant again. We were reassured that an incompetent cervix and what it does to induce preterm labor could be very preventable if monitored closely.

After that conversation, Felicia and I both felt like we had the green light, medically speaking, to start this new journey together, with the most likely outcome being a successful pregnancy.
And that is what we did. I'll save you all the details here because I think you know how a baby is created, so not much to share on how we constructed Rainbow Baby Plaza.

The one thing that I will touch on is Emilia 'The Baby Wrangler' and her involvement in this process. So, I go to a psychic every once in a while, named Margo, and I'm not ashamed to admit it. I love talking with Margo, and our conversations are a blast. You have to be open to seeing the world from all angles, and that is why I do it. Margo and I had just recently had our first session since Emilia's passing, sometime in late June, I think. At this time, the conversations around having another child were in full swing, so I thought this would be a great topic to consult with Margo about.

In our conversation, I had asked Margo if she could speak to the deceased. This is something that she and I had never discussed before. To my surprise, Margo informed me that she can and that she could actually hear Emilia at this moment. She said, "I hear all of the other voices telling me that they call Emilia by the nickname, The Baby Wrangler. She continued that she heard from Emilia that, "She couldn't wait for more brothers and sisters and had them lined up and ready to go for us."

I laughed and thought, "That is so Emilia. She's amazing and the most perfect older sister the world has ever known." Margo told me specifically that she had at least three or maybe four ready to go. "Four!" I thought, "Whoa, let's pump the brakes here, Emilia. No one ever talked about five children someday, but hey, who knows?" I told Felicia later that night. She laughed and said, "No way," but she did like the idea that Emilia was known as The Baby Wrangler.

With the seal of approval from our experts in Dr. Scifres and Margo the Giggling Guru, we were officially cleared to begin construction and let God and The Baby Wrangler do their thing. So, that July, we officially started trying for our second child. The first month of trying, Felicia actually got pregnant again, but we didn't know if it was fully real or not as the little blue line on the pregnancy test wasn't crazy bright. We thought, "This can't really be that easy, can it?" After all, it took us three years to get pregnant with Emilia, although we weren't really trying like we were now, to be fair. Felicia had a plan this time and was really going to do everything she could to try and time all this stuff right to increase our odds.

After a few days of testing and re-testing, the blue line on the pregnancy stick slowly started to fade, and we were pregnant no more. Damn! Felicia said it was probably something called a "chemical pregnancy." The only reason we even caught it is because we were so closely monitoring this stuff. We thought, "Oh well. We knew this wouldn't be so easy."
Well, we were wrong!

The following month in August 2020, The Baby Wrangler delivered again, and this time, to our surprise, we really were pregnant! We couldn't believe how easy this process was the second time around. Here we were, off to the races on building Rainbow Baby Plaza with expected completion and grand opening to be May 9th, 2021.

The Andre Agassi National Tennis and Racquet Center: Don't Forget to Have Some Fun

As we continue our tour around our new city, our next stop will be the Andre Agassi National Tennis Center Complex. My core values kept leading me back to tennis as a way to express myself and have some fun in my new city. I made sure to build state-of-the-art tennis, pickleball, and athletic center affectionately named Andre Agassi National Tennis Center, after my favorite tennis player of all time.

I was always going to name this building after Andre, as he is my tennis hero, and reading his memoir, Open, this past year only solidified that. I'm not really big into reading memoirs, but I couldn't resist picking up a book about the life of my childhood sports hero. Boy, was I glad I went on this adventure with Andre. After reading the first chapter, where he gave a riveting account and behind-the-scenes look at one of his last matches at his final US Open before retiring, I was hooked and couldn't wait to read more.

While Andre began his memoir with what you'd expect, a detailed account of his mindset before, during, and after one of his last triumphant matches, I was shocked to find that this memoir wasn't so much about tennis, but life in general. Sure, tennis was an important throughline across the whole memoir, but this was really all about Andre's search to find his why, core values, and mission in life, and how once he did, everything started to change.

I learned that Andre actually hated tennis with a passion. He wanted to do anything and everything besides tennis, but he never really had a choice. His dad forced him to play his whole childhood, against his will, in hopes that he would be a champion someday. Before he knew it, tennis was all he knew. He was so good at it that he felt like he had no choice but to play whether he wanted to or not. That inner conflict of not being able to choose his own path and be his own person tormented him for most of his tennis career. Whether he was winning or losing, he felt torn and conflicted.

It wasn't until hitting rock bottom that he started to discover who he really was, what was important to him, and why he was even playing tennis in the first place. In the rubble of his own life, depressed, divorced, alone, with his career crumbling and fighting off internal demons, Andre found his real mission. He dedicated his life, his time, and his fortune to helping young children have access to quality education through the Andre Agassi College Preparatory Academy in his hometown, Las Vegas. Andre was a high school dropout himself but had come to understand the importance of education and learning. He wanted to make sure at-risk children could have a different path in life, and that is how this project came to be.

His whole life and career trajectory changed. He realized that he was no longer playing a game that he hated for himself but for something way bigger than him. That is when his career rebirth began as he picked himself up out of the rubble and came back to the game better than ever. He was winning more than he ever had, and his life all finally made sense. The lifetime of trauma and pain he had endured on the tennis courts somehow now was all worth it, and he could see the bigger purpose. His paradigms had shifted, and he was a whole new person.

After finishing Agassi's memoir, I couldn't help but draw so many corollaries to my own life and personal journey. As I had mentioned before, I never really had a why, mission, or purpose until I met Emilia and then subsequently hit my own rock bottom. I slowly started to reframe my own paradigms until I felt my life truly had purpose and meaning. For the first time ever, everything that I do now means something. I'm not a lost soul in this world anymore. I have my map and compass, and I'm going to make the most of the time I have left on Earth. I couldn't help but feel a little more connected to my childhood hero after reading his story. That crystalized the fact that the National Tennis Center could be named after no one other than Andre Agassi.

During this whole summer/fall/winter of 2020-2021, I was playing more tennis than I had since I was a kid and loving every minute of it. I was back in my USTA leagues, playing in local singles challenge ladders, playing in some weekly fun doubles' leagues, meeting new players all over the city, and setting up hitting sessions with them a few times a week. I was a tennis-playing machine and couldn't get enough. I was playing at least three times a week in competitive matches and having a blast. I was also getting better and better than I have ever played in my life. I began to start to crush guys that I used to struggle against regularly.

I couldn't believe the leaps I was seeing in my game, and neither could some of my friends that I've always played with. They were starting to ask me, "What are you doing that is making this happen?" Of course, I knew the answer, but it would be too hard to explain all the magical changes that were taking place in my life while out on the tennis court. The truth was that I had found my why and my personal mission in life. I was "living for two" and being guided by my core values in all that I did, and that meant tennis as well.

All of the books I was reading really started to help me imagine and see the game differently. I was pulling inspiration from all kinds of new sources that were helping me to question my own game and why I did what I did in each match. It was helping me to strategize and be more versatile in practice and match play versus being the one-trick pony of my past, trying to hammer away at people with my powerful forehand no matter if it was working or not on that day. It was all the daily exercising, training, HIIT workouts, and longer and faster runs that I was doing every day that was making me stronger than I had ever been in my life. It was looking down at my reminder bands in the middle of a match and seeing "Emilia Quinn Sears" and "Remember the Why" whenever I would start to get frustrated with myself.

That summer, I got second in a challenge ladder of 50 people and was competing and beating former collegiate tennis players along the way. I even started to feel so confident that in late August, I entered into the NTRP USTA Midwest championship tournaments that were to be hosted in Dayton, OH, on clay courts, nonetheless (I never play on clay.) I hadn't really played in a real individual single-event tennis tournament since I was 13 years old. Well, I signed up, drove to Dayton, and played my ass off over four matches in 2 days and won! I was so shocked and even had a little trophy to bring back home to show Felicia. I knew I was playing well, but clearly, this was proof of the progress I was making. I had so much fun there that I decided to enter into another tournament in the Southern Indiana Open down in Evansville in September. While I didn't win that one, I did beat a 19-year-old current college athlete in my first-round match, which felt like a huge win for me, as I'm 36! I lost my second-round match to an 18-year-old kid who was a giant and looked like Ivan Drago from Rocky. I honestly could have beat him, but my body was tired as hell by the time I had to play my second match that day after the bruising 3 set affair in the morning with the 19-year-old. I'll get them next time!

All in all, in official matches, since the pandemic restrictions were limited, I'm 30-4 as of March, 2021. In unofficial matches, I'm probably more like 100-15 since the summer of 2020 with all the challenger ladder matches, doubles leagues, hitting sessions with friends, etc. The Andre Agassi National Tennis Center has been rocking and rolling this past year, and we aren't stopping anytime soon. So, stop by and play some tennis (pickleball, ping pong, and racquetball players are welcome as well). We're always open!

The Derek Zoolander Center for Kids Who Can't Read Good and Want to Learn How to Do Other Things Good Also! - Learning is a Lifestyle

The next building on our tour is our amazing new library named affectionately after Ben Stiller's classic character, the spectacularly dumb model that couldn't turn left, Derek Zoolander. If you've seen the movie, you will get the reference and why this is funny. If you haven't, go watch!

Learning and having a growth mindset has always been something I've said I valued, but it wasn't something I lived each and every day. This is a classic example of one of those stolen core values that I heard others talk about and thought I needed to value as well. I'll be the first to admit that I did not live this "learn every day" core value in my life before Emilia. Sure, I did concentrated learning activities every once in a while, but it was all over the place and sporadic at best.

That wouldn't be the case in my new city! I have spent the past year embracing this growth mindset and learning something new each and every day. I've never been more excited and passionate about acquiring new knowledge in my life. Learning was going to be a huge cornerstone of the new city, and we would need a majestic library that could hold all the books and new knowledge that I wanted to consume.

When you truly make learning every day a part of your life, the possibilities of what you can explore are endless, and that is what I was finding out as we constructed this library. I know the name of our library, "The Derek Zoolander for Kids Who Can't Read Good," is meant as a joke, but there is some truth behind why I picked it as well. Between the completion of my college degree in 2006 and January 1st, 2020, I had probably read a total of seven books. Looking back, I've been severely learning deprived. While I did regularly listen to educational podcasts, watch documentaries, and read Wikipedia all the time, I wasn't learning and living with a growth mindset every day. I'm so angry at myself for all the things that I missed out on in these past 14 years of my life. Well, luckily for me, I now have the rest of my life to make up for lost time and embrace all the curiosity and questions that my imagination can dream up.

Ironically, one of the goals that I set and publicly stated to my work team at Salesforce in January of 2020 was to read one book a month over the course of the 2020 (so 12 total). I thought 12 was a huge stretch for someone that didn't read regularly, but I was willing to give it a go. I had successfully completed my first two books in January and February before Emilia arrived that March. I'm glad I had already started this new habit earlier that year because the more time we spent in the NICU, the more time I kept reading. The more I read, the more I was loving all the new thoughts filling my mind.

By May, I had already finished my goal of 12 books for the year, and I was ready to take this newfound passion for learning into overdrive. As of today, I've lost count of all the books I've read in the past year. I stopped caring after I hit 60 or so at some point in the fall. It was no longer about the physical number of books consumed anymore and more about the journey. I embraced the act of truly learning something new every single day and looked forward to all the unread books out there that I hadn't read yet. It reminds me of another Nasim Talib quote from The Black Swan where he discusses Umberto Eco's library. Here is the quote:

"The writer Umberto Eco belongs to that small class of scholars who are encyclopedic, insightful, and non-dull. He is the owner of a large personal library (containing 30,000 books) and separates visitors into two categories: those who react with "Wow! Signore, professore Dottore Eco, what a library you have! How many of these books have you read?" and the others - a very small minority - who get the point that a private library is not an ego-boosting appendage but a research tool. Read books are far less valuable than unread ones. The library should contain as much of what you don't know as your financial means, mortgage rates, and the currently tight real-estate market allows you to put it there. You will accumulate more knowledge and more books as you grow older, and the growing number of unread books on the shelves will look at you menacingly. Indeed, the more you know, the larger the rows of unread books. Let us call this collection of unread books an antilibrary."

I always think of Umberto Eco's antilibrary these days when I'm looking for my next book to read from the hundreds of unread books I've saved in my Amazon account. It's all about the growing library of unread books that I'm amassing rather than how many books I've read so far. If I had to guess, I've consumed (I like audiobooks) at least 100 books since March, 2020 at this point. I'm about to hit my 500th hour "Master" level in the next few weeks on my Amazon Audible app and, while it feels pretty damn good to see that, it really doesn't matter at the end of the day. No one really cares about that other than me, and that is how it should be. Hell, I don't even know that I even really care about it.

I've learned more in this past year than ever before. A lot of what I've learned and the questions that it generated went into creating the lessons that I'm sharing with you in this book. The biggest change in me was that I started to learn about stuff every day that I wanted to learn about. Just like those famous European explorers that traveled the world for one nugget of knowledge, I was on my own quest. The beauty of it is that I had access to a limitless amount of knowledge, right in the palm of my hand!

In case you are one of the, "Wow! Signore, professore Dottore Eco, what a library you have! How many of these books have you read?" type of people (which is totally fine) and want to see what is currently in the "read" section of the Derek Zoolander for Center for Kids Who Can't Read Good library, here are some of my favorite recommendations from a few different categories to wet your whistle.

Psychology, Thinking, Creativity – *The Happiness Hypothesis, Thinking Fast and Slow, A More Beautiful Question, The Black Swan, Think Like a Rocket Scientist, The Outliers, What the Dog Saw, Unbroken, The Biggest Bluff, Think Again, Late Bloomers, The Inner Game of Tennis, Nudge, The Body Keeps the Score, The Drama of the Gifted Child*

Personal Growth and Communication – *The Ultimate Jim Rohn Library, The Compound Effect, 48 Laws of Power, Atomic Habits, UltraLearning, How to Win Friends and Influence People, The War of Art, Option B, On Writing*

Core Values and Paradigms – *Start with Why, The Infinite Game, The 7 Habits of Highly Effective People, The Go Giver, Give and Take, The Warrior Within*

Humanity and Philosophy – *Sapiens, The Culture Code, When, Endure, Range, The Lessons of History, The Design of Everyday Things, Enlightenment Now, The Socrates Express, Endurance, Tuesdays with Morrie, 101 Essays that will Change the Way You Think, A Year of Magical Thinking, The Geography of Genius, Open*

Business – *The Hard Things about Hard Things, Blue Ocean Strategy, Platform Revolution, Good to Great, Great by Choice, Alchemy, Creativity Inc, The Culture Code, Originals, Loonshots, Let My People Go Surfing, The Entrepreneur Roller Coaster, Who Moved My Cheese. Grit, Principles by Ray Dalio*

Spirituality and Meaning - *The Alchemist, Why Buddhism is True, Love Does, A Man's Search for Meaning, The Kaballion, Zen Mind Beginner's Mind, The Practicing Stoic, Meditations, The 4 Agreements, Ikigai, The Purpose Driven Life*

Natural History and Science: *The Entangled Life, On the Origin of Species, The Hidden Lives of Trees, The Body, A Short History of Nearly Everything, At Home with Bill Bryson, Why We Sleep, Other Minds, Rain, Why Fish Don't Exist, The Botany of Desire, I Contain Multitudes*

ENJOY!!!

The Hardy-Meyer Center for Thought and Inquiry - The Imagination Factory

Every morning for the past year, I've woken up and started my day (no matter where I was) with two things, reading Joyce Meyer's *Trusting God Day by Day* daily reflection and listening to Darren Hardy's morning video called DarrenDaily. DarrenDaily has been a staple of my morning routine for the past five years. However, Joyce's reflections were the new addition over the past year.

If you remember back in the story, *Trusting God Day by Day* was the book that our friends had gifted us a few days after Emilia was born to help us find additional daily strength and courage as we endured the NICU every day. Well, it worked. I had been reading each daily reflection since Ashley and Nick gifted us this book, and consuming Joyce's reflections had become an integral part of my daily routine.

Every day I looked forward to the unique perspective I gained from Darren and Joyce's thoughts and reflections. They talked about all kinds of fun topics that helped to start off each day fresh and new. Joyce's are a little more spiritual leaning, and Darren has a decidedly business world perspective for the most part, but each provided plenty of spark to get my mind working. If Darren or Joyce ever happen to read this, I really appreciate all the hard work that you do to help others seeking a fresh perspective each day. In a way, your words helped to change my life.

After I was done reading and listening to their thoughts and reflections each morning, I would take them and metaphorically walk around the new city, reflecting and thinking a little on what I had just heard and learned. One morning, as I was out walking and thinking, I came across a building that was really old and cool looking that I had never noticed before on my previous strolls. It had one of those classic, Elizabethan looks to it, seeming as though it had been there since the beginning of time. I had no idea how I had never noticed it before that particular morning stroll, but I decided to walk up and get a closer look.

As I approached the front door and turned the knob, I found that the door was locked. I thought, "Damn. Oh well," until I saw a note next to the door that read, "If you'd like to enter, ask any question you want, and the key will appear." I started to think about Darren and Joyce's message for the day, and a question popped into my mind. I reached into my pocket and surprisingly found a key that fit perfectly in the old wooden door, so I opened the door and started to walk in.

As I entered, I saw a great hall immediately before me. There wasn't much furniture or any decorations. As a matter of fact, the place was pretty barren. No one else was inside. There was only one great big room that was completely empty except for a little table and one chair in the center of it. Still, it still somehow felt warm and inviting enough that I decided that I would take a break from my walk and hang out a little while. I eventually parked myself in the chair to sit and think about the question I had just asked that provided the key to the door. I sat there and thought for a while until I felt refreshed and ready to resume my stroll. I got up, left, and set off for the rest of the day's adventures to come.

I enjoyed the feeling enough that I thought I would try it again the next day. So I came back with my fresh thoughts and questions inspired by the messages I had heard from Darren and Joyce, opened the door, parked myself on the chair, and just sat there thinking. I did this for a few days in a row.

One day, a dude appeared out of nowhere and scared the crap out of me. He asked what I was thinking about and if I wanted someone to talk through it with. I said, "Sure, why not?" I told him about the thoughts that Joyce and Darren had shared that morning and some of the questions it provoked in my mind. We ended up having a great chat as we discussed the topics together.

At the end of the conversation, he encouraged me to write down our findings and handed me a pen and paper. He let me know that if I ever wanted him to come back to talk, just pull out a pen and paper, and he would be there to help me work through my thoughts. I sat there for a few more minutes and wrote down what this random guy and I had talked through together. I enjoyed it so much that I couldn't wait to come back the next day. It felt freeing to get our thoughts down on paper.

I arrived the next morning, walked in, sat down, pulled out a pen and paper, and he appeared again. I shared my new thoughts and questions, we talked it out, I wrote, and then I left. I kept coming back to this building and found this guy waiting for me to talk through whatever I wanted each day. It became really fun. He didn't say much but rather asked more questions for me to ponder. I loved that he was getting me to think about more things than I ever had in my life.

One day after a few months of this, I finally asked who he was. He replied, "You may know me as God." It turns out that I had unknowingly walked into God's house, he was happy to see me, and was excited to have someone new to talk to who was bringing fresh thoughts and questions about life. He said jokingly, "What the hell took you so long to get here? I've been waiting for 36 years!" I thought, "Holy Shit. This is God's house! How did I end up here? Well, this isn't what I imagined God to be growing up, but this is pretty damn cool. Let's keep it rolling."

It was in this place every morning that God and I found a dedicated space to talk about what I had just learned and then work through my thoughts and questions on life. We would talk about whether I agreed or didn't agree with Darren and Joyce's message. If I did agree, why and how could I implement them into my own life? If I didn't agree, why and how would I like to adjust them to make them align with my core values? I would then write down our conversation in my journal, thank him for his time, and then I would head out ready to keep working on building my city.

Every once in a while, I stayed for an extra few minutes, and we would open up the discussion to anything else I wanted to speak about as well. This is when the magic really started to happen. We started talking about the most random things in that extra bonus time together. I had been reading so much and had a lot on my mind regarding all kinds of topics like business, culture, humanity, philosophy, friendship, marriage, work, life, children, core values, God, Emilia, and so on. When we had those extended sessions, the questions and ideas were organically flying out of my mouth, seemingly coming from nowhere. I did my best to capture all the craziness, fun, and fresh perspectives that were coming out of me with God's help and wrote them down in my journal under a section I labeled "Random Notes." If it was a really fun idea or thought, we would come back to it in the future, which we often did.

In essence, this daily time with God became my de facto imagination laboratory. It is with God that I rediscovered the curiosity that I had lost as a child. It was like I had my best friend back with me again. I'm so grateful that I found this old building and, in turn, my curiosity, ability to question, and imagination. I promised God that I would make sure that I would capture our conversations in my journals so I could help spread that message someday. Many of these ideas and conversations became the basis for this book (Emilia Tower) and a lot of the other construction that was going on in the city. Reflecting back on this, it is mind-blowing to me how little time I had spent talking to God over the course of my life. It's also mind-blowing how easy it was to find God on demand. All I had to do was carve out 15 minutes, bring a thought and a piece of paper, and let the magic ensue.

God has always given us all the keys to talk to Him with the gift of our consciousness if we choose to use it. The key is that we have to use it. If you aren't using it, I hope this book might be the little nudge you need to go start your own conversations with God again. Just ask a question, think a thought, look in your pocket, and you will find the key to the old building that has been in your own city since the beginning of time.

The ClubAny Work/Life Balance Complex - The Infinite Game and Forever Mission

The final stop on our tour of the new city is to serve as the functioning heart of the city for as long as this rebuild can endure. The ClubAny Work/Life Balance Complex is to be my infinite game in which I can always express our "living for two" mission for the rest of my days here on Earth. It will never be complete, and it will constantly be growing in size and scope for the rest of my life and, God willing, beyond. It will serve as the beating heart of the new city, and It will serve as the beating heart of the new city, and it will fund all the other projects and additional construction to come in the future. It is the ultimate expression of Emilia and my shared core values and the way we'll get our message out to the world. Pain always leaves a gift, and this will be our gift to the world.

It kind of came out of nowhere, heavily influenced by my time with God over at the Hardy-Meyer Center for Thought and Inquiry, which I will walk you through over the next few pages. This isn't hyperbole either. This new hybrid approach to work and life, in an effort to live a more balanced and purpose-driven existence, will have a dramatic impact on this world for generations to come. I can feel and see it starting to happen already in the few short months since we broke ground.

Humans living in a world that I can't imagine in far-off future centuries will hopefully still be feeling the positive effects of the groundwork that we hope to put in place today through ClubAny. I like to think that this may end up being a *Black Swan* type of event that will redefine how we live and work in the not-too-distant future. Mark my words, in just 50 short years from now, people will be wondering how we ever did work and life any other way. Now that I've hyped up "The ClubAny Work/Life Balance Complex," you are probably wondering, "What the hell is ClubAny?

Short Answer - ClubAny is a work and life balanced ecosystem for purpose-driven human beings. ClubAny lies directly at the heart of where we connect what we value most in our personal lives, the people we surround ourselves with, and the work we create.

Long Answer - ClubAny emerged out of the countless hours, days, and months, wandering around the rubble and talking with God. So stick with me as I try to put it all together for you.

You might be starting to think, "I think Chris might have left his mind back in the rubble!" Well, yes and no. Yes, I did lose my mind in a lot of ways over the past year. All the learning, reflection, and writing were unintentionally beginning to change me and open my mind up to a whole new world, unlocking my creativity in the process. My curiosity began to explode, and I was questioning and challenging everything that came across my path.

Whether it was big questions like what is life all about? What is my purpose? What do I value most? Is there a God? To the absurdly dumb questions like, what if another species had language like humans? How funny would it be to see a dog as a TV reporter covering a dog riot and reporting about all the crazy antics that the Pitbulls were doing for equal rights? Do dogs think like this about us? If I was an alien that landed on Earth today, what questions would I ask about things like houses, roads, and cars? Where do florists get their flowers? Are there flower farms somewhere? How do they make the flowers bloom at just the right time to get flowers ready for Valentine's Day? Why have I never seen a flower farm before? Wouldn't that be a cool place to see if it did exist?

My mind was becoming a questioning machine again. The more I read, the more questions I asked, and the more God and I had to talk about in our daily reflection time. For the first time that I can remember since I was a child, I was allowing my mind to imagine, play, and mash-up whatever it desired to reframe anything and everything I came across in this world. As an adult, I now had the power that I didn't have as a kid to take these ideas and do something with them. I wasn't going to waste it. All of this crazy questioning is where the genesis of ClubAny was born.

Before I can explain what ClubAny is, I have to take a quick step back and provide a little context as to how we got here in the first place, my life pre-Emilia, what I cared about then, and my lack of mission, core values, and why. I had mentioned this already in my story from the rubble of Ben Horowitz and The Hard Things About Hard Things discussion of what it takes to be a CEO, but I'll reiterate it here as it is important context. For about 10 years of my past life before Emilia, I've been trying to build and launch multiple companies, unsuccessfully.

A few of them have gotten some traction, but I've just never been able to break through. I've studied, networked, pitched, built, failed, learned, tried again, pitched some more, again and again to no avail. Society tells us that you have to be relentless, have grit, and never quit if you want to achieve your dreams. I'm no quitter, as evidenced by the fact that "never quit" is one of my core values. In fact, never quitting has always been a core value of mine. Before Emilia, never quit meant literally never giving up on something. It meant being relentless toward goals, having the grit to dig deeper, embrace the suck, fall in love with the process, etc. It was this never-quit mindset with which I approached starting a company in my past life. I was doing what I was told I was supposed to do to achieve my dream, and come hell or high water, I would make it happen.

I was trying to follow the blueprint of what everyone told me was the model for success if you wanted to have a successful startup someday. Have an idea, build an MVP (minimum viable product), gain a little traction, get some angel investors, add a few co-founders, gain some more traction, get funded from a venture capital firm, hire a lot, scale, get more funding, hire faster, scale more, and then sell and do it all over again. If you look up any business school, incubator, accelerator program, or business book, this is the process they will tell you to follow if you want success in this world.

If you talk to anyone that is a current or former entrepreneur, this is most likely the guidance and blueprint they will lay out for you as well. What I just described is basically what books like, *The Hard Things about Hard Things* talk about for the most part. It is a dog-eat-dog world, and there will be winners, and there will be losers. We're all told the winners are the visionaries and heroes of the business world like Steve Jobs, Mark Zuckerberg, Jeff Bezos, Ben Horowitz, and Elon Musk. These guys are just smarter and better than everyone else because they founded businesses that now have valuations in the billions and trillions. They did all this on sheer grit, determination, expert strategy, and execution. They were the ones that, when faced with the hard decisions, were able to step up, lead, take decisive action, and bring their people to the promised land.

This is what never quitting meant to me before Emilia. After Emilia, the definition changed dramatically as I watched her battle for a chance at life, holding on for seven additional hours as she laid in her mother's arms after extubating her. Never quit now represents what I saw in Emilia every day. It means to endure, to love life, and to make the most of each and every day here on this Earth. It is a reminder to embrace humanity, all the things that life will bring, good or bad, and to keep moving until you can't any longer.

In a weird twist of fate, I now find that quitting something is totally fine and sometimes often the right thing to do. Relentlessly trying to drill deeper in a dry well won't bring you oil, just misery, and pain. Sometimes you need to take a step back to reframe a problem, look at it differently, and find a new path forward. So, that is exactly what I did. I QUIT! I quit trying to be like everyone else. I quit trying to drill deeper into an empty well.

Before Emilia, the exciting world of startups and venture capital captivated me. After the atomic bomb was dropped on my life, this is the world that I was happy to leave behind and never revisit again in the future. I just didn't care anymore and didn't want to be a part of the rat race that seemed so dumb to me now. I was going to find my own path, one that aligned with my newfound mission and core values. That is when ClubAny began to take shape.

Okay, still with me? I provide all that context to let you know that while my desire for "traditional" success may have left me after we lost Emilia, my core values and "living for two" mission were continually leading me back to my roots of what I love the most. I love being curious, challenging things, and asking a lot of questions. So naturally, that led me to more and more books about all kinds of things that I found fascinating about this world. I slowly stopped reading the business books like *The Hard Things about Hard Things* and *Good to Great* because they all said the same thing without any fresh perspectives to offer. They told me how to be the person that I didn't want to be anymore. So I went over to the Derek Zoolander Center for Kids that Can't Read Really Good and Want to Learn How to Do Other Stuff Good as Well and picked up some new books in other genres. I searched the shelves for anything that wasn't business-related until I found anything that was new to me and piqued my curiosity.

Slowly but surely, I started to become captivated with reading about humanity, our bodies, minds, culture, psychology, thinking, creativity, and spirituality. Specifically, culture and humanity started to become my favorite subjects to explore. I devoured every new book I could get my hands on. My mind was filled with all kinds of new thoughts and questions to talk through with God. We would talk for hours sometimes about how I wanted to live my life. We went down rabbit hole after rabbit hole and had a blast. After months and months of talking about everything over at the Hardy-Meyer Center for Thought and Inquiry, this became my working model of the life that God and I co-created:

The Lessons Learned (so far):

1. I know nothing and never will know anything, but the journey for new knowledge and learning, thinking, and growing every day is everything.

2. It's all random. Life, success, and failure are as random as they come. There are no magical patterns or paths to follow. No one knows what they are doing, and thinking that we do is our biggest weakness.

3. Because life is random, the volume of our activity is really all that matters, statistically speaking. The more you do, the more likely you are to have success in something eventually.

4. Our imagination is our individual superpower.

5. Culture is the most important thing to all of humanity and our collective superpower. Our ability to unite around an idea and will it into existence is truly remarkable.

6. The only thing we truly have control over is deciding what we value most in our lives and doing our best to live those values in all that we do. That is the holy grail of happiness and the path toward living a balanced existence. It is also unobtainable, but SO WORTH STRIVING FOR EVERY SINGLE DAY!

After God and I had settled on these fundamental truths of life, we began using them as a basis to ask questions, play, and reframe how I looked at the world. We started to spend a lot of time revisiting my previous love of business but applying this new frame based on what I had learned and my new paradigms. Applying these lessons to the traditional business world led me to these questions to discuss with God:

1. If culture is the most important thing to humanity, what is truly at the core of the most successful cultures in the world (business or otherwise)?

2. Why do traditional businesses and their cultures always seem to fizzle out well before other longer-standing cultures like religions, clubs, nation-states, or fraternities, no matter how successful they were at one point? For example, which "culture" is more likely to exist in 500 years, Google or the Catholic Church? I think we all know the answer to that.

3. What truly is work/life balance? Is it even possible to obtain? Why are there no dominant cultures dedicated to this mission? You have successful work cultures like Google, Salesforce, and Facebook. You have successful life cultures like Buddhism, Stoicism, and Christianity. Why can't you have something that merges the two together? Why does it seem like you can have either life balance or work balance but not both? How can we create an environment where work and life balance is truly possible and sustainable?

4. How can we reimagine the traditional business model, applying these findings, to create an ecosystem that can be an enduring culture and still be a thriving business doing meaningful work based on individual core values for everyone involved? As my views started to take shape on the questions above, I kept going back to something that I had heard a lot of business gurus saying over the past 15 years, in one form or another, that "culture eats strategy for breakfast."

Striving to cultivate amazing cultures is not a new concept in the business world. Everyone who was anyone was focusing on their company cultures to gain a competitive advantage in the marketplace. To me, culture is a combination of all the foundational elements we've discussed like, core values, missions, visions, and finding your why. The best businesses did this stuff at a collective level. It really does help produce better results, and employees feel a deeper sense of purpose and meaning.

This "culture eating strategy for breakfast" mantra has become something of a business necessity if you truly want to grow and scale at the breakneck paces of Airbnb, Amazon, Uber, Facebook, and Salesforce. Business people could see that if you bring people together, uniting them around a cause they all cared about, and slapped together a few core values for everyone to get behind, employees become highly engaged, and productivity skyrockets.

Work doesn't feel like work when there is purpose and meaning behind the activity, when you are around a bunch of like-minded people and solving a problem or idea that you are passionate about. Problems just get solved, innovation organically happens, people bring their friends, and these cultures grow rapidly. When people come together and unite on a shared common vision, the sky truly is the limit.

So my question then became, if everyone knows this, why is it so rare to see successful business cultures that have been around for more than 100 years? What makes these cultures burn so bright and fast and then die out almost as quickly? That's not how cultures have worked throughout the history of humanity. On the flip side, what makes these 1,000-year-old thriving cultures, like the Catholic Church, for instance, continue to slowly burn bigger and brighter year after year?

If you drew a Venn Diagram of Salesforce and the Catholic Church, there really isn't much difference between the two entities when you boil them way down to their cores. They are both founded on a powerful idea that united a bunch of humans around a shared vision. Core values and missions were established, and an ultimate living breathing culture was formed and created. Hell, they even both have large buildings (skyscrapers and cathedrals) dotting the planet with their names plastered on them to act as recruitment tools for the masses to want to learn more.

So, what's the real difference? Why did the culture of the Catholic Church endure for 1,000+ years and the cultures of great companies like Salesforce, Facebook, Google seem to come and go at will?
God and I pondered on this one for a long time until I finally think we cracked the code. We came up with three main differences:

1. The Catholic Church is open to everyone. If you want to live that culture (mission and core values), you are welcome. On the contrary, these businesses are not open to everyone. Companies like Facebook, Google, and Salesforce make it a point to hire only the "best of the best." They let it be known that not all are welcome.

2. The culture is authentic with the Catholic Church. Its members actually choose to live and embrace the ideas, core values, and mission (to the best of their abilities). If you don't, you are welcome to leave. These businesses, on the other hand, pay mercenaries to adopt their mission and values. Sure, some

employees may really truly believe in the mission and values, but most don't, and the gaps only increase as the organizations get bigger.

3. The Catholic Church will only ever listen to itself and its people. It answers to no one outside their own universe (other than God). Salesforce, Google, and Facebook will always have investors to answer to that surely have a different mission and value structure.
These businesses are caught in a cultural identity crisis. They say they want to live and act a certain way, they preach their core values to their people, but the employees don't truly understand it or fully live it. Sure, a few of them (especially the earliest employees) do, but as the organizations grow, the further and further away they get from really embodying their core values.

The best of these companies spend a maximum of a few days talking to new employees about the vision, mission, and core values of the organization during new hire orientation. After you've heard what they have to say, they then send you on your way to living a completely different existence than what you were just told. Your job is to make money and grow the business and if you can find the time, live the core values and mission. Employees intuitively know this to their core. These companies are lying or simply too blind to see and admit what their real mission and core values are to the world. The real core values of all traditional businesses are dictated by its investors, who, by definition, are only in this for money and growth.

You can choose not to agree, but when push comes to shove, and shit hits the fan, and the money and growth dry up, their cultures die with them. I've lived this three different times in my career. It is the saddest thing in the world to see. All the people that thought they were a part of this beautiful idea, mission, and "family" have it yanked away in an instant. This is due to the fact that the real culture is driven by outside investors that only care about the mission of making money and the values of constant growth. The Catholic Church, on the other hand, takes the opposite approach. When shit gets real in their world, they double down on their mission and people, and in doing so, can weather any storm. Most importantly, no one outside of their tribe can have any say in the direction they collectively take, effectively ensuring that it will always be guided by their true founding principles, values, and mission. That is the real key to longevity...never let anyone hijack your mission, vision, and core values.

After God and I had this epiphany, I started to think, "What if that didn't have to be the case? What if you could take all that was great with these

1,000-year-old cultures, apply it to the business world, and create a hybrid of the two worlds?" After all, if you want to live a balanced existence, meaningful work is certainly a part of that equation. Based on this thought, a vision began to take shape; An entity that was made up of a true work/life balance, core values, and mission-driven culture that always puts its people first. It wasn't the same old "Culture Eats Strategy for Breakfast" mantra. I wanted to rebrand this as saying to be, "CULTURE IS THE STRATEGY!" When you always focus on culture, the mission, and your people first, you can build a 1,000-year-old organization.

With the seed of that idea planted in my mind, I started to dust off some of my old business plans and looked at them through this new lens. I got to work and completely reconstructed one of those dead ideas. Step 1 was to scrap all goals about what (meaning the product or service) I was trying to build and first focus only on the why (the mission and the core values). I rewrote the mission statement, which was to create our own universe where we could live a truly balanced work and life existence. From there, I started to focus on the core values of the business. After that, I then started to write down all the ways we could live and express these core values in our day-to-day operations to build our culture.

I got to a point where I felt really good about where this was headed and thought, "You can't have a culture with just one person. Culture is always founded on an idea that is planted in a garden. For that garden to grow, you need others to believe in the same thing. I have to grow this idea as fast as possible and get as many people on board as I can." I then took this message to the universe (the internet and a few chat forums). Before I knew it, the universe had delivered me a conversation with a few potential co-founders who cared about the same things and were curious to learn more.

When we started chatting, our conversations weren't about what I was hoping to build. Who cares what we were going to build together? What I wanted to talk about was the why, core values, and mission. I told my story about Emilia, how I arrived at this conversation we were having, and the idea that "Culture is the Strategy." The approach was resonating. It felt like co-founder speed dating. We weren't even hardly talking about the actual business at all, and I loved it.

One of these conversations eventually introduced me to a gentleman named Trieu. We were like a match made in heaven from the first time we started to chat. I could instantly tell that he was a life marathoner, and the feelings were mutual. He had been searching for balance for a long time in his own life and career. He is a technological wizard that, at one point in his career, had achieved a lot of what we would define in traditional business as a success. However, no matter how much he achieved, he never seemed to truly feel fulfilled in life, and that led him to seek a different path.

After I shared the story about Emilia and how this all came to be, Trieu was all in on trying to turn this mission into a reality. It's a funny thing how fragile an idea truly can be; it is like a little spark of fire. Once it is lit, you have to feed the tiny ember of light with energy for it to turn into a flame and grow. Getting others to believe is the fuel for any idea to go from an ember to a flame. The goal is then to spread that idea to feed the flame, turn it into a raging fire, and ensure that it never goes out. For an idea to make it out of your mind and into the world, someone else has to believe. As long as more than one person truly believes, an idea has life. The second that leaves, that idea is dead. Luckily for me, Trieu believed, and we got right to work.

Trieu and I began to meet every single night for an hour to work through our ideas, create and live our culture, and build our new universe dedicated to work/life balance. We still do this today, and that isn't going to stop anytime soon. Those nightly sessions became our forum to define our shared core values and share how we are living them each and every single day. We began to pull from a lot of the activities and habits I had been living the past few months. We began to read a lot together, and that became one of our core values for the new culture. We would read on our own, think constantly, and then come back the next night to tell each other all about it and discuss every off-the-wall idea we came up with. Every once in a while, we would do a little actual "work" on what we were trying to build, but the real fun was living the mission of a balanced life.

Slowly but surely, we started to incorporate more and more activities based on our shared core values and having a blast in the process. It felt great to live the way I wanted to live and build a business with someone who felt the same way. After a few weeks of doing this, we were having so much fun that we decided that we needed to get others involved in this new mission. That is when Nichol and Blake joined the mission.

Now, we were all co-creating our core values, having regular discussions about books, what we were reading, thinking, ideating, and building together. Rarely were we ever even focused on any particular thing that we were actually going to build. In one of these sessions, I started to tell the group about how this culture that we were forming was so much more than a business. This is a book club, a place to express ideas, a therapy session, etc.

Nichol, who is the best listener you will ever meet in your life, was doing what he does best and deeply listening to what I was saying. He then jumped in and jokingly said, "I'm hearing this is like a club? I'm also hearing that this is like a company? Maybe we should call it ClubAny?" We all laughed and then emphatically said, "THAT'S IT! That's what we are going to call this thing. CLUBANY!" As the months passed, we started to define what ClubAny really is and how we could turn this into a true work/life balanced ecosystem that could be an infinite game for others to join and participate in.

This idea was officially no longer my own, and the flame was growing stronger. Others were beginning to believe and starting to talk about how we were going to grow this culture that was becoming so much fun for us all. We decided together that we needed to figure out a way to help others live our culture before they could ever call themselves a true ClubAny member. What does living our culture mean? Well, we had to invent that! How were we going to do that? We came up with the following guidelines to get us started.

What is ClubAny culture?

1. Culture is the strategy – our people and culture will ALWAYS be put first over any business project, money, growth, etc.
2. Our culture will be centered around:
    1. Balance - Blending the activities of work and life together using core values as the universal binder.
    2. Working harder on yourself than you do on your job - We do this by always putting "first things first" in our personal and professional lives and letting our core values guide the way.

These guidelines were simple and easy to understand. It centered around truly knowing yourself and living that life on purpose while being supported by a tribe of like-minded people striving for the same thing.

It was that simple.

The first step to make this happen is to ensure that everyone truly knew themselves and their personal why, mission, and core values before being able to enter this ecosystem. That sounds easy in theory, but it is really the biggest challenge to this whole puzzle.

To solve this challenge, we decided on a solution that we affectionately began to call a Core Values Quest. The idea was simple but powerful. We devised a 90 day guided program around activities that reflected our shared ClubAny core values. Those activities we chose were 30 minutes of daily reading, writing, and exercise to help the prospective ClubAny member to learn, reflect, act, and challenge themselves every day in some capacity.

We called the prospective ClubAny member an "explorer" and assigned them a "guide" to mentor them and serve as an "accountabilibuddy" (accountability buddy) on this 90-day journey. The goal of the "explorer" was only to find out who they are, their personal core values, and their personal life mission to share with the group at the end of their quest at their "graduation."

Once the explorer had graduated, we would open up the doors to the ClubAny universe where we could all be speaking from the same knowledge base, truly understand each other and ourselves, and begin to start projects to collaborate on together that would unite their individual core values with work passions.

The idea and vision sounded great in theory, but at this point, it was just an idea. Trieu and I had been doing similar activities for months together, so we knew how life-changing this process could be as we could see it in ourselves. What remained to be seen was whether or not we could successfully recreate what we were experiencing and make this possible for someone else to experience something similar.

There were a lot of questions to answer. What were we going to have them read? What were they supposed to write about? How could we help them write? How long do they need to do this? What were they going to present each month? How were we going to make sure this was focused on them but still help guide the journey? How could we support any new explorer through this whole process?

Nichol, Blake, Trieu, and I started working through all of this until we had settled on the idea to try a 3-month program that would be designed around helping people to exercise for 30 minutes, learn for 30 minutes, and write for 30 minutes each day. We put together a few books to read for each month that Trieu and I had read together over the past few months and decided to give this a try.

Since Trieu and I had been really "living" this journey together and doing these activities already, we turned to Blake and asked him if he wanted to be the guinea pig on this project. Blake said, "Let's do this," and jumped right in. I volunteered to be his guide and "acountabilibuddy" on this journey. That meant that we would check in every single night for five minutes to see if he was on track, sticking with the daily reading, writing, and exercise habits, and quickly discuss any questions he may have. We then set up an end-of-the-week mentor meeting to talk about his week, what he was writing about, his core values, what he was learning, answer any questions, etc.

Blake and I embarked on this journey together over the next 90 days. He did his daily reading, writing, and exercise, and we would check in each night on progress, feedback, and questions. Slowly but surely, unexpected and magical changes started to occur in his life as the journey progressed. It is hard to describe in words, but I could see the visible changes in his actions, thoughts, the questions he was asking, and the way he was challenging himself and opening up. It was like he was blossoming before our eyes.

Trieu and Nichol could see it as well. Even Blake's wife made comments all the time about all the great changes she was indirectly seeing in her husband. Most importantly, Blake could feel it. He was growing stronger, understanding himself and his values, and feeling more confident and connected to his purpose each and every day. We were all growing together as we lived our shared core values, and something magical was brewing.

After Blake completed the first core values quest, we all immediately thought, "We have to get more people involved and do this again and again!" We got to work refining our program and convinced a few new prospective explorers to take this leap with us. Some brave soles named Cole, Amanda, and David were to be our next class to go through this grand core values quest.

After a few weeks on the quest, we all started to see the same changes happening with them as well. By the time they had "graduated" and completed their journeys, they presented their newly cemented personal why, missions, and core values to the rest of the ClubAny members, and it was incredible to witness. They really knew themselves so much better through this process and were seeing the compound effect from all the personal work in their own lives. Best of all, the rest of the group knew them as well through witnessing their monthly presentations and guiding them through the process.

We were really on to something. We brought in our next class and saw the same thing happen again. We are growing this delicate new culture the right way, living our shared core values together, and helping to promote putting first things first. We all felt so energized.

You might be saying at this point, "This is great, but where does the company part of this ecosystem come into play? It just sounds like a personal growth club at this point." You're right, but we had been thinking about this all along as well and had a bigger plan in mind. The idea behind the program in the first place was simply to design a way to ensure that we all spoke a common language, to develop consistent daily habits and accountability, to get to know each other on a more meaningful level and to live our personal and collective core values in all that we do. It was designed to set the stage and build the foundation for our culture. The core values quest was the minimum bar we had determined just to be able to open the door to the rest of the ClubAny ecosystem that was beginning to take shape on the other side.

After all, ClubAny is supposed to be a work and life balanced ecosystem. Our master plan became to help leverage the momentum of the quest to propel innovation, ideation, and generate a ton of new projects to collaborate on. The quest had been intelligently designed to have everything lead up to this goal as well as set the cultural baseline.

- Month 1 of the quest had been designed to solely focus on the explorer, helping them to understand themselves and helping them to find their core values and personal missions through various books and writing prompts.
- Month 2 was designed to focus on humanity and life in general. The goal was to open their eyes to shift personal paradigms to start to see the world a little differently and think beyond just themselves.
- Month 3 was to bring it all home and designed to unleash their curiosity, encourage them to ask their own questions, and unlock the creativity and imagination hidden deep inside.

In the 3rd month, we encouraged the explorers to ask a question each and every morning and write about their thoughts in their journals. We asked them to pull from all the shifting paradigms in their lives and try to look at things a little differently to come up with some creative new questions to explore and play around with in their minds. From this, we offered them the opportunity to help "coach" them through taking that new lens on life and newfound creativity to start to come up with some new business ideas that they could present to the group at graduation if that was appealing to them. The idea behind this was to leverage this newfound surge of creativity in their lives to generate ideas that the rest of the ClubAny could work on together if that aligned with their individual core values and unique skill sets.

We thought this might be our solution to fight the "life is random" and "volume of output is the key to success" rules discussed earlier. We hoped this process might generate a consistent trickle of new projects to break ground on in hopes that one of them would lead to financial success to help fund the mission further.

That is the logic on the company side of everything; harvest ideas from people going through a transformational personal journey and then marry up people's newly cemented core values with projects that mirrored these values to get to work. You ideate in month three and then throw those ideas out into the ecosystem, and other ClubAny members can pair up, use their unique skills and backgrounds, and see if they can make something of it, if they want to. No one was being mandated to do this stuff unless they wanted to contribute. If business ideation and creating new ventures wasn't appealing to a new ClubAny member, we would still have a ton of club activities that they could participate in to grow with their newfound tribe. The only rule, once your quest was complete, was to always put first things first in your life and live your core values in as many daily activities as you can. That was it! As long as you do that, you're a ClubAny member for life.

If we could figure out how to scale this plan and make it a reality, we could avoid ever needing to take on an investor and be subjected to them hijacking our mission and core values like traditional business cultures. After all, what do you even need money for to build a business? It's mainly to hire employees. In the ClubAny universe, we wouldn't need to hire anyone. As the membership grows, eventually, we will have so many people in our ecosystem with all different kinds of backgrounds and skillsets that we will be able to tackle any project. We don't limit who can join like a traditional business. If you want to live your life this way, come on down. We don't care if you are young, old, rich, poor, a seasoned vet, or a newbie. You are welcome in ClubAny if this life appeals to you, and we will find a way to maximize your unique talents if that is appealing to you. Come one and come all. We can't wait to have you join the fun and help us to build our vision for how work and life should be conducted in the modern age to come.

Whew. Let's take a break. I hope all that made sense. To be clear, this ClubAny Work / Life Balance Complex is still incredibly new, and we have a ton of work left to do to perfect this unique and new model. It has been a wild and fun ride but worth every second. I've never felt happier and more balanced in my entire adult life, and I know my other co-founders feel the same. That is all that really matters. Rest assured, the only way that construction will stop on this complex is if the idea dies, and Trieu and I will never let this happen. We will never be controlled by any outside entity or investor that wants to use this to make money and therefore trump the amazing culture that we are trying to build. Our people will control every aspect of this organization and structure. It may not be quick, but check back in 1,000 years, and I'm sure we have a better chance of still being here than Facebook or Google.

Open pitch to all:

If you are reading this book and this thing sounds fun to you, come find us at www.clubany.org. We will get you aligned to a guide and started on your own core values quest in the next class. EVERYONE IS WELCOME! We don't care what industry you are in, your age, gender, sex, background, work history, etc. If you are willing to put in the time to understand and live your core values in all that you do, we are willing to invest in you.

Note about future construction projects:

So that concludes the tour of our new city rising from the rubble as of this writing on 3/4/2021. I wanted to end this section with a quick note about the buildings we've discussed here in the past few pages. These are all just the start of Emilia and my new city. These buildings that we've already built are amazing, we are so proud of them, and our citizens are LOVING them. They will continue to be the anchors and cornerstones for future development. However, just like life, where we are today isn't the end all be all, and we still have so much more to build and create. We will do everything we can while we have time in this world to leave a foundation for the future to keep building.

In the meantime, our construction crews are ready and can't wait to see what future projects spin out of the Hardy-Meyer Center for Thought and Inquiry. We currently have a long backlog and waitlist for construction cranes, so check back in the next few decades to see the progress, and we'll be happy to tell you all about it.

Just remember, DON'T EVER STOP BUILDING!

CHAPTER 6

Fix Your Basement! – The Magic of the Compound Effect in Action

With our new city slowly rising from the ashes and taking shape, I was truly "living for two" and expressing Emilia and my core shared values in everything that I did in my life. You could say that we were doing okay and life had meaning and purpose again. Emilia and I had found a way through the worst thing that any of us could have ever imagined and had turned that pain into a gift that was unfolding before our very eyes.

If the story ended here, I think we would all agree that it was a happy ending. However, as it turns out, the fun was just beginning, and Emilia and God had the craziest series of events in store for our family over the next few months. I can't even make this stuff up.

Ready for the exciting conclusion? LET'S DO THIS!

Before we jump in, let's reconnect on a little story called *The Compound Effect*, written by Darren Hardy, that we touched on earlier in the story. *The Compound Effect* is actually the first book that I read and completed while sitting next to Emilia all day long in the NICU at Riley's Hospital for Children. This book has had a pretty profound impact on my life, to say the least. It is fitting that the lessons learned in this book would be how our story concludes.

A quick reminder about what it is about: The compound effect is the cumulative outcome that occurs when you take small, seemingly insignificant steps toward your mission in all that you do each and every day. Individually, each step may seem meaningless, but when you keep at them over time, they start to compound together, and magic starts to happen. This compound effect is exactly what started to happen in my life in the months that followed Emilia's tragic passing. Taking the tiny actions of reading a little each day, writing a little each day, and exercising a little each day snowballed into winning tennis tournaments, consuming 100+ books in a year, writing this book, starting a movement with ClubAny, and finding my tribe. Most importantly, it helped me to find God, save my marriage, discover my core values, and bring hope for the future.

I didn't plan for any of this. The only goal I had in mind was to not let Emilia down and to honor her life. That's the beauty of the compound effect in life; it comes out of nowhere and leads you to places your own imagination could never have conceived. This final story that I'm about to share is the ultimate compound effect manifestation. It still blows my mind thinking about it. I bet even the most imaginative Hollywood writer couldn't have conceived of this one. I affectionately call it, FIX YOUR BASEMENT!

It all began in October of 2020. ClubAny was in full swing, and Blake was just embarking on our inaugural "core values quest" plan we had concocted. I had been living my own personal quest of sorts for about six months, and I was searching for more ways to express my core values in my everyday life. Well, luckily, one of my (and ClubAny's) core values is to "challenge." With this in mind, I figured that I would challenge myself to keep pushing for new and crazy ways to express more of my core values and to provide a good example to Blake in hopes of motivating him as he was embarking on this new quest himself.

Reading, writing, and exercising every day were no longer challenges for me; they were just a part of my day-to-day life at this stage. My days looked like this: I would wake up, make a cup of coffee, listen to DarrenDaily, go to my office and write about my thoughts, read *Trusting God Day by Day*, write more about my thoughts, write any random notes that I wanted to share with God, write for Emilia's book for an hour, go workout, listen to an audiobook for 30 minutes, take a shower, and get to work on my day job at Salesforce. After work, Trieu and I had our nightly meeting, and then two to three nights a week, I would go play tennis after that. It sounds exhausting just writing that, but I was actually in my comfort zone at this point. When you are living your core values in all that you do, it is remarkable what you can accomplish seemingly effortlessly. Your activities provide a source of energy versus depleting you, which means you can do more and more. I could handle it all pretty easily, and it was no longer a challenge for me to manage, which meant that I was no longer living my core values. So, I decided I'd try to change that.

In September 2020, I decided I would try to throw in a new challenge each month where I would try a new skill, habit, or activity that reflected another one of my core values which I could then try to incorporate into my day in addition to all that other stuff I mentioned above. September's challenge had been meditation for 15 minutes a day. That was pretty interesting, fun, and I learned a lot as it led me to explore a lot of new books about Eastern philosophy. I'm so glad that I did because they have a really good grasp on the mind and body connection. When October rolled around, I thought that I'd keep trying this new monthly challenge. I choose my core value "give more than I take" as an area I wanted to improve upon. I thought, "What if I tried to do a random act of kindness each day and see what happens?" So that is what I did. Every morning in October, after I was done with listening to Darren and Joyce, I completed writing my thoughts and reflections, and before I started writing for the book, I spent some time thinking about what I could do for a RAK (random act of kindness) on that day. The first few were easy enough to perform as I would do something nice for Felicia or my closest friends. However, after a few days, figuring out who and what to perform my RAK for the day on started to get really freaking hard. Having to intentionally think about someone else, what would make them happy, how I could help them or do something nice for them is super challenging. This is like the ultimate platinum rule activity in action. It was mind-blowing how hard it was to actually do this each and every day. You really had to think hard and get creative. I didn't want these to be some elaborate gesture, just something small, nice, and natural that wasn't forced or fake.

One morning, I had been writing about core values in my daily reflections, and it led me to think about my granny, Big Momma. I thought about how much I've always looked up to her in how she lived her life and the way she carried herself. We called her Big Momma for a reason. She knows who she is, and she lives life on purpose and with conviction. She is the definition of a rock-solid human, and you always know what you are going to get from her. Big Momma has been through so much in her life that I honestly can't imagine (there it is again). She's endured two husbands passing away from chronic and devastating illnesses, losing her mother, brother and his wife in a tragic car accident, raising her brother's four children as her own, and so much more! However, she would never let any of that get her down. If anything, it always seemed like she just got stronger and stronger as time passed.

As I was writing and reflecting about her, I thought, "That's core values and purpose in action! I finally got it! I finally get why I've always looked up to Big Momma!" I decided that I would use that as my RAK for the day, and I sent her an email saying exactly what I just wrote. The subject line of the email read, "I finally get it…" In the email, I laid out all the reasons why she was an inspiration and the journey that I was on to explore my core values and understand my purpose. I also thanked her for being her.

After I finished the email, I hit send and marked my RAK complete for the day. I can't begin to tell you how out of character this action was for me. I don't think I've ever sent something like that to anyone I've ever known. I waited all day for a response back to see what she would say. She replied back later that night because she was serving at the food pantry (of course she was. Core values anyone?) when she first read it and wanted to give the response the proper time it required. She wrote back saying how touched she was by the gesture and offered to have Felicia and me over for dinner to talk more about core values, how she found her own purpose, stories from her life, etc. I replied back, "Let's do it," and we locked down a dinner date at her house in late October. When the night of the dinner date arrived, Felicia was about 10 to 12 weeks pregnant. She was having a REALLY rough pregnancy. I won't get into details here for privacy's sake, but we thought we lost our rainbow baby a few times along the way. With what we had experienced with Emilia, we were being super cautious and trying to diligently listen to what her body was telling us. On this particular day, I could tell that Felicia was just feeling like total shit. She was moving really slowly and experiencing a lot of cramping.

We made dessert to take to Big Momma's, got the food ready to transport, and then Felicia slowly walked to the car and got in the front passenger seat. I looked over at her, and she just looked miserable. I could sense a little bit of anxiety and panic in her face as well. I said, "You should stay home. It's fine." She protested back in a whimper, "No, I can go if you need me to." I said, "Nope. Go back in the house. I promise I'm not going to get mad, and I'll make up an excuse to tell Big Momma or something." Felicia reluctantly agreed and went back inside to lay down and rest for the night. I continued on to Big Momma's house solo.

As I drove away, I wasn't mad, but I was thinking, "What am I going to tell Granny?" as she had made dinner for three, and now I felt bad. Also, on a personal level, I was oddly now a bit more nervous for this conversation without Felicia by my side. I don't think that I've ever had an extended one-on-one conversation by myself with Big Momma in my entire adult life. Sure, we saw each other all the time, and we'd had some in-depth chats in the past, but they were never just her and I over dinner by ourselves. This was a totally unique experience, and I had no idea what to really expect, so I was a bit anxious. I decided on the drive down that I would just tell Big Momma the truth when I arrived. I walked up, gave her a hug, and told her that Felicia wouldn't be joining us because she was feeling really bad, and we didn't want to risk anything with the pregnancy. Big Momma said, "I understand. I was just looking forward to seeing you both." With that out of the way, we grabbed a plate and sat down to start our dinner.

Our conversation began by talking about the email I had sent to her earlier that month. She said that she wanted to share some stories about how she found God and her own core values in her life. She asked me, "Do you know that story about how your grandpa and I came to adopt your aunts and uncle?" I said, "Of course I know that story. I think?" I told her I knew that my Great Aunt Teresa and Great Uncle Joe died in a car accident along with Teresa's parents, and that is how she came to adopt them. She said, "Yes, but did you know that your grandfather and I were supposed to be with them in the car that night?" I said, "Not at all. I guess I have never heard the full story before. Please share."

I told her what I knew that Great Aunt Teresa and Great Uncle Joe died in a car accident along with Great Grandmother Feltz (Joe and my grandma's mother), and that is how she came to adopt them. She said, "Yes, but did you know that your grandfather and I were supposed to be with them in the car that night?" I said, "Not at all. I guess I have never heard the full story before. Please share."

Big Momma started telling me the story of how she and Grandpa Pete came to adopt my aunts and uncle. She said, the night that Great Aunt Teresa and Uncle Joe tragically passed away, they were all supposed to be going to the Frank Sinatra concert down at Market Square Arena in downtown Indianapolis. They had a crew of seven that were all really excited for the concert and had bought tickets six months in advance to see Frank (this was in the 1970s, so I'm sure this was a big deal and the equivalent of us seeing Beyonce or something now.) A few weeks prior to the date of the concert, my grandma said that she and my grandpa had been discussing fixing up their basement for years, and she had finally had enough of waiting for the project to kick off. They needed more space at home as the house was pretty packed with the three kids they already had at this time. Big Momma was done waiting for my grandpa to get to work on his own, so she decided to force the issue. She told me that she came home from work one evening, walked into the kitchen, grabbed a hammer out of the drawer, walked to the basement, and pounded a big hole in the wall. She then walked back up the stairs and told Grandpa Pete it was time to get this basement renovation started and to get to work. Classic Big Momma move!

Grandpa Pete reluctantly accepted the challenge, and over the next few weeks, he and my great grandfathers came over to help work on the remodel. The day the big Frank Sinatra concert arrived, my grandpa had been working in the basement all day on the remodel. As my grandma's brother and his wife came down the street from their house to pick them up for the concert, my grandpa apparently decided that he didn't want to go anymore, seemingly out of the blue. My grandma said, "It was weird, and that he didn't really have a reason, he just didn't want to go anymore." She thought, "Fine, screw you. I'll go by myself."

As she walked out to get in her brother's car, she said she stopped and thought she shouldn't go either for some mysterious reason. She informed her brother of her decision as he waited in the car in her driveway. She said that she didn't know why she decided to do this as she had no problem going without my grandpa. She said she just didn't feel right for some reason and decided to stay home at the last minute. She told me that after she told her brother of their decision not to attend, the last words he said to her as he was pulling out of the driveway was, "Your husband's an asshole."

Joe and Teresa left and continued on to their next stop to go pick up my Grandma and Joe's Mother (My Great Grandma Feltz). After picking her up, they were on their way down to Great Aunt Ruthie's house when a drunk driver flipped over a medium and landed on top of their car, instantly killing all three people in the vehicle. My grandma said, "*THAT* is why I felt we *HAD TO ADOPT* your aunts and uncles after the tragic event."

She and my grandpa were supposed to be in that car that night. Something out of their control had created the series of events that somehow spared their lives and allowed them to remain here on Earth. She felt that all this happened for a reason, and they were being called to step in and help her nieces and nephew, who had just lost their parents and grandparents in one single night. My grandparents immediately asked to adopt the four young children and took them into their home.

In another weird twist of fate, that newly fixed-up basement would now become a necessity because their already cramped house with three kids was about to become one with seven. God had unknowingly been preparing them with the resources needed for this very moment. The basement remodel began as a nice-to-have when my grandma decided to grab a hammer and smash a hole in the wall, and just a few short months later, it became a must-have.

I was blown away as I listened to this story. I spent the rest of the night hearing about how she found purpose and meaning in her life. As we sat and ate, I was learning more and more about how she felt called by God and how she found her core values through Him and the Catholic Church. That is why she was always so religious and had lived her life the way she did. It was an amazing discussion, and I'm so glad that we ended up having it. I stayed way later than we initially had planned, and it was a great night.

As I was driving back home after dinner, I started to think about the words "fix your basement" as a metaphor for my own life and what that meant to me. Sometimes you just have to do the things you don't understand and trust that there is a reason behind it all. We don't know the answers to everything in life, and we aren't supposed to. What we are supposed to do is live our lives guided by God, our purpose, our core values, and it will eventually all be revealed over time. I think that is called faith!

I started thinking about my own literal basement back at home. When Felicia and I bought our house back in 2013, we bought it for a ton of reasons, but mainly to start and grow a family there one day. It has a huge yard, four bedrooms, and this old unfinished basement with a ton of open space that I knew could come in handy someday. From the day we bought the house, I knew that I always wanted to remodel that basement to give our kids more space to play and explore. Also, because BASEMENTS ARE THE BEST! A basement can be whatever you want them to be. They are beautiful blank canvases of space with which you can create whatever family needs during a specific period of time. They can be an additional family room, movie room, man cave, she-shed, art studio, woodworking studio, personal gym, laundry room, kids playroom, arcade, etc. To me, I always envisioned our basement as the kid's fun space to play and be creative. It is where I wanted to banish them to go play with their friends, watch their cartoons, play video games, draw on the walls, and just go be kids.

When we found out we were pregnant with Emilia, Felicia not-so-gently informed me that it was time for my office to relocate in our house as that was to be Emilia's nursery. After putting up a small fight, I eventually relented. Instead of sulking about my lost office space, I thought I'd use this as an opportunity. I informed Felicia, "This is the perfect time to remodel our basement and create that fun family space that I had always wanted down there. That way, my office can go into the bonus loft space upstairs, and we won't lose our second living room. Everyone will be happy, happy, happy." Felicia said, "Fine. Do whatever you want. Just relocate your office out of Emilia's nursery."

When I had this epiphany, we were still only ten weeks into Emilia's pregnancy, so I figured I had TONS of time to get the renovation completed and the house reconfigured before Emilia's arrival. I didn't start right away, but the plan was in place. In late February 2020, I had just started to get quotes from contractors on the basement remodel because I thought we had until July 13th before Emilia would be arriving. Well, we all know what happened in mid-March. With her urgent situation in the NICU taking precedence, I postponed the plans to start the remodel and figured I'd revisit all of this once Emilia was getting closer to coming home. When we lost her, the grand vision of the basement remodel was scrapped altogether. We were back to being the childless couple, so no new space was needed. My office stayed my office, and we had no nursery. Emilia and I shared that space with a memorial to her in a quarter of the room, but it was not a nursery.

When we found out we were pregnant again in late August, I thought, "I'm not waiting around this time. I'm going to get this basement done way early." Well, here we were in late October, and I still hadn't even gotten a quote yet for the basement. After hearing Big Momma's story, I thought, "It's time to make this happen!" I went home and told Felicia about our dinner conversations and all the symbolism I saw in our own life. She agreed. I went to bed that night and couldn't stop thinking about those words, "FIX YOUR BASEMENT!"

The next morning I woke up and started my day off with my usual routine. I made a cup of coffee and listened to my DarrenDaily as it was brewing. Right below our coffee maker happens to be a little utility kitchen drawer with a bunch of random things in it like screwdrivers, nails, and a hammer. I opened up the drawer, picked up the hammer, walked down into the basement, and hit a big old hole into one of the walls. Smiling, I walked back up the stairs, and Felicia asked, "Did you just go hammer a hole in the basement?" I said, "YEP! Time to FIX THE BASEMENT!" I then called a good friend of mine, Ryan, who owns a construction company, and asked him to come over to give me a quote on this basement remodel. I shared with him the whole story, and he said he'd be over later in the week to get us a quote. Just like that, the basement remodel was underway.

By early November, Ryan and I had come to terms on the project specifications and a price that felt comfortable for both of us. I started buying materials to prepare for Ryan's team when they were ready to get to work. They had a little backlog of projects, so we weren't projected to start until Mid-December, 2020. On December 15th, 2020, demo day began, and we were officially off to the races on the long-awaited basement remodel. Over the next two months, they were in our basement basically every single day, gutting the entire space and re-constructing this amazing new work of art in our home. I couldn't wait to see the finished product.

All the while, Felicia and her pregnancy were progressing, albeit with a lot of complications, but progressing, nonetheless. We had always expected that this little baby would come early as well and had been working feverishly to do everything we could to keep Felicia pregnant as long as we possibly could. We had always set the "safe date" in our minds at 28 weeks, which happened to be February 14th, 2021. We knew enough about preemie life that the chance of survival at 28 weeks is like 95%. That was the date that we could metaphorically kick back and hopefully ride this whole thing out until May 9th, when our little boy would be at full term, the basement would be done, the nursery would be remodeled, and the whole house would be reconfigured to adjust for this new entry into our family.

On Friday, February 12th, 2021, the finishing touch of laying the carpet in the main big room of the basement was finally completed. We now officially had a 97% finished basement remodel, and it was the space that I had always envisioned. Ryan and the construction team still had some really tiny little things to finish up, but enough was completed that we could officially start to move back in and fill up that space. I was beyond excited and relieved that we got this all done before anything unexpected happened with the pregnancy.

On Saturday, February 13th, 2021, I had planned to have two of my life marathoner friends, Kevin and Mike, along with my parents, over to the house to show off the new space and to help us reorganize our house that had been a dirty construction zone for the past few months. We were going to move all the furniture around in the house, get the new office configured upstairs in the old second living room space, and then move all of that stuff down to the basement so we could get the nursery cleared and ready to decorate. We worked all day Saturday moving stuff around, building the new treadmill and Ikea couch in the basement, hanging flat screens, artwork, etc.

By 8 p.m., we were finally done, and everyone was out of the house. Felicia and I sat there in the basement for two hours, enjoying our new space in peace and quiet, without contractors, dust, or crap everywhere. The house was in order, the basement was complete, we were officially at our "safe date" of 28 weeks the next day, and we could breathe a sigh of relief. We went to bed.

The next morning, February 14th, 2021, I woke up, looked over at Felicia, and she had this distressed and pained look on her face as she laid next to me. She had been having random contractions almost daily for the past eight weeks. To her, this had become par for the course in this pregnancy. She had adjusted by basically putting herself on bedrest and worked remotely from our house. She had also found some strategies to manage the contractions when they came on, and it seemed to be working for the most part. However, on this particular morning, the pained looks on her face were different. I had seen them before. They immediately took me back to the day before Emilia was born. This was the same look on her face I remembered seeing as we walked around Whole Foods the night when we were all concerned about her but didn't know if something was really wrong. At this moment, I could tell that those weren't just random contractions like we'd seen over the past eight weeks. Those were labor pains!

I looked at her and said, "We're going to the hospital right now!" She started to push back a little and then relented and said, "You're right. Let's go." We went to the OB Triage area back at IU Methodist, where this all began less than a year ago. We were back in the little exam room again with Felicia on the bed and me tucked in the corner behind her holding her hand. The OBGYN on call began to examine Felicia. They confirmed that she was indeed in labor and was currently 1centimeter dilated. They informed us that they were going to admit her into Labor and Delivery to try and stop this baby from coming. This was around 11:30 a.m. at this point.

We were wheeled back over to Labor and Delivery. I hadn't been in this section of the hospital since we had Emilia in LDR Room 20. I was praying we wouldn't go by that room on our walk through this section of the hospital. As we got to the sign that read, "LDR Rooms 1-19" with an arrow pointing to the left and "LDR Rooms 20-30" with the arrow pointing to the right, we turned left. I was so relieved. They put us in LDR 12. Apparently, LDR 12 also happened to be what all the nurses called The Suite because the room was so huge and one of the biggest on the floor (lucky us). This whole experience couldn't feel more different than with Emilia. We were all calm, cool, collected, had a plan, and were ready for this. It almost felt like it was a movie, and someone was behind the scenes directing the past few months of our life. The nurses got to work administering all the drugs they could to stop labor, along with some magnesium and a shot of steroids to help the baby should he arrive anytime in the next two weeks. They strapped some contraction monitors on Felicia, and then we waited. The NICU team came back in to talk to us about protocols and what to expect. I thought, "Yeah, yeah, we know." We spoke with the doctors about the importance of the steroids for the baby and walked through the plan. They said, "If we can stop labor, in 24 hours Felicia will get a second dose for the baby. It takes two full days for the steroids to have max effectiveness, and then every day for the next two weeks is like a week of equivalent development in the womb if he still comes early." We were praying we could make those two days happen, but it was still undecided if we would be able to get there at this point.

Felicia's contractions were happening more and more frequently, and the decision was made to remove her cerclage that we had put into place back in week 14 to keep her cervix from shortening out of nowhere like what happened with Emilia. Once the cerclage was removed, we found out that Felicia was actually four centimeters dilated, and her contractions were increasing. "This could literally go either way at this point," the doctors were telling us.

Slowly but surely, over the next few hours, Felicia's contractions started to space out a little wider by each passing hour. By 7 p.m. that evening, they were only happening once an hour. By the next morning, she was hardly having any at all. We had stopped delivery and bought some more time. The doctors informed us that Felicia would be in the hospital for the remainder of the pregnancy because the baby was still in a breech position, and a C-Section would be required should labor resume and delivery become imminent. We were stuck in LDR 12 for the foreseeable future, just patiently waiting on what God would bring next.

On Monday, Feb 15th, at midday, Felicia got her second dose of steroids for the baby, and contractions had basically stopped. By later that night, they weren't even regularly monitoring Felicia as she was officially no longer considered to be in active labor. Tuesday came and passed with not even a peep to be heard or any change at all. Felicia and I started to think maybe we could go until 30 or 32 weeks and eliminate all concerns for Baby Boy Sears.

That night, Tuesday, Feb 16th, we barely slept at all. Sleeping at the hospital is the worst, and Felicia and I both kept waking up throughout the night. We both got up around 7 a.m., and I asked Felicia how she was feeling? She said, "Fine. My stomach is starting to hurt because I haven't really used the bathroom much the past few days." She continued, "I think I'm going to call the nurse in to see if they can give me something to help me go to the bathroom or something." I said, "Okay," and got up to start getting cleaned up for the day. The nurse came in, Felicia shared her stomach pain issues, and they both agreed it is probably a constipation thing at this point. Around 7:30 a.m., Felicia made mention that her pain was starting to hurt a little more, but nothing too bad. The nurse said, "Just out of precaution, go to the bathroom, come back, and let's put the monitors back on you to make sure these aren't contractions." Felicia did just that and returned to bed.

Around 7:40 a.m., the nurse started trying to get everything all hooked back up to monitor for contractions. For ten minutes or so, they fumbled around trying to find the baby's heartbeat, and it just wasn't working well. It was about this time that Felicia said, "This is REALLY starting to hurt!" Around 7:50 a.m., the nurse said she would call the doctor. As the nurse was on the phone waiting to speak to someone, Felicia started yelling, "Somethings going on. THIS REALLY HURTS!" This was around 7:52 a.m. By 7:55 a.m., Felicia was screaming, "He's coming, he's coming, I can feel it!" The nurse was still waiting on hold for the doctor. She dropped the phone, hit the panic button on the wall, and 20 doctors and nurses came flooding into the Labor and Delivery room suite. Dr. Scifres, our doctor, was the OB delivering that week and checked Felicia quickly. She said, "She is fully dilated, and we need to get her to the OR ASAP." They rushed Felicia out of the room. On the way to the OR, her water broke. At 8:00 a.m. on the dot, little LUCA FRANCISCO SEARS was born at 28 weeks and three days with his full course of steroids. It was a wild freaking scene, and my heart was racing like it was about to fly out of my chest.

I was left back in LDR 12 as everyone rushed out of the room. I had no idea what was going on, but I felt calm and at peace. I knew we had someone really special watching over all these events that would never let anything happen. Eventually, a nurse came back to the room to let me know that everyone was okay. Dr. Scifres came back a few minutes after that to check on me and tell me everything was okay, but it would be an hour or so before I could see Luca or Felicia. "What a relief," I thought. I sat back in my chair and picked up my old friend, my journal, and started writing and smiling. I felt at ease.

After about an hour, my heartbeat had come back down to Earth, and a nurse came by to let me know I could go and see Felicia. Felicia and I talked about how wild that whole thing was and how we wouldn't have expected anything less from our children, given our track record. The nurse tending to Felicia shared with us that a lot of women say they had an emergency c-section, but that isn't true. She continued, "Felicia really did just have an emergency c-section, and that was pretty dramatic." She called it a "splash and slash" or something like that. Meaning, they splashed some iodine on Felicia, knocked her out, and delivered the baby in about three minutes total. It is crazy what modern medicine is able to do. We sat there talking for a while until I was getting impatient and asked, "When can I go see Luca?" I couldn't wait to meet my son. After a few hours, the nurses finally led me to the NICU, the same NICU where Emilia spent her first three days before moving to Riley, to meet my beautiful son, Luca Francisco Sears!

Important background on how this NICU at IU Methodist is set up: there are 32 beds in one big room. The beds are broken up into little pod stations of two beds for nurses to manage two babies at once. As I entered the NICU and turned the corner to head into the section with all the babies, wouldn't you know it, Luca's bed was in Emilia's same pod and right next to her original bed. Emilia had been in bed 15, and Luca was now right next to her in bed 16. I got chills as I turned the corner and saw where his bed was located. It was like Emilia was looking out for him the whole freaking time, and she wanted to make sure that she was right next to him. Instead of the wing with LDR 20, we were in LDR 12. Instead of being born the day we got admitted, we had three full days for the steroids to work their magic.

This time I could feel that this experience was going to be different with Luca. Emilia was watching over us all, and I knew that she would never let anything happen to her little brother. That is what big sisters do! It is almost as if Emilia was symbolically passing the baton to finish her NICU marathon over to her little brother so we could all get home safe and sound as a family. Her hands were all over this entire process. From the core values quest that I had been on for the past year, which led me to random acts of kindness, which led to the conversation with my grandma, which led to the basement remodel being finished and our house put back into order the day before Luca arrived, to getting us to the hospital early, to buying an extra three days for the steroids to do their thing, and to now watching over her little brother in the bed next to her old bed at the same NICU less than a year later.

If you still don't believe that Emilia and God were the ones orchestrating this whole thing, here are the final kickers to set you straight. As I got back to Felicia in the post-op recovery area and they wheeled her over to the Mother/Baby Unit, I told her where Luca's bed was located in the NICU.

She could feel the same chills I was feeling. I then asked her, "How old again, gestationally speaking, would Emilia have been when she passed away?" Felicia added it up in her head and said, "28 weeks and 2 days." I said, "And Luca was born at 28 weeks and 3 days? What the hell is going on?" To top it all off, when they officially put us in our Mother/Baby recovery room, we found out we were staying in the SAME DAMN MOTHER/BABY ROOM that we were in after Emilia's birth. This was all just too crazy to believe, and Felicia agreed. Emilia has been there with us this whole time and will be there with us forever! I don't have to imagine that anymore. It is just our reality.

Fix Your Own Basement!

On February 18th, 2021, a day after Luca was born, I was back at our house, picking up a few things before heading back to the hospital. As I was looking out our sunroom window, drinking a cup of coffee, I broke down crying, thinking of all that we had gone through and this entire journey I've written about in this story. I just couldn't hold back the tears. I realized that it took an atomic bomb going off in my life to wake me up and allow me to be open to trusting God, seeing things for what they are, and truly living my own life for the first time (but with my daughter right next to me all along).

If you take anything from this story, don't wait to fix the metaphorical basement in your own life. Be open to receiving the signs and omens that life brings to us all the time and then act on them. Understand that you aren't meant to understand any of this and just get to work on doing your best each and every day. Trust that God is with you and truly does have a plan that works in crazy and mysterious ways.

EPILOGUE

I Can Imagine!

I end our journey by revisiting the question that I posed in the introduction, "Why is the phrase, "I can't imagine," so commonly the first words out of someone's mouth when confronted with another's human being's personal tragedies and life traumas?"

After I had completed the first draft of the manuscript for this book, I was reading a new book called *The Socrates Express: In Search of Life Lessons from Dead Philosophers*. This book, upon completion, instantly became one of my top five favorite reads of all time, and I highly recommend it to any reader of this story. On a personal level, I enjoyed it so much because I had always struggled with the concept of philosophy and philosophers. I would always think, "Who the hell did these people think they were? Why were they so special? Out of the unquantifiable number of thoughts and ideas that humans have had over the course of our existence, somehow these assholes figured it all out and were now going to share their answers with the world on how to live our best lives?" The pure arrogance of a "philosopher" is something I just could never get over. Trust me, I tried and tried to listen to them, consume their thoughts, and be open to their wisdom. I slogged my way through *Meditations by Marcus Aurelius*, I fought kicking and screaming until the end of *Why Buddhism is True*, I've started and stopped the first section of *Walden* about five different times, and I fought my desire to pull my hair out as I listened to a 27-year-old give me life lessons in *101 Essays That Will Change the Way You Think*. After each book I read, I left more confused and unfulfilled than when I began. It happened every time, without fail. I eventually accepted the fact that philosophy was just something that would never be for me. That was until I found *The Socrates Express*. The author, Eric Weiner, did a magnificent job of pulling out little nuggets that he found valuable from a wide range of famous philosophers and ancient wisdoms and weaving them back together to form his own unique take and thoughts on life. That was the first time that I've ever read a philosophy book that was more about life and how to pull from all different kinds of sources to form your own meaning. That was the first time that anyone has ever made philosophy understandable and relatable to me, and I'm so grateful to the author. For me, pulling from all different kinds of sources of wisdom to find your own path is the real beauty of life. It is how I think and how I learn in my own world. Listen, observe, and learn as much as you can and then go out in the world to see what works and what doesn't for you. Eric's book showed me that this was possible with philosophers as well, and it has opened my eyes to a whole new source of knowledge and ideas.

I mention all this because, as I was consuming his book, I came across a new concept in the chapter titled "How to Cope like Epictetus." In this chapter, Mr. Weiner spent a lot of time detailing a teaching of Stoicism and Epictetus that I had not heard of before. It was a concept called premeditated adversity. I've read at least three books on Stoicism this year, and I must have missed this one, but I'm glad Mr. Weiner made it so easy to understand.

Premeditated adversity, I learned, is the concept of imagining the worst-case scenario, letting your mind see it happening to you, how your life would change, what emotions you would have, and how you will or won't react in the moment. Modern Stoics do the premeditation as a visualization exercise, essentially running a movie in one's mind that plays out the likely scenario, over and over until one is habituated to it and anxiety diminishes. The goal is to de-catastrophize the situation by shifting the focus on the development of coping plans aimed at handling the problematic situation. The moment I heard of this concept, I immediately thought, "This is why I wrote, I Can't Imagine."

As a society, most of us are trained to run as fast as we can from someone else's personal traumas. The moment we hear of a tragedy, most of us say, "I can't imagine," and go back to our life as quickly as we can. We dream all day about a better life and visualize success. We are taught about the power that visualization can bring toward positive outcomes in our lives from childhood. We often hear, "If you can dream it, you can do it." I've heard those sentiments in some capacity at every stage of my life. What I've never heard is someone telling me to use visualization techniques to imagine the worst-case scenarios that life can bring. This is honestly a shame because we're missing out on the profound lessons and growth that can come from pain. We can't pretend like it doesn't happen, or else we will never know what to do when it happens to us.

I hope to change that conversation. I hope that after taking this journey with my family and me, any reader will be more receptive to, and maybe even seek out, stories of people's pain and suffering to embrace them for all the positive things they can offer to this world. My dream is that by hearing my family's tragic atomic bomb event, and others like ours, someone else out there can benefit from the lessons and growth that tragedy can bring without having to endure their own. Finally, should any reader tragically find themselves waking up after an unexpected blast in their own life, I pray that this story may help to provide them with some tools to guide them through the rubble of their own lives. I hope that they can rediscover their own imaginations, rebuild their own shiny new city from the ashes, and keep enduring.

I want to finish our journey by sharing a question that I asked myself one day, a few months after Emilia had passed, as my mind aimlessly wandered one afternoon. I asked, "What does it truly mean to be alive? Does Emilia have to physically be here with me to enjoy a long and happy life together as father and daughter? Can I still teach her tennis and lessons about life? Can we still go on long runs together and enjoy the park down the street? Can I still be a dad, the verb? Can Emilia still be an amazing sister and play an active role in her future siblings' lives? Can we stay connected spiritually and carry on a thriving relationship until we are one-day reunited again?" I think you know my answer at this point! Just in case you don't, my answer is an emphatic yes! I CAN DEFINITELY IMAGINE THAT!

End Credits and Acknowledgements

When construction first began on Emilia Tower back on 3/15/2020, and those first few words were written in our journals to document this whole experience, I had no idea that this is where we would end up. It is sometimes hard to believe that this is where we are after it is all said and done.

After I realized that construction wouldn't be completed in my original timeline, I quickly set my sights on getting most of the construction completed by Emilia's first birthday, 3/15/2021, to give her an amazing first birthday present. Well, I'm happy to say that I'm writing these final words on 3/4/2021 and will be able to deliver on that promise to my precious daughter. This was only made possible by my little man, Luca, taking a world of weight off our shoulders and crushing it back in the NICU, to allow me the time and mental relief to write and get this completed in time for his big sister's birthday. Thank you so much, and we can't wait to get you home and tell you all about Emilia as you grow.

Also, thank you to Salesforce for doing everything you can to develop an amazing culture of putting your employees first as best as possible. Without your policies of liberal paternity leave to celebrate and enjoy life with our families, I certainly would never have had the time to get this done in time for her first birthday. I actually wrote the final 40 to 50 pages the past two weeks since Luca was born in a flurry of activity in between trips back and forth to the NICU. With that in mind, I would definitely say my writing has been very unbalanced the past few weeks as I've been plugging away all Stephen King-style and cranking out page after page versus my normal one-to-two page a day balanced pace.

However, my imbalance has been worth it to deliver a special birthday gift to my daughter that neither of us will ever forget.

HAPPY 1st BIRTHDAY, MY SWEET EMILIA QUINN!

Now it is time to get back to the mission of balance and "living for two." So, I'm off to go take a run with Emilia while listening to a book together and getting our minds right so we can complete the second leg of this NICU marathon for Luca.

P.S. - I couldn't leave you all hanging without an update on how Luca's doing. Well, I'm happy to report that after 92 days in the NICU, little Luca the Lion triumphantly made it home safe and sound. He is doing great, and Felicia and I are so blessed to have him in our lives. Emilia has taken him under her wings and will ensure that he always has his big sister to protect him. Volume two of my family's story, a children's book called Luca the Lion, is coming soon to a bookshelf near you.

See you all at our next ClubAny event! Let's go change the world together!

Love,
Emilia, Luca, Felicia, and Chris

Printed in the United States
by Baker & Taylor Publisher Services